MARVEL COMICS #1

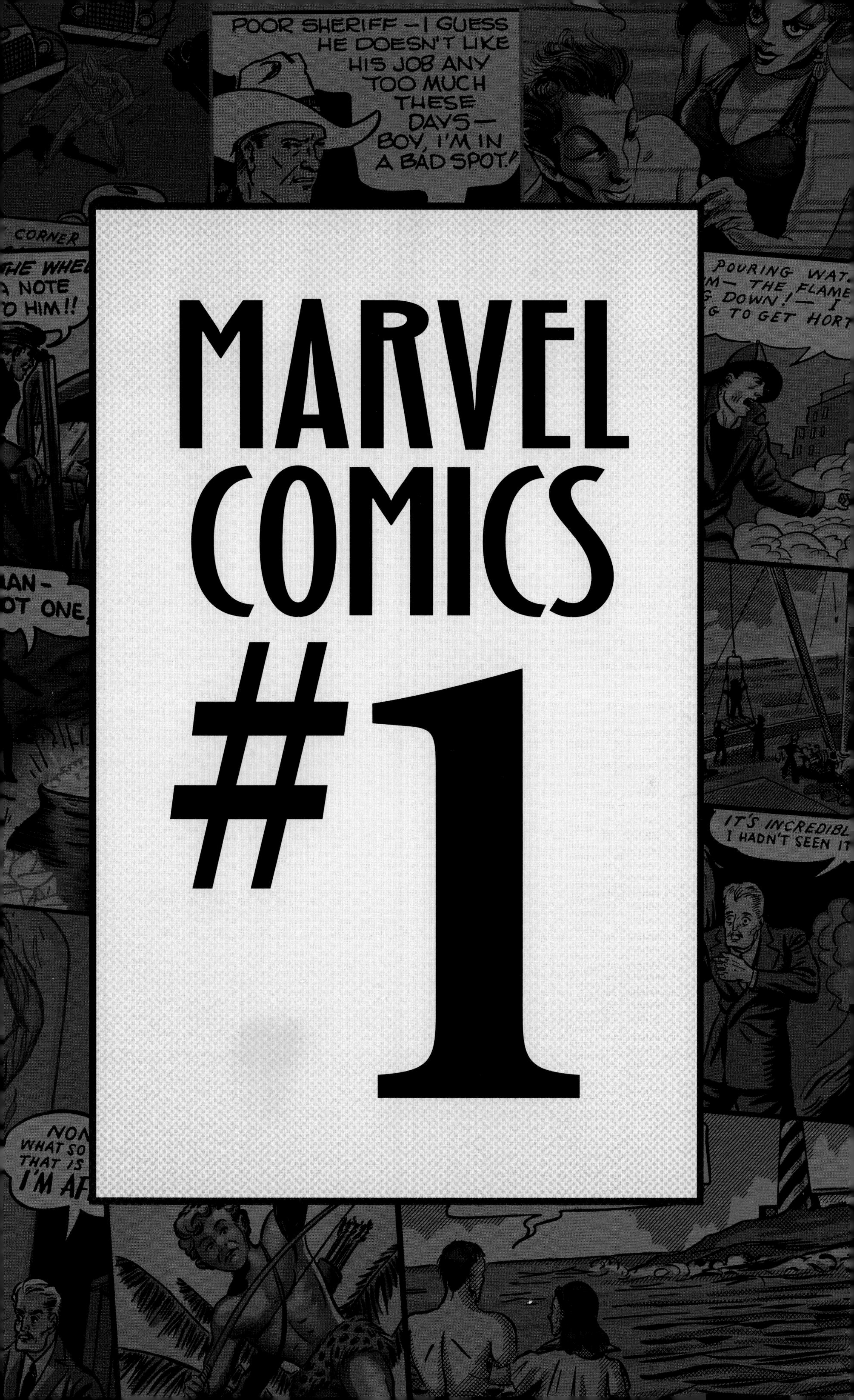
POOR SHERIFF — I GUESS HE DOESN'T LIKE HIS JOB ANY TOO MUCH THESE DAYS— BOY, I'M IN A BAD SPOT.!
CORNER

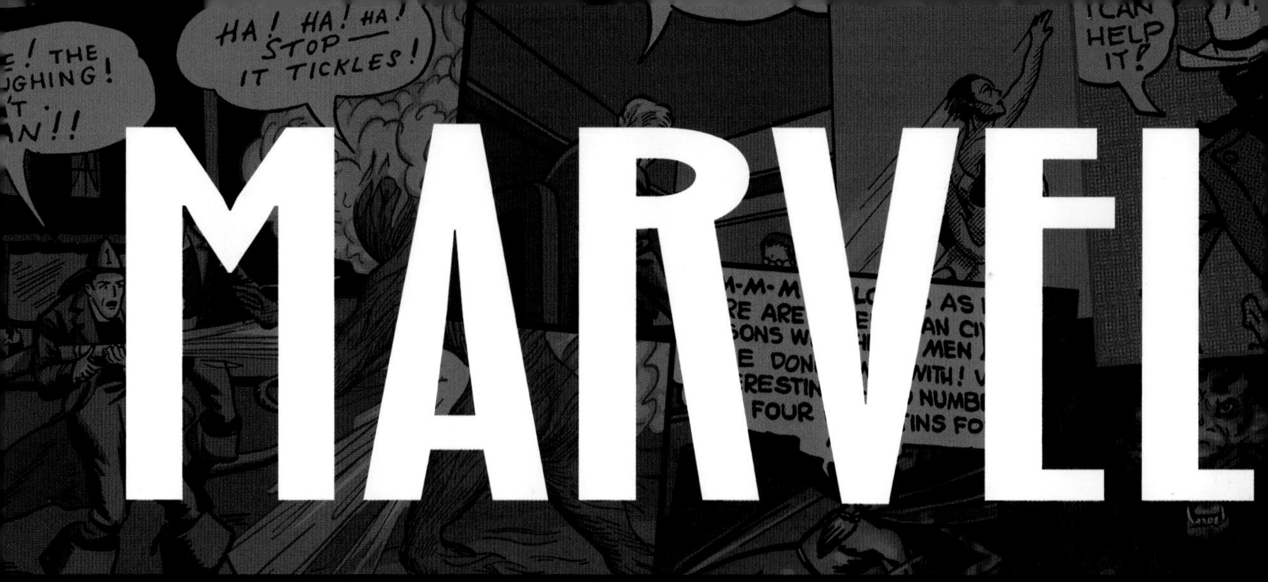
HA! HA! HA! STOP— IT TICKLES!

MARVEL

MARVEL COMICS #1
OCTOBER 1939

"NOW I'LL TELL ONE!"
by **Fred Schwab** (as **Ed Wood**)

"THE HUMAN TORCH"
by **Carl Burgos**

"THE ANGEL"
by **Paul Gustavson**

"THE SUB-MARINER"
by **Bill Everett**

"THE MASKED RAIDER"
by **Al Anders**

"JUNGLE TERROR"
by **Art Pinajian** (as **Tomm Dixon**)

"BURNING RUBBER"
Writer **Ray Gill**
Artist **Sam Gilman**

"ADVENTURES OF KA-ZAR THE GREAT"
by **Ben Thompson**

COVER ART **FRANK R. PAUL**
EDITOR **MARTIN GOODMAN**

SAGA OF THE ORIGINAL HUMAN TORCH #1
APRIL 1990

Writer **Roy Thomas**
Penciler **Rich Buckler**
Inker **Danny Bulanadi**
Colorist **Bob Sharen**
Letterer **Janice Chiang**
Cover Art **Rich Buckler & Danny Bulanadi**
Managing Editor **Mike Rockwitz**
Editor **Ralph Macchio**

MARVELS #0
AUGUST 1994

Writers **Alex Ross & Steve Darnall**
Artist **Alex Ross**
Letterer **Richard Starkings & Comicraft**
Cover Art **John Romita Sr. & Alex Ross**
Editor **Marcus McLaurin**
Book Concept **Kurt Busiek**

MARVEL COMICS #1 70TH ANNIVERSARY EDITION

OCTOBER 2009

"THE HUMAN TORCH"
by **Carl Burgos**
Colorist: **Dave McCaig**

"THE ANGEL"
by **Paul Gustavson**
Colorist: **Frank D'Armata**

"THE SUB-MARINER"
by **Bill Everett**
Colorist **José Villarrubia**

"THE MASKED RAIDER"
by **Al Anders**
Colorist **John Rauch**

"JUNGLE TERROR"
by **Art Pinajian** (as **Tomm Dixon**)
Colorist **Morry Hollowell**

"BURNING RUBBER"
Writer **Ray Gill**
Artist **Sam Gilman**
Colorist **Morry Hollowell**

"ADVENTURES OF KA-ZAR THE GREAT"
by **Ben Thompson**
Colorist **Justin Ponsor**

COVER ART **JELENA KEVIC DJURDJEVIC**

VARIANT COVER ART **FRANK R. PAUL & DEAN WHITE**

COLLECTION EDITORS **CORY SEDLMEIER & CORY LEVINE**

MARVEL COMICS #1 NOTES:
IT WAS NOT INDUSTRY STANDARD IN THE GOLDEN AGE OF COMICS TO PROVIDE DETAILED CREDITS FOR EACH STORY. THE CREDITS IN THIS VOLUME REPRESENT THE MOST ACCURATE INFORMATION AVAILABLE AT THE TIME OF PUBLICATION.

ART RECONSTRUCTION **PACIFIC RIM GRAPHICS & MICHAEL KELLEHER**

COLOR RECONSTRUCTION **WESLEY WONG**

COVER RECONSTRUCTION **MICHAEL KELLEHER**

COLLECTION EDITOR **MARK D. BEAZLEY**
ASSISTANT EDITOR **CAITLIN O'CONNELL**
ASSOCIATE MANAGING EDITOR **KATERI WOODY**
ASSOCIATE MANAGER, DIGITAL ASSETS **JOE HOCHSTEIN**
MASTERWORKS EDITOR **CORY SEDLMEIER**
SENIOR EDITOR, SPECIAL PROJECTS **JENNIFER GRÜNWALD**
VP PRODUCTION & SPECIAL PROJECTS **JEFF YOUNGQUIST**
RESEARCH & LAYOUT **JEPH YORK**
PRODUCTION **JOE FRONTIRRE**
BOOK DESIGNER **JAY BOWEN**
SVP PRINT, SALES & MARKETING **DAVID GABRIEL**

EDITOR IN CHIEF **C.B. CEBULSKI**
CHIEF CREATIVE OFFICER **JOE QUESADA**
PRESIDENT **DAN BUCKLEY**
EXECUTIVE PRODUCER **ALAN FINE**

SPECIAL THANKS TO **MIKE HANSEN**

CONTENTS

Bonus Material

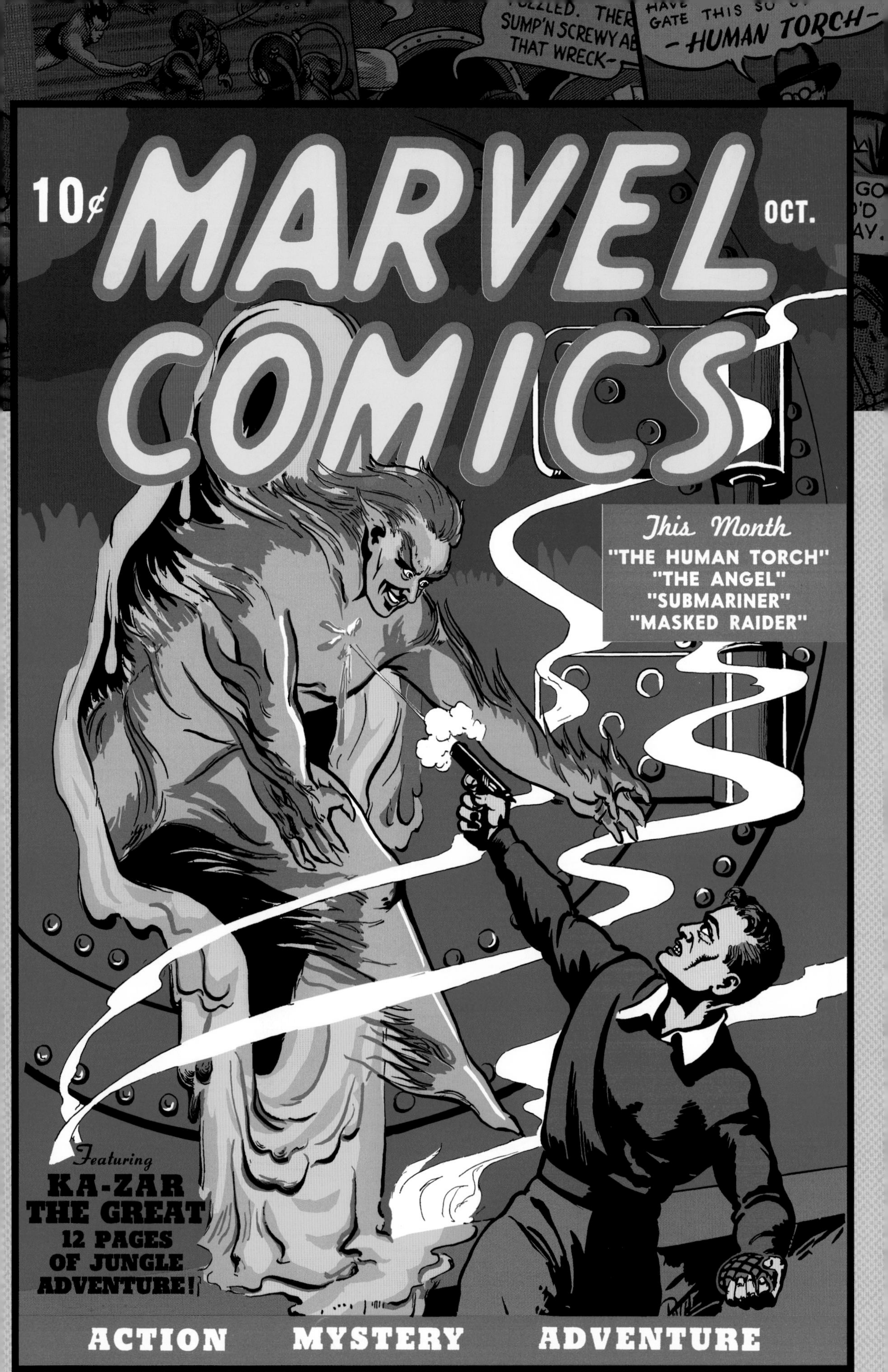

-HUMAN TORCH-
10¢
MARVEL COMICS
OCT.
This Month
"THE HUMAN TORCH"
"THE ANGEL"
"SUBMARINER"
"MASKED RAIDER"
Featuring
KA-ZAR THE GREAT
12 PAGES OF JUNGLE ADVENTURE!
ACTION MYSTERY ADVENTURE

Vol. I, No. I, MARVEL COMICS, Oct., 1939. Published monthly by Timely Publications, publication office, 81 Spring St., Newark, N. J. Executive office, 330 W. 42nd St., New York, N. Y. Art and editorial by Funnies Incorporated, 45 W. 45th St., New York, N. Y. Application for entry as Second Class Matter pending at the Post Office at Newark, N. J. Yearly subscription in U. S. and Canada, $1.50; elsewhere, $2.00. No actual person is named or delineated in this magazine. Copyright, 1939 by Timely Publications. Printed in U.S.A.

THE HUMAN TORCH

by CARL BURGOS

GENTLEMEN OF THE PRESS · I CALLED YOU TO MY LABORATORY BECAUSE I, PROFESSOR HORTON, HAVE A DIFFICULT PROBLEM IN MY LATEST DISCOVERY··

AS YOU ALL KNOW, I'VE BEEN WORKING ON A SYNTHETIC MAN — AN EXACT REPLICA OF A HUMAN BEING!!

WHEN I FINISHED, I FOUND I HAD SURPASSED ANYTHING THAT ANY SCIENTIST HAD EVER DONE —

IF YOU'LL FOLLOW ME · I'LL SHOW YOU WHY, EVEN I FEAR THE MONSTROSITY, WHICH I'VE CREATED!!

IN THIS AIR-TIGHT GLASS CAGE, LIVES MY CREATION·· I CALL HIM — THE HUMAN TORCH!

SOMETHING WENT WRONG WITH MY FIGURINGS SOMEWHERE · EVERY TIME THIS ROBOT, THE HUMAN TORCH, CONTACTS OXYGEN IN THE AIR, HE BURSTS INTO FLAME! NOW WATCH!

AS HORTON ALLOWS SOME AIR INTO THE CAGE, THE OTHERS GASP IN TERROR!—

GOOD LORD! THAT FIGURE IS A WALL OF FIRE!!

HORTON, DESTROY THAT MAN, BEFORE SOME MAD-MAN CAN GRASP ITS PRINCIPLES AND HURL IT AGAINST OUR CIVILIZATION!

NO!

SORRY, GENTLEMEN, BUT YOU SEE, DESTROYING HIM, DOES NOT ANSWER ANYTHING!!

THEN PERHAPS THE POWER OF THE PRESS WILL HELP CHANGE YOUR MIND!

WITHIN THE HOUR NEWSIES ARE ON THE STREET WITH AN *EXTRA!*

EXTRA! - READ ALL ABOUT THE MAN OF FIRE - THE - *HUMAN TORCH!*

FIREMAN

-HELLO!-YES THIS IS HORTON! WHO IS THIS? ··· THE SCIENTISTS' GUILD? ··· YOU WANT TO SEE MY CREATION? — CERTAINLY! ANYTIME YOU SAY - TONIGHT? ·· VERY WELL ··· AT EIGHT!

AS HORTON READS THE PAPER IN HIS STUDY, THE PHONE BUZZES, BREAKING THE ROOM'S EERIE SILENCE.

THAT EVENING

EIGHT BELLS! - YOU'RE ON TIME BOYS!

YOU KNOW, HORTON, THOSE NEWSPAPERS HAVE AROUSED THE PUBLIC AND WE THREE HAVE BEEN SENT TO INVESTIGATE THIS SO CALLED - *HUMAN TORCH* -

I THOUGHT SO, MY FRIENDS ·· COME THIS WAY PLEASE — AND I WILL SHOW YOU EVERYTHING!

TO BE TRUTHFUL, EVEN I CAN'T UNDERSTAND THIS STRANGE PHENOMENON! IT'S HARD TO SAY WHAT IT IS IT MIGHT BE SPONTANEOUS COMBUSTION — BUT WHO KNOWS?

PERHAPS WE MIGHT BE ABLE TO ANALYSE HIM, HORTON -

- HE LOOKS HARMLESS ENOUGH ·· DO YOU MIND FEEDING HIM SOME AIR, HORTON? - SO WE CAN MEASURE THE HEAT GIVEN WITH THIS PYROMETER? -

VERY WELL! -

NONE WHAT SO EVER - THAT IS WHY *I'M AFRAID!*

AS AIR LEAKS IN THE WEIRD FLAME LIVENS LIKE A HELLISH FIRE!!

GOOD LORD - THE HANDS OF THE METERS HAVE ALREADY GONE OFF THE DIALS! -

WHAT?

THE METER SNAPPED THE HEAT IS TOO GREAT! -

- AND YOU HAVE NO CONTROL OVER THE FLAME?

2

AND NOW THAT YOU'VE SEEN IT ·· WHAT IS YOUR OPINION? —

HORTON, THIS MAY HURT·· BUT SINCE YOU'VE NO CONTROL OVER HIM, I'M INCLINED TO AGREE WITH THE NEWSPAPERS! — DESTROY HIM!

SURELY, THERE MUST BE SOME OTHER WAY THAN TO BREAK HIM UP! — FOR WHO KNOWS, IN THE COURSE OF EXPERIMENTATION, I MIGHT HIT ON A DEVICE TO GAIN CONTROL OF, AND MASTER THIS MECHANICAL TORCH!

— THERE IS A WAY OUT, HORTON! — ENTOMB HIM IN A CONCRETE BLOCK, SO THAT IF · · —

—THAT'S IT! — IF I FIND THE SOLUTION, I CAN DIG HIM OUT, AND THAT WAY THERE'S NO DANGER · —EUREKA! — THAT'S THE ANSWER! —

THE NEXT DAY, WORKERS BEGIN BUILDING A MOULD IN WHICH TO BURY THE HUMAN TORCH—

WHILE IN THE HOUSE — AS OFFICIAL WITNESSES OF THE PRESS, YOU'VE SEEN ME SEAL THE HUMAN TORCH IN THIS STEEL TUBE — PERHAPS FOREVER!

LIFTING THE STEEL-TUBE, WHERIN LIES THE HUMAN TORCH, TWO HUSKIES CARRY IT FROM THE ROOM—

AND FIT IT TO A HOOK, DANGLING FROM THE TOP OF A DERRICK! —

O·K! —LET 'ER GO!

3

AS THE TUBE HITS THE WET CEMENT MIXTURE AND SINKS, HORTON MAKES A VOW TO FIND A SOLUTION TO CONTROL THE FLAME! —

TIME WENT BY—AND EVERYBODY HAD FORGOTTEN ABOUT THE FIRE-MAN, UNTIL, ONE EARLY MORNING, THERE WAS A TERRIFYING BLAST AND THE EARTH SPLIT OPEN!

BOOM

THE WINDOWS OF HORTON'S NEARBY HOME WERE SHATTERED TO BITS!—

GOOD HEAVENS—WHAT WAS THAT?—I WONDER?! COULD IT BE--?

IN HORTONS BEDROOM—

—YE GODS! THAT WAS THE HUMAN-TORCH'S TOMB! COULD HE HAVE BEEN DESTROYED?

HORTON RUSHES TO THE SHATTERED WINDOW!—

—HE MUST HAVE BEEN!— NOTHING COULD SURVIVE A BLAST LIKE THAT · ···NOTHING·· UNLESS—

—UNLESS THERE WAS A LEAK IN THE AIR-TIGHT TUBE IN WHICH HE WAS BURIED·· A LEAK?! BUT THAT'S IMPOSSIBLE— I SEALED IT MYSELF!!—

—BUT THERE HAD BEEN A LEAK—A SLOW LEAK, ALLOWING THE OXYGEN TO SEEP IN SLOWLY! THE HUMAN TORCH, IN CONTACT WITH AIR, SPREADS TERROR THROUGH THE CITY, AS EVERYTHING HE TOUCHES TURNS INTO AN INFERNO!!—

FIRE! IT'S THE HUMAN TORCH! HE'S ON THE LOOSE!!

I'M BURNING ALIVE! —WHY MUST EVERYTHING I TOUCH, TURN TO FLAME?—

ATTRACTED BY THE CLANG OF FIRE-ENGINES, AFTER SOMEBODY HAD TURNED IN A FIRE ALARM, THE HUMAN TORCH TURNS

LOOK! — THE HUMAN TORCH! BUSY, MEN!

CLANG! CLANG!

HAH! — I LIKE THE SOUND OF THE BELL··

WELL, WHAT ARE YOU GUYS WAITING FOR? C'MON — GET THE HOSE INTO ACTION!

YESSIR.

HURRY! — THAT GUY'S STILL HERE!·· WATER OUGHT TO DO THE TRICK! —

AS THE WATER SPURTS ONTO THE **HUMAN-TORCH** — A HISSING SOUND BELLOWS — A CLOUD OF SMOKE RISES·· BUT THE FIREMEN ARE DUMBFOUNDED, AS···

GLORY BE! THE GUY'S LAUGHING! IT AIN'T· HUMAN!!

HA! HA! HA! STOP — IT TICKLES!

KEEP POURING WATER ON HIM — THE FLAME'S DYING DOWN! — I'M GOING TO GET HORTON!

AS THE **HUMAN TORCH** STEPS ON A HOSE, IT BURNS THROUGH, AND THE WATER SPURTS OUT

THE FLAMES ONCE AGAIN SHOOT UP, AND THE **HUMAN TORCH** IS ON THE LOOSE AGAIN! —

11

I MUST FIND A RETREAT · I'VE ALREADY CAUSED TOO MUCH DAMAGE···

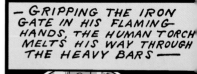

IT LOOKS LIKE A POOL IN THERE··· PERHAPS THAT WILL PUT OUT THIS FLAME! —

COMING TO AN IRON GATE, THE HUMAN-TORCH PAUSES··

— GRIPPING THE IRON GATE IN HIS FLAMING HANDS, THE HUMAN TORCH MELTS HIS WAY THROUGH THE HEAVY BARS —

THOSE IRON BARS CAN'T STOP ME!

LEAVING A TRAIL OF BLAZING GRASS, THE HUMAN-TORCH DIVES INTO THE POOL···

MEANWHILE, IN THE HOUSE ON THE ESTATE WITH THE POOL

DAT'S FUNNY — DE GRASS 'ROUND DE POOL IS BOININ', SARDO!

YOU'RE NUTS, RED!

HUMAN-TORCH ON LOOSE!

WAIT A MINUTE — DID YOU SAY BURNING?!! — THAT MEANS BUT ONE THING!

HUH?

NOW LISTEN — GET THE WINTER GLASS-COVER, THAT FITS THE POOL — DRAW THE AIR OUT··· THEN DRAIN THE WATER OUT! — HURRY! — DON'T ASK ANY QUESTIONS!

LATER! HAH! — I THOUGHT SO! — IT'S THE HUMAN TORCH!!

SO WOT?

THAT'S WHAT I LIKE ABOUT YOU RED — YOU'RE SO STUPID!

I DON'T LIKE DAT KIND OF TALK — SARDO!

FORGET IT RED — WE GOT A MILLION-DOLLAR RACKET, AND DON'T NEED TO WORRY ABOUT COPS NOW!

6

FROM NOW, ON, RED, WE'RE IN THE *FIRE-INSURANCE BUSINESS*.

OK! IF YOUSE SEZ SO, SARDO!

SARDO TRIES EXPLAINING TO RED HIS PLAN TO USE THE HUMAN TORCH.

AND OUR FIRST CUSTOMER WILL BE THE ACMEN WAREHOUSES, INC.

-BUT STEEL CAN'T BOIN!

LOOK DOPE - THAT GUY IN THE POOL IS TH *HUMAN TORCH* - AND HE CAN MELT STEEL!!

DO YA TINK HE'LL WOIK FOR US?

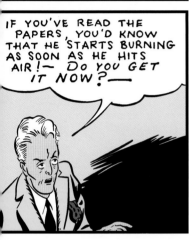

IF YOU'VE READ THE PAPERS, YOU'D KNOW THAT HE STARTS BURNING AS SOON AS HE HITS AIR! - *DO YOU GET IT NOW?* -

YEAH! - BUT, WHAT'S OUR NEXT MOVE NOW - SARDO?

GET THE CAR OUT! WE'RE GOIN' TO CALL ON THE ACMEN WAREHOUSES - INC.

BUT, I STILL DON'T SEE HOW THAT FREAK CAN BE OP ANY USE TO US IN OUR RACKET, BOSS -

ATER

I'LL SHOW YOU - YOU STAY HERE, RED, WHILE I HAVE A SALES - TALK WITH THE COMPANY'S *PRESIDENT!* -

- YESSIR, WHAT CAN I DO FOR YOU?

I'D LIKE TO SEE MR. HARRIS, PLEASE.

- AND WHO SHALL I SAY IS CALLING? -

-ER, JUST SAY - MR. SARDO - AND TELL HIM IT'S *HOT STUFF!*

THERE'S A MR. SARDO OUTSIDE TO SEE YOU... HE SAYS - IT'S "HOT STUFF!"

"HOT STUFF?" - WHAT'S THAT? - OH WELL, SEND HIM IN -

7

MR. HARRIS, I'LL BE BRIEF - UNLESS YOU SIGN UP FOR MY *PROTECTION INSURANCE* - YOU WON'T HAVE ANY MORE RAW-STEEL LEFT IN YOUR WAREHOUSES!

OH! - A RACKETEER, EH?! -

LISTEN, SARDO, - I DON'T NEED ANY INSURANCE - AND I HATE PUNKS LIKE YOU - SO GET OUT - NOW!

I WAS ONLY DOIN' YOU A FAVOR HARRIS - YOU'LL BE SORRY - *WATCH!*

DID YA HAVE ANY LUCK, SARDO?

NO, GET MOVING — WE GOT WORK TO DO! — AND FAST!!

SARDO JUMPS INTO ACTION!!

SARDO AND HIS LIEUTENANT HEAD FOR THEIR MANSION — WHERE THEY STRANGELY HOLD THE HUMAN TORCH

NOW, RED, FILL THE POOL WITH WATER. THEN GET A DIVING-SUIT AND A GLASS-TUBE TO FIT THE HUMAN TORCH — YOU'LL FIND THEM IN MY LAB!

YEAH — OK-SARDO!

AFTER DONNING THE DIVING-SUIT SARDO LOWERS HIMSELF INTO THE POOL AND FITS THE TUBE ON THE HUMAN TORCH, WHO THINKS SARDO IS HELPING HIM —

OK-RED — LOWER A ROPE, THEN HAUL AWAY — EVERYTHING IS OKEH — SO FAR!

TAKE IT EASY NOW — OR YOU'LL BREAK THE GLASS!!

THE GLASS CASE IS THEN PLACED ON AN OPERATING COT AND THEN WHEELED TO THE BACK OF A TRUCK.

OK- NOW HEAD FOR THOSE WAREHOUSES, WHERE HARRIS KEEPS HIS STEEL!

THE TRUCK BEARING THE TORCH SPEEDS THROUGH THE NIGHT!

THERE'S THE WAREHOUSE, SARDO — THAT BIG ONE, THERE! —

DON'T BREAK THE CASE — NOT TOO FAST — MOVE HIM SLOWLY! —

8

IT'S ALL YOURS, TORCH! — BURN IT TO THE GROUND! HAH! — I ONLY WISH HARRIS COULD SEE THIS! —

SARDO TAKES CAREFUL AIM AND THROWS A WEIGHT AT THE PROTECTING GLASS CASE ··· THE OXYGEN OF THE AIR MAKES TORCH BURST INTO FLAMES!!

I CONFESS I DON'T UNDERSTAND.. I THOUGHT SARDO WAS TRYING TO HELP ME!

AS THE HUMAN TORCH WALKS ABOUT, UNABLE TO GRASP THE MEANING OF IT ALL, THE WAREHOUSE BECOMES A MASS OF FLAME!—

— THEN HE BRINGS ME HERE, AND BREAKS THE COVER... I WONDER IF HE MIGHT BE JUST A LOW-DOWN RACKETEER?

THE HUMAN TORCH TRIES TO FIGURE THE REASON SARDO IS USING HIM.

THAT'S IT!— HE MUST BE!— ELSE WHY LET ME LOOSE IN THIS TINDER BOX?—

SARDO IS A BUSINESS WRECKER. I'VE GOT TO GET OUT AND SEE HIM!—

UH-OH!— THE ROOF CAVED IN!—THAT'S MY WAY OUT!—

I HOPE IT WORKS!!

TAKING A RUNNING START THROUGH THE MOLTEN STEEL, THE TORCH LEAPS UPWARDS—

EVEN THE HUMAN TORCH IS SURPRISED AS HIS LEAP TURNS OUT TO BE A FLIGHT THROUGH SPACE!— THE REASON WAS THAT THE BLUE AND COMBINED RED FLAMES MADE THE HUMAN TORCH LIGHTER THAN AIR!—

THE GOGGLE-EYED SPECTATORS FLEE AS THE HUMAN TORCH LANDS IN THEIR MIDST, MANY BLOCKS AWAY—

— NOW FOR THAT CROOK SARDO AND HIS MOB OF RATS!!—

15

WHAT'S THIS FLASH OF FIRE COMING INTO MY PLACE? WHY— IT'S THE HUMAN TORCH!!

SARDO IS TAKEN BY SURPRISE BY THE TORCH'S SUDDEN APPEARANCE ON HIS GROUNDS — BUT...

HA! YOU'RE A FOOL, SARDO· WHY LOCK THE DOOR? —

BAM

SARDO RUNS INTO THE HOUSE- SLAMMING THE DOOR, IN AN EFFORT TO ESCAPE THE HUMAN TORCH!

I'LL GET YOU IN THE END! —

A CLOSED DOOR CAN'T STOP THE HUMAN TORCH— HE WALKS RIGHT THROUGH IT!

GOOD LORD! — HE'S BURNING THROUGH THE DOORS — I'VE GOT TO HIDE! — BUT WHERE? — I GOT IT! — MY UNDERGROUND LAB- IT'S STEEL- IT'LL STOP HIM!

—HE'LL NEVER GET ME THERE! — THE WALLS ARE MADE OF TWELVE INCH BATTLE- SHIP CHROMIUM STEEL PLATES! —

SARDO RUNS TO HIS SECRET UNDERGROUND LAB! —

I WONDER WHERE SARDO DISAPPEARED TO! — I SAW HIM RUN IN HERE! —

WHILE IN THE HOUSE ABOVE—

IT'S FUNNY, BUT I CAN'T FIND SARDO IN THESE RUINS — ··I WONDER?···

—AS THE HOUSE COLLAPSES, A LONE FIGURE STANDS ERECT— IT'S THE HUMAN TORCH, UN- TOUCHED IN THE FIERY INFERNO, HELPING THE DESTRUCTION WITH HIS OWN HEAT! —

—HA!—HA!—HA— IT WAS EASY TO BURN SARDO'S HOME DOWN!

WE CAN'T WAIT FOR SARDO· LET'S DUCK QUICK ·· SAY— IT'S THE TORCH— HE FIRED THE HOUSE! —

SARDO'S MOB LEAVE THEIR LEADER, AND TRY TO RUN AWAY, WHEN THEY SEE THE TORCH!

AS THE HUMAN TORCH LEAPS FORWARD THE OTHERS SPREAD OUT- SOME DIVING INTO THE POOL···· SARDO'S MAN, RED, DUCKS UNDER A NEARBY CAR! —

10

JUMPING THRU SPACE LIKE A COMET, THE HUMAN TORCH LANDS ON THE CAR AND MELTS THE BODY AS IF IT WERE MADE OF BUTTER!—

HELP! THE HEAT'S KILLING ME!

THE HEAT IS TERRIFIC—AND, UNDER THE AUTO...

THAT RAT BURNED—ALL RIGHT! AND THOSE FELLOWS IN THE POOL WONT COME UP FOR AIR—NOW FOR—-—SARDO!!

THE HUMAN TORCH, HAVING SCALDED THE GANGSTERS IN THE POOL, BY TURNING WATER TO STEAM—

HMM—A STEEL DOOR. —FUNNY, I DIDN'T NOTICE IT BEFORE!

—RUNS BACK INTO THE FLAMING HOUSE, SEEKING SARDO'S HIDEOUT—

PLACING HIS HANDS ON THE DOOR, IT REACTS LIKE AN ACETEYLENE TORCH—BORING A HOLE THRU THE STEEL!—

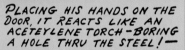

SO—THIS IS SARDO'S LABORATORY—AND I'M NOT SUPPOSED TO GET BY THAT SPECIAL DOOR EH?!—

THE DOOR LEADS TO SARDO'S UNDERGROUND LAB!—

HEH-HEH—.SO YOU THINK YOU'LL GET ME, EH?.—NOT IN A MILLION YEARS, MR. TORCH!—

SARDO FEELS SECURE, BEHIND SUPER-STEEL WALLS—

HELLO, RAT!

BUT SARDO'S LAUGH WASN'T FUNNY, AS THE HUMAN TORCH MELTS THRU THE STEEL DOOR, WITHOUT EKERTION...

SARDO, IN AN ATTEMPT TO BRING THE TORCH UNDER HIS CONTROL, DONS A GAS-MASK AND HURLS A GAS BOMB AT HIM—WITH NO EFFECT—THE HEAT CAUSING IT TO FIZZ BEFORE IT CAN EVEN TOUCH THE HUMAN TORCH!

HAVING FUN, SARDO?

FIZZ-Z

11

THE HUMAN TORCH LAUGHS AND BIDS SARDO TO WATCH HIM — AS HE PICKS UP A BOMB — INSTANTLY IT MELTS!!

SARDO — NOW HALF-CRAZED, PICKS UP A TANK OF LIQUIDAR. JUST AS HE IS ABOUT TO FLING IT, THE CLANG OF FIRE ENGINES CATCHES THE ATTENTION OF BOTH MEN! —

CLANG CLANG

— DON'T GO IN THERE! — YOU'LL BE BLOWN TO BITS!

I HAVE TO GET THAT NITRO-TANK OUT OF THERE!

WHILE THE FIREMEN FIGHT THE ROARING BLAZE FROM THE OUTSIDE, — HORTON SPOTS A TANK FULL OF NITROGEN — HE RUSHES INTO THE FLAMES! —

BUT JUST THEN, THE HUMAN-TORCH APPEARS ON THE SCENE, AND HE TOO, SEES THE TANK —

WITH A MIGHTY LEAP HIS ARMS CLOSE AROUND THE SLIM TANK, MELTING IT — AND THE NITRO GAS SHOOTS UP —

WHILE HORTON'S EYES POP WITH AMAZEMENT —

IT'S INCREDIBLE! — IF I HADN'T SEEN IT, I —

THE FLAMES DIE DOWN ··· AND THE TORCH IS HIMSELF AGAIN!

12

THIS'LL BE A BETTER WORLD WITHOUT YOU — MR. TORCH!

THE FIRE CHIEF SEEING THIS, DRAWS HIS GUN AND FIRES —

BUT THE STILL SUPER-HOT SKIN, SAVES THE TORCH FROM DESTRUCTION ·· THE LEAD PELLET MELTS, AS IT LANDS BETWEEN THE EYES!

WITH A GURGLING LAUGH, THE HUMAN TORCH WHIRLS AND MAKES A SUDDEN DASH BACK INTO THE BLAZING EMBERS!!—

HE'S BACK— BUT WAIT!— WHAT'S THIS?— HIS FLAME IS OUT!— WHY?!

THERE WAS A TANK OF NITRO UPSTAIRS... COULD IT HAVE BEEN THAT?— IT HAS POSSIBILITIES!!

—BUT AS THE HUMAN TORCH APPROACHES SARDO, HE AGAIN BURSTS INTO FLAME..

—NOW I'M SURE IT WAS THE NITRO!!— THIS GIVES ME A CHANCE TO STRIKE A BARGAIN!

HERE, YOU CAN HAVE THIS NITRO — IF YOU'LL LET ME GO!

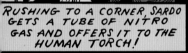

RUSHING TO A CORNER, SARDO GETS A TUBE OF NITRO GAS AND OFFERS IT TO THE HUMAN TORCH!

—BUT THE HUMAN TORCH FLIES FORWARD AND QUICKLY WRESTS THE TANK FROM SARDO'S GRIP!

THANKS! SARDO— THIS'LL COME IN HANDY!—

—BUT AS FOR LETTING YOU GO — NEVER!—

LISTEN,— I'LL DO ANYTHING YOU SAY — ONLY DON'T BURN ME!—

—YOU RAT!— YOU SHOULD HAVE THOUGHT OF THAT BEFORE YOU DECIDED TO MAKE ME THE GOAT FOR YOUR RACKET!—

13

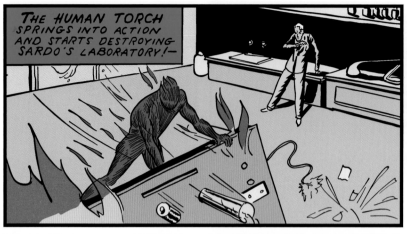

THE HUMAN TORCH SPRINGS INTO ACTION AND STARTS DESTROYING SARDO'S LABORATORY!—

THEN LEAPING IN APE-LIKE FASHION—HE RIPS THE CHEMICAL-LADEN SHELVES DOWN!

NOW'S MY LAST—AND FINAL CHANCE TO GET HIM!—

WITH SEEMINGLY FIENDISH DELIGHT, THE HUMAN-TORCH COMPLETELY WRECKS THE LAB—AS SARDO SNEAKS AWAY TO A CORNER...

···WHERE HE GRIPS A TANK OF SULPHURIC ACID—THEN SNEAKS UP BEHIND THE TORCH!

BOOM

HURLING THE TANK—IT EXPLODES BEFORE IT EVEN TOUCHES THE HUMAN TORCH!—

POOR FOOL—KILLED BY HIS OWN HAND—

GRABBING AN INSULATED TANK OF NITROGEN, THE ONLY GAS THAT WILL CONTROL HIS FLAME, THE TORCH WALKS OUT OF THE BURNING LAB—

WE HEARD AN EXPLOSION OUT HERE!—WHAT WAS IT?—

—A RAT DEALT OUT JUSTICE TO HIMSELF HORTON!

14

HEY CHIEF!—I JUST SAW HORTON TALK-ING TO THE TORCH!

SO!—IT'S MORE OF THE TORCH'S WORK, EH?—

THE POLICE, ATTRACTED BY THE BLAZE AND EXPLOSION, RUSH TO THE SCENE!—

MEANWHILE THE TORCH LEAVES HORTON AND MOVES INTO THE FLAMES TO EXPERIMENT WITH THE NITRO!—

I HOPE THIS NITRO WILL BRING COMPLETE CONTROL OVER THE FLAME!

LATER

IT WORKS!! I CAN NOW CONTROL THE FLAME, WITHOUT THE NITRO!

GOOD LORD—I CAN THROW THE FLAME AS I WOULD A BALL!—

THEN TURNING BACK TO HIS FLAME—THE TORCH FINDS THAT HE CAN FLING THE BLUE FLAME FROM HIS BODY!

ATTENTION—ALL CARS!—CLOSE IN ON TORCH!!—HE'S HEADED DOWN SPRUCE STREET!—HURRY—I'LL TRAIL HIM JUST IN CASE!—

MEANWHILE, THE CHIEF RUNS BACK TO HIS CAR AND SENDS A MESSAGE OVER THE ETHER

—I WONDER IF THAT CAR IS FOLLOWING ME?—

HIS SUSPICIONS CONFIRMED—THE TORCH SHOOTS AHEAD LIKE A COMET—THE CAR BEING LEFT FAR BACK IN THE DISTANCE!

BUT AT THE CORNER, A BLOCKADE OF POLICE CARS SEEMINGLY TRAP THE TORCH!—

OK—COME AND GET ME—

IT'S NO USE! THE HEAT'S TOO GREAT. WE CAN'T EVEN GET NEAR HIM!

WAIT!—DON'T GO—WATCH!—

LOOK THE FLAME IS OUT!

—SORRY, I CAUSED YOU SO MUCH TROUBLE·· I DIDN'T KNOW YOU WERE AFTER ME··· IT'S OK!—YOU CAN TAKE ME—MY BODY'S COLD!—

15

TORCH, YOU'VE COMMITTED A MOST DASTARDLY CRIME — BURNING A WAREHOUSE AND THEN PROCEEDING TO DESTROY SARDO'S ESTATE — WHY?

BURNING THE WAREHOUSE WAS SARDO'S PLAN TO SHAKE DOWN THE COMPANY FOR PROTECTION — AS FOR ME — I WAS A VICTIM OF CIRCUMSTANCES!

LATER — AT POLICE HEADQUARTERS

— ALL OF WHICH WAS PART OF SARDO'S PLAN FOR A RACKET! — YES, I AM GUILTY OF BURNING SARDO'S ESTATE, BUT IT WAS OF HIS OWN DOING — HE SET ME FREE IN AIR, THEREBY ALLOWING ME TO IGNITE! —

CAP'N, LEAVE THE TORCH IN MY CUSTODY — I'LL BE RESPONSIBLE —

VERY WELL, HORTON — THE TORCH IS IN YOUR CUSTODY! — HA! — HE'D PROBABLY BURN THE JAIL DOW IF I DIDN'T DO SO! —

THIS MIGHT INTEREST YOU, HORTON, I HAVE COMPLETE CONTROL OVER THE FLAME! —

WHAT?

HORTON LEADS THE TORCH TO HIS CAR AND HEAD AT ONCE FOR HORTON'S HOME —

IF HE HAS COMPLETE CONTROL, I CAN MAKE A FORTUNE THRU HIM!

— TORCH — I'D LIKE TO SEE AN EXAMPLE OF YOUR CONTROL, PLEASE —

LATER — INSIDE HORTON'S LAB —

YOU SEE, I TURN MY FLAME ON, AND MERELY POINT! — AH — THERE! — YOUR CIGAR IS LIT — A PERFECT EXAMPLE OF FLAME CONTROL!

THE TORCH ORDERS NORTON TO PLACE AN UNLIT CIGAR IN HIS MOUTH —

HOW'S THAT, PROF?

IT'S AMAZING! WE COULD MAKE A FORTUNE! —

THEN AS A FURTHER EXAMPLE OF CONTROL — THE TORCH SNAPS HIS FLAME ON AND OFF!

SO! — EVEN YOU'VE BEEN TOUCHED BY THE POSSIBILITY OF A FORTUNE IN ME, EH HORTON?

— NO HORTON, I'LL BE FREE, AND NO ONE WILL EVER USE ME FOR SELFISH GAIN — OR CRIME!

— THE CEILING'S BURNING

"PUTTING ON" THE FLAME, HE GESTURES AT THE CEILING IN A CIRCULAR MOTION —

THEN WITH A LAUGH AND A MIGHTY LEAP, CRASHING THRU THE UNBURNT OPENING IN THE ROOF — THE TORCH SAILS THRU SPACE LIKE A COMET! —

CRASH!

NEXT MONTH — ANOTHER HUMAN TORCH PICTURE-ACTION-STORY

22

The ANGEL

by Paul Gustavson

AT THE POINT OF A GUN, A GROUP OF RACKETEERS, KNOWN AS THE "SIX BIG MEN", HAVE TAKEN OVER AN ENTIRE CITY.... STRIKING EVERYWHERE WITH ONLY A MOMENTS NOTICE....

YOU'RE FINISHED, BUD — SO SAY YOUR PRAYERS!

I - I'LL PAY! I'LL PAY!

RESTAURANT

YOU HAD YOUR CHANCE TO PAY — — BUT YOU DIDN'T NEED ANY PROTECTION!

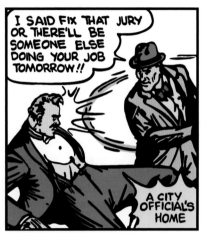

I SAID FIX THAT JURY OR THERE'LL BE SOMEONE ELSE DOING YOUR JOB TOMORROW!!

A CITY OFFICIAL'S HOME

A WIFE AN' THREE KIDS, EH?? YOU SHOULD'A TOLD THAT TO YOUR BOSSES!

SUBWAY STATION

A NIGHT CLUB

FROM NOW ON YOU'RE SELLIN' OUR BRAND OF LICQUOR!

GET RID OF 'IM — I'M GONNA RUN THIS JOINT MY WAY!

OUT ON THE ISLAND AN' DUMP 'IM IN TH' SWAMPS!

A GAMBLING HOUSE

ONE OF YOUR TRUCKS IS DOWN THERE — TAKE A LOOK!!

A DELIVERY SYNDICATE

A MOMENT LATER, THE ENGINE OF THE DELIVERY TRUCK BURSTS INTO FLAMES AND EXPLODES.

A GROUP OF CIVIC-MINDED MEN CALL UPON THE MAYOR.

THE MAYOR WILL SEE YOU AT ONCE!

YES, YES — BUT LET THE POLICE COMMISSIONER TELL YOU HIS SIDE OF THE STORY!

AFTER HEARING ABOUT THE OUTRAGES, THE MAYOR CALLS IN THE COMMISSIONER.

WE'RE HELPLESS!! THERE HASN'T BEEN ONE WITNESS TO TESTIFY FOR THE STATE IN THE TWO HUNDRED ARRESTS WE'VE MADE WHILE THESE RATS HAVE HAD DOZENS EACH TO SWEAR THEY WERE SOMEWHERE ELSE!

THERE'S NOTHING I CAN DO WITHOUT THE PEOPLE'S CONFIDENCE!

WE'LL TAKE THE LAW IN OUR OWN HANDS THEN!

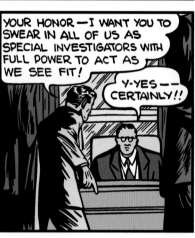

YOUR HONOR — I WANT YOU TO SWEAR IN ALL OF US AS SPECIAL INVESTIGATORS WITH FULL POWER TO ACT AS WE SEE FIT!

Y-YES — CERTAINLY!!

WAIT, GENTLEMEN! I STARTED THIS CAMPAIGN AGAINST THE CRIME WAVE AND I'D LIKE TO SUGGEST SOMETHING! HAVE ANY OF YOU HEARD OF THE ANGEL?!

IF YOU'RE THINKING OF HIRING THE ANGEL TO CLEAN UP THIS MESS, YOU'RE GOING A BIT TOO FAR! HE'LL STOP AT NOTHING!

PRECISELY!

NO TRIALS OR LEGAL FORMALITIES TO CONTEND WITH — — THESE SO-CALLED "SIX BIG MEN" WILL SIMPLY BE WIPED OUT! I'LL START FOR PARIS IMMEDIATELY, WHERE THE ANGEL WAS — — LOOK OUT!

A STONE WITH A NOTE WRAPPED AROUND IT!

WHAT DOES IT SAY?? OPEN IT UP!

WAIT A MINUTE! HOLY CATS — — LOOK AT THIS!!

"...one by one they'll go

The Six Big Men!"

Name

Gus Ronson — — Restaurant Business

Mike Malone — — Restaurant Protection

John Dillon — — Crooked Gambling Houses

Trigger Bolo — — Subway Protection

Steve Sribel — — Retail Delivery Protection

Dutch Hansen — — Night-Club Protection

"The Big Boss!!" — — Political Fixer

Political

WELL — YOU GOT WHAT YOU WANTED, DR. LANG — — EXCEPT THAT THE ANGEL IS ONE STEP AHEAD OF YOU!

YES — AND NOW THE "SIX BIG MEN" WILL KNOW THEIR DOOM!

"....AND HE'S MADE ONE MORE ADDITION TO THE LIST — — THE BIG BOSS!! BESIDES THAT, MY PLANS ARE WORKING VERY WELL! HUH — HE'LL NEVER FIND OUT WHO THE REAL BOSS IS — THAT I'M SURE OF!

BUT DR. LANG WAS SAYING TO HIMSELF...

SEVERAL DAYS LATER, GUS RONSON, HEAD OF THE RESTAURANT PROTECTIVE ASSOCIATION IS FREED FROM A MANSLAUGHTER CHARGE BY A FIXED JURY...

WELL — IF IT ISN'T THE COMMISSIONER! I'VE A SURPRISE FOR YOU, RONSON! *THE ANGEL* HAS YOU ON HIS LIST! RIGHT UP ON TOP!

HEE — HAW — HAW — HAW !! D'YOU HEAR THAT! *THE ANGEL'S* AFTER ME! LISTEN COPPER — I DON'T BELIEVE IN SPOOKS OR FAIRY TALES!!

RONSON'S BOASTING IS SUDDENLY CUT SHORT BY A COLD WIND BLOWING ACROSS HIS FACE...

...AND A SHADOW FORMS ON THE BUILDING ACROSS THE STREET — — SHAPING ITSELF INTO A HUGE ANGEL.

L-LOOK — *THE ANGEL* !!

GEES — JUST LIKE A C-COLD WIND OUT OF A GR-GRAVE !

TH' SHADOW'S FADIN'!! M-MAYBE I'M LOOSIN' MY GUTS — BUT I GOT TH' JITTERS! I-I'M GETTIN' OUTA HERE !

LIKE A WILD MANIAC, GUS RONSON RUNS FOR HIS CAR

OUTA ME WAY!!

AT THE SAME TIME, A STRANGE FIGURE JUMPS FROM THE ROOF OF THE COURT HOUSE TO THE NEARBY LAMP POST AND TO THE GROUND IN FRONT OF RONSON'S CAR.

LIKE A FLASH HE JUMPS INTO THE BACK SEAT OF THE CAR ...

UNAWARE THAT THE MYSTERIOUS STRANGER IS IN THE BACK OF HIS CAR, RONSON DRIVES OFF AT FULL SPEED.

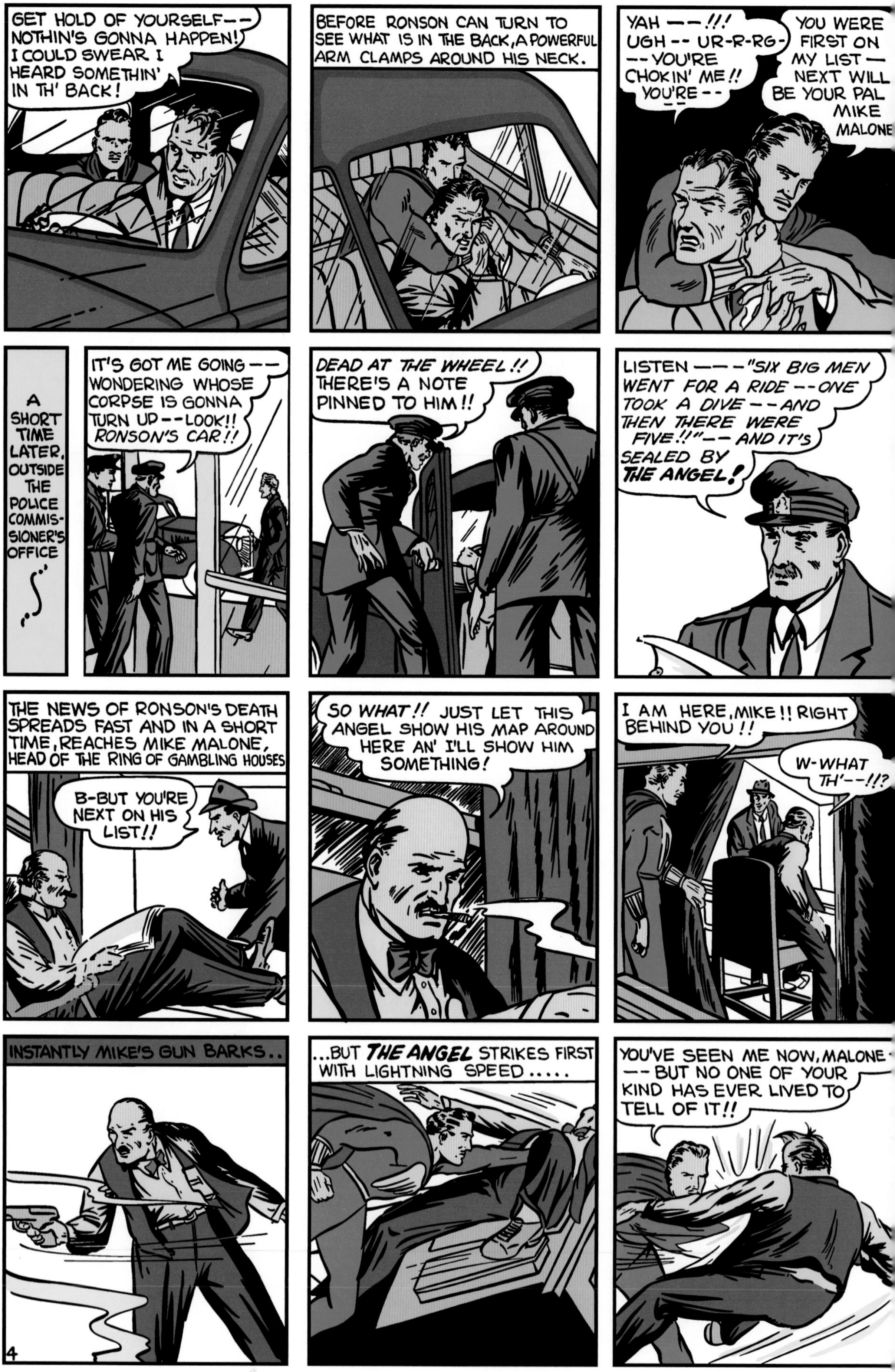

GET HOLD OF YOURSELF-- NOTHIN'S GONNA HAPPEN! I COULD SWEAR I HEARD SOMETHIN' IN TH' BACK!
BEFORE RONSON CAN TURN TO SEE WHAT IS IN THE BACK, A POWERFUL ARM CLAMPS AROUND HIS NECK.
YAH --!!! UGH -- UR-R-RG- --YOU'RE CHOKIN' ME!! YOU'RE -- --
YOU WERE FIRST ON MY LIST — NEXT WILL BE YOUR PAL MIKE MALONE
A SHORT TIME LATER, OUTSIDE THE POLICE COMMISSIONER'S OFFICE
IT'S GOT ME GOING -- WONDERING WHOSE CORPSE IS GONNA TURN UP--LOOK!! RONSON'S CAR!!
DEAD AT THE WHEEL!! THERE'S A NOTE PINNED TO HIM!!
LISTEN ---"SIX BIG MEN WENT FOR A RIDE --ONE TOOK A DIVE --AND THEN THERE WERE FIVE!!"-- AND IT'S SEALED BY THE ANGEL!
THE NEWS OF RONSON'S DEATH SPREADS FAST AND IN A SHORT TIME, REACHES MIKE MALONE, HEAD OF THE RING OF GAMBLING HOUSES
B-BUT YOU'RE NEXT ON HIS LIST!!
SO WHAT!! JUST LET THIS ANGEL SHOW HIS MAP AROUND HERE AN' I'LL SHOW HIM SOMETHING!
I AM HERE, MIKE!! RIGHT BEHIND YOU!!
W-WHAT TH'--!!?
INSTANTLY MIKE'S GUN BARKS..
4
...BUT THE ANGEL STRIKES FIRST WITH LIGHTNING SPEED.....
YOU'VE SEEN ME NOW, MALONE -- BUT NO ONE OF YOUR KIND HAS EVER LIVED TO TELL OF IT!!

AFTER LITERALLY MASHING HIM INTO A PULP, MIKE MALONE CRUMBLES INTO A HEAP. INSTANTLY THE ANGEL TURNS TO MIKE'S PAL...

...WHO MAKES FOR THE NEAREST EXIT --- A WINDOW ....

Y-Y-YOU WON'T G-GET ME!! N-NO YOU WON'T!!

IN THE CONFUSION, THE THUG PICKED THE WRONG WINDOW-- -INSTEAD OF THE ONE TO THE FIRE-ESCAPE....

MEANWHILE, A WOMAN QUIETLY OPENS THE DOOR AND PLACES A NOTE ON THE TABLE FOR THE ANGEL ...

"YOU CAN CROSS NUMBER THREE OFF YOUR LIST -- HE WAS THE ONE THAT WENT THROUGH THE WINDOW! NUMBER FOUR IS WAITING FOR YOU-- BE CAREFUL!!"

QUICKLY, THE ANGEL RUSHES INTO THE HALL TO SEE WHO HAD LEFT THE NOTE FOR HIM, ONLY TO GET A GLIMPSE OF A WOMAN ENTERING THE ELEVATOR....

H-M-M-M!! IT LOOKS AS IF THERE ARE OTHER THAN CIVIC REASONS WHY THESE MEN ARE TO BE DONE AWAY WITH! VERY INTERESTING --! SO NUMBER FOUR IS WAITING FOR ME!!

WHILE IN ONE OF THE UNDERWORLD'S DENS, TRIGGER BOLO, HEAD OF THE RETAIL-DELIVERY PROTECTIVE ASSOCIATION, WAITS FOR THE ANGEL.

ALL SET TRIGGER!

SO THE ANGEL'S GONNA DO AWAY WITH ME EH?! MY TRIGGER FINGER'S ITCHIN', SO SEE THAT YOU BRING HIM IN HERE!!

WE GOTCHA, BOSS!

NICE HOLE TRIGGER HAS -- FIT FOR ONLY RATS TO LIVE IN!!

THAT'S RIGHT-- BE NICE AND QUIET!!

IN THE STRUGGLE, THE THUG KNOCKS OVER A STACK OF CRATES....

...ATTRACTING THE ATTENTION OF THE OTHER MEN IN BOLO'S DEN.

HE'S GOT SHORTY!!

NO RODS— TRIGGER WANTS 'IM ALIVE!

SEEING THE GUN-MEN RUSHING TOWARD HIM, *THE ANGEL* COUNTER-ATTACKS WITH THE FURY OF A CHARGING LION!

BUT CANNOT WITHSTAND THE TREMENDOUS ODDS AGAINST HIM.

GOT HIS HANDS TIED?

YEAH!

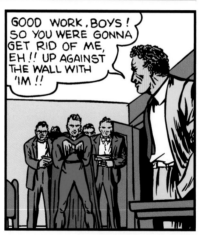

GOOD WORK, BOYS! SO YOU WERE GONNA GET RID OF ME, EH!! UP AGAINST THE WALL WITH 'IM!!

AT THAT MOMENT, THE MYSTERIOUS WOMAN, THAT LEFT THE WARNING NOTE FOR *THE ANGEL*, STEPS INTO THE ROOM.

NOT HERE, TRIGGER! THAT'S AN ORDER!

SEE THIS TOMMY-GUN! IT'S GONNA CUT YOU TO PIECES--VERY SLOWLY!

O.K.— STAND BACK, BOYS!

6

I'LL TAKE ORDERS HOW TO RUN THIS RACKET BUT NOT HOW TO GET RID OF GUYS! YOU CAN TELL THAT TO TH' BOSS!

THE WOMAN'S FACE TURNS STERN AND HER HAND FLASHES A SMALL AUTOMATIC !

TRIGGER— YOU'RE STEPPING OUT TOO FAR !

I-I'M SORRY LIL !! I-I'M JUST KINDA JITTERY AN' NERVOUS!! WHAT'S THE ORDERS??

STEVE ENKEL IS WAITING UPSTAIRS — WE THREE ARE TO TAKE THE ANGEL TO THE WOODS OUTSIDE OF THE CITY!

WELL—MY HUNCH ABOUT A BIG BOSS WAS RIGHT! SO STEVE ENKEL, THE POLITICAL FIXER, TRIGGER BOLO AND THE BIG BOSSES GO-BETWEEN ARE GOING TO TAKE ME FOR A RIDE! H-M-M-M !!

A FEW MINUTES LATER, THE ANGEL IS PLACED IN A CAR BETWEEN TRIGGER BOLO AND STEVE ENKEL, WHILE LIL FOLLOWS THE THREE IN HER OWN CAR...

SOON, THE TWO CARS STOP.

TIE HIM TO THAT TREE!

C'MON, YOU!

I THINK I LET THIS SO TOO FAR !

I WANT TO MAKE SURE HE'S TIED SECUREDLY!

AS LIL STEPS BEHIND THE TREE, SHE CUTS THE ROPES WITH A SHARP PEN-KNIFE....

WHAT THE—!!

ASK ENKEL FOR A CIGARETTE —— THE REST IS UP TO YOU!

AS STEVE ENKEL IS ABOUT TO LIGHT THE CIGARETTE, THE ANGEL STRIKES

SET AWAY FROM THERE YOU FOOL — I'M GONNA SHOOT!

N-NO !! YOU'LL GET ME TOO!!

THAT'S YOUR TOUGH LUCK !! I'M JUST CARRYING OUT ORDERS FROM TH' BOSS !

TO SAVE HIMSELF, STEVE ENKEL OPENS FIRE TOO....

KILLED EACH OTHER—FOUR AND FIVE! THANKS FOR SAVING MY LIFE! WAIT!

I DIDN'T SAVE IT—I'M JUST OBEYIN' ORDERS! JUST FORGET ABOUT THE WHOLE THING!

UNABLE TO CATCH THE FAST CAR OF LIL, *THE ANGEL* TURNS TO NUMBER SIX—DUTCH HANSEN.

AN HOUR'S NOTICE TO CLOSE THE BOOKS AN MAKE A DEPOSIT——IT'S TOO SHORT A TIME! WHO OPENED THAT WINDOW?? THAT BREEZE SEEMS ICE COLD!!

AS DUTCH TURNS, HE SEES *THE ANGEL!* INSTANTLY HE REACHES FOR THE GUN ON THE DESK...

...BUT *THE ANGEL* HURLES A HEAVY CHAIR AND SENDS HIM CRASHING INTO THE STONE FIRE-PLACE.

ALL THIS MONEY AND A KEY TO THE CITY BANK, SAFE DEPOSIT VAULTS—— I THINK I'M BEGINNING TO SEE THINGS! AND THIS NOTE FROM THE BOSS TO DEPOSIT IT BY TEN O'CLOCK SO HE CAN CHECK IT OVER! IT'S NINE-THIRTY——I'LL HAVE TO MOVE FAST!!

REACHING THE CITY BANK BUT A FEW MINUTES BEFORE TEN, *THE ANGEL* SEES LIL WALKING INTO IT WITH A FAMILIAR MAN...

DR. LANG — WHO STARTED THIS WAR ON CRIME! SO HE'S THE BIG BOSS!!

LIL — DUTCH HASN'T BEEN HERE !!

NO—AND HE NEVER WILL EITHER

THE ANGEL QUICKLY ENTERS THE VAULT UNNOTICED....

A PERFECT PLAN, EH!! EXCEPT YOU MISSED UP AT THE END! WILL YOU TELL YOUR STORY TO THE POLICE OR WILL I !?!

DR. LANG AND LIL PLANNED THE RACKETS THE PROCEEDS WHICH WERE TO BE DEPOSITED IN THIS VAULT AND SPLIT SEVEN WAYS AT THE END OF A YEAR! THAT WAS WHY THEY WANTED THE "SIX BIG MEN" DONE AWAY WITH——SO THERE WOULDN'T BE ANY SPLITTING TO DO AND THEY WOULD HAVE IT ALL TO THEMSELVES!

THE ANGEL FLIES TO ANOTHER....

ADVENTURE!

WATCH FOR THE NEXT EPISODE of "THE ANGEL" IN THE NEXT ISSUE...

The Sub-Mariner

HERE IS THE SUB-MARINER! ··AN ULTRA-MAN OF THE DEEP... LIVES ON LAND AND IN THE SEA... FLIES IN THE AIR... HAS THE STRENGTH OF A THOUSAND MEN... IS A YOUTH OF DYNAMIC PERSONALITY... QUICK THOUGHT AND FAST ACTION... FROM WHENCE DOES HE COME, AND WHAT IS HIS MISSION?

By Bill Everett

A SALVAGE SHIP'S DIVER COMES UP ~

THE DIVING PLATFORM IS HOISTED, AND SWUNG TO THE DECK OF THE SALVAGE SHIP "S.S. RECOVERY" —

HOW DO YOU FEEL, NELSON?

OKAY, CHIEF - BUT KINDA PUZZLED. THERE'S SUMP'N SCREWY ABOUT THAT WRECK ~

SOME TIME LATER, THE DIVER, ROD NELSON, STEPS FROM THE DECOMPRESSION CHAMBER, AND IS ASKED WHAT HE FOUND ON THE BOTTOM —

I FOUND THE SAFE IN THE MAIN SALOON, ALL RIGHT, BUT IT LOOKS LIKE SOMEBODY GOT HERE BEFORE WE DID ~ THE SAFE'S EMPTY! THEN, TOO, IT LOOKS LIKE WHOEVER RIFLED IT HASN'T BEEN GONE LONG - THERE WAS A KNIFE ON THE DECK, AND IT HADN'T EVEN RUSTED —

31

THAT'S STRANGE, NELSON – THERE'S BEEN NO REPORT OF ANY OTHER SALVAGE SHIP IN THESE WATERS FOR THREE YEARS – WE OURSELVES HAVE BEEN CRUISING HERE FOR A WEEK, AND WE'VE SEEN NO SIGN OF LIFE AT ALL

WELL, THERE'S ONLY ONE THING TO DO – I'LL HAVE TO SEND YOU DOWN AGAIN WITH CARLEY, TO SEE WHAT EVIDENCE YOU CAN PICK UP – THEY MAY HAVE LEFT SOMETHING BY WHICH WE CAN IDENTIFY THEM.

OKAY – SEND CARLEY AHEAD – I'LL BE WITH YOU IN A MINUTE....

ALL SET, CARLEY? I'LL DROP THE ACETYLENE TORCH AS SOON AS YOU HIT BOTTOM

AND SO CARLEY SETTLES BENEATH THE SURFACE, LITTLE KNOWING THE PHENOMENA HE AND NELSON ARE ABOUT TO WITNESS ~

SAY, ROD, DID YOU LEAVE THAT SIDE HATCH OPEN? OR WAS IT SPRUNG IN THE WRECK?

NO – IT WAS CLOSED WHEN I WAS DOWN BEFORE – THERE'S SOMETHING UNCANNY ABOUT THIS –

ON THE SEA BOTTOM THEY CONVERSE BY TELEPHONE~

COME ON, ROD—LET'S GET INSIDE—TURN ON YOUR LIGHT—WE MAY NEED IT

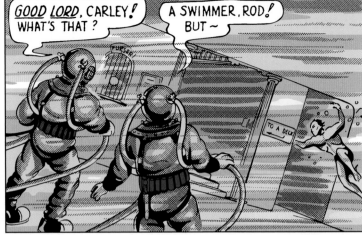

GOOD LORD, CARLEY! WHAT'S THAT?

A SWIMMER, ROD! BUT ~

IT CAN'T BE! NO HUMAN COULD LIVE IN THIS PRESSURE ~ YET NOW HE'S DISAPPEARED ~ AND HE WAS SWIMMING ~ HE CAN'T BE DEAD!

COME ON—LET'S FOLLOW HIM—HE CAN'T HAVE GONE FAR

BUT THE SWIMMER ELUDES THEM, AND WITH LONG STROKES OF HIS POWERFUL ARMS, RISES TO THE DECK OF THE SUNKEN SHIP —

HERE HE LOOKS CAUTIOUSLY ABOUT HIM, AND SEES THE CABLES RUNNING FROM THE DIVERS TO THE SURFACE OF THE WATER

THOSE ROBOTS—THEY CAN'T BE MEN! WHY, THEY'RE MECHANICAL—AND SO PONDEROUS—YET THEY'RE SHAPED LIKE MEN, AND CERTAINLY THEY'RE NOT FISH — I WONDER ...... ONE OF THEM HAD SOME KIND OF FIRE-WEAPON — I'D BETTER GET OUT OF HERE!

THESE MUST BE THE CONTROL WIRES —I'LL FIX IT SO THEY CAN'T FOLLOW ME!

WITH FIVE QUICK STROKES THE SWIMMER CUTS THE AIR-HOSES, TELEPHONE CABLES, AND ACETYLENE TORCH TUBE —!

33

HOLY SMOKE! OUR LINES ARE CUT! CALLING SURFACE - CALLING SURFACE! NO ANSWER!

THE DIVERS, REALIZING THEIR PREDICAMENT, QUICKLY SHUT THE AIR-VALVES IN THEIR HELMETS, THUS IMPRISONING THE AIR IN THEIR SUITS - TELEPHONE WIRES SEVERED THEY ARE CUT OFF FROM ALL COMMUNICATION

THE SUB-MARINER DARTS THROUGH THE DOOR, AND ATTACKS THE DIVERS!

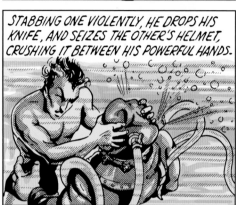

STABBING ONE VIOLENTLY, HE DROPS HIS KNIFE, AND SEIZES THE OTHER'S HELMET, CRUSHING IT BETWEEN HIS POWERFUL HANDS.

ON DECK OF THE "RECOVERY," THE MATE SEES BUBBLES ON THE WATER'S SURFACE WHICH WARN HIM OF THE TRAGEDY BELOW

NELSON - CARLEY! NELSON! - THE WIRES ARE DEAD!

ANDERSON - GET INTO YOUR SUIT - YOU'LL HAVE TO GO BELOW - TAKE LIFE-LINES, A KNIFE, AND ANOTHER TORCH - AND HURRY!

AYE, SIR!

ALL RIGHT - SEND HIM DOWN FAST, BO'S'N!

AND IN A MOMENT, BELOW ~

ANDERSON FINDS THE CRUSHED BODIES OF CARLEY AND NELSON. - THE SUB-MARINER WATCHES FROM SECLUSION -

FRIGHTENED, AND RISKING "THE BENDS," ANDERSON HAULS HIMSELF RAPIDLY TO THE SURFACE -

BACK ON DECK, IN THE DECOMPRESSION CHAMBER, ANDERSON GASPS OUT HIS REPORT - THE MATE ORDERS ALL HANDS TO GET THE SHIP UNDER WEIGH ~

WE'LL HAVE TO REPORT THIS TO THE COAST-GUARD - PETERS, MAN THE ANCHOR WINCH!

FROM THE DEPTHS, THE SUB-MARINER SEES THE POWERFUL PROPELLORS BEGIN TO CHURN, AS THE ANCHOR IS HOISTED ~

WITH THE SPEED OF A BULLET, HE SPRINGS UPWARD, AND WITH SUPERHUMAN STRENGTH, SEIZES THE RUDDER!

JAMMING IT TO THE RIGHT, HE STOPS THE STARBOARD PROPELLOR WITH BARE HANDS!

IN THE ENGINE ROOM, THE FIRST ASSISTANT REPORTS EXCITEDLY TO THE BRIDGE ~

STARBOARD PROPELLER FOULED, SIR!

WHAT'S THAT?!

GOOD LORD, SIR - THE RUDDER WINCH SEEMS OUT OF ORDER! THE SHIP WON'T RESPOND!

UNABLE TO REPAIR THE UNKNOWN DAMAGE, THE CAPTAIN ORDERS THE ENGINES STOPPED, BUT UNCANNILY THE SHIP PROCEEDS, HEADED FOR A COASTAL REEF!

THE CREW BECOMES PANICKY!

WITH EXTRAORDINARY STRENGTH, THE SUBMARINER GIVES THE UNFORTUNATE SHIP A TERRIFIC SHOVE - AND THE "RECOVERY" CRASHES HIGH ONTO THE ROCKS, SPLITTING COMPLETELY IN TWO

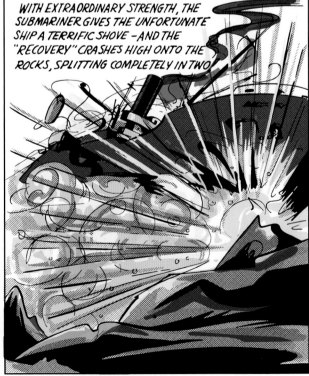

ELATED AT THIS FEAT OF HIS OWN STRENGTH, THE SUB-MARINER DIVES BACK TO THE SUBMERGED WRECK ~

GATHERING THE DIVERS' BODIES IN HIS ARMS, HE SPEEDS OFF THROUGH THE WATER ~ HIS WINGED FEET PROPEL HIM, ROCKET-LIKE, INTO GREATER DEPTHS, AND PRESENTLY HE FACES A MAMMOTH DOOR IN A SECLUDED GROTTO — IT OPENS AT HIS COMMAND ~

DOMMA! OPEN!

HE ENTERS A HUGE, CHAPEL-LIKE CHAMBER ~

AND IS ADDRESSED BY A BEAUTIFULLY ROBED CREATURE ON THE THRONE AT THE FAR END OF THE HALL ~

WELL, NAMOR, PRIVILEGED ONE, WHAT MANNER OF PRIZE DOST THOU BRING US TODAY?

THAT I CANNOT TRUTHFULLY SAY, HOLY ONE – BUT THOU SHALT SEE FOR THYSELF – THESE I CAME UPON AND CONQUERED, SURPRISING THEM AS THEY RAIDED THE EARTH-MEN'S DERELICT ~ THEY CAME FROM A FLOATING SHIP, WHICH I HAVE WRECKED WITH MY GREAT STRENGTH ~ I GIVE THEM TO YOU, AND PRAY YOU MAY BE PLEASED!

GREAT SHARKS, NAMOR! WHAT TYPE OF PRIZE DOST THOU CALL THESE? OPEN THEIR ENCASEMENTS – LET US SEE OF WHAT THEY ARE MADE!

WITH INFINITE CAUTION, THE HELMETS ARE UNSCREWED AND LIFTED OFF ~

HOLY MOTHER OF NEPTUNE! THEY ARE EARTH-MEN!!

CONGRATULATIONS, MY SON! YOU HAVE MADE A GOOD BEGINNING IN OUR WAR OF REVENGE!

WHY MOTHER!

KARAL, I COMMAND THEE TO OSSIFY THESE CREATURES ~ SET THEM IN THE ROYAL CHAMBER, WHERE THEY MAY BE SEEN AS EXAMPLES TO OUR WORTHY PEOPLE

DONE, YOUR HIGHNESS!

BUT MOTHER, I DON'T QUITE UNDERSTAND ~ WHY ARE THE EARTH-PEOPLE SO BAD? WASN'T MY FATHER AN EARTH-MAN?

YES, MY SON ~ AND A FINE MAN ~ BUT HIS PEOPLE WERE CRUEL ~ THEY INVADED OUR ANCIENT HOME DEEP IN THE WATERS AT THE SOUTH POLE, AND NEARLY EXTERMINATED OUR ENTIRE RACE ~ I MET YOUR FATHER IN THE YEAR 1920, WHEN.......

"A GREAT SHIP, THE 'ORACLE', CAME FROM AMERICA ON A SCIENTIFIC EXPEDITION ~ YOUR FATHER, COMMANDER LEONARD M'KENZIE, WAS THE CAPTAIN, AND THEY MADE THEIR BASE ON AN ICE-FLOE DIRECTLY ABOVE OUR CITY..."

"DURING THE WEEKS THAT FOLLOWED, WE WERE TORMENTED WITH BOMBARDMENTS OF NIGH EXPLOSIVES ~ OUR CASTLES WERE DEMOLISHED ~ OUR HUSBANDS, WIVES, MOTHERS, AND EVEN CHILDREN, WERE KILLED IN DROVES.........."

"THE WHITE EARTH-MEN WERE BLASTING US OUT OF EXISTENCE WITH THEIR INFERNAL 'SCIENTIFIC' INVESTIGATIONS' ~ SOON MANY MORE SHIPS ARRIVED, AND FINALLY, IN DESPERATION, OUR ELDERS COMMANDED AN ARMY TO BE FORMED, AND I, MOST NEARLY RESEMBLING THE FEMALE OF THE WHITE RACE, WAS INVESTED AS A SPY......."

THOU, FEN ~ BEAUTIFUL GODDESS OF THE SEALS ~ THOU SHALT FIND THY WAY INTO THE HANDS OF THESE WHITE MONSTERS, THERE TO WORK YOUR FEMININE WILES TO OUR RACIAL ADVANTAGE ~ GET THEE HENCE, WHILE THERE IS YET TIME!

"AND SO IT WAS, THAT, ON THE SAME NIGHT, I WAS FOUND HUNCHED UP AND SHIVERING, IN A SHIP'S HOLD, JUST AFT OF THE MAIN-MAST....."

GREAT HEAVENS! A STOWAWAY! CAPTAIN, COME QUICKLY!

"NOT REALIZING WHAT I WAS, OR WHY I WAS THERE, AND THINKING ME ONE OF THEIR OWN RACE, THEY HURRIED ME TO THE COMMANDER, WHO, GOOD MAN THAT HE WAS, DECIDED THAT I WAS INSUFFICIENTLY CLAD FOR THAT CLIMATE ~ AFTER GIVING ME HEAVY CLOTHES, IN WHICH I NEARLY SUFFOCATED, THEY FED ME SOME OF THEIR FOOD - WHAT IT WAS, I DIDN'T KNOW, BUT IT MADE ME VIOLENTLY ILL ~ THE COMMANDER TOOK PITY ON ME, AND, ALTHOUGH I COULD NOT UNDERSTAND HIS LANGUAGE, TRIED TO COMFORT ME WITH WORDS... "

"WITHIN A VERY SHORT TIME WE BECAME FAST FRIENDS, AND I BEGAN TO LEARN THEIR STRANGE TONGUE ~ THEY COULD NEVER UNDERSTAND, THOUGH, HOW I COULD SWIM SO MUCH IN THE EXTREMELY COLD WATER ~

OF COURSE I HAD TO, FREQUENTLY, FOR WE SUB-MARINERS CANNOT LIVE OUT OF WATER FOR LONGER THAN FIVE HOURS AT A STRETCH ~ AND MANY OF US CANNOT LIVE EVEN THAT LONG ~ "

"WELL, AS TIME WENT ON, THE COMMANDER AND I FELL IN LOVE, AND WERE MARRIED BY THEIR OWN RITUAL ~ AND ALL THE WHILE I WAS GIVING SECRET INFORMATION BACK TO OUR PEOPLE......"

WE CANNOT WIN, MASTER - THEY ARE TOO MIGHTY!

"AND THEY WERE TOO MIGHTY, FOR EVEN AS OUR ARMY ASSEMBLED FOR THE FIRST COUNTER-ATTACK, THERE CAME A TERRIBLE BOMBARDMENT FROM ABOVE - WHICH DESTROYED ALL BUT A MERE HANDFUL OF US!

AND SO, MY SON, IT HAS TAKEN US TWENTY YEARS TO BUILD UP A RACE TO AVENGE THE BRUTAL HARM DONE US THEN ~ NOW, SINCE YOU ARE THE ONLY ONE OF US LEFT WHO CAN LIVE ON LAND AND IN WATER, AND WHO CAN ALSO FLY IN THE AIR, AND BECAUSE YOU HAVE THE STRENGTH OF A THOUSAND EARTH-MEN, IT IS YOUR DUTY TO LEAD US INTO BATTLE! YOU HAVE BEGUN WELL, BUT YOU MUST USE STRATEGY AND GREAT CARE ~ GO NOW TO THE LAND OF THE WHITE PEOPLE!

AND SO NAMOR, THE AVENGING SON, FACES THE SURFACE MEN OF THE WORLD, IN WHAT PROMISES TO BE MORTAL COMBAT!

38

IN THE ADJOINING CHAMBER, NAMOR MEETS HIS COUSIN, YOUNG DORMA - HE TELLS HER OF HIS COMMISSION, AND HIS PROPOSED TRIP -

OH NAMOR! HOW WONDERFUL! TAKE ME WITH YOU - PLEASE!

IT WILL BE TOO DANGEROUS, DORMA - BUT YOU MAY ACCOMPANY ME PART WAY - COME, NOW - WE MUST HURRY!

BUT WON'T WE HAVE TO TAKE SOME EQUIPMENT WITH US, NAMOR?

DECIDING THAT EQUIPMENT WILL ONLY HAMPER THEIR PROGRESS, THEY TRAVEL "LIGHT", AND LEAVE THE UNDERWATER CASTLE WITH THE HEARTFELT BEST WISHES OF THE ENTIRE TRIBE .....

AFTER TRAVELING FOR TWO DAYS AT LIGHTNING SPEED, THEY STOP FOR REST, AND COME TO THE SURFACE AT THE FIRST SIGN OF CIVILIZATION ....

THIS MUST BE CAPE ANNA LIGHTHOUSE, DORMA - IT GIVES ME AN IDEA - WE CAN START OUR CRUSADE RIGHT HERE - YOU SEE, IF WE DEMOLISH THIS LIGHT, IT WILL ENDANGER MANY SHIPS, AND PERHAPS DESTROY THEM! - IT WILL BE OUR FIRST MOVE!

THERE'S NO TELLING HOW MANY PEOPLE OCCUPY THE LIGHTHOUSE, SO WE MUST TAKE NO CHANCES - WHEN THE GUARD OPENS THE DOOR, I'LL JUMP HIM AND RUSH INSIDE TO WRECK THE CONTROLS - IF ANYONE COMES, YELL TO ME!

QUIETLY, NOW! I HEAR SOMEONE COMING!

39

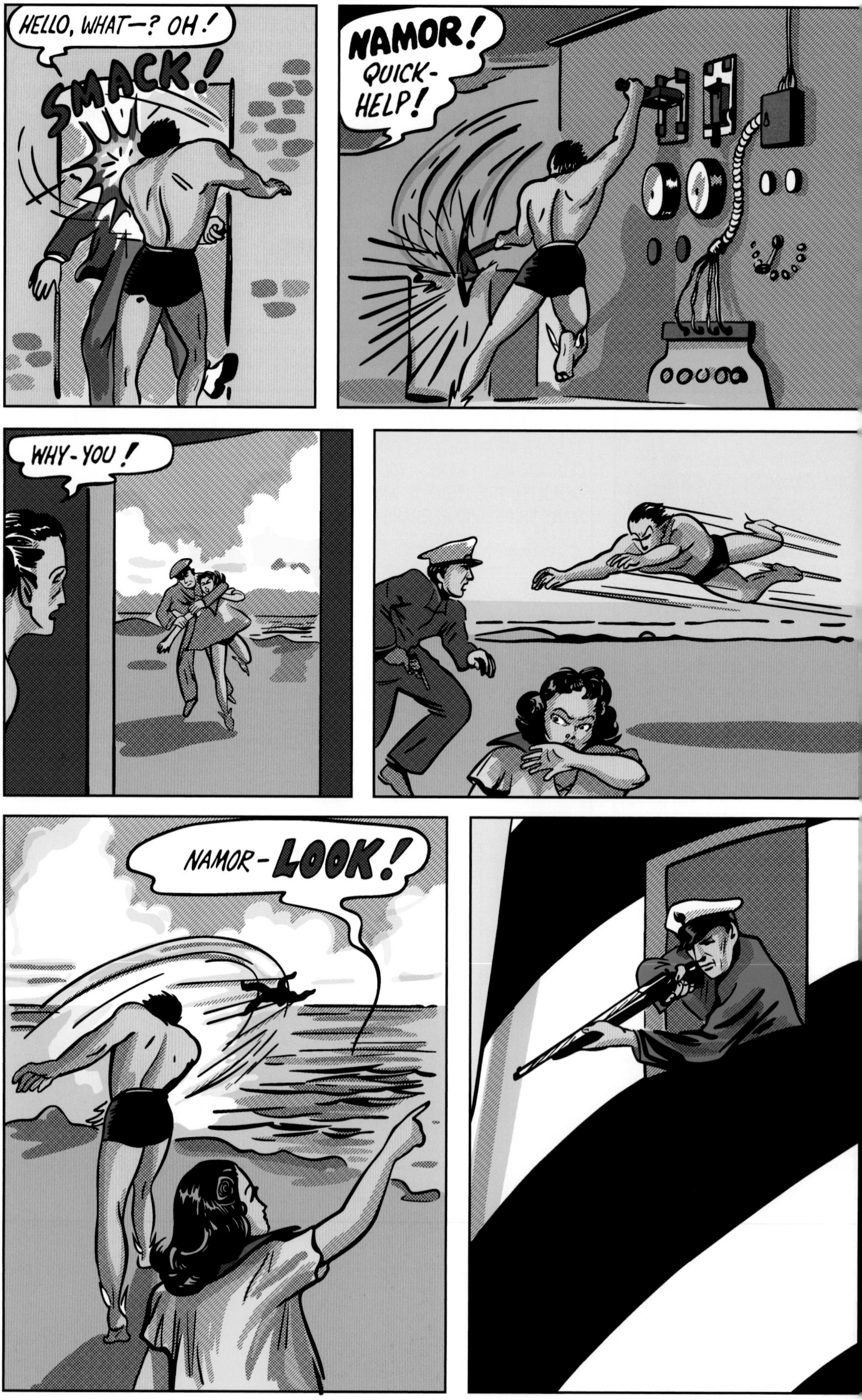
HELLO, WHAT—? OH!
SMACK!
NAMOR! QUICK- HELP!
WHY-YOU!
NAMOR-LOOK!

LIKE A FLASH, NAMOR LEAPS TO THE WINDOW!

OH NO, MY FRIEND! YOU DON'T GET AWAY *THAT* EASY!

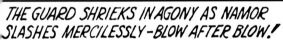

THE GUARD SHRIEKS IN AGONY AS NAMOR SLASHES MERCILESSLY — BLOW AFTER BLOW!

NAMOR! WHAT ARE YOU DOING?!

LOOK OUT, DORMA! COMING DOWN!

COME ON, GIRL — WE'VE GOT TO GET TO THE TOP! WE'LL WRECK THE BEACON LIGHT, AND TAKE OFF AS SOON AS WE CAN....

HURRY, NAMOR! WE'RE BEING *SURROUNDED*!

SAY, WHO ARE THESE PEOPLE? WHERE DID THEY COME FROM?

I DUNNO, CHIEF, BUT THEY'RE SURE RAISIN' HECK WITH THE LIGHT!

DORMA! THERE'S OUR ESCAPE! WHEN THAT PLANE FLIES NEARER, WE'LL MAKE A DIVE FOR IT! HOLD TIGHT, NOW!

WITH THE SPEED OF AN ARROW, NAMOR'S WINGED FEET SHOOT THEM STRAIGHT FOR THE PLANE!

QUIETLY, NOW, AND HURRY! WE MUST GET RID OF THE PILOT!

NAMOR HURLS HIMSELF UPWARD, AND GRAPPLES WITH THE PILOT —

THE AIRMAN IS NO TEST FOR NAMOR'S SUPERHUMAN STRENGTH, AND WITH A TERRIFIC BLOW, NAMOR SENDS HIM FLYING INTO SPACE!

DORMA, I'LL HAVE TO LEAVE YOU NOW — WRECK THE SHIP SOMEWHERE, AND SWIM BACK HOME ~ I'LL GET IN TOUCH WITH YOU LATER —

AND SO NAMOR DIVES INTO THE OCEAN AGAIN — ON HIS WAY TO FURTHER ADVENTURES IN HIS CRUSADE AGAINST WHITE MEN!

42

THE MASKED RAIDER.

CAL BRUNDER, POWERFUL RULER OF CACTUSVILLE, IS ATTEMPTING TO FORCE ALL OF THE SMALLER RANCHERS TO SELL OUT TO HIM, AT HIS OWN PRICE. BRUNDER SEND HIS GUN-MEN TO CALL ON JIM — GARDLEY —

NOW YUH GIT BACK AN' TELL BRUNDER I'M NOT SELLING OUT!

UNSEEN BY GARDLEY ONE OF BRUNDER'S MEN SNEAKS UP BEHIND HIM.

UP WITH 'EM GARDLEY! BRUNDER AIN'T GONNA LIKE WOT YUH DID!

AWRIGHT SLICK! LET'S TAKE HIM BACK T'TOWN!

AND DON'T TRY TUH MAKE NO GIT AWAY—IT AIN'T HEALTHY!

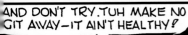

SOME DAY "SLICK", PEOPLE ARE GOING TO RUN YOUR CORRUPT GANG OUT OF THE COUNTRY. BRUNDER CAN'T KEEP BULL DOZIN' THE LITTLE RANCHERS MUCH LONGER!

WHY DON'T YOU GIT WISE TUH YORE SELF? WE COULD USE A MAN LIKE YOU IN OUR OUTFIT!

GARDLEY IS BROUGHT BEFORE BRUNDER, WHO IS THE REAL POWER IN CACTUSVILLE

HE LIKE TUH KILLED BENDS WIT' A BUSY ON THE JAW—HE SAID HE WOULDN'T SELL NOTHIN' EITHER

ALL RIGHT! SLICK!

SLICK YOU TALK TO THE OTHER RANCHERS..I'LL HANDLE FRIEND GARDLEY ALONE!

BRUNTER SOON REALIZES THAT GARDLEY IS UNAFRAID OF HIS THREATS.

NO USE WASTING ANY WORDS ON YOU — NOW I'LL GIVE SOME MEDICINE THAT WILL IN TIME CHANGE YOUR MIND!

BRUNDER SENDS FOR THE SHERIFF

WHAT'S ON YORE MIND CAL? GARDLEY?? WHAT, ARE YUH TIED UP FER?

SHERIFF, MY BOY'S CAUGHT GARDLEY RED HANDED — RUSTLING MY STOCK!

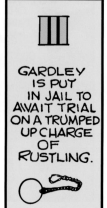

III

GARDLEY IS PUT IN JAIL TO AWAIT TRIAL ON A TRUMPED UP CHARGE OF RUSTLING.

GOSH A'MIGHTY KID — WHAT MADE YUH STEAL CATTLE —? YUH HAD A GOOD START, BUT NOW LOOK AT YUH!

BUT.. STEVE!

GARDLEY HAS PLENTY OF TIME TO THINK THINGS OVER.

POOR SHERIFF — I GUESS HE DOESN'T LIKE HIS JOB ANY TOO MUCH THESE DAYS — BOY, I'M IN A BAD SPOT!

IT'S TIME SOMEONE DID SOMETHING ABOUT THE BRUNDER GANG, AND I'M BEGINNING TO GET IDEAS.

YESSIR! IT MIGHT WORK!! I'M YOUNG AND STRONG— ...I'LL TRY IT — HEY— SHERIFF

I HEARD YUH — WHA'D'YA WANT — HOMESICK A'READY?

HURRY STEVE! I'M — DYING.. oooOH.. I CAN'T STAND THIS.. OH MY STOMACH..... STEVE!

I'M COMIN' — YUH CAIN'T TAKE ON LIKE THIS — AN' YUH CAIN'T DIE! 'CAUSE YUH GOTTA GO ON TRIAL

②

44

SHERIFF.. LEAN CLOSER.... I'M DYING! — I WANT TO... CONFESS!

AS THE SHERIFF BENDS A LITTLE CLOSER — A FIST, CRASHES INTO HIS CHIN —

SORRY STEVE, BUT I JUST COULDN'T STAY - I'LL ALSO NEED YOUR GUN!

LOCKING UP THE SHERIFF, GARDLEY STEPS OUTSIDE. THE STREET IS QUITE DESERTED.

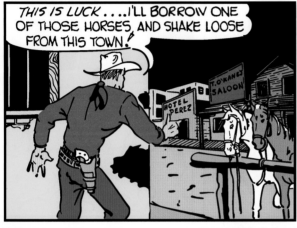

THIS IS LUCK ....I'LL BORROW ONE OF THOSE HORSES, AND SHAKE LOOSE FROM THIS TOWN!

GARDLEY HEADS FOR THE HILLS.

SAFE, FOR THE MOMENT, GARDLEY MAKES A CAMP IN THE HILLS

NOW OLD BOY, YOU, PRESENT SOMEWHAT OF A PROBLEM.

I HATE TO LET YOU GO OLD BOY — BUT YOU'D BE A DEAD GIVE A - WAY!

THEN, ONE NIGHT, GARDLEY, UNDER COVER OF DARKNESS, RAIDS HIS OWN RANCH FOR SUPPLIES. THE DAYS OF HIS DISAPPEARANCE BECOME WEEKS.

AT LAST MY DRAW IS FAST AND SMOOTH, AND OF LATE I HAVE MISSED ANY SHOTS!

NOW I MUST GET A TOP-NOTCH HORSE SOMEWHERE!

ONE DAY GARDLEY DISCOVERS A MAGNIFICENT WILD HORSE.

BOY! HE SURE IS A BEAUTY — HE'LL FILL THE BILL, PERFECTLY!

IN SPITE OF GARDLEY'S EFFORT THE HORSE REMAINS FREE

— THEN ONE DAY —

DOGGONE! HE'S CAUGHT HIMSELF!

THEN CAME DAYS OF THE UTMOST PATIENCE GRADUALLY JIM WON THE FRIENDSHIP OF THE HORSE, HE CALLED "LIGHTNING"

NOW FELLOW THE FUN IS GOING TO START

LIGHTNING IS SADDLED AND GARDLEY CLIMBS ABOARD HIS MOUNT PREPARED FOR THE WORST.

LIGHTNING BREAKS INTO A RUN —

...and GARDLEY IS MASTER.

PEOPLE ARE GOING TO HEAR A LOT ABOUT US, FROM NOW ON LIGHTNING!

④

JUBILANT OVER LIGHTNING'S ABILITIES, GARDLEY MAKES READY TO ADOPT A NEW ROLE THAT OF THE MASKED RAIDER.

I, JIM GARDLEY HEREBY MAKE A SOLEMN VOW TO FOREVER FIGHT THE LAWLESS...BRING JUSTICE TO THE OPPRESSED, AND HELP THE POOR—TO THIS END, I, THE MASKED RAIDER, DEDICATE MY LIFE TO THIS OATH!

SLICK, ROUND THE BOYS— BURN THE BLECK'S PLACE. WHEN THEY SEE THAT I MEAN BUSINESS...THEY WONT ACT SO VERY TOUGH!

I DON'T CARE IF ROWDY *HAS* FIVE ACES..THE GAMES OVER...WE'RE RIDIN'!

AWRIGHT!

SLICK AND BRUNDER'S GUNSLINGERS, SET OUT FOR THE BLECK'S RANCH.

BUT BLECK A SMALL RANCHER SEES THEM FIRST—

DON'T YOU FELLOW'S COME NO CLOSER!

A BULLET REMOVES BLECK FROM THEIR PATH.

PING

THET'S DONE...LOOK'S LIKE MRS BLECK DIDN'T MAKE IT!

NEWS OF THE BURNING OF THE BLECK RANCH SPREAD LIKE WILD-FIRE.

BUT, KILLIN' AND BURNIN' THET'S GOIN' TO FAR

SHUT UP! WHAT RIGHT HAVE YOU TO THINK?

IF YUH ASK ME – I BET PEOPLE ARE GONNA GIT READY AND DO A BIT OF SELLIN' OUT!

THE DESPERATE RANCHERS AT LAST DECIDE TO TRY AND FIND A SOLUTION TO THEIR PROBLEM.

WE BETTER DO SOMETHING ABOUT BRUNDER! I'LL HEAD SOUTH — YUH GIT THE RANCHERS NORTH OF HERE!

..AND WE MEET IN LORDIN'S BARN AT EIGHT T'MORROW!

YUH BET WE'LL BE THERE! IT'S TIME WE HAD A MEETIN'!

LORDIN, A WISE AND RESPECTED MAN IS CHOSEN TO SPEAK TO THE WORRIED RANCHERS.

AS MUCH AS I HATE TUH ADMIT DEFEAT I SAY SELL — WE DON'T WANT NO MORE KILLIN'S.

HE'S RIGHT!

I'M STICKIN'.

YER FREE T'DECIDE FER YORE SELVES... BUT TUH MORRER I'M A'SELLIN' LORDIN'S RIGHT!

BACK IN TOWN BRUNDER HEARS OF THEIR DECISION.

HO! HO! I KNEW THEY'D SEE IT THAT WAY.

HEY SLICK! CALL BRUNDER.

IT'S ROWDY, BOSS

WHAT TH-?

THIS WAS PINNED TUH ROWDY'S BACK.. HE'S SHOT UP BAD!

48

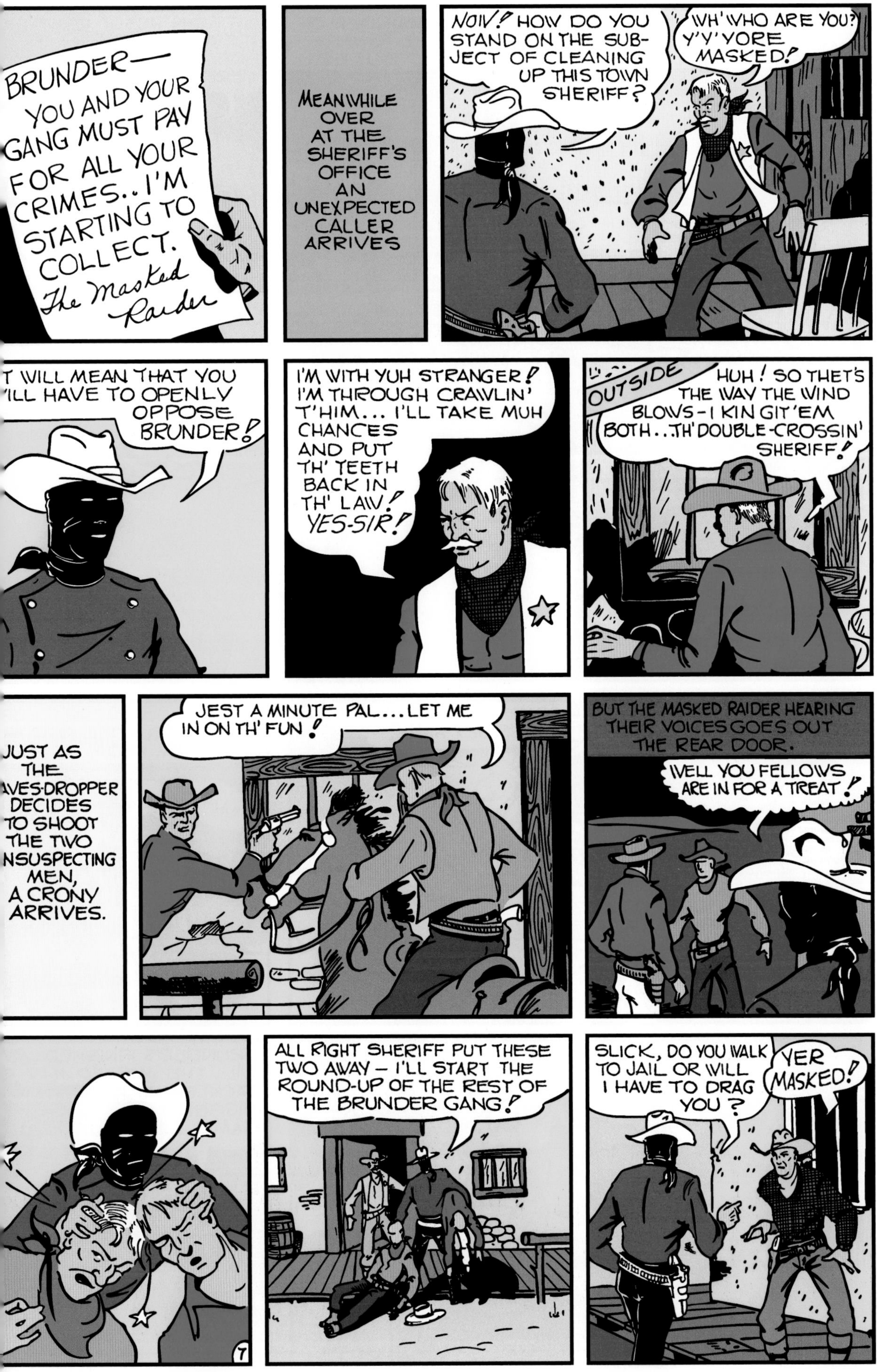
BRUNDER— YOU AND YOUR GANG MUST PAY FOR ALL YOUR CRIMES..I'M STARTING TO COLLECT. The Masked Raider
MEANWHILE OVER AT THE SHERIFF'S OFFICE AN UNEXPECTED CALLER ARRIVES
NOW! HOW DO YOU STAND ON THE SUBJECT OF CLEANING UP THIS TOWN SHERIFF?
WH' WHO ARE YOU? Y'Y' YORE MASKED!
T WILL MEAN THAT YOU 'ILL HAVE TO OPENLY OPPOSE BRUNDER!
I'M WITH YUH STRANGER! I'M THROUGH CRAWLIN' T'HIM... I'LL TAKE MUH CHANCES AND PUT TH' TEETH BACK IN TH' LAW! YES-SIR!
OUTSIDE
HUH! SO THET'S THE WAY THE WIND BLOWS - I KIN GIT 'EM BOTH..TH' DOUBLE-CROSSIN' SHERIFF!
JUST AS THE AVES-DROPPER DECIDES TO SHOOT THE TWO NSUSPECTING MEN, A CRONY ARRIVES.
JEST A MINUTE PAL...LET ME IN ON TH' FUN!
BUT THE MASKED RAIDER HEARING THEIR VOICES GOES OUT THE REAR DOOR.
WELL YOU FELLOWS ARE IN FOR A TREAT!
7
ALL RIGHT SHERIFF PUT THESE TWO AWAY - I'LL START THE ROUND-UP OF THE REST OF THE BRUNDER GANG!
SLICK, DO YOU WALK TO JAIL OR WILL I HAVE TO DRAG YOU?
YER MASKED!

THE LOUD VOICE OF SLICK BRINGS THE REMAINDER OF BRUNDER'S GANG TO HIS AID — BUT THE TOWNSMEN RUSH TO THE AID OF THE "MASKED RAIDER".

GIT GOIN' 'HOSS! IT'S TOO HOT HERE!

AH! SO BRUNDER IS TRYING TO RUN OUT — NOT IF I CAN HELP IT!

COME ON LIGHTNING! LET'S GET HIM!!

THE MASKED RAIDER'S ROPE SNAGS BRUNDER AND — JERKS HIM FROM HIS HORSE

WHAT TH.!

THERE YOU ARE MEN — THE BRUNDER GANG IS NO MORE!

ANDERS

BRUNDER'S FINISHED.. BUT WILL THE MASKED MAN TACKLE THE BIGGER GAME.?

The End

50

JUNGLE TERROR

A COMPLETE ADVENTURE STORY

by TOHM DIXON

AT THE FLORIDA PLANTATION HOME OF PROFESSOR ROBERTS, KEN MASTERS AND TIM ROBERTS, THE PROFESSOR'S NEPHEW ARE TALKING....

I TELL YOU, TIM — WE SHOULDN'T HAVE LET THE PROFESSOR GO INTO THAT JUNGLE! THREE MONTHS HAVE GONE BY AND WE HAVE NOT HEARD FROM HIM AS YET!

JUST BECAUSE SOMEONE TOLD HIM THAT A CERTAIN INDIAN TRIBE HAS A DIAMOND POSSESSING HYPNOTIC POWERS IS NO REASON FOR HIM TO GO ALONE INTO THE JUNGLE! WE'VE GOT TO FIND HIM, TIM — LET'S TAKE A LOOK AT THE MAP!

YES—HERE'S THE SPOT THE PROF. MARKED BEFORE HE LEFT, TIM!

GEE—IT SURE IS A DESOLATE SPOT, KEN!

I'LL SAY, SON! LOOK—DEEP IN THE AMAZON JUNGLE! WELL, THAT SETTLES IT. TIM——

—WE'RE LEAVING THE FIRST THING IN THE MORNING, TIM! —AND WE'RE GOING BY AIR!

WHEE!! I CAN'T WAIT TILL MORNING, KEN!!

BUT OUTSIDE THE WINDOW, A FIGURE LISTENS—

—AND A FEW MINUTES LATER!

THE FIGURE RUSHES INTO THE HOME OF JOHN CRAFTON, OWNER OF THE ADJOINING PLANTATION.

BOSS! THEY'RE LEAVING IN THE MORNIN'! I HEARD MASTERS TELL TH' KID!

GOOD! TELL THE BOYS TO GET READY! WE FOLLOW!

THE NEXT MORNING KEN AND TIM ARE READY TO LEAVE.

OKAY, KEN LET'S GO!

TAKE A LAST LOOK AT FLORIDA, TIM, WE'RE HEADED TOWARD THE CARIBBEAN!

KEN!! THERE'S A PLANE FOLLOWING US -- SAY!! IT LOOKS LIKE -- IT IS --- THAT'S CRAFTON'S PLANE!! NOW I WONDER WHAT HE'S UP TO!!

HOURS LATER!

THEY'RE STILL FOLLOWING US, KEN!

LET 'EM COME! WE'RE OVER THE JUNGLE, TIM!

OH-OH! SOMETHING'S WRONG! MOTOR'S MISSING!! HOLD TIGHT, TIM — WE'RE GOIN' TO LAND IN THE TREES!

KEN CLIMBS FROM THE WRECK PLANE CARRYING TIM WITH HIM

OW—MY HEAD! ARE YOU OKAY, KEN?

YES, TIM—TAKE IT EASY! YOU'LL BE ALL RIGHT IN A FEW MINUTE

BUT A FIGURE FOLLOWS KEN AND THE BOY AS THEY MAKE THEIR WAY THROUGH THE JUNGLE!

DON'T BE AFRAID, TIM— BUT I THINK WE'RE BEING FOLLOWED!

GOSH— SAVAGES!

A MOMENT LATER—

WHITE MAN STOP WE TAKE TO CHIEF! COME

MEANTIME, CRAFTON AND HIS MEN LAND IN THE JUNGLE AND SET OUT TO FIND KEN AND TIM.

STRAIGHT AHEAD, BOYS, AND STEP ON IT!

I'M KEEPIN MY GUN HANDY, BOSS!

HERE'S WHAT WE DO—WE FOLLOW MASTERS AND TH' KID UNTIL THEY FIND PROFESSOR ROBERTS—THEN WE WAIT, AND WHEN THEY GET THE DIAMOND WE LET 'EM HAVE IT AND MAKE OUR WAY BACK TO THE PLANE!

HEY, BOSS, TAKE IT EASY, MY FEET HURT!

B-BOSS! H-HELP! DO SOMETHING QUICK!

I GOT 'IM, BOSS!!

BANG! BANG!

NICE WORK, MIKE, BUT C'MON LET'S GET GOIN'! WE'VE GOT TO FIND WHAT'S HAPPENED TO MASTERS AN' THE KID!

I'LL SHOW THESE SAVAGES WHO'S BOSS 'ROUND HERE—

COMIN' BOSS!

—SUDDENLY A WHIZZING SOUND PIERCES THE AIR AND——

OW!

ZING!

HE'S DEAD, SLUG! MUST'VE BEEN A POISONED ARROW—

DON'T MOVE BOSS! THEY'RE ALL AROUND US— I CAN SEE 'EM THROUGH THE BUSHES!

A MOMENT LATER THEY ARE SURROUNDED BY SAVAGES!

THEY'RE MOTIONING FOR US TO FOLLOW 'EM!

WE'D BETTER DO AS THEY SAY, BOSS— I DON'T LIKE THE WAY THEY'RE LOOKIN' AT US!

THE TWO MEN ARE LED TO THE NATIVE VILLAGE.

MEANWHILE KEN AND TIM ARE LED TO THE CHIEF'S HUT!

I'M OKAY NOW, KEN!

GOOD, TIM!

TAKE THEM TO THE PRISONER'S HUT—WE WILL KILL THEM LATER!

THIS IS GOOD! WE COME DOWN HERE TO GET YOUR UNCLE OUT OF A JAM AND WE GET IN ONE OURSELVES!

IN THERE— DO NOT TRY TO ESCAPE!

GOSH, KEN! NOW WE'LL NEVER FIND UNCLE JOHN!

—AND AS THEY ENTER THE HUT!

KEN—LOOK! IT'S UNCLE JOHN!

TIM! KEN— WHAT ARE YOU TWO DOING DOWN HERE?

WE CAME AFTER YOU, PROF! BUT WHY ARE YOU A PRISONER? I THOUGHT YOU KNEW THIS TRIBE!

AT FIRST THEY WERE FRIENDLY, KEN—BUT WHEN THEY SAW I WAS AFTER THE HYPNOTIC DIAMOND THEY THREW ME IN HERE!

BUT LOOK! I'VE FOUND AN OPENING IN THIS CORNER—IT MUST LEAD SOMEWHERE—I'LL GO FIRST—WHEN THE COAST IS CLEAR, FOLLOW ME!

GO AHEAD, TIM! YOU'RE NEXT— BUT TAKE IT EASY—IT MIGHT BE A BIG DROP!

UNCLE JOHN IS HELPIN' ME FROM BELOW—C'MON, KEN!

SHALL I LET GO, UNCLE JOHN!

YES, TIM! GOSH—I HAD NO IDEA THIS PLACE WAS SO DEEP!

A FEW MINUTES LATER KEN JOINS THEM AND THE THREE SET OUT IN THE DARKNESS!

HANG CLOSE, TIM! SEE ANYTHING, KEN?

NO--WAIT YES --A LIGHT!

GREAT SCOTT, KEN! THAT LIGHT—IT'S AS HOT AS A FURNACE—WHAT IS IT?

WOW! YOU'LL SEE, PROF! GET CLOSER!

4.

DIAMONDS —MAN— DIAMONDS! NOT ONE, THOUSANDS!

ER—— I THINK I'LL TAKE——

STOP! DON'T TOUCH THOSE DIAMONDS! HANDS UP, ALL O' YOU!

LOOK! IT'S CRAFTON!

WELL I'LL BE— IT IS! HOW DID YOU GET DOWN HERE CRAFTON?

IF YOU MUST KNOW, MASTERS— WE LANDED AFTER YOU CRACKED UP, AND WERE CAPTURED BY THOSE SAVAGES—THEY PUT US IN A HUT —WE ESCAPED INTO THE JUNGLE AND FOUND A CAVE! THIS IS WHERE IT LED TO—HAH!

THEN HERE 'S A WAY OUT O' HERE!

SURE BUT YOU'LL NEVER GET TO USE IT—OKAY, SLUG, FILL YOUR POCKETS AND MINE—THEN WE'LL RUN OUT OF HERE! THE SAVAGES WILL TAKE CARE O' THESE THREE!

BUT AS SLUG STEPS FORWARD TO TOUCH THE DIAMONDS —

ZING!

SLUG! HE'S DEAD! THEY'RE COMIN'—— WE'LL BE KILLED—— —I'M GETTING OUT O' ———

KEN! ANOTHER ARROW—LOOK OUT!

UH—

WHIZZ-Z

—AND AS CRAFTON FALLS TO THE GROUND KEN DIVES FOR THE GUN!

KEN—LISTEN— THEY'RE COMIN' DOWN THE TUNNEL!

RUN FOR IT, MEN — I'LL HOLD 'EM OFF—WE'VE GOT TO FIND CRAFTON'S PLANE—IT'S OUR ONLY CHANCE!

BANG! BANG!

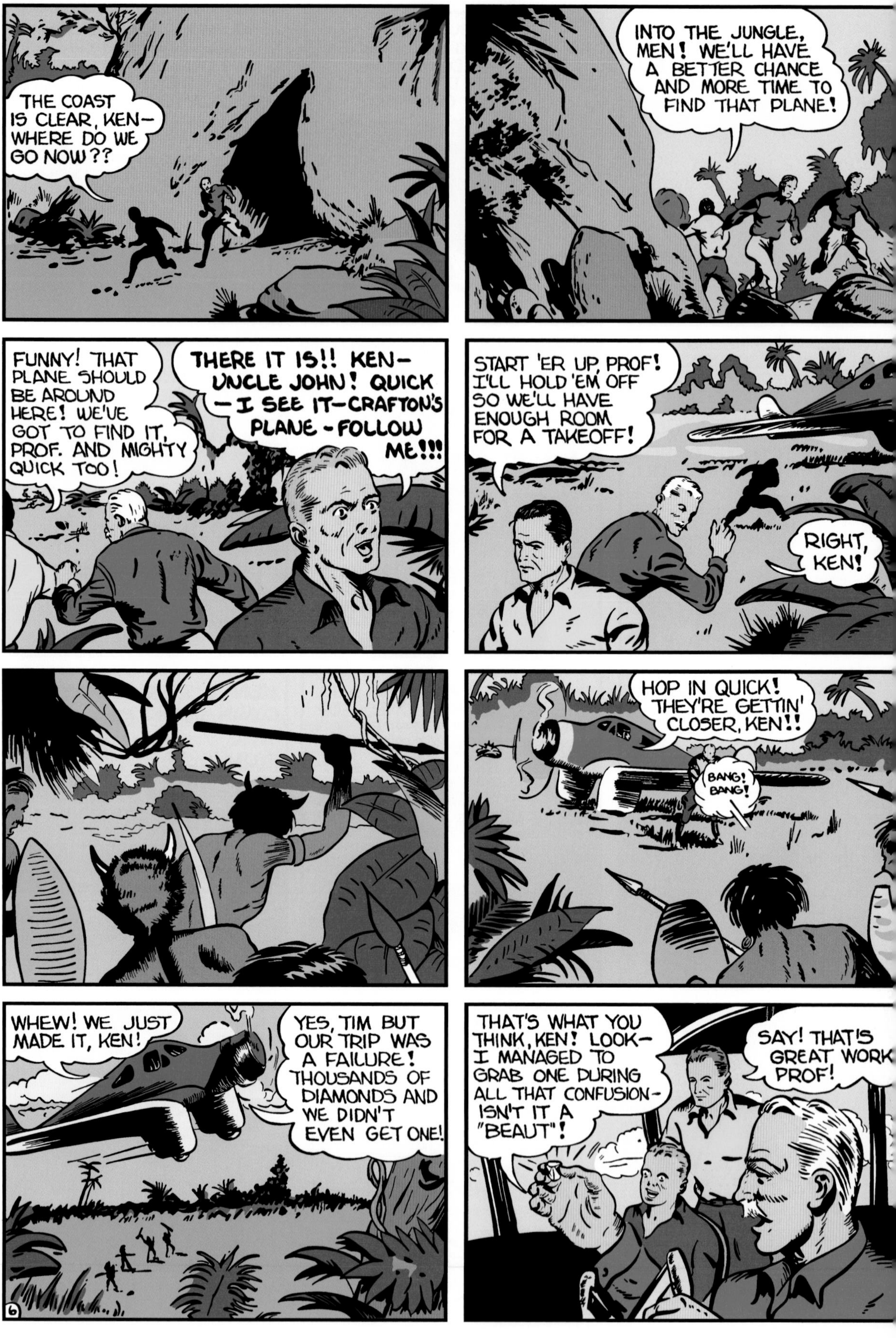
THE COAST IS CLEAR, KEN—WHERE DO WE GO NOW??
INTO THE JUNGLE, MEN! WE'LL HAVE A BETTER CHANCE AND MORE TIME TO FIND THAT PLANE!
FUNNY! THAT PLANE SHOULD BE AROUND HERE! WE'VE GOT TO FIND IT, PROF. AND MIGHTY QUICK TOO!
THERE IT IS!! KEN—UNCLE JOHN! QUICK—I SEE IT—CRAFTON'S PLANE—FOLLOW ME!!!
START 'ER UP, PROF! I'LL HOLD 'EM OFF SO WE'LL HAVE ENOUGH ROOM FOR A TAKEOFF!
RIGHT, KEN!
HOP IN QUICK! THEY'RE GETTIN' CLOSER, KEN!!
BANG! BANG!
WHEW! WE JUST MADE IT, KEN!
YES, TIM BUT OUR TRIP WAS A FAILURE! THOUSANDS OF DIAMONDS AND WE DIDN'T EVEN GET ONE!
THAT'S WHAT YOU THINK, KEN! LOOK—I MANAGED TO GRAB ONE DURING ALL THAT CONFUSION—ISN'T IT A "BEAUT"!
SAY! THAT'S GREAT WORK PROF!

BURNING RUBBER

A Short Short Story About
The Auto Race Tracks

By Raymond Gill

THE crowd roared . . . with laughter! Bill Williams knew what they were laughing at, his coveted Blue Bird. Compared to the other cars in the race, the Blue Bird did look a bit shabby. But one thing was certain, there weren't any better mechanics or drivers than Bill and his able mechanic, Fred Turner.

"Everything's shipshape, Bill. You know, I feel kind of sorry for those other mugs. I'd hate to lose a race if I spent a lot of dough on a two tone chrom plated model."

"Fine. Well, I don't know, I'd give a lot to dress my Lady Bird here up with a lot of new feathers. I don't give a hoot what the crowd thinks myself, but I feel sorry for my Laddie's' sake.

"Cut it fella, I think you did pretty well digging up the entry fee. After all, you spent plenty for parts for your new super-charger."

"Yep, that's our only hope now. Don't kid yourself that we have any cinch. We have the best drivers in the business here today."

"What's the matter with you today Bill, I've never heard you talk like this before. You sound as though you've lost faith in our Blue Bird."

"No, not on your life. That's one thing I'll never do. I guess it got under my skin a little bit . . . those people laughing at her, I mean."

"That's better. By the way, doesn't Ann ever complain about your spending so much time with your 'Lady' here?"

"Yea, she was kidding me the other night."

"Well, there goes the signal, Bill. Move over."

"Oh, ah. . . . Listen old man, let me take it alone this time. . . . I don't know why I want to. I . . . well, humor me this once, will you? I know I'll feel a lot better if I get out there alone. . . ."

"Ah, sure . . . sure, Bill. Anything you say. Only, be careful."

BILL shot ahead with a roar that surprised the smiling crowd that had gathered around to poke fun at the Blue Bird.

He was hardly topped on the line when the second starting signal was given. There were eight cars in the race besides the Blue Bird. The combined noise of dozens of unmuffeled explosions thundered out into an increasing crescendo that thrilled some and annoyed others.

To Bill it was sweet music . . . the powerful voice of his Lady Bird. Bill was in his glory, he could feel his whole body grow taught with a passionate desire to go faster, faster, faster. The stiffer his body grew, the harder his foot pressed the accelerator.

He was setting the pace, the other cars directly behind him, weaving back and forth. He was at his perfect ease now, he felt that the Lady Bird was standing still and that the track was some never ending ribbon that kept unfolding in front of him. He was in a new world, a world all his own.

Ann, the girl was literally sitting on the edge of her seat as she watched the Blue Bird madly rush on in meaningless velocity. Or so it seemed to her.

"Hello, Ann. Enjoying the race?"

"Fred! What are you doing up here? Why aren't you in there with Bill?"

"Whoa, take it easy. He's just a bit moody, I guess. He vants to be alone."

"Oh, Fred, I always feel better when you're with him. If it's possible to feel good when he's throwing himself bodily into the face ot fate. You shouldn't have let him take it out there alone."

"Well, it's too late now to do anything about that, besides, there's something you can do to help Bill. That's why I came up here."

"Yes, Fred. You know I'll do anything for that grease monkey."

"That's the idea, calm down. I don't know what it is that's got everybody keyed up today. We've all gone through these races before together."

"Yes, we have, Fred. But somehow I feel that today it's all got to end. One way or the other."

"Ann, you know that we've spent a lot of time working on the Blue Bird these last few months. We always work hard on her before a race, but this time we've done something more than that. We've perfected a new gas feeder. I know Bill wouldn't want me to tell you, but I feel that you have a right to know. Bill is in there right now, risking his life to test it. This test is the final step. If it works, Bill will retire from the track. He told me so. If it fails . . . well . . ."

"Fred! Tell me. What if it doesn't work, what will happen? What can a gas feeder do that will possibly crack him up?"

"Just this. That new feeder is mounted over the engine, it feeds with a combined force of gravity and pressure. If anything should go wrong, if it should spring the smallest leak . . . that hot motor will blow both him and the Blue Bird to kingdom come."

"Tell me, quickly Fred. What can I do that will help?"

"Well, you and Ruth Clerk, the daughter of the big motor magnet, C. G. Clark, are on pretty good terms, aren't you?"

"Why, yes. Ruth and I went to school together. Why?"

"Here's why. If you can get Ruth to get you in to see her father, now, before it's too late, we may be able to save the day . . . and Bill's neck."

"What am I supposed to do after I get in?"

"Here, show him these plans. It's the g[as] feeder. If you can sell him on the idea [of] manufacturing it, Bill could be flagged out [of] the race before that temporary mountin[g] should blow."

"It's a deal. Give me those plans. You ju[st] watch . . . he won't make more than on[e] more circle of the track . . . I'll see to that[.]"

BILL, still madly kicking the gas pedal, w[as] now unconsciously wiping oil off his fa[ce] . . . suddenly he jerked himself back into sta[rk] reality. The oil he's wiping off is thin. . . . To[o] thin. . . . GASOLENE!

On the stands, Fred saw the thin shred [of] smoke trailing the Blue Bird. Terror grippin[g] his heart, he called to Ann to hurry. . . . [In] another moment. . . .

But Ann hadn't wasted any time. Fred['s] nervous, scanning eyes finally located he[r] down talking to the starter.

He also saw the Blue Bird, never slowin[g,] round the turn and come rocketing up t[he] straightway in front of the stands. Just as [he] crossed the line the checkered flag wave[d] him out of the race. The other cars shot rig[ht] past him for the final lap. Bill leaped out [of] the Blue Bird and took the situation in at [a] glance. Of course, just like a woman. A[nn] became nervous . . . couldn't stand a litt[le] smoke . . . so she had him flagged out. S[he] didn't care if she was throwing all of his har[d] work out of the window.

"Well, Ann, you did a beautiful job. [I] couldn't have done better myself. And yo[u] claim you care for me. Why, all you care abo[ut] is yourself. . . ."

"See here, see here. This young lady ju[st] saved your life. A most ungrateful exhibitio[n] young man. A most ungrateful exhibition."

"Why, Mr. Clark. I . . . Oh, whats' t[he] use . . . she's probably queered that too. A[t] least if she let me finish the race I'd be in th[at] much. Oh, well."

"Young man, this young lady just explain[ed] the fine points of your new gas feeder to m[e.] I'd like to have you drop in to my office th[is] afternoon, if you will, and we can come [to] terms."

"What? Why didn't you tell me this befor[e?] Wheeeeee? Oh, Ann, forgive me. . . . To th[e] devil with the race."

"Oh, ah, pardon me. But do remember m[e,] I'm Fred, your mechanic?"

"Fred. You old sonofagun. Isn't it wo[n]derful?"

"It certinly is. The darn thing works! Yo[u] did manage to gain a whole lap on those birds[.] They all had to go around an extra lap t[o] compete for second place!"

ADVENTURES OF
KA-ZAR THE GREAT

CHAKA

from the FAMOUS CHARACTER
CREATED BY
BOB BYRD

ZAR

TRAJAH

Ben Thompson

John Rand, young owner of a rich diamond field in the Transvaal, is flying from Johannesburg to Cairo with his wife and their three-year-old son David. Over the heart of the **BELGIAN CONGO** the plane develops motor trouble and Rand is forced to come down in the thick, wild **TROPICAL FOREST!!**

CONSTANCE!! HOLD DAVID..... I'M GOING TO LAND!!

THE PLANE DIVES INTO THE DENSE CONGO JUNGLE!

CONSTANCE! DAVID! ARE YOU HURT?

JOHN RAND STAGGERS OUT OF THE WRECK!!

TENDERLY, HE LIFTS HIS WIFE OUT OF THE BROKEN PLANE

MUMMY HURT?

MY LEG.... I THINK IT'S BROKEN!!

THERE'S A MEDICAL KIT IN THE PLANE....I'LL FIX YOU UP IN A JIFFY!

WHILE HIS MOTHER WAS RECOVERING, YOUNG DAVID QUICKLY MADE FRIENDS WITH THE SMALL JUNGLE ANIMALS

DAILY, ZAR, LORD OF THE JUNGLE, WATCHES THE STRANGE TWO-LEGGED CUB!!

ANOTHER PAIR OF KEEN EYES WATCH THE BOY AS HE PLAYS NEAR THE EDGE OF THE SMALL CLEARING.

N'JAGA, THE LEOPARD, COULD WAIT NO LONGER!

LOOK, DADDY!

A WARNING CRY FROM DAVID'S MOTHER BRINGS JOHN RAND WITH A RIFLE ....

ONE QUICK SHOT STOPS N'JAGA AND THE WOUNDED LEOPARD DASHES INTO THE JUNGLE WITHOUT HARMING DAVID.

3

YOU HURT HIM... NOW HE WON'T COME BACK..

DAVID HAS NO FEAR OF JUNGLE ANIMALS --

STRANGE...HE DOESN'T SEEM TO BE AFRAID OF ANY BEAST!!

RAND MARVELS AT THE BOY'S LACK OF INSTINCTIVE FEAR.

LATER, THE FATHER'S AUTOMATIC SAVES DAVID FROM AN EMERALD GREEN SNAKE! EVEN THEN, THE BOY MOURNS THE PASSING OF A FELLOW DENIZEN OF THE WILD!

BACK! DAVID...

DADDY— HE'S MY FRIEND!

JOHN RAND'S ANNOUNCE-MENT THAT SEARCHING PLANES WOULD SOON FIND THEM DID NOT CHEER DAVID, UNHAPPY WITH THE THOUGHT OF HAVING TO LEAVE HIS NEW JUNGLE COMPANIONS.

DAYS FOLLOWED WITH NO SIGN OF RESCUE, DURING WHICH TIME RAND BUILT A SAFE AND COMFORTABLE DWELLING FOR HIS FAMILY OUT OF PARTS OF THE WRECKED PLANE. CONSTANCE RECOVERED RAPIDLY AND DAVID'S SKIN BRONZED UNTIL IN THE REMNANTS OF HIS TORN CLOTHING HE RESEMBLED A STURDY YOUNG SAVAGE!

JOHN! I HEAR A PLANE!

WATER AND FUEL WERE WITHIN EASY REACH AND THE PARENTS WERE BECOMING RECONCILED TO THE STRANGE ENVIRONMENT, WHEN--

I'LL LIGHT THE SIGNAL FIRE!

IN THE CLEARING, SMOKE ROLLS HIGH AS THE DRONE OF THE PLANE GROWS LOUDER.

RAND SPLASHES OUT INTO THE LAKE, AWAY FROM THE TOWERING TREES, AND WAVES A TARPAULIN.

NOT A SIGN OF RAND OR HIS PLANE..... NO CHANCE OF FINDING THEM IN THIS JUNGLE!

TURNING, THE PILOT CIRCLES TO THE NORTH WITHOUT SEEING THE SMOKE!

WITH A SINKING FEELING, RAND AND HIS WIFE WATCH THE PLANE DISAPPEAR!

POOH! THIS IS A BUSY HIGHWAY...THERE'LL BE ANOTHER ALONG SOON!

TRUE, THE PLANE CAME AGAIN THE NEXT DAY....AND ONE THE DAY AFTER, BUT EACH TIME IT WAS FARTHER FROM THEIR LONELY CAMP, UNTIL FINALLY, THEY CAME NO MORE.

THE DAY CAME WHEN CONSTANCE LAY IN THE HUT, CONSUMED BY A RAGING FEVER!!

SOON SHE DIED FROM THE RAVAGES OF THE TROPICAL FEVER. RAND WAS HEART-BROKEN...MORBIDLY HE TOYED WITH THE IDEA OF ENDING IT ALL.....LIFE HELD NO MEANING FOR HIM.

HIS WIFE'S LAST WISH HAD BEEN THAT THE BOY MUST LIVE. THAT THOUGHT, THAT CONVICTION, BROUGHT RAND BACK TO HIS SENSES. IMMEDIATELY HE BEGAN MAKING PLANS TO TREK BACK TO CIVILIZATION.

IT'S ABOUT 200 MILES TO THE NEAREST WHITE OUTPOST!

THE HEAVY RAINS STOPPED AND RAND STUDIES THE MAP HE CARRIED IN THE AIRPLANE.

DAVID KNEW WHERE THE SWEETEST FLOWERS GREW FOR HIS MOTHER'S GRAVE.

THAT EVENING, A TERRIBLE STORM LASHED THE JUNGLE.

AS GIANT BAOBAB TREES PLUNGED AND FELL, RAND SWEPT YOUNG DAVID INTO HIS ARMS AND RAN FOR THE SHELTER OF A CAVE.

A SIZZLING BOLT OF LIGHTNING SENDS A MAMMOTH TREE CRASHING DOWN ON **THEIR HEADS!**

RAND THRUSTS THE LAD ASIDE AS THE FALLING BAOBAB SENDS HIM SPINNING!

DO WE STILL HAVE TO START HOME SOON?

HOME?

QUICKLY, THE STORM PASSED AND RAND WAS NEXT CONSCIOUS OF BEING LED BACK TO THE HUT!

WHY THIS IS HOME, SON... HERE IN THIS CLEARING WHERE YOUR MOTHER IS!

I'M GLAD

J OHN RAND NEVER RECOVERED MENTALLY FROM THE BLOW THAT THE FALLING TREE STRUCK HIM. THOUGH RATIONAL IN EVERY OTHER RESPECT, HE LABORED UNDER THE DELUSION THAT THE JUNGLE WAS HIS HOME!

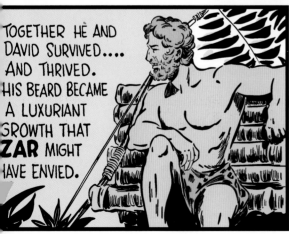

TOGETHER HE AND DAVID SURVIVED.... AND THRIVED. HIS BEARD BECAME A LUXURIANT GROWTH THAT **ZAR** MIGHT HAVE ENVIED.

SOME LATENT IMPULSE HAD MADE JOHN RAND TEACH HIS SON TO READ AND WRITE .... BUT DAVID PREFERRED PLAYING WITH HIS FRIENDS TO EVEN SUCH SIMPLE SCHOOLING.

AS DAVID GREW OLDER HE LIKED TO ROAM THE FOREST. HE COULD SWIM LIKE **NYASSA** THE FISH, AND CLIMB TREES WITH ALL THE AGILITY OF **NONO**, THE MONKEY.

HE KNEW NOW WHY HIS FATHER HAD FIRED AT **N'JAGA** AND WHY HE KILLED THE GREEN SNAKE. HIS WAS THE CODE OF THE JUNGLE...KILL ONLY WHEN NECESSARY.

SOON HE LEARNED TO TALK TO THE ANIMALS WITH STRANGE GUTTURAL SOUNDS AND FROM THAT DAY HE LIVED A HAPPIER LIFE.

THE JUNGLE LAD MET **QUOG**, THE WILD PIG, AND STAYED THAT BEAST'S STARTLED FLIGHT WITH A FRIENDLY CALL.

WHILE SWIMMING IN THE LAKE, HE WAS IN TURN STARTLED BY A GREAT BEAST THAT ROSE FROM THE SHALLOWS **...WAL-LAH**, THE HIPPOTAMUS.

HE HAD HIS FIRST VIEW OF **TRAJAH** AND LONGED TO RIDE ON THAT GREAT GRAY BACK!

THOUGH HE DID NOT KNOW IT, DAVID HAD ANOTHER COMPANION....**ZAR** KEPT PACE WITH HIM AS HE RACED THROUGH THE JUNGLE!

A FLOATING SPECK IN THE SKY BROUGHT HIS EYES UPWARD. HE WATCHED **KRU**, THE BUZZARD, DROP TOWARDS THE EARTH.

QUICKLY, DAVID RAN TO WHERE KRU PERCHED IN A TREE-TOP.

THE STILLNESS WAS RENT BY A BLOOD-CURDLING ROAR...THAT OF ZAR...AND WITH A NOTE OF FEAR!

FOR, THE WISE MONARCH OF THE JUNGLE HAD ERRED! HE HAD MADE A FATAL MISSTEP AND LAY TRAPPED IN QUICKSAND!!

ZAR WAS UP TO HIS HAUNCHES NOW AND COULD NOT HOPE TO GAIN SOLID GROUND.

DAVID COULD SEE THE HOPELESS LIGHT IN THE LION'S AMBER EYES AND COULD NOT RESIST THE FORLORN APPEAL.

DESPERATELY HE SEIZED FALLEN BRANCHES AND THRUST THEM TOWARD ZAR....

INCH BY INCH ZAR DREW HIS TIRING BODY ACROSS THE TANGLE OF BOUGHS UNTIL....

FOR A FEW MINUTES ZAR LAY PANTING IN THE TALL GRASS WHILE SHA, HIS MATE, NUZZLED CLOSE. ZAR SURVEYED THE MAN CUB AND THERE A STRANGE PACT OF TRUCE WAS MADE.

....AT LAST HE STOOD FREE OF THE CLINGING SANDS!

I SMELL SMOKE!

NONSENSE! WE PUT OUR FIRE OUT BEFORE LEAVING

A WEEK AFTER THE RESCUE OF **ZAR**, DAVID AND HIS FATHER WERE EXPLORING THE FOREST, WHEN.....

THERE IT IS!!

SWIFTLY THEY TRAVELLED THROUGH THE TREES IN THE DIRECTION OF THE STRANGE SMOKE.

PEERING THROUGH THE BRANCHES, THEY SAW A BLACK MAN SQUATTING BEFORE A FIRE.

A SHORT DISTANCE AWAY, TWO OTHER BLACKS SCOOPED GRAVEL FROM A STREAM.... WATCHED BY A FAT WHITE MAN.

DROPPING TO THE GROUND RAND STEPPED INTO THE CLEARING AND WALKED STRAIGHT TO THE GROUP.

FROM THEIR ACTIONS, DAVID KNEW THEY WERE ARGUING AND THAT HIS FATHER WAS COMMANDING THEM TO LEAVE!

HE ALSO SAW HIS FATHER TURN SLOWLY ON HIS HEEL AND START BACK TOWARDS THE BRUSH.

AT THAT MOMENT, **PAUL DE KRAFT**, WITH A HEART AS GREASY AS THE ROLLS OF FAT THAT COVERED HIS BODY, RAISED HIS GUN AND POINTED IT AT RAND'S BACK!

66

QUICKLY, DAVID FITTED AN ARROW TO HIS BOW.

 OHN RAND WAS AWARE OF A SUDDEN HUMMING BESIDE HIS EAR!

IN DE KRAFT'S ARM AN ARROW QUIVERED AND THE AUTOMATIC REVOLVER DROPPED TO THE GROUND!

DAVID AND HIS FATHER SILENTLY FADED INTO THE JUNGLE..... BUT, IF DAVID COULD HAVE SEEN THE DEVILS OF HATE LEERING OUT OF DE KRAFT'S EYES, HE WOULD HAVE PLACED ANOTHER ARROW IN THE MAN'S THROAT!

THIS JUNGLE IS SACRED TO YOUR MOTHER.... REMEMBER THAT, SON. NO ONE MUST BE ALLOWED TO PROFANE IT!

THAT NIGHT........

EMERALDS!! THAT'S WHAT I'VE STUMBLED ON IN THIS GOD-FORSAKEN STREAM!

AND SOME HALF-CRAZED HERMIT THINKS HE CAN ORDER ME FROM HERE! MUBANGI... GO FIND HIS CAMP AND SEE IF THERE ARE OTHERS!

IN A SHORT WHILE THE NATIVE RETURNS.....

I SAW, **INKOSI**, THE MAN AND BOY... NO OTHERS. **THEY HAVE NO GUNS!**

GOOD! THAT WILL MAKE IT EASIER!

AT DAWN DAVID WATCHED THE OTHER CAMP FROM A HIGH ROCK. IT APPEARED DESERTED. HAD THEY OBEYED HIS FATHER AND FLED IN THE NIGHT?

CAUTIOUSLY, DAVID APPROACHES THE TENT, PUZZLED THAT THEY COULD HAVE LEFT THEIR POSSESSIONS BEHIND.

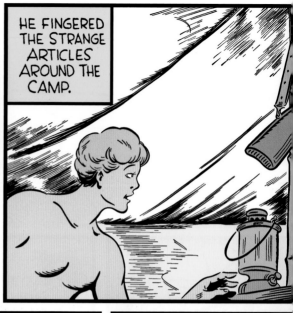

HE FINGERED THE STRANGE ARTICLES AROUND THE CAMP.

FASCINATED, THE BOY STUDIES HIS REFLECTION IN A MIRROR!

HE DECIDES TO RETURN HOME .....TO TELL HIS FATHER OF THE MANY WONDERFUL THINGS THE STRANGERS LEFT BEHIND.

A STACATTO CRACK PIERCES THE STILLNESS...... DAVID REMEMBERS FAINTLY THE TIME HIS FATHER HAD FIRED AT **N'JAGA** AND SENSES .....**DANGER!!**

A **SECOND SHOT** ECHOES FROM THE DIRECTION OF HIS HOME AND DAVID WAITS NO LONGER!

THE HUT IS **AFIRE!!** DAVID LEAPS FORWARD WITH THE THOUGHT THAT HIS FATHER IS **INSIDE!**

AN OBJECT ON THE GROUND CAUGHT HIS EYE.

RAND, SHOT AND PAINFULLY WOUNDED, CRAWLED ALONG THE GROUND!

FATHER! WHAT HAPPENED?

WEAKLY, RAND MUMBLES A WARNING AS THE BOY, WITH THE STRENGTH OF A GROWN MAN, CARRIES HIS FATHER AWAY FROM THE FIRE.

DAVID FAILS TO SEE A NATIVE SNEAK AROUND THE BURNING SHELTER!

A SHARP SPEAR PRICKED THE MIDDLE OF HIS BACK!

BEFORE HE COULD ACT, DE KRAFT CAME ON THE RUN FROM THE JUNGLE.

FAT-FACE HAS WOUNDED MY FATHER.... AND FOR THAT FAT-FACE SHALL DIE!

DE KRAFT LAUGHED AT DAVID'S THREAT.

SPUNKY, EH? BUT, YOU'RE WRONG, KID. I DON'T WANT ANY WITNESSES TO THIS PARTY....AND I'M GOING TO KILL YOU ...... SEE?

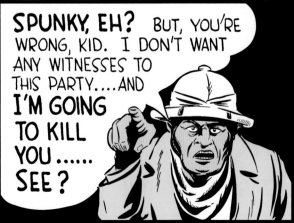

As David bent to grasp a knife at his father's side, **De Kraft's** gun whipped up!

DEAD MEN TELL NO TALES!

Another spectator watched the grim drama ....ZAR

Roaring, **ZAR** bursts into the clearing!

That lion will finish the job for me!!

De Kraft escapes!

Look, **ZAR** has killed two of them and driven fat-faced away

Too late son..I'm dying!

With the death of his father, David was alone in the jungle.

At twilight he lingered in the clearing...where his home was a heap of ashes.

ZAR sensed the grief of the boy who once saved his life, and with a low guttural call, stepped into the clearing.

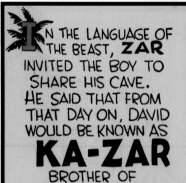
In the language of the beast, **ZAR** invited the boy to share his cave. He said that from that day on, David would be known as **KA-ZAR** brother of **ZAR, the mighty!**

And so, the strange pair strode off through the jungle, side by side, to begin a new life for the son of John Rand.

More Adventures of **KA-ZAR** in the NEXT ISSUE!

70

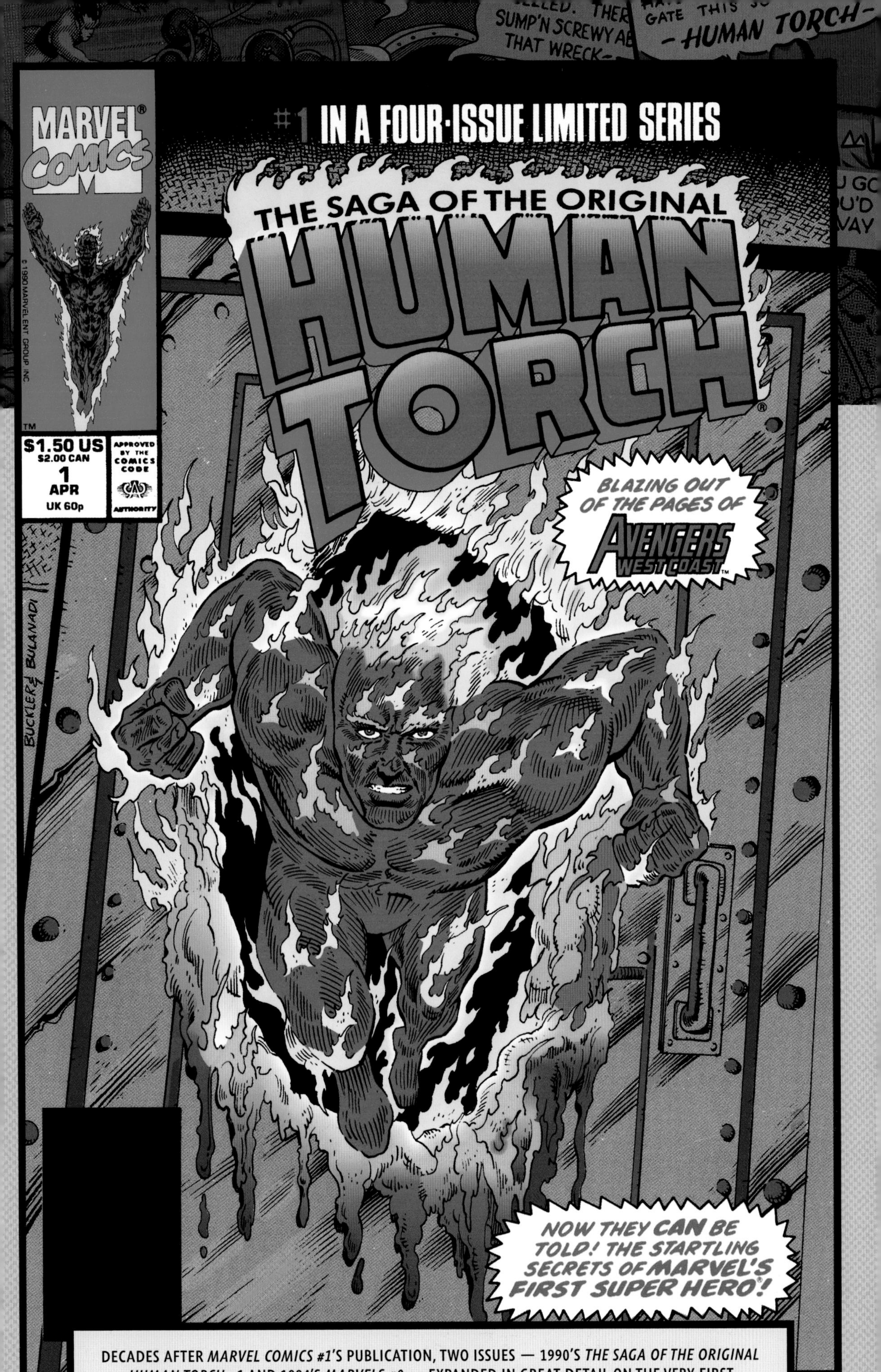
MARVEL® COMICS
#1 IN A FOUR-ISSUE LIMITED SERIES
THE SAGA OF THE ORIGINAL
HUMAN TORCH®
$1.50 US
$2.00 CAN
1
APR
UK 60p
APPROVED BY THE COMICS CODE AUTHORITY
BLAZING OUT OF THE PAGES OF AVENGERS WEST COAST™
NOW THEY CAN BE TOLD! THE STARTLING SECRETS OF MARVEL'S FIRST SUPER HERO®!
BUCKLER/BULANADI

DECADES AFTER *MARVEL COMICS #1*'S PUBLICATION, TWO ISSUES — 1990'S *THE SAGA OF THE ORIGINAL HUMAN TORCH #1* AND 1994'S *MARVELS #0* — EXPANDED IN GREAT DETAIL ON THE VERY FIRST PUBLISHED EVENT IN MARVEL COMICS HISTORY, THE DEBUT OF THE ORIGINAL HUMAN TORCH.

IN THE BEGINNING?

THE VERY BEGINNING?

IT WAS DARK.

AND THEN THERE WAS LIGHT.

LIGHT.

AND SOUND.

...DUNNIT...

BY HEAVEN, I'VE DONE IT!

TOO MUCH SOUND.

A MOMENT MORE, AND IT WAS DARK AGAIN.

DARK...AND SILENT.

OF COURSE, AT THAT TIME, I DIDN'T KNOW THE WORDS FOR SUCH CONCEPTS...

...OR FOR ANYTHING ELSE.

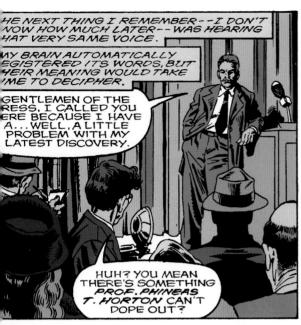

THE NEXT THING I REMEMBER--I DON'T KNOW HOW MUCH LATER--WAS HEARING THAT VERY SAME VOICE.

MY BRAIN AUTOMATICALLY REGISTERED ITS WORDS, BUT THEIR MEANING WOULD TAKE TIME TO DECIPHER.

GENTLEMEN OF THE PRESS, I CALLED YOU HERE BECAUSE I HAVE A...WELL, A LITTLE PROBLEM WITH MY LATEST DISCOVERY.

HUH? YOU MEAN THERE'S SOMETHING PROF. PHINEAS T. HORTON CAN'T DOPE OUT?

THE LATE GREAT ROGERS ONCE SAID, "WE'RE ALL IGNORANT, ONLY ON DIFFERENT SUBJECTS."

AS MANY OF YOU KNOW, I'VE BEEN LABORING ALL THIS YEAR OF 1939, TO CREATE A SYNTHETIC MAN--AN EXACT REPLICA OF A HUMAN BEING.

WELL, BEHIND THIS CURTAIN IS THE END PRODUCT OF MY QUEST.

HUH? IS HE KIDDING OR WHAT?

YOU'RE, UH, PULLING OUR LEG WITH THAT BIT, RIGHT, PROF?

WRONG! LET ME SHOW YOU!

HERE--IN SUSPENDED ANIMATION--IS THE MONSTROSITY I HAVE DEVELOPED.

"MONSTROSITY"? JUST LOOKS LIKE SOME GUY IN RED LONG-JOHNS TO ME!

YEAH, BUT--HEY! HE DOESN'T APPEAR TO BE BREATHING!

VERY OBSERVANT. HE HAS BEEN DESIGNED TO BE, EVERY INCH A TRUE MAN--

--ONE WHO'LL COMMENCE BREATHING AS SOON AS I ALLOW OXYGEN INTO HIS AIR-TIGHT TUBE.

HSSSSSSSSSSS

BUT THE INSTANT I DO, YOU WILL SEE WHY I'VE CHRISTENED MY NEW CREATION--

HSSSSS

73

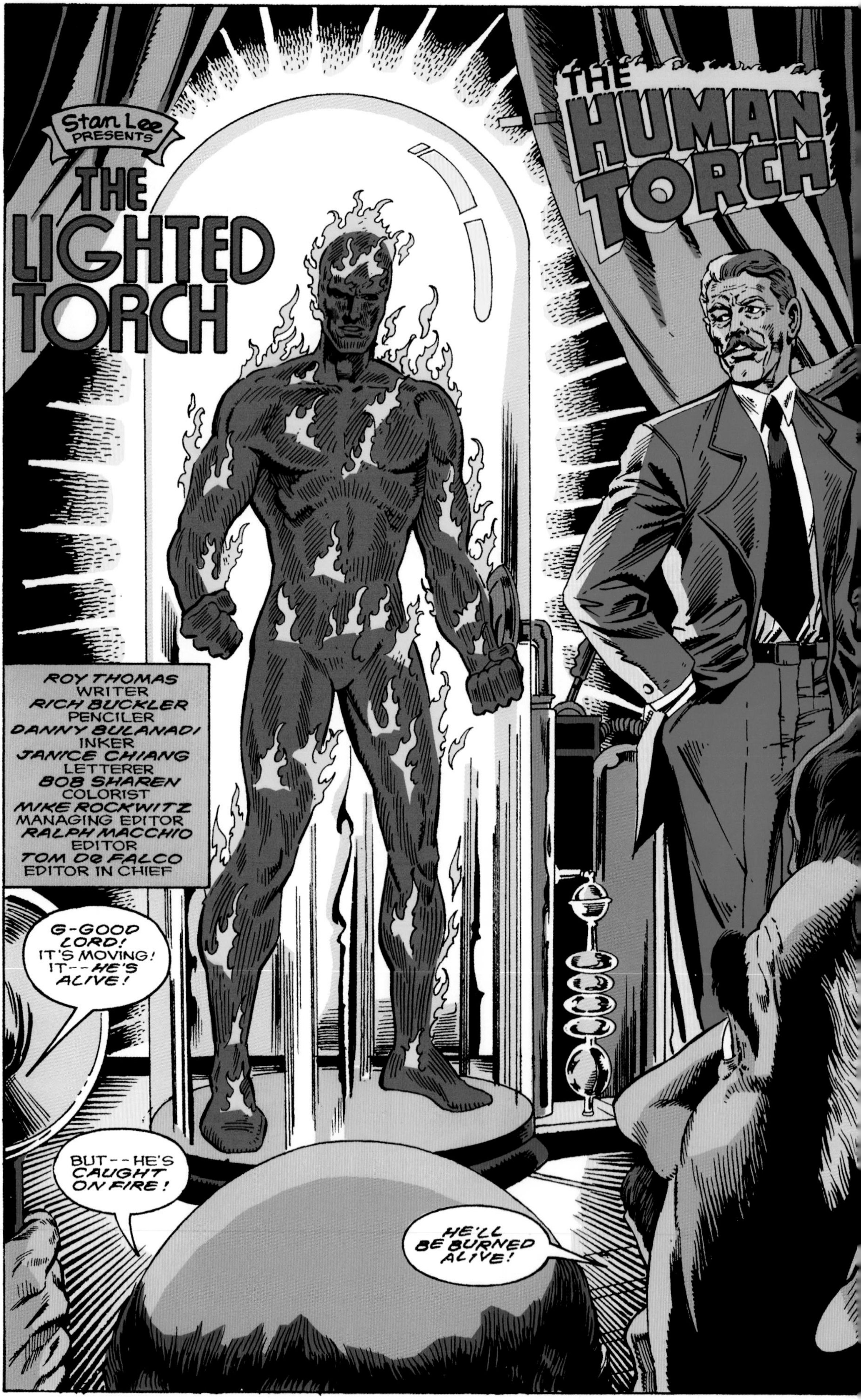
Stan Lee PRESENTS
THE LIGHTED TORCH
THE HUMAN TORCH
ROY THOMAS WRITER
RICH BUCKLER PENCILER
DANNY BULANADI INKER
JANICE CHIANG LETTERER
BOB SHAREN COLORIST
MIKE ROCKWITZ MANAGING EDITOR
RALPH MACCHIO EDITOR
TOM DeFALCO EDITOR IN CHIEF
G-GOOD LORD! IT'S MOVING! IT--HE'S ALIVE!
BUT--HE'S CAUGHT ON FIRE!
HE'LL BE BURNED ALIVE!

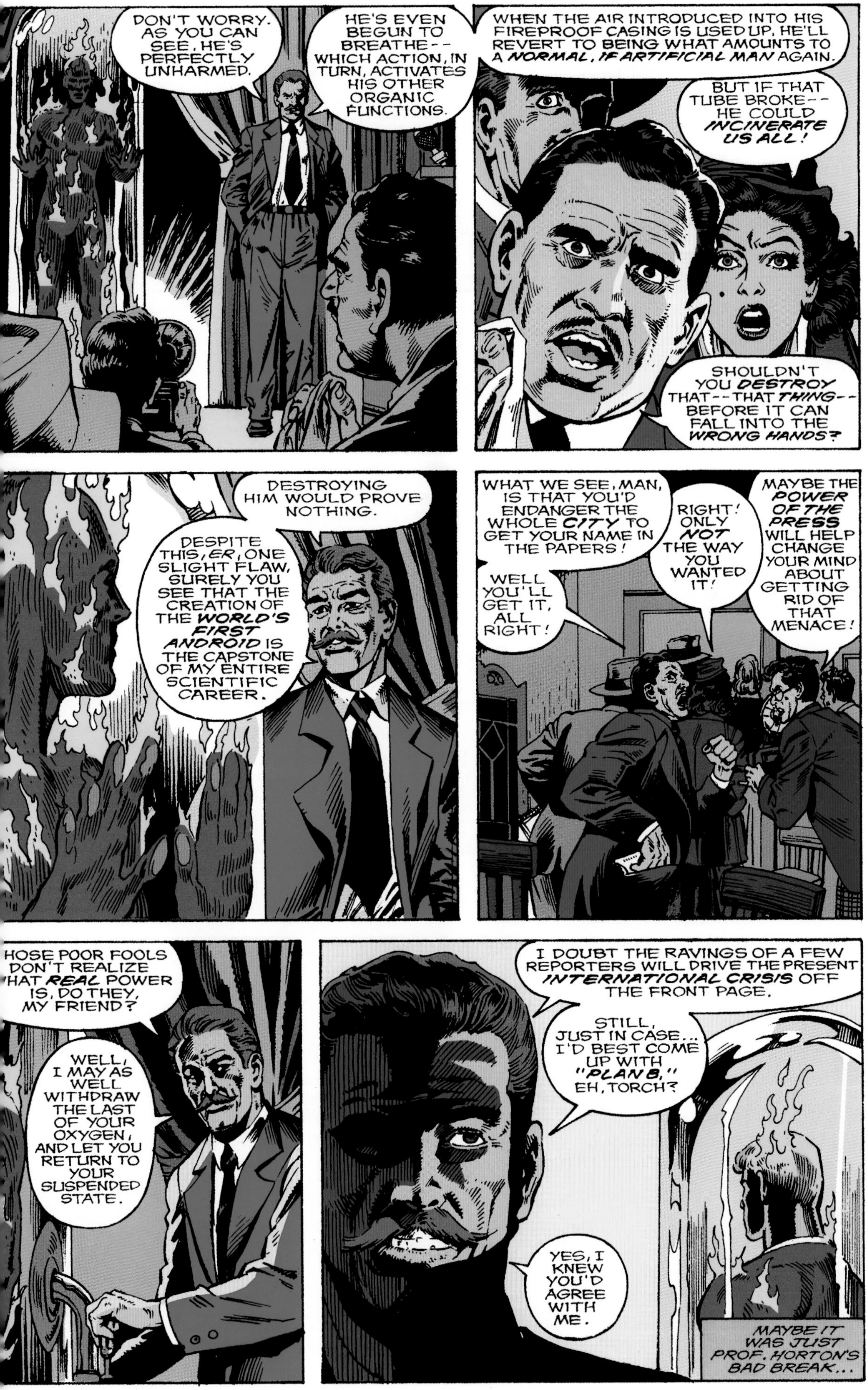

DON'T WORRY. AS YOU CAN SEE, HE'S PERFECTLY UNHARMED.
HE'S EVEN BEGUN TO BREATHE-- WHICH ACTION, IN TURN, ACTIVATES HIS OTHER ORGANIC FUNCTIONS.
WHEN THE AIR INTRODUCED INTO HIS FIREPROOF CASING IS USED UP, HE'LL REVERT TO BEING WHAT AMOUNTS TO A NORMAL, IF ARTIFICIAL MAN AGAIN.
BUT IF THAT TUBE BROKE-- HE COULD INCINERATE US ALL!
SHOULDN'T YOU DESTROY THAT--THAT THING-- BEFORE IT CAN FALL INTO THE WRONG HANDS?
DESTROYING HIM WOULD PROVE NOTHING.
DESPITE THIS, ER, ONE SLIGHT FLAW, SURELY YOU SEE THAT THE CREATION OF THE WORLD'S FIRST ANDROID IS THE CAPSTONE OF MY ENTIRE SCIENTIFIC CAREER.
WHAT WE SEE, MAN, IS THAT YOU'D ENDANGER THE WHOLE CITY TO GET YOUR NAME IN THE PAPERS!
WELL YOU'LL GET IT, ALL RIGHT!
RIGHT! ONLY NOT THE WAY YOU WANTED IT!
MAYBE THE POWER OF THE PRESS WILL HELP CHANGE YOUR MIND ABOUT GETTING RID OF THAT MENACE!
HOSE POOR FOOLS DON'T REALIZE HAT REAL POWER IS, DO THEY, MY FRIEND?
WELL, I MAY AS WELL WITHDRAW THE LAST OF YOUR OXYGEN, AND LET YOU RETURN TO YOUR SUSPENDED STATE.
I DOUBT THE RAVINGS OF A FEW REPORTERS WILL DRIVE THE PRESENT INTERNATIONAL CRISIS OFF THE FRONT PAGE.
STILL, JUST IN CASE... I'D BEST COME UP WITH "PLAN B," EH, TORCH?
YES, I KNEW YOU'D AGREE WITH ME.
MAYBE IT WAS JUST PROF. HORTON'S BAD BREAK...

...THAT THE NAZIS WERE LYING LOW, THE MORNING MY STORY BROKE...

WUXTRY! WUXTRY! READ ALL ABOUT THE MAN OF FIRE--

--"THE HUMAN TORCH"!

DAILY NEWS
FIRE-BREATHING ROBOT CALLED A MENACE!

--AND JUST IMAGINE IF ADOLF HITLER GOT HIS HANDS ON THIS WALKING FLAME-THROWER!

THIS IS THE SCARIEST THING SINCE THAT "INVASION FROM MARS" LAST YEAR!

BUT THAT WAS JUST ON RADIO! THIS IS FOR REAL!

PUBLIC PRESSURE FORCED HORTON TO LET THE SCIENTISTS' GUILD EXAMINE ME--AND THEIR CONCLUSION, TOO, WAS THAT I SHOULD BE DISPOSED OF.

HE WAS 'WAY AHEAD OF THEM, THOUGH.

IN FRONT OF MORE SELF-RIGHTEOUS WITNESSES THAN YOU COULD SHAKE A BIRCH-ROD AT--

--HE HAD MY TRANSPARENT TUBE ENCASED IN PLATES OF SOLID AIRPROOF STEEL--

--AND THE WHOLE BUSINESS DUMPED INTO A REINFORCED POOL OF FAST-DRYING CEMENT.

WELL, I GUESS IT'S BACK TO THE OL' DRAWING BOARD, HUH, PROF?

THAT'S THE LAST WE'LL BE SEEING OF THE NOT-SO-HUMAN HUMAN TORCH!

PROF. HORTON SAID NOTHING.

HE WAS CONTENT TO GRIT HIS TEETH... AND BIDE HIS TIME.

IN EUROPE, *ADOLF HITLER* AND *JOSEF STALIN* WERE CONSIDERABLY LESS PATIENT.

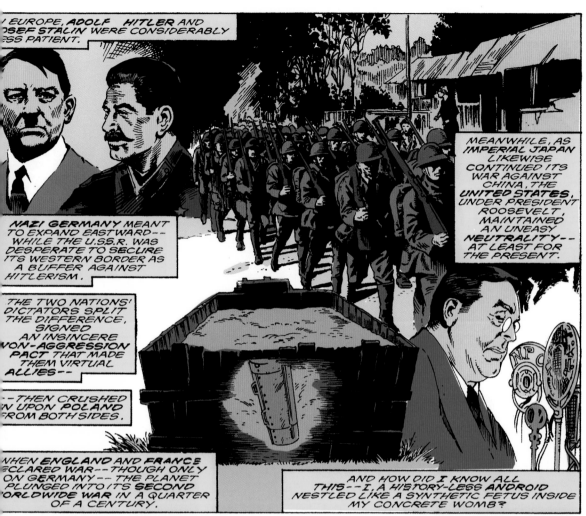

NAZI GERMANY MEANT TO EXPAND EASTWARD-- WHILE THE *U.S.S.R.* WAS DESPERATE TO SECURE ITS WESTERN BORDER AS A BUFFER AGAINST HITLERISM.

THE TWO NATIONS' DICTATORS SPLIT THE DIFFERENCE, SIGNED AN INSINCERE NON-AGGRESSION PACT THAT MADE THEM VIRTUAL ALLIES--

--THEN CRUSHED IN UPON *POLAND* FROM BOTH SIDES.

WHEN *ENGLAND* AND *FRANCE* DECLARED WAR--THOUGH ONLY ON GERMANY--THE PLANET PLUNGED INTO ITS *SECOND* WORLDWIDE WAR IN A QUARTER OF A CENTURY.

MEANWHILE, AS IMPERIAL JAPAN LIKEWISE CONTINUED ITS WAR AGAINST CHINA, THE *UNITED STATES,* UNDER PRESIDENT *ROOSEVELT,* MAINTAINED AN UNEASY *NEUTRALITY--* AT LEAST FOR THE PRESENT.

AND HOW DID *I* KNOW ALL THIS--I, A HISTORY-LESS *ANDROID* NESTLED LIKE A SYNTHETIC FETUS INSIDE MY CONCRETE WOMB?

ALL THAT KNOWLEDGE--AND MUCH MORE--WAS *PUMPED* INTO ME VIA RADIO AND RECORDING-DEVICE, ALL INSTALLED BY PROF. HORTON BEFORE THE FIRST DROP OF CEMENT WAS POURED.

CLEARLY, MY CREATOR DID NOT INTEND TO LET ME LIE FALLOW FOREVER...

...YET HE WANTED IT TO BE A *HUMAN TORCH EDUCATED FOR CIVILIZATION* WHICH HE WOULD EVENTUALLY RELEASE FOR HIS OWN PURPOSES.

BUT WHAT HE DIDN'T NOTICE WAS THAT THERE WAS A *CRACK* IN THE SUPPOSEDLY SOLID BLOCK OF CONCRETE.

OVER A FEW WEEKS' TIME, BOTH IT AND MY AIRTIGHT TUBE SPRANG A *SLOW LEAK,* WHICH FINALLY ALLOWED *OXYGEN* TO SEEP INTO ME--

-- WITH PREDICTABLE RESULTS.

BAOOOM!!

WHAT WAS THAT?

IT CAME FROM THE DIRECTION OF THE TORCH'S "TOMB"!

IT'S BURST WIDE OPEN, AS IF A THUNDERBOLT--

YE GODS! HE'S DOWN THERE -- FREE!

TORCH! THIS IS PROF. HORTON!

I ORDER YOU TO STAY WHERE YOU ARE, UNTIL I COME DOWN!

THE PIPED-IN LANGUAGE LESSONS LET ME UNDERSTAND FOR THE FIRST TIME, WORDS THAT WERE BEING SPOKEN TO ME.

I KNEW I WAS BEING GIVEN A COMMAND--

--AND I DIDN'T MUCH LIKE THE IDEA.

TORCH! COME BACK--!

HORTON'S WIRE-RECORDINGS HAD FILLED MY BRAIN WITH MANY THINGS --

--AMONG THEM, IMAGES OF PEOPLE KILLED BY FIRE IN CHICAGO, LONDON, POMPEII.

I-I'M BURNING ALIVE!

LOOK! IT'S THAT "HUMAN TORCH"!

HE'S ON THE LOOSE!

78

WHY MUST EVERYTHING I TOUCH-- TURN TO FLAME?

EVERYONE-- KEEP OUT OF MY WAY!

BUT, IF A MAN OF FIRE CAREENED THROUGH THE STREETS OF NEW YORK CITY--

--COULD THE SO-CALLED "FIREMEN" BE FAR BEHIND?

KLANGKLANGKLANG

WHAT'S BEEN THROUGH HERE, ANYWAY?

WHATEVER IT IS-- IT'S BURNED FOOTPRINTS INTO THE STREET!

LIKE THE CHILD I STILL WAS, IN MANY WAYS, I FOUND MYSELF ATTRACTED BY THE FIRE-FIGHTERS' BELL...

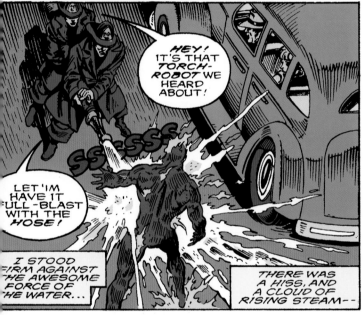

HEY! IT'S THAT TORCH-ROBOT WE HEARD ABOUT!

LET 'IM HAVE IT FULL-BLAST WITH THE HOSE!

SSSSSS

I STOOD FIRM AGAINST THE AWESOME FORCE OF THE WATER...

THERE WAS A HISS, AND A CLOUD OF RISING STEAM--

--AND A MOST UNEXPECTED REACTION, ALL AROUND.

HAHAHAHA

SPLOOSSH

S-STOP-- PLEASE--!

TURN IT OFF A SECOND, MEN! GIVE THE POOR DEVIL A CHANCE TO SURRENDER!

HURT? I DID NOT HURT ME. NOR WAS IT STRONG ENOUGH TO PUT OUT MY FLAME.

BUT IF THAT WATER-BLAST HURT YOU, HOTSHOT, WHY IN BLAZES WERE YOU LAUGHING?

IT ONLY-- TICKLED!

TICKLED?! I DON'T BELIEVE I'M *HEARING* THIS!

OKAY, MEN, WE BETTER--

WATCH OUT! HE'S GRABBING THE HOSE!

I DO NOT WANT TO HARM YOU--

--BUT NEITHER CAN I LET YOU HARM *ME!*

SSSSS

SSPZZZ

MY GENERAL INTENTIONS WERE A STEP OR TWO AHEAD OF MY GRASP OF THE COLLOQUIAL...

STEP TO THE SIDE, MALES AND FEMALES!

Y-YOU BET!

I KNEW I MUST FIND A RETREAT... A PLACE WHERE I COULD HIDE, AND THINK, AND NOT DO DAMAGE THAT WOULD BRING THE WRATH OF THIS STRANGE NEW WORLD DOWN UPON MY BLAZING BROW.

INSTINCTIVELY, I FELT MYSELF DRAWN TOWARD A SPRAWLING SUBURBAN ESTATE WITH SPRAWLING GROUNDS--

--AND AN IRON GATE.

THE METAL BARS WERE TOO HARD, TOO THICK, TO GIVE WAY AS I ADVANCED UPON THEM.

BUT WHEN I GRASPED THEM IN MY FIERY HANDS--

--AND THE HEAT OF MY GROWING FRUSTRATION POURED OUT THROUGH MY EVERY PORE.

--THEY MELTED LIKE THE SPRING FROST BEFORE THE BURNING SUN.

NOT FAR AHEAD, I SENSED, WAS THE THING I NEEDED TO COOL THE FIRE WHICH RAGED BOTH WITHIN-- AND WITHOUT-- ME.

80

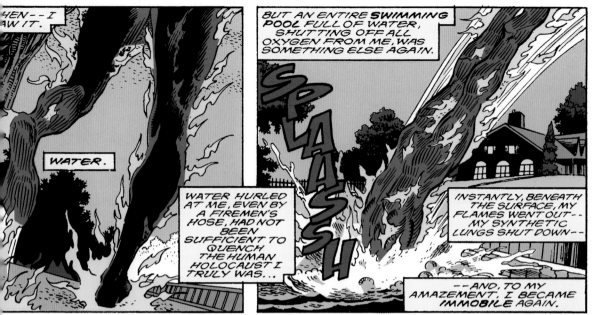

HEN -- I
AW IT.

WATER.

WATER HURLED AT ME, EVEN BY A FIREMEN'S HOSE, HAD NOT BEEN SUFFICIENT TO QUENCH THE HUMAN HOLOCAUST I TRULY WAS...

BUT AN ENTIRE *SWIMMING POOL* FULL OF WATER, SHUTTING OFF ALL OXYGEN FROM ME, WAS SOMETHING ELSE AGAIN.

S P L A A S H

INSTANTLY, BENEATH THE SURFACE, MY FLAMES WENT OUT-- MY SYNTHETIC LUNGS SHUT DOWN--

--AND, TO MY AMAZEMENT, I BECAME IMMOBILE AGAIN.

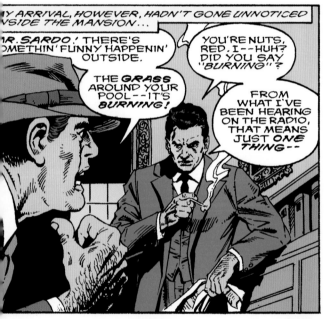

MY ARRIVAL, HOWEVER, HADN'T GONE UNNOTICED NSIDE THE MANSION...

R. SARDO! THERE'S OMETHIN' FUNNY HAPPENIN' OUTSIDE.

THE *GRASS* AROUND YOUR POOL--IT'S *BURNING*!

YOU'RE NUTS, RED. I--HUH? DID YOU SAY "BURNING"?

FROM WHAT I'VE BEEN HEARING ON THE RADIO, THAT MEANS JUST *ONE THING*--

PUT THE *WINTER-GLASS* COVER OVER THE POOL!

HURRY UP! DON'T STOP TO ASK ANY QUESTIONS!

HE DIDN'T.

SONUVAGUN! HERE'S SOMEBODY OWN THERE, ALL RIGHT--STANDIN' TIFF AS A STATUE!

THAT THE ONE YOU FIGURED, MR. SARDO?

IT SURE IS.

NOW, RED, I'VE GOT A FEW *OTHER* ITEMS FOR YOU TO PICK UP...

SOMETIME LATER, THE ONE CALLED SARDO ENTERED THE POOL, CLAD IN DIVING GEAR...

--AND HOLDING A TRANSPARENT TUBE WHICH WAS EASILY PUT OVER ME IN MY SUSPENDED STATE.

81

CUT OFF FROM OXYGEN BY THE SURROUNDING WATER, I COULD ONLY WATCH AND WONDER...

OKAY UP THERE--

--TAKE HIM TOPSIDE!

AS I SAY, I WAS NOT UNLIKE A CHILD...NAIVE, UNSOPHISTICATED.

I HALF IMAGINED THAT THIS FIRST HUMAN BEING I HAD ENCOUNTERED CLOSE-UP MIGHT EVEN BE...A FRIEND.

IT WOULD NOT TAKE LONG TO DISABUSE ME OF THAT NOTION.

LIFT HIM IN THE TRUCK REAL EASY, BOYS.

HOT-PANTS HERE'S GOING TO MAKE US A FORTUNE!

HOW YOU FIGURE THAT, MR. SARDO?

WE'RE IN THE PROTECTION BUSINESS, RIGHT?

PEOPLE PAY US OFF, OR THEIR HAPPY LITTLE BUSINESS GOES UP IN SMOKE.

WELL, LADY LUCK JUST PLOPPED THE GREATEST ENFORCER OF ALL TIME RIGHT IN OUR LAPS!

AND THOSE HOLDOUTS AT ACMEN WAREHOUSE, INC., ARE ABOUT TO GET OUR VERY FIRST FREE HOME DEMONSTRATION...!

THEY GOT EVERYTHING IN HERE, MR. SARDO-- CRATES, BOXES, EVEN HEAVY EQUIPMENT!

EXACTLY! LOTS OF THIS STUFF WON'T CATCH ON FIRE REAL FAST, IF WE USE OUR OLD TRIED- AND-TRUE ARSON METHODS...

BUT TONIGHT-- SOMETHING *NEW* HAS BEEN ADDED!

LET'S GO, BOYS! WHEN THE WORD GETS AROUND THAT THE *"HUMAN TORCH"* WAS SEEN IN A BURNING WAREHOUSE THAT DIDN'T PAY PROTECTION MONEY TO SARDO--

--WE'LL HAVE TO OPEN OUR OWN BANK JUST TO HANDLE ALL THE DOUGH THAT'LL COME ROLLING IN!

SMASH

ALL RIGHT, HOT STUFF-- IT'S ALL YOURS!

EVEN AS FULL CONSCIOUSNESS SLOWLY RETURNED TO ME, MY CASCADING FLAME SET THE WAREHOUSE ALIGHT--

--BEGAN TO MELT EVEN THE METAL MACHINERY STORED THERE.

SARDO? WHERE ARE YOU?

WHY DID YOU BRING ME HERE--

--KNOWING MY FIRE WOULD *DESTROY* EVERYTHING AROUND ME?

AND THEN, AS PROF. HORTON'S SYNTHETICALLY GENERATED SYNAPSES MADE THE LAST CONNECTIONS WITHIN MY ARTIFICIAL BRAIN, IT ALL FELL INTO PLACE.

THERE WERE *WORDS* I HAD BEEN FED WHICH FIT WHAT I HAD HEARD OF THE MAN SARDO'S CONVERSATION:

"CRIMINAL.

"GANGSTER.

"RACKETEER"!

83

IN THAT MOMENT, ALL THE ARTIFICIAL INTELLIGENCE WITH WHICH MY MORTAL CREATOR HAD ENDOWED ME CAME CRASHING IN UPON ME--

--LIKE THE FIRE-DEVASTATED CEILING OF WOOD AND METAL EVEN THEN COLLAPSING ABOUT MY HEAD--

THRAKKK

--AND, FOR THE FIRST TIME, THEN AND FOREVER--

-- I BECAME A TRULY *HUMAN* TORCH.

NOR HAD I TIME TO BEMOAN AN INFANCY I HAD NEVER PHYSICALLY POSSESSED--

--A *CHILDHOOD* AND *ADOLESCENCE* TELESCOPED INTO A FEW SHORT WAKING WEEKS--

--BEFORE THE REALIZATION THUNDERED IN UPON ME THAT I MUST *LEAVE* THIS SEARING, SMOLDERING RUIN.

THAT'S WHEN I FIRST DISCOVERED--

--THAT I COULD *FLY.*

THINGS LOOKED STRANGELY DIFFERENT FROM UP ABOVE.

IN MY ALTERED PERSPECTIVE, MEN BECAME THE TINY CREATURES THEY REALLY WERE, RATHER THAN THE GIANTS THEY WERE IN THEIR OWN FLACCID IMAGINATIONS.

BUT I KNEW THE VEHICLE RACING AWAY FROM THE WAREHOUSE MUST CONTAIN THE MAN CALLED SARDO--

--AND I HATED HIM.

HATED HIM FOR WHAT HE HAD TRIED TO MAKE ME--

--NOT AN ENGINE OF DESTRUCTION, WHICH I HAD BEEN FROM THE MOMENT OF MY CONCEPTION--

--BUT A SLAVE, AND THEREFORE LESS THAN FULLY HUMAN.

STILL, BY SOME INBORN INSTINCT, I HOVERED ABOVE HIS AUTOMOBILE--

--BIDING MY TIME.

--UNTIL HE REACHED HIS SPRAWLING ESTATE.

THERE, FAR FROM THE MADDENED CROWD--

--I WOULD DEAL WITH HIM.

YOU?!

I'M NOT CERTAIN I KNEW, AT THAT MOMENT, PRECISELY WHAT I INTENDED TO DO TO SARDO.

BUT HIS RABID FEAR FANNED THE RISING FLAMES OF MY INNATE LONGING AFTER JUSTICE.

G-GET AWAY FROM ME!

SLAM

OR PERHAPS IT WAS MERELY RETALIATION-- NAKED, INCANDESCENT REVENGE-- WHICH FUELED MY ACTIONS.

IN ANY EVENT, THE THICKEST OAKEN DOOR WAS NO MORE THAN A MOMENTARY BARRIER TO MY PASSAGE...

SARDO!

YOU CAN'T ESCAPE ME, SARDO!

NO MATTER WHERE YOU HIDE--

--THE GLOW OF MY RAGE WILL SEEK YOU OUT!

PERHAPS, AT THAT INSTANT, SARDO'S BRAIN TOLD HIM THE SAME THING.

STILL, WITH THAT TERRIBLE DESPERATION WITH WHICH HUMAN BEINGS CLING, ALL ACHING FINGERTIPS, TO PRECIOUS LIFE--

--HE COULD NOT TURN AND FACE HIS DESTINY.

PERHAPS STEEL WOULD SUFFICE, WHERE THREE INCHES OF WOOD HAD FAILED.

A FEW SECONDS MORE, AND I WOULD HAVE FOUND THE UNDERGROUND TUNNEL WHICH LED TO THE REINFORCED BOMB SHELTER, BUT JUST THEN--

SARDO!

RECOGNIZING THE VOICE FROM OUTSIDE, I FORMULATED IN MY MIND A NEW TRUISM, FROM THE LESSONS AND LORE WHICH HAD BEEN PIPED IN TO ME:

"TWO BIRDS IN THE BUSH ARE WORTH ONE ALMOST IN HAND."

CRIPES -- FORGET ABOUT HIM! HE AIN'T WALKIN' OUT OF THAT INFERNO!

GUESS YOU'RE RIGHT...

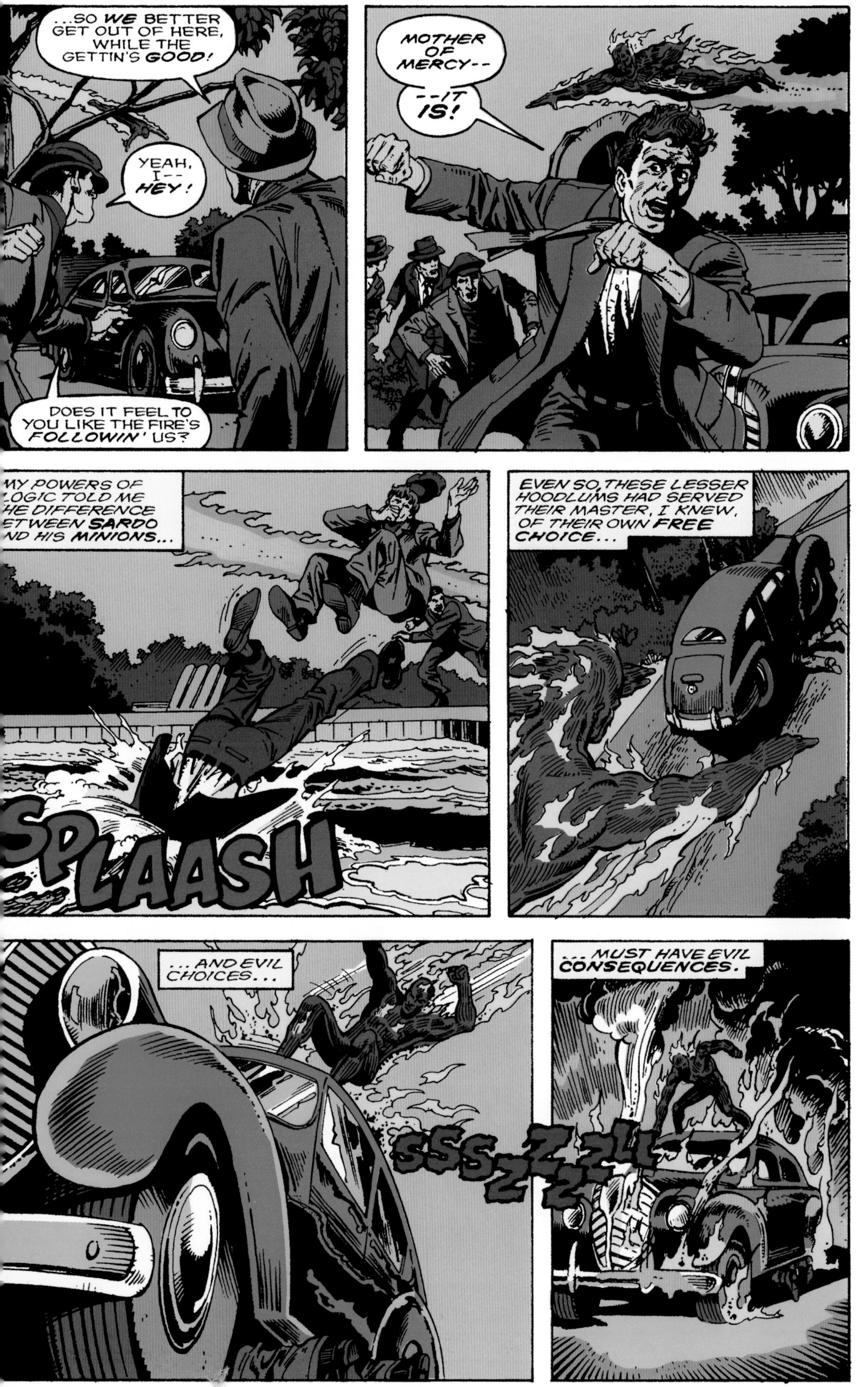
...SO WE BETTER GET OUT OF HERE, WHILE THE GETTIN'S GOOD!
YEAH, I-- HEY!
DOES IT FEEL TO YOU LIKE THE FIRE'S FOLLOWIN' US?
MOTHER OF MERCY--
--IT IS!
MY POWERS OF LOGIC TOLD ME THE DIFFERENCE BETWEEN SARDO AND HIS MINIONS...
SPLAASH
EVEN SO, THESE LESSER HOODLUMS HAD SERVED THEIR MASTER, I KNEW, OF THEIR OWN FREE CHOICE...
...AND EVIL CHOICES...
SSSZZZZZZ
...MUST HAVE EVIL CONSEQUENCES.

I'M NOT CERTAIN THAT THE MAN CALLED **RED** APPRECIATED THAT, IN HIS FINAL, FLICKERING MOMENTS OF EXISTENCE.

AAAAA

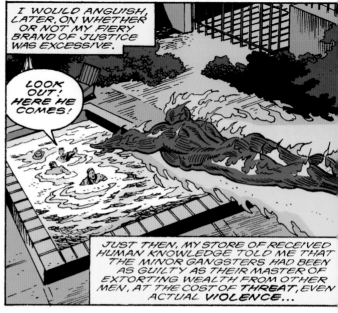

I WOULD ANGUISH, LATER, ON WHETHER OR NOT MY FIERY BRAND OF JUSTICE WAS EXCESSIVE.

LOOK OUT! HERE HE COMES!

JUST THEN, MY STORE OF RECEIVED HUMAN KNOWLEDGE TOLD ME THAT THE MINOR GANGSTERS HAD BEEN AS GUILTY AS THEIR MASTER OF EXTORTING WEALTH FROM OTHER MEN, AT THE COST OF **THREAT**, EVEN ACTUAL **VIOLENCE**...

...AND IF THIS WAS A CASE OF "AN EYE FOR AN EYELASH," I WAS NOT YET INTELLECTUALLY PREPARED TO MAKE SUCH SUBTLE DISTINCTIONS.

YYAAAA

TH-THE POOL WATER'S **BOILING**!

GOTTA GET OUTTA HERE!

YET PERHAPS, AFTER ALL, THE BEGINNINGS OF A FINE **BALANCE** WERE FORMING IN MY RAPIDLY MATURING MIND.

WHY ELSE DID I LET THE CHASTENED CRIMINALS **FLEE** TO NURSE THEIR PAINFUL WOUNDS, RATHER THAN CUT THEM DOWN AS THE BRUSHFIRE DOES THE ROTTED UNDERGROWTH?

YES, THERE WOULD BE MUCH TO THINK ABOUT?

LATER.

PERHAPS I SENSED THAT **ONE MAN**, AND ONE ALONE, DESERVED THE FULL, DEADLY RANGE OF MY RIGHTEOUS RETRIBUTION.

SARDO...

AS THE RISING CONFLAGRATION INSIDE WASHED OVER ME, AS A WELCOME RAIN TO MORTAL MEN, I SPIED THE METAL TRAP DOOR...

...AND KNEW THAT ULTIMATE CONFRONTATION WAS AT HAND.

NOTHING IN MY EXPERIENCE TO DATE HAD CONVINCED ME THAT I SHOULD LEAVE SUCH MATTERS TO MANKIND'S **POLICE**.

REEEE

N.Y.P.D.

IN TIME TO COME, I WOULD SEE THE **IRONY** THAT SARDO HAD ONCE MEANT HIS BOMB SHELTER TO BE HIS LAST-DITCH PLACE OF REFUGE FROM SUCH MEN...

...AND THAT NOW, HE WOULD ALMOST HAVE **WELCOMED** THEIR ARRIVAL.

H-HOT IN HERE--BUT AT LEAST--

...O...

SOMEWHERE AMID PROF. HORTON'S PIPED-IN WIRE-TAPES I WAS DIMLY AWARE OF A CHILDREN'S STORY ABOUT THREE MINIATURE PIGS.

BUT TO THE HUMAN TORCH, **EVERYTHING** WAS A HOUSE OF STRAW, NOT OF BRICKS.

THROW DOWN YOUR WEAPON, SARDO.

NOT ON YOUR **LIFE**--

--WHICH JUST NOW **RAN OUT!**

BLAMM

CLEARLY, SARDO'S UNDERSTANDING OF MY ORGANIC PROCESSES WAS EXTREMELY **LIMITED**.

EVEN IF HIS BULLET HAD **NOT** MELTED BEFORE IT STRUCK ME, IT WOULD HAVE DONE ME ONLY SLIGHT DAMAGE.

BUT IT DID **NOT** TOUCH ME--ONLY THE FIERY AURA AROUND ME.

HAVING FUN, SARDO?

SSZZZL

EH? WHAT'S THIS **TANK** YOU'VE TAKEN REFUGE BEHIND?

I--I JUST REALIZED-- IT'S FULL OF **NITRO!**

GET AWAY FROM IT, YOU FOOL!

YOU'LL BLOW US **BOTH** UP!

YET, EVEN AS I STROVE--JUST HOW, I HAD NO IDEA--TO **LESSEN** MY FLAMES, MY INCANDESCENT HANDS BURNED THROUGH THE METAL--

--AND **NITRO GAS** SHOT UP AT ME!

HSSSS

BUT, TO SARDO'S AMAZEMENT, AS WELL AS MY OWN HALF-EDUCATED WONDER--THERE WAS NO EXPLOSION.

WHAT'S MORE, THOUGH THE NITRO HAD ALL BUT PUT OUT MY FIRE, I WAS STILL CAPABLE OF MOVEMENT.

YOU'VE **ABSORBED** THE NITRO SOMEHOW-- AND IT'S **CHANGED** YOU!

WHY--SO IT HAS!

NITRO DANGER

BUT THAT DOESN'T MEAN I'M NOT GOING TO FRY **YOUR** HIDE, SARDO!

S-STAY BACK! LOOK! YOU C-CAN HAVE THIS **OTHER** CAN OF NITRO--

--IF YOU'LL JUST **LET** ME GO!

YOU'RE IN NO POSITION TO STRIKE A **BARGAIN,** RAT!

"RAT"--A TERM I'D PICKED UP FROM SOME PIPED-IN RADIO MELODRAMAS, NO DOUBT.

NITRO DANGER

LISTEN, TORCH--I CAN MAKE YOU **RICH!**

YOU WANT TO BE A **CHUMP**--FIGHTING FIRE AND GUYS LIKE ME FOR PEANUTS, LIKE THOSE **COPS** AND **FIREMEN** OUTSIDE?

SARDO, YOU'RE STARTING TO ANNOY ME.

SLAM

THINK I'LL JUST STAND BY AND LET YOU TRASH MY LAB, DO YOU?

WELL, LET'S SEE HOW HOT AND BOTHERED YOU ARE--

--AFTER A BATH OF *SULPHURIC ACID!*

I'LL ADMIT IT -- I WAS CARELESS.

IF I'D BEEN AS *VULNERABLE* TO THAT ACID AS SARDO HOPED, THE WORLD'S *FIRST* ANDROID WOULD HAVE *BEEN* HISTORY BEFORE HE COULD *MAKE* VERY MUCH OF IT.

BUT, IN THE *INTENSE HEAT,* THE SMALL TANK *EXPLODED* BEFORE IT EVER HIT ME--

BTHOO!

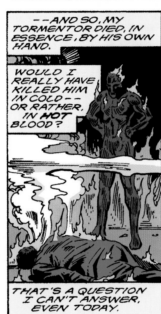

--AND SO, MY *TORMENTOR* DIED, IN ESSENCE, BY HIS OWN HAND.

WOULD I *REALLY* HAVE KILLED HIM IN *COLD* -- OR RATHER, IN *HOT* BLOOD?

THAT'S A QUESTION I CAN'T ANSWER, EVEN TODAY.

AT THE TIME, I WAS MORE CONCERNED WITH HANDLING THAT REMAINING TANK OF *NITRO* BEFORE MY RESTORED FLAMES BURNED *THROUGH* IT...

..SO I COULD FIND OUT IF THE LATE MR. SARDO'S IMPROMPTU THEORIES WERE ON TARGET.

SSSS

THEY WERE.

ON AN IMPULSE, I *BATHED* MYSELF IN THE NITRO -- AND FOUND THAT NOW, NOT ONLY COULD I *CONTROL* THE FIRES RAGING WITHIN ME, BUT WHEN I WANTED TO--

FLAME ON!

--THE FLAMES WOULD COME AND GO AT MY MENTAL COMMAND.

THE "*FLAME ON!*" WAS SIMPLY A *WAR CRY,* TO HELP MY CONCENTRATION.

I COULD TOSS *FIREBALLS* NOW, TOO -- WHICH I SUSPECTED WOULD COME IN HANDY ONE DAY SOON.

91

FOR THE MOMENT HOWEVER, I DECIDED I'D BETTER ABANDON THE INFERNO WHICH HAD BEEN SARDO'S HOME.

THERE WAS ALWAYS THE CHANCE THAT SOMETHING WOULD LAND ON ME THAT MY FLAMES WOULDN'T MELT QUITE QUICKLY ENOUGH.

I SHOULD HAVE REALIZED THE BLAZE WOULD HAVE ATTRACTED AN AUDIENCE.

ALL RIGHT, YOU WALKING HOT PLATE UP WITH 'EM!

AND IF HE DOESN'T? WHAT DO WE DO THEN?

WHY, WE WRITE OUT A NICE LONG REPORT FOR MAYOR LaGUARDIA!

HE'S STILL COMIN'! HE'LL COOK US IF HE GETS ANY CLOSER!

WAIT--!

LET 'IM HAVE IT, BOYS!

BLAM SSZZZL BLAM

HUH? WE MIGHT AS WELL BE TOSSING CHOCOLATE KISSES AT HIM, FOR ALL THE GOOD IT'S DOING.

AND THE HEAT'S SO TERRIFIC-- WE CAN'T EVEN GET NEAR HIM!

DON'T YOU HUMANS EVER LISTEN?

I SAID TO WAIT...

...BECAUSE I'VE GOT SOMETHING TO SHOW YOU.

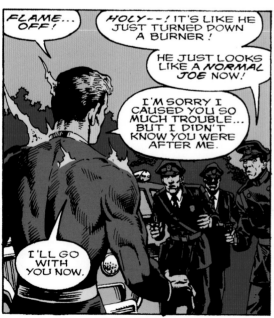

FLAME... OFF!

HOLY--! IT'S LIKE HE JUST TURNED DOWN A BURNER!

HE JUST LOOKS LIKE A NORMAL JOE NOW!

I'M SORRY I CAUSED YOU SO MUCH TROUBLE... BUT I DIDN'T KNOW YOU WERE AFTER ME.

I'LL GO WITH YOU NOW.

OKAY--BUT THE LAW SAYS WE GOTTA CUFF YOU. IS THAT-- I MEAN--

GO AHEAD, OFFICER MY BODY IS COLD NOW.

LIKE THE FEELING IN MY SYNTHETIC HEART.

LATER, WHEN I STOOD BEFORE THE POLICE COMMISSIONER...

PROF. HORTON, HERE, TOLD ME WHAT HAPPENED-- UH, MR. TORCH.

--AND FRANKLY, I'M AT A LOSS AS TO WHAT TO DO ABOUT YOU.

COMMISSIONER, YOU TALK AS IF MY CREATION WERE A *MAN,* INSTEAD OF A *ROBOT*--OR AN *ANDROID,* TO USE A MORE PRECISE TERM.

WELL, PROFESSOR, YOU DID CALL HIM A *HUMAN* TORCH, DIDN'T YOU?

MERELY A FIGURE OF SPEECH-- AND A POSSIBLE *TRADEMARKING* TERM I ASSURE YOU.

SINCE HE'S NOT REALLY HUMAN, THAT MAKES HIM MY *PROPERTY.*

HE--I MEAN, *IT* CAN'T BE PUNISHED FOR ITS ACTIONS, ANY MORE THAN YOU'D JAIL A *RUNAWAY TRACTOR!*

I SUPPOSE THAT MAKES SENSE.

BUT--I--

QUIET! HORTON, I MAY TAKE SOME HEAT ON THIS-- NO PUN INTENDED.

--BUT I HEREBY RESTORE YOUR... *PROPERTY...* TO YOU.

THANK YOU, COMMISSIONER. YOU WON'T REGRET THIS.

JUST KEEP YOUR ROBOT UNDER WRAPS, UNTIL IT *ACTS* AS HUMAN AS IT *LOOKS.*

COME ALONG, TORCH!

AND FOR HEAVEN'S SAKE, DON'T *"FLAME ON"* ON MY NEW UPHOLSTERY!

I DIDN'T EVEN NOTICE THE POLICE CHIEF'S CURIOUS EYES ON ME.

BEFORE LONG...

NO BLAZING HERE, EITHER! I DON'T WANT MY LABORATORY TO WIND UP LIKE THAT WAREHOUSE.

IT MIGHT INTEREST YOU TO KNOW, PROF. HORTON--

--THAT I NOW HAVE *COMPLETE CONTROL* OVER MY FLAME.

YOU SEE?

I--I SURE *DO!*

THIS IS AMAZING! IF THE *FIRE-THREAT* YOU POSE CAN BE MINIMIZED-- I CAN MAKE A *FORTUNE* WITH YOU!

NO, HORTON.

WHAT--?

IN MY BRIEF SPAN OF LIFE, I HAVE ALREADY SEEN THOSE CALLED *FIREMEN* AND *POLICEMEN* RISK THEIR LIVES-- WITHOUT *"MAKING A FORTUNE,"* AS YOU PUT IT.

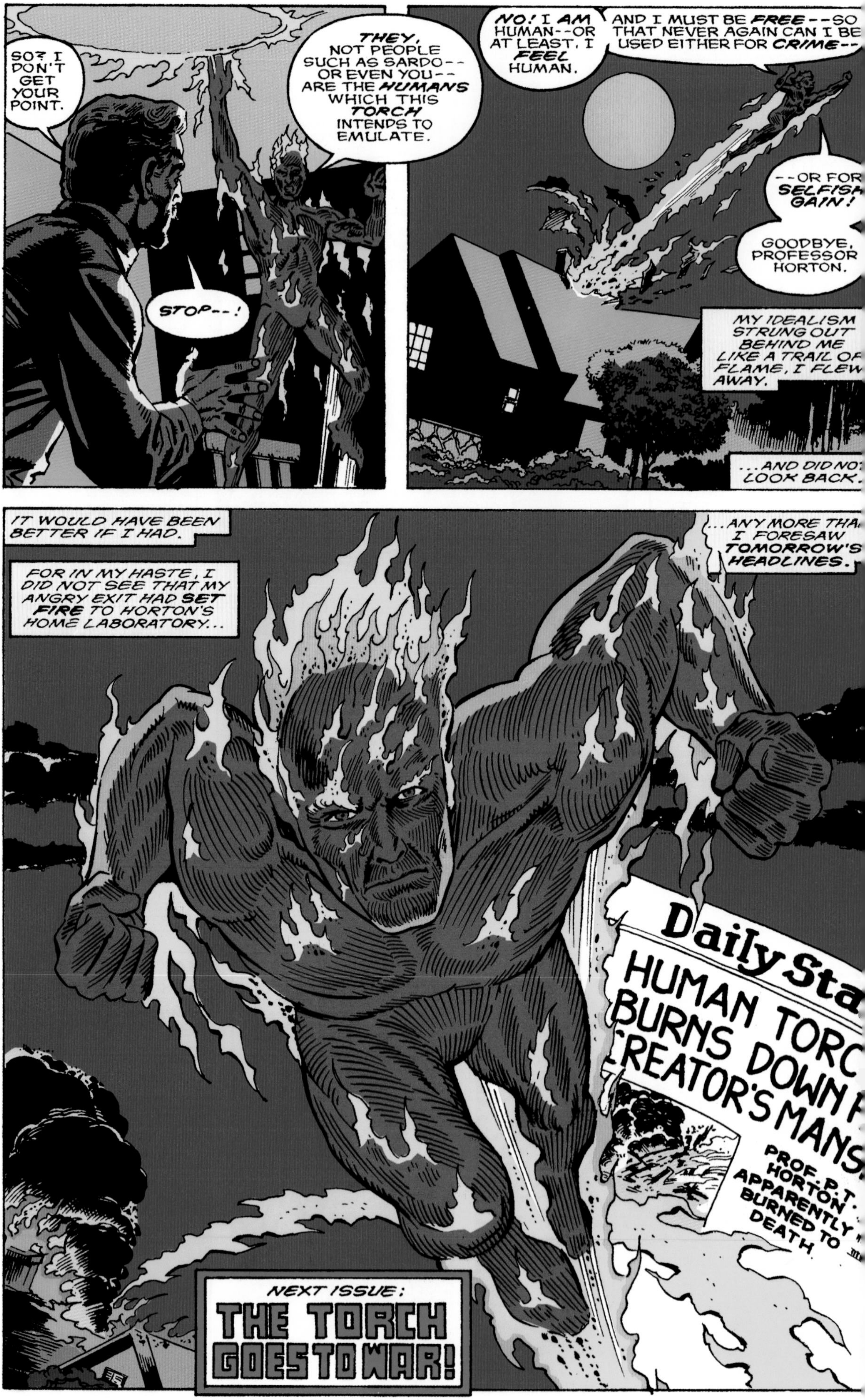
SO? I DON'T GET YOUR POINT.
THEY, NOT PEOPLE SUCH AS SARDO--OR EVEN YOU--ARE THE HUMANS WHICH THIS TORCH INTENDS TO EMULATE.
STOP--!
NO! I AM HUMAN--OR AT LEAST, I FEEL HUMAN.
AND I MUST BE FREE--SO THAT NEVER AGAIN CAN I BE USED EITHER FOR CRIME--
--OR FOR SELFISH GAIN!
GOODBYE, PROFESSOR HORTON.
MY IDEALISM STRUNG OUT BEHIND ME LIKE A TRAIL OF FLAME, I FLEW AWAY.
...AND DID NOT LOOK BACK.
IT WOULD HAVE BEEN BETTER IF I HAD.
FOR IN MY HASTE, I DID NOT SEE THAT MY ANGRY EXIT HAD SET FIRE TO HORTON'S HOME LABORATORY...
...ANY MORE THAN I FORESAW TOMORROW'S HEADLINES.
Daily Sta
HUMAN TORC BURNS DOWN CREATOR'S MANS
PROF. P.T. HORTON APPARENTLY BURNED TO DEATH
NEXT ISSUE:
THE TORCH GOES TO WAR!

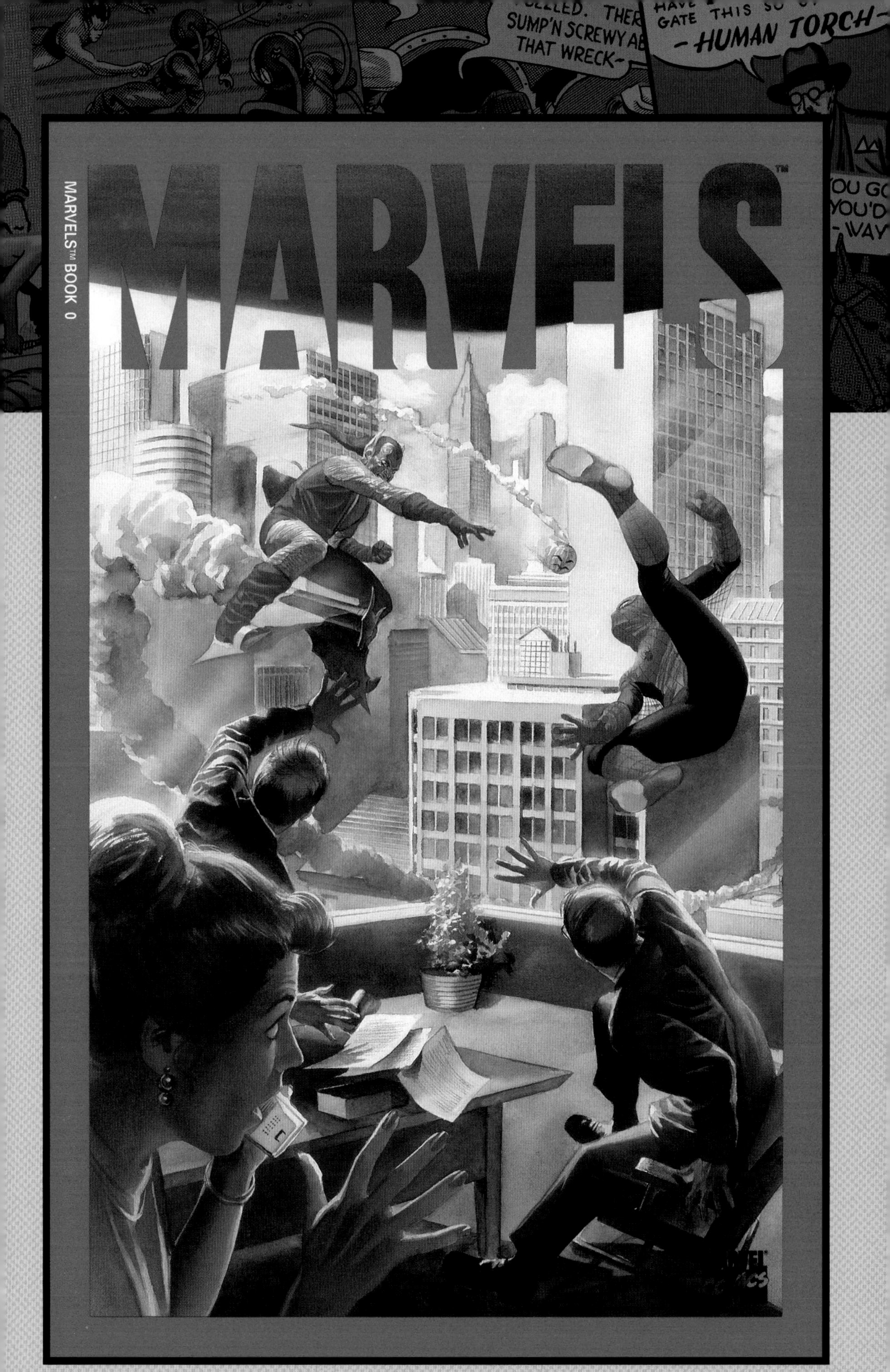

SUMP'N SCREWY
THAT WRECK-
GATE THIS
-HUMAN TORCH-
MARVELS™ BOOK 0
MARVELS™

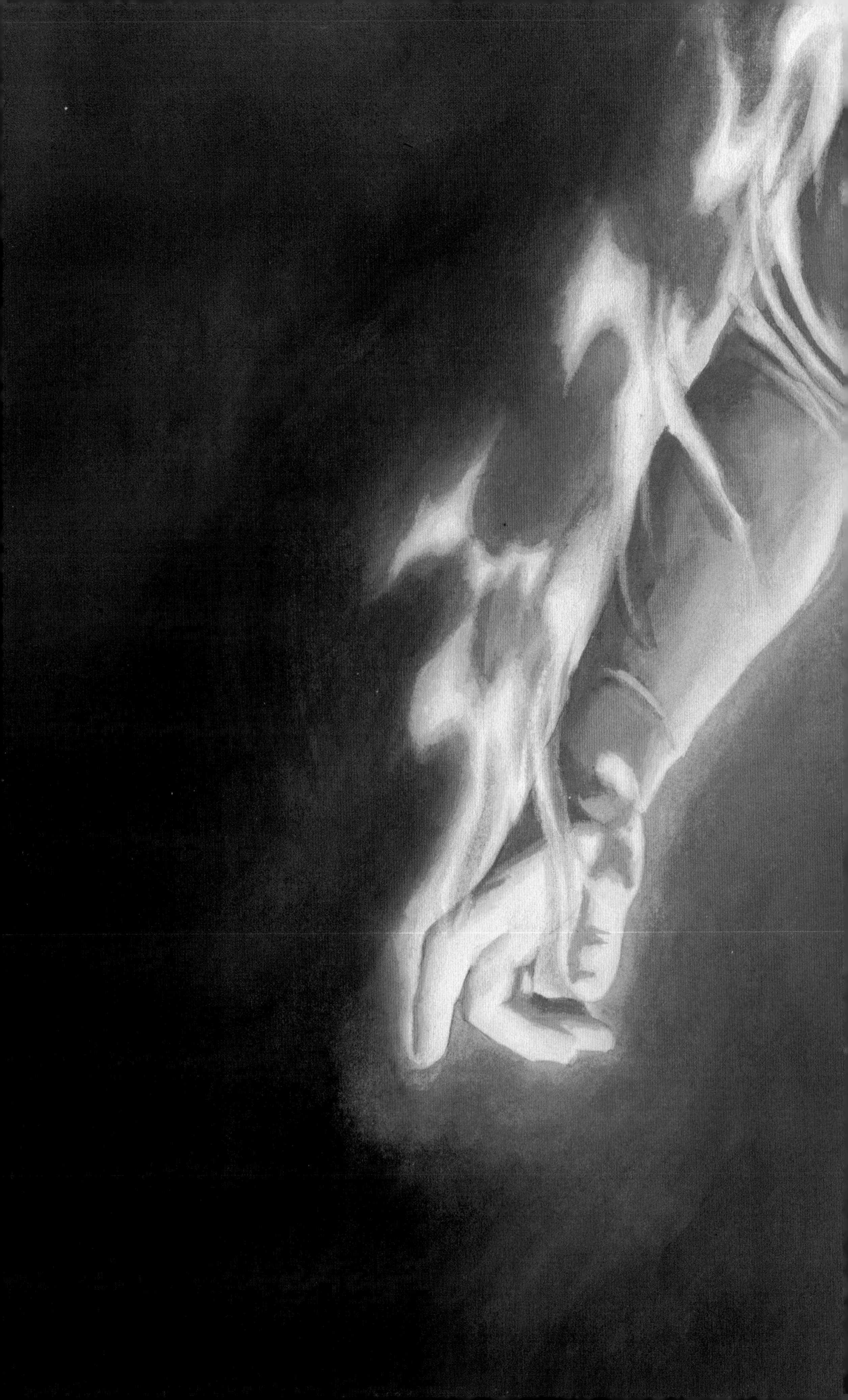

"IT IS WITH CONSIDERABLE DIFFICULTY
THAT I REMEMBER THE ORIGINAL
ERA OF MY BEING...."

MARY SHELLEY
FRANKENSTEIN

HORTON

PHINEAS THOMAS HORTON

QUITE POSSIBLY THE GREATEST
SCIENTIST OF HIS TIME.

HE WAS MY FATHER.

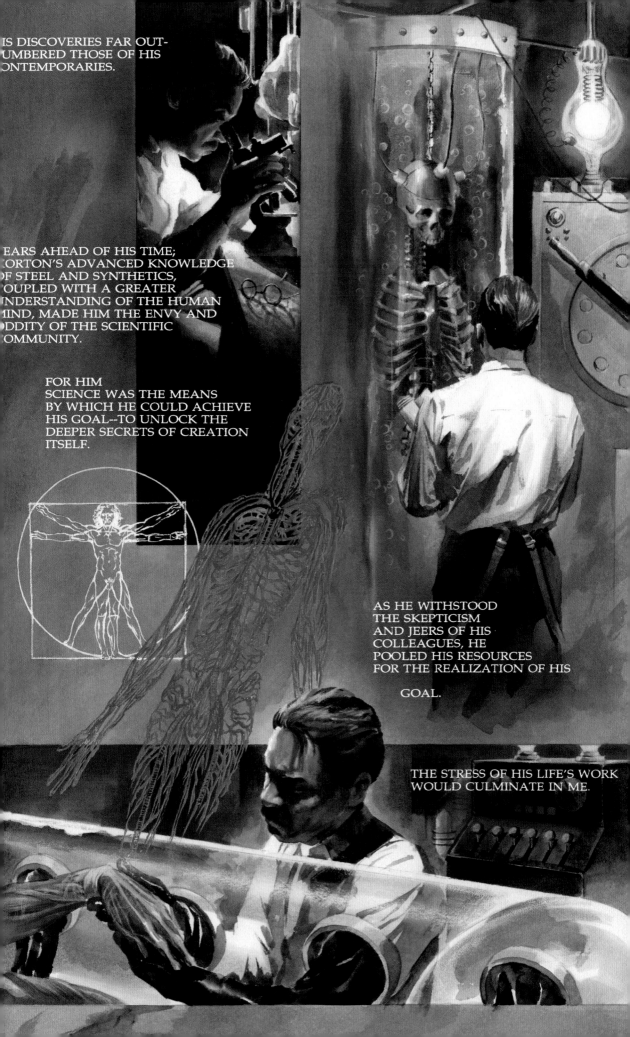

IS DISCOVERIES FAR OUT-
UMBERED THOSE OF HIS
ONTEMPORARIES.

EARS AHEAD OF HIS TIME;
ORTON'S ADVANCED KNOWLEDGE
F STEEL AND SYNTHETICS,
OUPLED WITH A GREATER
NDERSTANDING OF THE HUMAN
IND, MADE HIM THE ENVY AND
DDITY OF THE SCIENTIFIC
OMMUNITY.

FOR HIM
SCIENCE WAS THE MEANS
BY WHICH HE COULD ACHIEVE
HIS GOAL--TO UNLOCK THE
DEEPER SECRETS OF CREATION
ITSELF.

AS HE WITHSTOOD
THE SKEPTICISM
AND JEERS OF HIS
COLLEAGUES, HE
POOLED HIS RESOURCES
FOR THE REALIZATION OF HIS

GOAL.

THE STRESS OF HIS LIFE'S WORK
WOULD CULMINATE IN ME.

I CANNOT RECALL IT PERFECTLY,
BUT IN MY FIRST MOMENT OF
CONSCIOUSNESS, SOMETHING
UNPREDICTED

OCCURRED.

DUE TO SOME FLAW IN MY
ORIGINAL CONCEPTION,
MY BODY HAD AN INCENDIARY
REACTION TO THE CONTACT
WITH AIR.

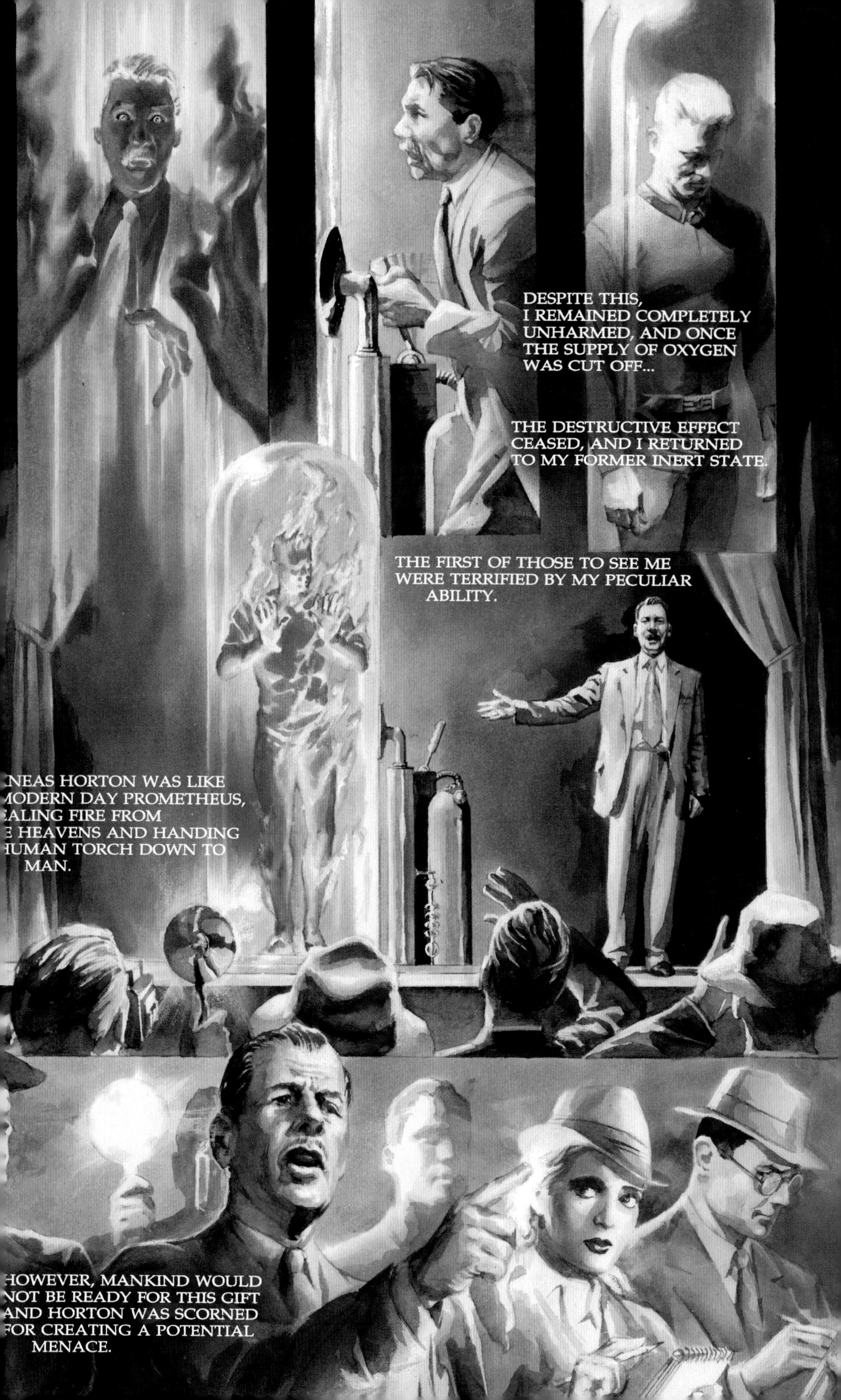
DESPITE THIS, I REMAINED COMPLETELY UNHARMED, AND ONCE THE SUPPLY OF OXYGEN WAS CUT OFF...
THE DESTRUCTIVE EFFECT CEASED, AND I RETURNED TO MY FORMER INERT STATE.
THE FIRST OF THOSE TO SEE ME WERE TERRIFIED BY MY PECULIAR ABILITY.
NEAS HORTON WAS LIKE MODERN DAY PROMETHEUS, ALING FIRE FROM HEAVENS AND HANDING HUMAN TORCH DOWN TO MAN.
HOWEVER, MANKIND WOULD NOT BE READY FOR THIS GIFT AND HORTON WAS SCORNED FOR CREATING A POTENTIAL MENACE.

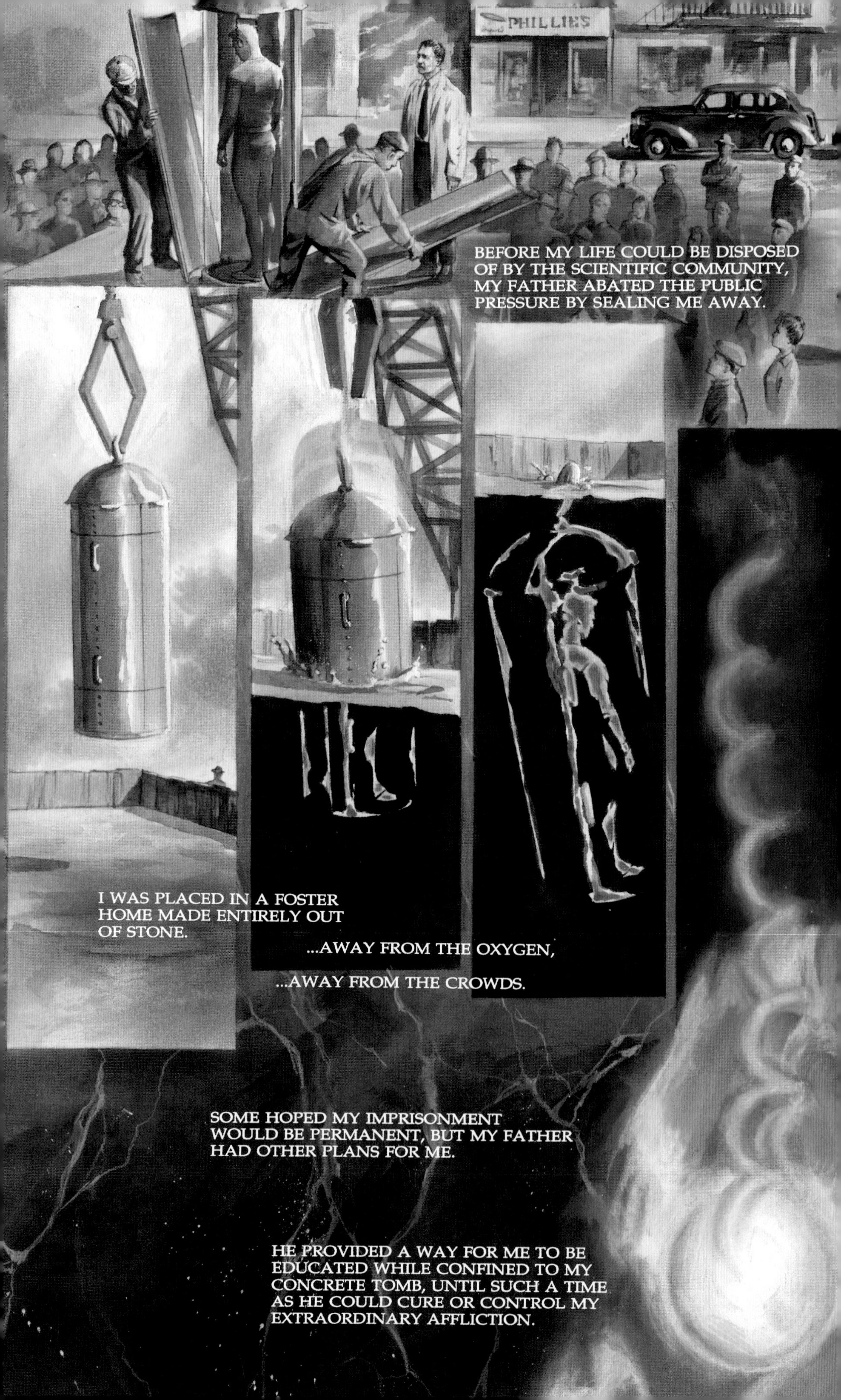
PHILLIES
BEFORE MY LIFE COULD BE DISPOSED OF BY THE SCIENTIFIC COMMUNITY, MY FATHER ABATED THE PUBLIC PRESSURE BY SEALING ME AWAY.
I WAS PLACED IN A FOSTER HOME MADE ENTIRELY OUT OF STONE.
...AWAY FROM THE OXYGEN,
...AWAY FROM THE CROWDS.
SOME HOPED MY IMPRISONMENT WOULD BE PERMANENT, BUT MY FATHER HAD OTHER PLANS FOR ME.
HE PROVIDED A WAY FOR ME TO BE EDUCATED WHILE CONFINED TO MY CONCRETE TOMB, UNTIL SUCH A TIME AS HE COULD CURE OR CONTROL MY EXTRAORDINARY AFFLICTION.

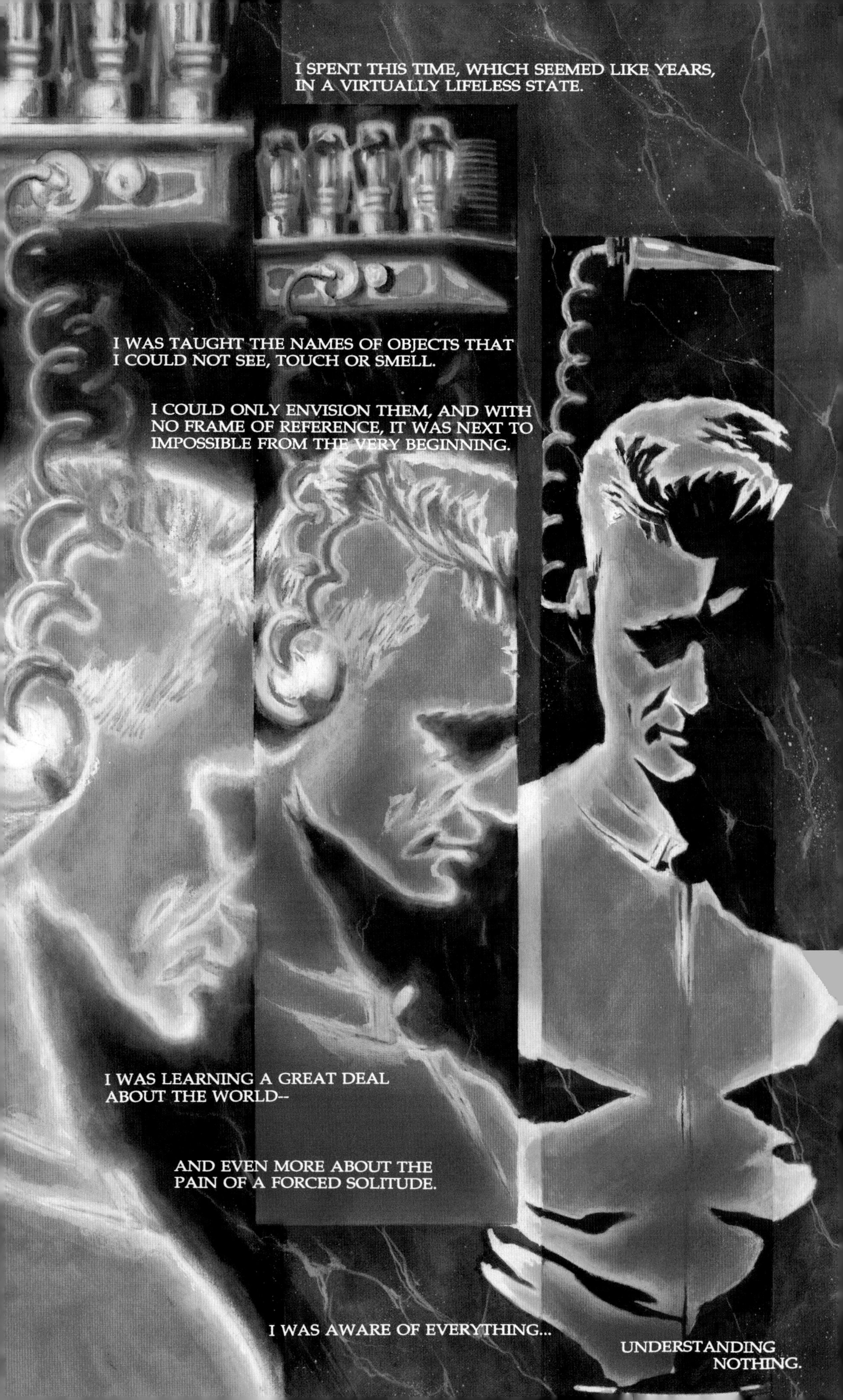

I SPENT THIS TIME, WHICH SEEMED LIKE YEARS, IN A VIRTUALLY LIFELESS STATE.
I WAS TAUGHT THE NAMES OF OBJECTS THAT I COULD NOT SEE, TOUCH OR SMELL.
I COULD ONLY ENVISION THEM, AND WITH NO FRAME OF REFERENCE, IT WAS NEXT TO IMPOSSIBLE FROM THE VERY BEGINNING.
I WAS LEARNING A GREAT DEAL ABOUT THE WORLD--
AND EVEN MORE ABOUT THE PAIN OF A FORCED SOLITUDE.
I WAS AWARE OF EVERYTHING...
UNDERSTANDING NOTHING.

I COULD BARELY COMPREHEND WHAT
HAD HAPPENED TO ME

IN THE COURSE OF MY SHORT
LIFE.

I HAD BEEN RIPPED FROM MY ORIGINAL
WOMB AND THRUST INTO A WORLD
WHERE EVERY NOISE WAS
WAS EQUAL TO A
SCREAM.

I HAD GONE FROM THE SECURITY
OF DARKNESS TO A PLACE WHERE
LIGHT BLAZED FROM EVERY DIRECTION.

AND YET,
AS I BECAME AWARE OF
THESE SENSATIONS,

AS MY EYES,
MY EARS, AND
MY SKIN WOULD
FOCUS UPON
THESE...

THEY DISAPPEARED.

AND I ONCE AGAIN WOULD
FALL BACK INTO THE DARK-
NESS AND THE SILENCE WHICH
LACKED THE COMFORT THEY
ONCE HELD.

THEY WERE NOW ONLY
MOCKING REMINDERS OF
ALL THAT WAS DENIED ME.

MY FATHER BROUGHT ME INTO THIS WORLD
AND KEPT ME ALIVE WHEN OTHERS WOULD HAV
ME DESTROYED.

WHY THEN,
DID HE ALLOW ME
THIS TORMENT?

WAS HE SO EASILY WILLING
TO FORSAKE ME...

WAS IT POSSIBLE THAT WHILE
I BELIEVED IN HIM AS A FATHER,

HE DID NOT BELIEVE IN M
AS A SON?

KNEW THE AIR THAT
HAD ONCE TASTED.

I KNEW I WANTED TO
TASTE IT AGAIN,
ALWAYS AND FOREVER.

ORE THAN ANYTHING ELSE, HOWEVER,
ANTED TO BE WITH YOU.
ANTED TO BE A PART OF YOUR WORLD.

AS MY YOUNG MIND HAD DEVELOPED,
I LEARNED TO RECOGNIZE THE BEAUTY
AND THE VALUE OF HUMAN LIFE.

LIFE AND FREEDOM COMMANDED
MY RESPECT AS THAT
I POSSESSED NEITHER.

AT THE SAME TIME,
I WAS BECOMING AWARE
OF MYSELF AS AN
INDIVIDUAL...

I WAS THE FIRST OF MY KIND.

WAS IT RIGHT THAT I
SHOULD BE GIVEN LIFE
ONLY TO BE PLACED
IN ETERNAL IMPRISONMENT?

TO BE TANTALIZED WITH
A KNOWLEDGE OF THE WORLD,
AND DENIED THE CHANCE
TO SAVOR IT?

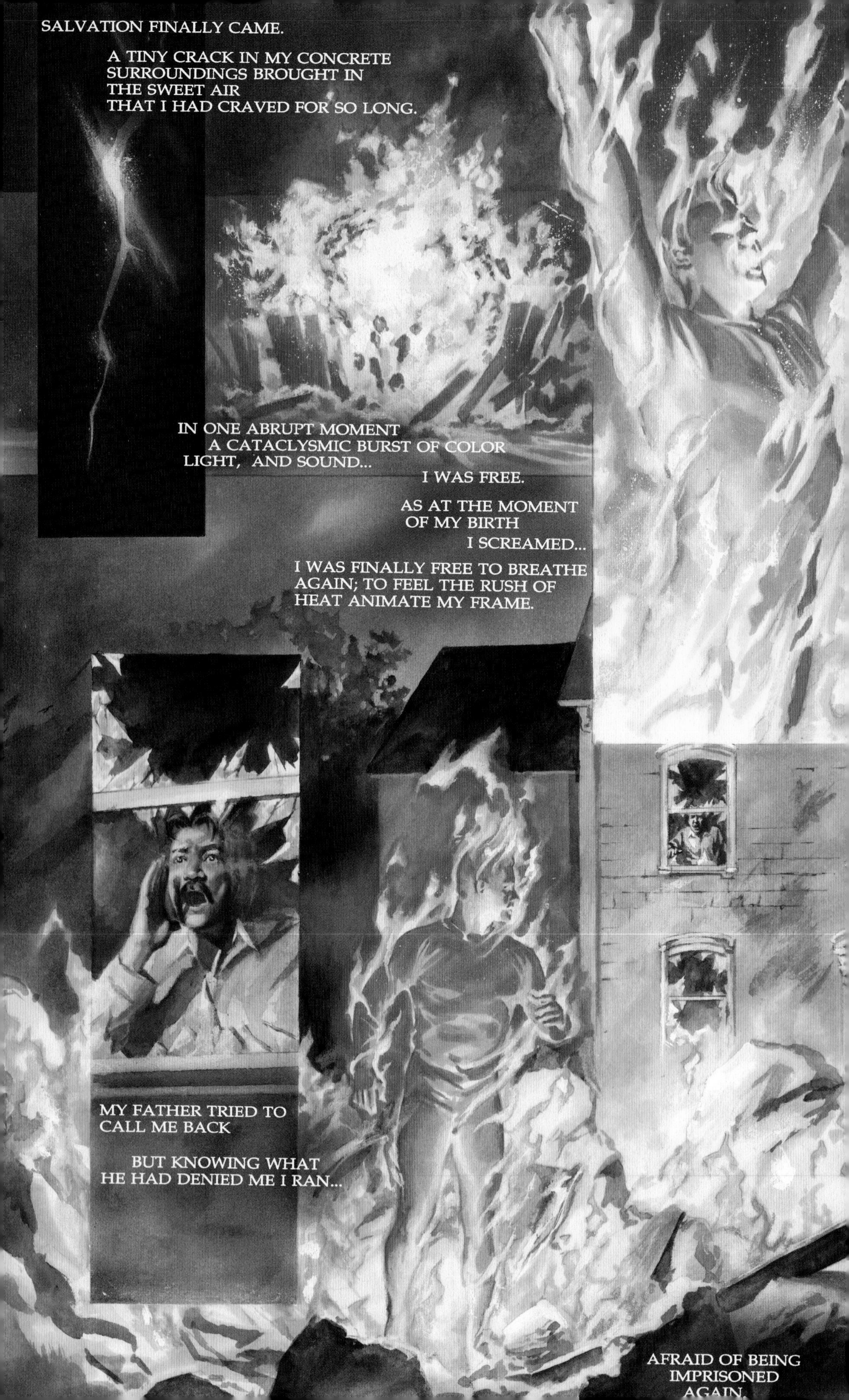
SALVATION FINALLY CAME.
A TINY CRACK IN MY CONCRETE SURROUNDINGS BROUGHT IN THE SWEET AIR THAT I HAD CRAVED FOR SO LONG.
IN ONE ABRUPT MOMENT A CATACLYSMIC BURST OF COLOR LIGHT, AND SOUND...
I WAS FREE.
AS AT THE MOMENT OF MY BIRTH
I SCREAMED...
I WAS FINALLY FREE TO BREATHE AGAIN; TO FEEL THE RUSH OF HEAT ANIMATE MY FRAME.
MY FATHER TRIED TO CALL ME BACK
BUT KNOWING WHAT HE HAD DENIED ME I RAN...
AFRAID OF BEING IMPRISONED AGAIN.

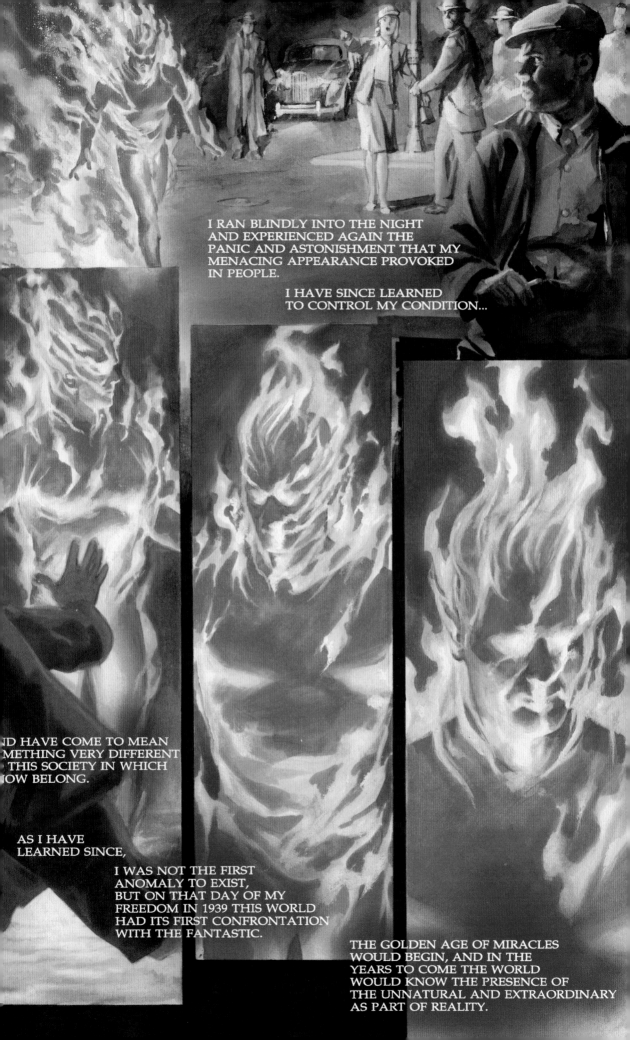

I RAN BLINDLY INTO THE NIGHT AND EXPERIENCED AGAIN THE PANIC AND ASTONISHMENT THAT MY MENACING APPEARANCE PROVOKED IN PEOPLE.

I HAVE SINCE LEARNED TO CONTROL MY CONDITION...

...ND HAVE COME TO MEAN ...METHING VERY DIFFERENT ... THIS SOCIETY IN WHICH ...OW BELONG.

AS I HAVE LEARNED SINCE,

I WAS NOT THE FIRST ANOMALY TO EXIST, BUT ON THAT DAY OF MY FREEDOM IN 1939 THIS WORLD HAD ITS FIRST CONFRONTATION WITH THE FANTASTIC.

THE GOLDEN AGE OF MIRACLES WOULD BEGIN, AND IN THE YEARS TO COME THE WORLD WOULD KNOW THE PRESENCE OF THE UNNATURAL AND EXTRAORDINARY AS PART OF REALITY.

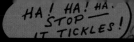

MARVEL COMICS

OCT.

This Month
"THE HUMAN TORCH"
"THE ANGEL"
"SUBMARINER"
"MASKED RAIDER"

Featuring
**KA-ZAR
THE GREAT**
**12 PAGES
OF JUNGLE
ADVENTURE!**

ACTION   MYSTERY   ADVENTURE

PUBLISHED IN 2009, THE *MARVEL COMICS #1 70TH ANNIVERSARY EDITION* WAS A 64-PAGE ONE-SHOT
SHOWCASING THE ORIGINAL *MARVEL COMICS #1*, NEWLY REMASTERED — AND FOR THIS EDITION,
RECOLORED IN MODERN STYLE BY SEVERAL OF MARVEL'S MOST NOTABLE COLORISTS.
COVER ART BY **JELENA KEVIC DJURDJEVIC**.

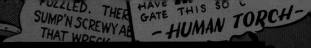

MARVEL COMICS

OCT.

Featuring
KA-ZAR THE GREAT
12 PAGES OF JUNGLE ADVENTURE!

ACTION   MYSTERY   ADVENTURE

THE HUMAN TORCH

BY CARL BURGOS

GENTLEMEN OF THE PRESS · I CALLED YOU TO MY LABORATORY BECAUSE I, PROFESSOR HORTON, HAVE A DIFFICULT PROBLEM IN MY LATEST DISCOVERY··

AS YOU ALL KNOW, I'VE BEEN WORKING ON A SYNTHETIC MAN — AN EXACT REPLICA OF A HUMAN BEING!!

WHEN I FINISHED, I FOUND I HAD SURPASSED ANYTHING THAT ANY SCIENTIST HAD EVER DONE —

IF YOU'LL FOLLOW ME, I'LL SHOW YOU WHY, EVEN I FEAR THE MONSTROSITY, WHICH I'VE CREATED!!

IN THIS AIR-TIGHT GLASS CAGE, LIVES MY CREATION·· I CALL HIM — THE HUMAN TORCH!

SOMETHING WENT WRONG WITH MY FIGURINGS SOMEWHERE · EVERY TIME THIS ROBOT, THE HUMAN TORCH, CONTACTS OXYGEN IN THE AIR, HE BURSTS INTO FLAME! NOW WATCH!

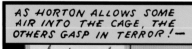

AS HORTON ALLOWS SOME AIR INTO THE CAGE, THE OTHERS GASP IN TERROR!—

GOOD LORD! THAT FIGURE IS A WALL OF FIRE!!

HORTON, DESTROY THAT MAN, BEFORE SOME MADMAN CAN GRASP IT'S PRINCIPLES AND HURL IT AGAINST OUR CIVILIZATION!

NO!

SORRY, GENTLEMEN, BUT YOU SE DESTROYING HIM, DOES NOT ANSWER ANYTHING!!

THEN PERHAPS THE POWER OF THE PRESS WIL HELP CHANGE YOUR MIND!

WITHIN THE HOUR NEWSIES ARE ON THE STREET WITH AN *EXTRA!*

EXTRA! - READ ALL ABOUT THE MAN OF FIRE - THE HUMAN TORCH!

-HELLO!- YES THIS IS HORTON! WHO IS THIS? ··· THE SCIENTISTS' GUILD? ··· YOU WANT TO SEE MY CREATION? — CERTAINLY! ANYTIME YOU SAY - TONIGHT? ·· VERY WELL ··· AT EIGHT!

AS HORTON READS THE PAPER IN HIS STUDY, THE PHONE BUZZES, BREAKING THE ROOM'S EERIE SILENCE.

THAT EVENING

EIGHT BELLS! - YOU'RE ON TIME BOYS!

YOU KNOW, HORTON, THOSE NEWSPAPERS HAVE AROUSED THE PUBLIC AND WE THREE HAVE BEEN SENT TO INVESTIGATE THIS SO CALLED — -HUMAN TORCH-

I THOUGHT SO, MY FRIENDS ·· COME THIS WAY PLEASE — AND I WILL SHOW YOU EVERYTHING!

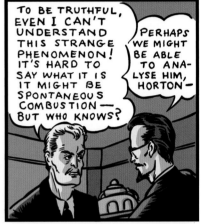

TO BE TRUTHFUL, EVEN I CAN'T UNDERSTAND THIS STRANGE PHENOMENON! IT'S HARD TO SAY WHAT IT IS IT MIGHT BE SPONTANEOUS COMBUSTION — BUT WHO KNOWS?

PERHAPS WE MIGHT BE ABLE TO ANALYSE HIM, HORTON-

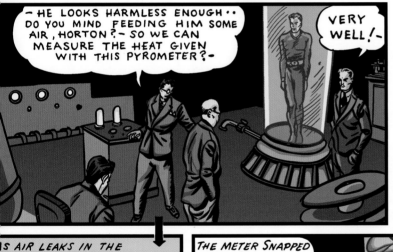

- HE LOOKS HARMLESS ENOUGH ·· DO YOU MIND FEEDING HIM SOME AIR, HORTON? - SO WE CAN MEASURE THE HEAT GIVEN WITH THIS PYROMETER? -

VERY WELL! -

NONE WHAT SO EVER - THAT IS WHY I'M AFRAID!

AS AIR LEAKS IN THE WEIRD FLAME LIVENS LIKE A HELLISH FIRE!!

GOOD LORD - THE HANDS OF THE METERS HAVE ALREADY GONE OFF THE DIALS! —

WHAT?

THE METER SNAPPED THE HEAT IS TOO GREAT! - — AND YOU HAVE NO CONTROL OVER THE FLAME?

2

AND NOW THAT YOU'VE SEEN IT·· WHAT IS YOUR OPINION?—

HORTON, THIS MAY HURT·· BUT SINCE YOU'VE NO CONTROL OVER HIM, I'M INCLINED TO AGREE WITH THE NEWSPAPERS!— DESTROY HIM!

SURELY, THERE MUST BE SOME OTHER WAY THAN TO BREAK HIM UP!— FOR WHO KNOWS, IN THE COURSE OF EXPERIMENTATION, I MIGHT HIT ON A DEVICE TO GAIN CONTROL OF, AND MASTER THIS MECHANICAL TORCH!

—THERE IS A WAY OUT, HORTON!— ENTOMB HIM IN A CONCRETE BLOCK, SO THAT IF·—

—THAT'S IT!— IF I FIND THE SOLUTION, I CAN DIG HIM OUT, AND THAT WAY THERE'S NO DANGER· —EUREKA!— THAT'S THE ANSWER!—

THE NEXT DAY. WORKERS BEGIN BUILDING A MOULD IN WHICH TO BURY THE HUMAN TORCH—

WHILE IN THE HOUSE— AS OFFICIAL WITNESSES OF THE PRESS, YOU'VE SEEN ME SEAL THE HUMAN TORCH IN THIS STEEL TUBE— PERHAPS FOREVER!

LIFTING THE STEEL·TUBE, WHEREIN LIES THE HUMAN TORCH, TWO HUSKIES CARRY IT FROM THE ROOM—

AND FIT IT TO A HOOK, DANGLING FROM THE TOP OF A DERRICK!

O·K! —LET 'ER GO!

AS THE TUBE HITS THE WET CEMENT MIXTURE AND SINKS, HORTON MAKES A VOW TO FIND A SOLUTION TO CONTROL THE FLAME!—

3

TIME WENT BY — AND EVERYBODY HAD FORGOTTEN ABOUT THE FIRE-MAN, UNTIL, ONE EARLY MORNING, THERE WAS A TERRIFYING BLAST AND THE EARTH SPLIT OPEN!

BOOM

THE WINDOWS OF HORTON'S NEARBY HOME WERE SHATTERED TO BITS! —

GOOD HEAVENS — WHAT WAS THAT? — I WONDER?! COULD IT BE — — ?

IN HORTON'S BEDROOM —

— YE GODS! THAT WAS THE HUMAN-TORCH'S TOMB! COULD HE HAVE BEEN DESTROYED?

HORTON RUSHES TO THE SHATTERED WINDOW! —

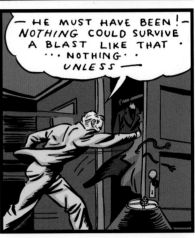

— HE MUST HAVE BEEN! — NOTHING COULD SURVIVE A BLAST LIKE THAT ··· NOTHING ·· UNLESS —

UNLESS THERE WAS A LEAK IN THE AIR-TIGHT TUBE IN WHICH HE WAS BURIED ·· A LEAK?! BUT THAT'S IMPOSSIBLE — I SEALED IT MYSELF!! —

— BUT THERE HAD BEEN A LEAK — A SLOW LEAK, ALLOWING THE OXYGEN TO SEEP IN SLOWLY! THE HUMAN TORCH, IN CONTACT WITH AIR, SPREADS TERROR THROUGH THE CITY, AS EVERYTHING HE TOUCHES TURNS INTO AN INFERNO!! —

FIRE! IT'S THE HUMAN TORCH! HE'S ON THE LOOSE!!

I'M BURNING ALIVE! — WHY MUST EVERYTHING I TOUCH, TURN TO FLAME? —

4

ATTRACTED BY THE CLANG OF FIRE-ENGINES, AFTER SOMEBODY HAD TURNED IN A FIRE ALARM, THE HUMAN TORCH TURNS

LOOK!— THE HUMAN TORCH! BUSY, MEN!

CLANG! CLANG!

HAH!— I LIKE THE SOUND OF THE BELL··

WELL, WHAT ARE YOU GUYS WAITING FOR? C'MON— GET THE HOSE INTO ACTION!

YESSIR.

HURRY!— THAT GUY'S STILL HERE!·· WATER OUGHT TO DO THE TRICK!—

AS THE WATER SPURTS ONTO THE HUMAN-TORCH — A HISSING SOUND BELLOWS— A CLOUD OF SMOKE RISES ·· BUT THE FIREMEN ARE DUMBFOUNDED, AS ···—

GLORY BE! THE GUY'S LAUGHING! IT AIN'T· HUMAN!!

HA! HA! HA! STOP— IT TICKLES!

KEEP POURING WATER ON HIM— THE FLAMES DYING DOWN!— I'M GOING TO GET HORTON!

AS THE HUMAN TORCH STEPS ON A HOSE, IT BURNS THROUGH, AND THE WATER SPURTS OUT

THE FLAMES ONCE AGAIN SHOOT UP, AND THE HUMAN TORCH IS ON THE LOOSE AGAIN!—

I MUST FIND A RETREAT· I'VE ALREADY CAUSED TOO MUCH DAMAGE···

?

IT LOOKS LIKE A POOL IN THERE··· PERHAPS THAT WILL PUT OUT THIS FLAME!—

COMING TO AN IRON GATE, THE HUMAN-TORCH PAUSES··

—GRIPPING THE IRON GATE IN HIS FLAMING HANDS, THE HUMAN TORCH MELTS HIS WAY THROUGH THE HEAVY BARS—

THOSE IRON BARS CAN'T STOP ME!

EAVING A TRAIL OF BLAZING GRASS, THE HUMAN-TORCH DIVES INTO THE POOL···

MEANWHILE, IN THE HOUSE ON THE ESTATE WITH THE POOL

DAT'S FUNNY— DE GRASS 'ROUND DE POOL IS BOININ', SARDO!

YOU'RE NUTS, RED!

HUMAN-TO... ON LOOSE!...

WAIT A MINUTE— DID YOU SAY BURNING?!!— THAT MEANS BUT ONE THING!

HUH?

NOW LISTEN—GET THE WINTER GLASS-COVER, THAT FITS THE POOL—DRAW THE AIR OUT··· THEN DRAIN THE WATER OUT!—HURRY!—DON'T ASK ANY QUESTIONS!

ATER!

HAH!—I THOUGHT SO!—IT'S THE HUMAN TORCH!!

SO WOT?

THAT'S WHAT I LIKE ABOUT YOU RED— YOU'RE SO STUPID!

I DON'T LIKE DAT KIND OF TALK— SARDO!

FORGET IT RED—WE GOT A MILLION-DOLLAR RACKET, AND DON'T NEED TO WORRY ABOUT COPS NOW!

FROM NOW ON, RED, WE'RE IN THE FIRE-INSURANCE BUSINESS.

OK! IF YOU'SE SEZ SO, SARDO!

SARDO TRIES EXPLAINING TO RED HIS PLAN TO USE THE HUMAN TORCH.

AND OUR FIRST CUSTOMER WILL BE THE ACMEN WAREHOUSES, INC.

-BUT STEEL CAN'T BOIN!

LOOK DOPE - THAT GUY IN THE POOL IS TH HUMAN TORCH - AND HE CAN MELT STEEL!!

DO YA TINK HE'LL WO FOR US?

IF YOU'VE READ THE PAPERS, YOU'D KNOW THAT HE STARTS BURNING AS SOON AS HE HITS AIR! - DO YOU GET IT NOW? -

YEAH! - BUT, WHAT'S OUR NEXT MOVE NOW - SARDO?

GET THE CAR OUT! WE'RE GOIN' TO CALL ON THE ACMEN WAREHOUSES - INC.

BUT, I STILL DON'T SEE HOW THAT FREAK CAN BE OP ANY USE TO US IN OUR RACKET, BOSS-

LATER

I'LL SHOW YOU - YOU STAY HERE, RED, WHILE I HAVE A SALES-TALK WITH THE COMPANY'S PRESIDENT! -

- YESSIR, WHAT CAN I DO FOR YOU?

I'D LIKE TO SEE MR. HARRIS, PLEASE.

-AND WHO SHALL I SAY IS CALLING? -

-ER, JUST SAY - MR. SARDO - AN TELL HIM IT'S HOT STUFF.

THERE'S A MR. SARDO OUTSIDE TO SEE YOU... HE SAYS - IT'S "HOT STUFF!"

"HOT STUFF?" - WHAT'S THAT? - OH WELL, SEND HIM IN -

MR. HARRIS, I'LL BE BRIEF- UNLESS YOU SIGN UP FOR MY PROTECTION INSUR-ANCE - YOU WON'T HAVE ANY MORE RAW-STEEL LEFT IN YOUR WAREHOUSES!

OH! - A RACKETEER, EH?! -

LISTEN, SARDO, - I DON'T NEED ANY INSURANCE - AND I HATE PUNKS LIKE YOU - SO GET OUT - NOW!

I WAS O DOIN' YO A FAVO HARRIS YOU'LL BE SORRY - WATCH

116

SARDO JUMPS INTO ACTION!!

SARDO AND HIS LIEUTENANT HEAD FOR THEIR MANSION—WHERE THEY STRANGELY HOLD THE HUMAN TORCH

AFTER DONNING THE DIVING-SUIT—SARDO LOWERS HIMSELF INTO THE POOL AND FITS THE TUBE ON THE HUMAN TORCH, WHO THINKS SARDO IS HELPING HIM—

THE GLASS CASE IS THEN PLACED ON AN OPERATING COT AND THEN WHEELED TO THE BACK OF A TRUCK.

THE TRUCK BEARING THE TORCH SPEEDS THROUGH THE NIGHT!

SARDO TAKES CAREFUL AIM AND THROWS A WEIGHT AT THE PROTECTING GLASS CASE··· THE OXYGEN OF THE AIR MAKES TORCH BURST INTO FLAMES!!—

I CONFESS I DON'T UNDERSTAND·· I THOUGHT SARDO WAS TRYING TO HELP ME!

AS THE HUMAN TORCH WALKS ABOUT, UNABLE TO GRASP THE MEANING OF IT ALL, THE WAREHOUSE BECOMES A MASS OF FLAME!—

—THEN HE BRINGS ME HERE, AND BREAKS THE COVER··· I WONDER IF HE MIGHT BE JUST A LOW-DOWN RACKETEER?

THE HUMAN TORCH TRIES TO FIGURE THE REASON SARDO IS USING HIM

THAT'S IT!—HE MUST BE!—ELSE WHY LET ME LOOSE IN THIS TINDER BOX?—

SARDO IS A BUSINESS WRECKER· I'VE GOT TO GET OUT AND SEE HIM!—

UH-OH!—THE ROOF CAVED IN!—THAT'S MY WAY OUT!—

I HOPE IT WORKS!!

TAKING A RUNNING START THROUGH THE MOLTEN STEEL, THE TORCH LEAPS UPWARDS—

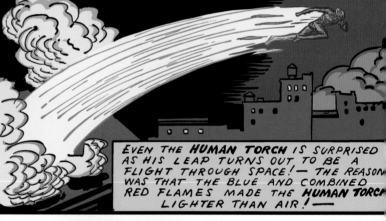

EVEN THE HUMAN TORCH IS SURPRISED AS HIS LEAP TURNS OUT TO BE A FLIGHT THROUGH SPACE!—THE REASON WAS THAT THE BLUE AND COMBINED RED FLAMES MADE THE HUMAN TORCH LIGHTER THAN AIR!—

THE GOGGLE-EYED SPECTATORS FLEE AS THE HUMAN TORCH LANDS IN THEIR MIDST, MANY BLOCKS AWAY—

—NOW FOR THAT CROOK SARDO AND HIS MOB OF RATS!!—

WHAT'S THIS FLASH OF FIRE COMING INTO MY PLACE? WHY- IT'S THE HUMAN TORCH!!

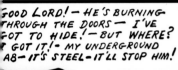

SARDO IS TAKEN BY SURPRISE BY THE TORCH'S SUDDEN APPEARANCE ON HIS GROUNDS — BUT···

HA! YOU'RE A FOOL, SAROO· · WHY LOCK THE DOOR? —

BAM

SARDO RUNS INTO THE HOUSE-SLAMMING THE DOOR, IN AN EFFORT TO ESCAPE THE HUMAN TORCH!

I'LL GET YOU IN THE END! —

A CLOSED DOOR CAN'T STOP THE HUMAN TORCH— HE WALKS RIGHT THROUGH IT!—

GOOD LORD! — HE'S BURNING THROUGH THE DOORS — I'VE GOT TO HIDE! — BUT WHERE? I GOT IT! — MY UNDERGROUND LAB — IT'S STEEL — IT'LL STOP HIM!

— HE'LL NEVER GET ME THERE! — THE WALLS ARE MADE OF TWELVE INCH BATTLESHIP CHROMIUM STEEL PLATES! —

SARDO RUNS TO HIS SECRET UNDERGROUND LAB!

I WONDER WHERE SARDO DISSAPPEARED TO! — I SAW HIM RUN IN HERE! —

WHILE IN THE HOUSE ABOVE —

IT'S FUNNY, BUT I CAN'T FIND SARDO IN THESE RUINS — ··I WONDER?···

— AS THE HOUSE COLLAPSES, A LONE FIGURE STANDS ERECT — IT'S THE HUMAN TORCH, UNTOUCHED IN THE FIERY INFERNO, HELPING THE DESTRUCTION WITH HIS OWN HEAT! —

— HA! — HA! — HA — IT WAS EASY TO BURN SARDO'S HOME DOWN!

WE CAN'T WAIT FOR SARDO — LET'S DUCK QUICK·· SAY— IT'S THE TORCH— HE FIRED THE HOUSE! —

SARDO'S MOB LEAVE THEIR LEADER, AND TRY TO RUN AWAY, WHEN THEY SEE THE TORCH!

AS THE HUMAN TORCH LEAPS FORWARD THE OTHERS SPREAD OUT — SOME DIVING INTO THE POOL···· SARDO'S MAN, RED, DUCKS UNDER A NEARBY CAR! —

10

119

JUMPING THRU SPACE LIKE A COMET, THE HUMAN TORCH LANDS ON THE CAR AND MELTS THE BODY AS IF IT WERE MADE OF BUTTER!—

HELP! THE HEAT'S KILLING ME!

THE HEAT IS TERRIFIC—AND, UNDER THE AUTO...

THAT RAT BURNED—ALL RIGHT! AND THOSE FELLOWS IN THE POOL WONT COME UP FOR AIR—NOW FOR————SARDO!!

THE HUMAN TORCH, HAVING SCALDED THE GANGSTERS IN THE POOL, BY TURNING WATER TO STEAM—

—RUNS BACK INTO THE FLAMING HOUSE, SEEKING SARDO'S HIDEOUT—

HMM—A STEEL DOOR.—FUNNY, I DIDN'T NOTICE IT BEFORE!

PLACING HIS HANDS ON THE DOOR, IT REACTS LIKE AN ACETEYLENE TORCH—BORING A HOLE THRU THE STEEL!

SO—THIS IS SARDO'S LABORATORY—AND I'M NOT SUPPOSED TO GET BY THAT SPECIAL DOOR EH?!—

THE DOOR LEADS TO SARDO'S UNDERGROUND LAB!—

HEH-HEH—SO YOU THINK YOU'LL GET ME, EH?—NOT IN A MILLION YEARS, MR. TORCH!—

SARDO FEELS SECURE, BEHIND SUPER-STEEL WALLS—

HELLO, RAT!

BUT SARDO'S LAUGH WASN'T FUNNY, AS THE HUMAN TORCH MELTS THRU THE STEEL DOOR, WITHOUT EKERTION...

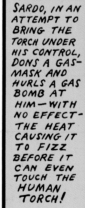

SARDO, IN AN ATTEMPT TO BRING THE TORCH UNDER HIS CONTROL, DONS A GAS-MASK AND HURLS A GAS BOMB AT HIM—WITH NO EFFECT—THE HEAT CAUSING IT TO FIZZ BEFORE IT CAN EVEN TOUCH THE HUMAN TORCH!

HAVING FUN, SARDO?

FIZZ-Z

THE HUMAN TORCH LAUGHS AND BIDS SARDO TO WATCH HIM — AS HE PICKS UP A BOMB — INSTANTLY IT MELTS!!

SARDO — NOW HALF-CRAZED, PICKS UP A TANK OF LIQUIDAR. JUST AS HE IS ABOUT TO FLING IT, THE CLANG OF FIRE ENGINES CATCHES THE ATTENTION OF BOTH MEN! —

CLANG CLANG

— DON'T GO IN THERE! — YOU'LL BE BLOWN TO BITS!

I HAVE TO GET THAT NITRO-TANK OUT OF THERE!

WHILE THE FIREMEN FIGHT THE ROARING BLAZE FROM THE OUTSIDE, — HORTON SPOTS A TANK FULL OF NITROGEN — HE RUSHES INTO THE FLAMES! —

BUT JUST THEN, THE HUMAN-TORCH APPEARS ON THE SCENE, AND, HE TOO, SEES THE TANK —

WITH A MIGHTY LEAP HIS ARMS CLOSE AROUND THE SLIM TANK, MELTING IT — AND THE NITRO GAS SHOOTS UP —

WHILE HORTON'S EYES POP WITH AMAZEMENT —

IT'S INCREDIBLE! — IF I HADN'T SEEN IT, I —

THE FLAMES DIE DOWN — AND THE TORCH IS HIMSELF AGAIN!

THIS'LL BE A BETTER WORLD WITHOUT YOU — MR. TORCH!

THE FIRE CHIEF SEEING THIS, DRAWS HIS GUN AND FIRES —

BUT THE STILL SUPER-HOT SKIN, SAVES THE TORCH FROM DESTRUCTION — THE LEAD PELLET MELTS, AS IT LANDS BETWEEN THE EYES! —

12

WITH A GURGLING LAUGH, THE HUMAN TORCH WHIRLS AND MAKES A SUDDEN DASH BACK INTO THE BLAZING EMBERS!!—

HE'S BACK — BUT WAIT! — WHAT'S THIS? — HIS FLAME IS OUT! — WHY?.

THERE WAS A TANK OF NITRO UPSTAIRS... COULD IT HAVE BEEN THAT? — IT HAS POSSIBILITIES!!—

—BUT AS THE HUMAN TORCH APPROACHES SARDO, HE AGAIN BURSTS INTO FLAME..

—NOW I'M SURE IT WAS THE NITRO!! — THIS GIVES ME A CHANCE TO STRIKE A BARGAIN!

HERE, YOU CAN HAVE THIS NITRO — IF YOU'LL LET ME GO!

RUSHING TO A CORNER, SARDO GETS A TUBE OF NITRO GAS AND OFFERS IT TO THE HUMAN TORCH!

—BUT THE HUMAN TORCH FLIES FORWARD AND QUICKLY WRESTS THE TANK FROM SARDO'S GRIP!

THANKS! SARDO— THIS'LL COME IN HANDY!—

—BUT AS FOR LETTING YOU GO — NEVER!—

LISTEN, — I'LL DO ANYTHING YOU SAY — ONLY DON'T BURN ME!—

— YOU RAT! — YOU SHOULD HAVE THOUGHT OF THAT BEFORE YOU DECIDED TO MAKE ME THE GOAT FOR YOUR RACKET!—

13

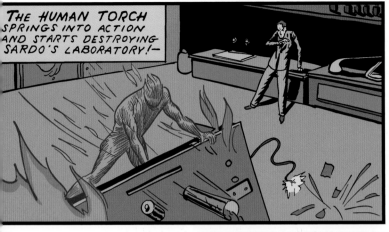

THE HUMAN TORCH SPRINGS INTO ACTION AND STARTS DESTROYING SARDO'S LABORATORY!—

THEN LEAPING IN A PE-LIKE FASHION — HE RIPS THE CHEMICAL-LADEN SHELVES DOWN!

NOW'S MY LAST — AND FINAL CHANCE TO GET HIM!—

WITH SEEMINGLY FIENDISH DELIGHT, THE HUMAN-TORCH COMPLETELY WRECKS THE LAB- AS SARDO SNEAKS AWAY TO A CORNER...

...WHERE HE GRIPS A TANK OF SULPHURIC ACID—THEN SNEAKS UP BEHIND THE TORCH!

BOOM

HURLING THE TANK — IT EXPLODES BEFORE IT EVEN TOUCHES THE HUMAN TORCH!—

POOR FOOL — KILLED BY HIS OWN HAND —

GRABBING AN INSULATED TANK OF NITROGEN, THE ONLY GAS THAT WILL CONTROL HIS FLAME, THE TORCH WALKS OUT OF THE BURNING LAB—

WE HEARD AN EXPLOSION OUT HERE!— WHAT WAS IT?—

—A RAT DEALT OUT JUSTICE TO HIMSELF HORTON!

14

HEY CHIEF!— I JUST SAW HORTON TALK-ING TO THE TORCH!

SO!— IT'S MORE OF THE TORCH'S WORK, EH?—

THE POLICE, ATTRACTED BY THE BLAZE AND EXPLOSION, RUSH TO THE SCENE!—

MEANWHILE THE TORCH LEAVES HORTON AND MOVES INTO THE FLAMES TO EXPERIMENT WITH THE NITRO!—

I HOPE THIS NITRO WILL BRING COMPLETE CONTROL OVER THE FLAME!

LATER

IT WORKS!! I CAN NOW CONTROL THE FLAME, WITHOUT THE NITRO!

GOOD LORD—I CAN THROW THE FLAME AS I WOULD A BALL!—

THEN TURNING BACK TO HIS FLAME—THE TORCH FINDS THAT HE CAN FLING THE BLUE FLAME FROM HIS BODY!

ATTENTION—ALL CARS!—CLOSE IN ON TORCH!!—HE'S HEADED DOWN SPRUCE STREET!—HURRY—I'LL TRAIL HIM JUST IN CASE!—

MEANWHILE, THE CHIEF RUNS BACK TO HIS CAR AND SENDS A MESSAGE OVER THE ETHER

— I WONDER IF THAT CAR IS FOLLOWING ME?—

HIS SUSPICIONS CONFIRMED—THE TORCH SHOOTS AHEAD LIKE A COMET—THE CAR BEING LEFT FAR BACK IN THE DISTANCE!

BUT AT THE CORNER, A BLOCKADE OF POLICE CARS SEEMINGLY TRAP THE TORCH!—

OK—COME AND GET ME—

IT'S NO USE! THE HEAT'S TOO GREAT. WE CAN'T EVEN GET NEAR HIM!

WAIT!—DON'T GO—WATCH!—

LOOK THE FLAME IS OUT!

—SORRY, I CAUSED YOU SO MUCH TROUBLE ·· I DIDN'T KNOW YOU WERE AFTER ME··· IT'S OK!—YOU CAN TAKE ME—MY BODY'S COLD!—

15

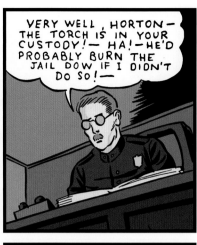

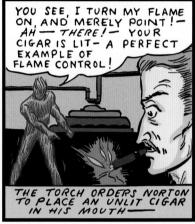

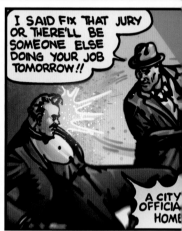

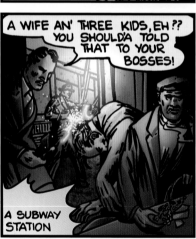

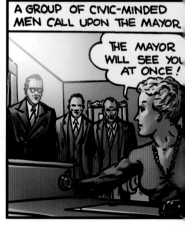

126

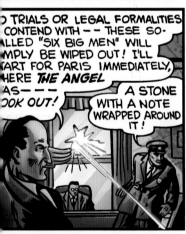

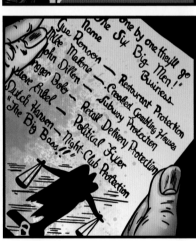

WELL—IF IT ISN'T THE COMMISSIONER!

I'VE A SURPRISE FOR YOU, RONSON! *THE ANGEL* HAS YOU ON HIS LIST! RIGHT UP ON TOP!

HEE-HAW-HAW-HAW!! D'YOU HEAR THAT! *THE ANGEL'S* AFTER ME! LISTEN COPPER—I DON'T BELIEVE IN SPOOKS OR FAIRY TALES!!

RONSON'S BOASTING IS SUDDENLY CUT SHORT BY A COLD WIND BLOWING ACROSS HIS FACE.

....AND A SHADOW FORMS ON THE BUILDING ACROSS THE STREET—— SHAPING ITSELF INTO A HUGE ANGEL.

L-LOOK— *THE ANGEL!!*

GEES— JUST LIKE A C-COLD WIND OUT OF A GR-GRAVE!

TH' SHADOW'S FADIN'!! M-MAYBE I'M LOOSIN' MY GUTS—BUT I GOT TH' JITTERS! I-I'M GETTIN' OUTA HERE!

LIKE A WILD MANIAC, GUS RONSON RUNS FOR HIS CAR

OUTA ME WAY!!

AT THE SAME TIME, A STRANGE FIGURE JUMPS FROM THE ROOF OF THE COURT HOUSE TO THE NEARBY LAMP POST AND TO THE GROUND IN FRONT OF RONSON'S CAR

LIKE A FLASH HE JUMPS INTO THE BACK SEAT OF THE CAR . . . .

UNAWARE THAT THE MYSTERIOUS STRANGER IS IN THE BACK OF HIS CAR, RONSON DRIVES OFF AT FULL SPEED.

3

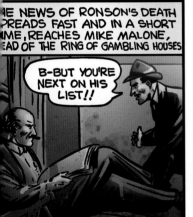

AFTER LITERALLY MASHING HIM INTO A PULP, MIKE MALONE CRUMBLES INTO A HEAP. INSTANTLY *THE ANGEL* TURNS TO MIKE'S PAL...

...WHO MAKES FOR THE NEAREST EXIT --- A WINDOW....

Y-Y-YOU WON'T G-GET ME!! N-NO YOU WON'T!!

IN THE CONFUSION, THE THUG PICKED THE WRONG WINDOW - INSTEAD OF THE ONE TO THE FIRE-ESCAPE....

MEANWHILE, A WOMAN QUIETLY OPENS THE DOOR AND PLACES A NOTE ON THE TABLE FOR *THE ANGEL*...

"YOU CAN CROSS NUMBER THREE OFF YOUR LIST -- HE WAS THE ONE THAT WENT THROUGH THE WINDOW! NUMBER FOUR IS WAITING FOR YOU -- BE CAREFUL!!"

QUICKLY, *THE ANGEL* RUSHES INTO THE HALL TO SEE WHO HAD LEFT THE NOTE FOR HIM, ONLY TO GET A GLIMPSE OF A WOMAN ENTERING THE ELEVATOR....

H-M-M-M!! IT LOOKS AS IF THERE ARE OTHER THAN CIVIC REASONS WHY THESE MEN ARE TO BE DONE AWAY WITH! VERY INTERESTING -! SO NUMBER FOUR IS WAITING FOR ME!!

WHILE IN ONE OF THE UNDERWORLD DENS, TRIGGER BOLO, HEAD OF THE RETAIL-DELIVERY PROTECTIVE ASSOCIATION, WAITS FOR *THE ANGEL*

ALL SET TRIGGER!

SO *THE ANGEL'S* GONNA DO AWAY WITH ME EH?! MY TRIGGER FINGER'S ITCHIN', SO SEE THAT YOU BRING HIM IN HERE!!

WE GOTCHA, BOSS!

NICE HOLE TRIGGER HAS -- FIT FOR ONLY RATS TO LIVE IN!!

THAT'S RIGHT BE NICE AND QUIET!!

THE STRUGGLE, THE THUG KNOCKS OVER A STACK OF CRATES....

...ATTRACTING THE ATTENTION OF THE OTHER MEN IN BOLO'S DEN.

HE'S GOT SHORTY!!

NO RODS—TRIGGER WANTS 'IM ALIVE!

USING THE GUN-MEN RUSHING TOWARD HIM, THE ANGEL COUNTER-ATTACKS WITH THE FURY OF A CHARGING LION!

BUT CANNOT WITHSTAND THE TREMENDOUS ODDS AGAINST HIM.

GOT HIS HANDS TIED?

YEAH!

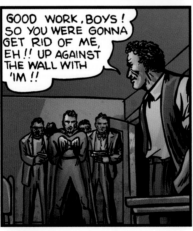

GOOD WORK, BOYS! SO YOU WERE GONNA GET RID OF ME, EH!! UP AGAINST THE WALL WITH 'IM!!

AT THAT MOMENT, THE MYSTERIOUS WOMAN, THAT LEFT THE WARNING NOTE FOR THE ANGEL, STEPS INTO THE ROOM.

NOT HERE, TRIGGER! THAT'S AN ORDER!

SEE THIS TOMMY-GUN! IT'S GONNA CUT YOU TO PIECES--VERY SLOWLY!

O.K.— STAND BACK, BOYS!

131

I'LL TAKE ORDERS HOW TO RUN THIS RACKET BUT NOT HOW TO GET RID OF GUYS! YOU CAN TELL THAT TO TH' BOSS!

THE WOMAN'S FACE TURNS STERN AND HER HAND FLASHES A SMALL AUTOMATIC :

TRIGGER— YOU'RE STEPPING OUT TOO FAR!

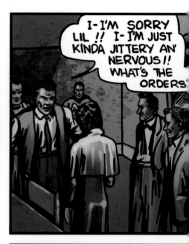

I-I'M SORRY LIL!! I-I'M JUST KINDA JITTERY AN' NERVOUS!! WHAT'S THE ORDERS

STEVE ENKEL IS WAITING UPSTAIRS —WE THREE ARE TO TAKE *THE ANGEL* TO THE WOODS OUTSIDE OF THE CITY!

WELL —MY HUNCH ABOUT A BIG BOSS WAS RIGHT! SO STEVE ENKEL, THE POLITICAL FIXER, TRIGGER BOLO AND THE BIG BOSSES GO-BETWEEN ARE GOING TO TAKE ME FOR A RIDE! H-M-M-M!!

A FEW MINUTES LATER, *THE ANGEL* IS PLACED IN A CAR BETWEEN TRIGGER BOLO AN' STEVE ENKEL, WHILE LIL FOLLOWS THE THREE IN HER OWN CAR..

SOON, THE TWO CARS STOP.

TIE HIM TO THAT TREE!

C'MON, YOU!

I THINK I LET THIS SO TOO FAR!

I WANT TO MAKE SURE HE'S TIED SECUREDLY!

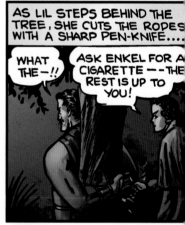

AS LIL STEPS BEHIND THE TREE, SHE CUTS THE ROPES WITH A SHARP PEN-KNIFE....

WHAT THE—!!

ASK ENKEL FOR A CIGARETTE — THE REST IS UP TO YOU!

AS STEVE ENKEL IS ABOUT TO LIGHT THE CIGARETTE, *THE ANGEL* STRIKES

7

SET AWAY FROM THERE YOU FOOL — I'M GONNA SHOOT!

N-NO!! YOU'LL GET ME TOO!!

THAT'S YOUR TOUGH LUCK!! I'M JUST CARRYING OUT ORDERS FROM TH' BOSS!

TO SAVE HIMSELF, STEVE
ENKEL OPENS FIRE TOO....

KILLED EACH OTHER—FOUR AND FIVE! THANKS FOR SAVING MY LIFE! WAIT!

I DIDN'T SAVE IT—I'M JUST OBEYIN' ORDERS! JUST FORGET ABOUT THE WHOLE THING!

UNABLE TO CATCH THE FAST CAR OF LIL, THE ANGEL TURNS TO NUMBER SIX——DUTCH HANSEN...

HOUR'S NOTICE TO CLOSE THE BOOKS AN MAKE A DEPOSIT—IT'S TOO SHORT A TIME! WHO OPENED THAT WINDOW?? THAT BREEZE SEEMS ICE COLD!!

AS DUTCH TURNS, HE SEES THE ANGEL! INSTANTLY HE REACHES FOR THE GUN ON THE DESK...

...BUT THE ANGEL HURLES A HEAVY CHAIR AND SENDS HIM CRASHING INTO THE STONE FIRE-PLACE.

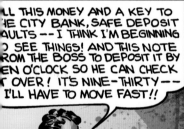

ALL THIS MONEY AND A KEY TO THE CITY BANK, SAFE DEPOSIT VAULTS—— I THINK I'M BEGINNING TO SEE THINGS! AND THIS NOTE FROM THE BOSS TO DEPOSIT IT BY TEN O'CLOCK SO HE CAN CHECK IT OVER! IT'S NINE-THIRTY—— I'LL HAVE TO MOVE FAST!!

REACHING THE CITY BANK BUT A FEW MINUTES BEFORE TEN, THE ANGEL SEES LIL WALKING INTO IT WITH A FAMILIAR MAN...

DR. LANG—WHO STARTED THIS WAR ON CRIME! SO HE'S THE BIG BOSS!!

LIL—DUTCH HASN'T BEEN HERE!!

NO—AND HE NEVER WILL EITHER!

THE ANGEL QUICKLY ENTERS THE VAULT UNNOTICED....

A PERFECT PLAN, EH!! EXCEPT YOU MISSED UP AT THE END! WILL YOU TELL YOUR STORY TO THE POLICE OR WILL I !?!

DR. LANG AND LIL PLANNED THE RACKETS THE PROCEEDS WHICH WERE TO BE DEPOSITED IN THIS VAULT AND SPLIT SEVEN WAYS AT THE END OF A YEAR! THAT WAS WHY THEY WANTED THE "SIX BIG MEN" DONE AWAY WITH——SO THERE WOULDN'T BE ANY SPLITTING TO DO AND THEY WOULD HAVE IT ALL TO THEMSELVES!

THE ANGEL FLIES TO ANOTHER....

ADVENTURE!
WATCH
FOR THE NEXT EPISODE OF "THE ANGEL" IN THE NEXT ISSUE!!

133

The Sub-Mariner

HERE IS THE SUB-MARINER! --AN ULTRA-MAN OF THE DEEP...LIVES ON LAND AND IN THE SEA...FLIES IN THE AIR...HAS THE STRENGTH OF A THOUSAND MEN...IS A YOUTH OF DYNAMIC PERSONALITY...QUICK THOUGHT AND FAST ACTION...FROM WHENCE DOES HE COME, AND WHAT IS HIS MISSION?

A SALVAGE SHIP'S DIVER COMES UP ~

THE DIVING PLATFORM IS HOISTED, AND SWUNG TO THE DECK OF THE SALVAGE SHIP "S.S. RECOVERY"—

HOW DO YOU FEEL, NELSON?

OKAY, CHIEF - BUT KINDA PUZZLED. THERE'S SUMP'N SCREWY ABOUT THAT WRECK—

SOME TIME LATER, THE DIVER, ROD NELSON, STEPS FROM THE DECOMPRESSION CHAMBER, AND IS ASKED WHAT HE FOUND ON THE BOTTOM—

I FOUND THE SAFE IN THE MAIN SALOON, ALL RIGHT, BUT IT LOOKS LIKE SOMEBODY GOT HERE BEFORE WE DID— THE SAFE'S EMPTY! THEN, TOO, IT LOOKS LIKE WHOEVER RIFLED IT HASN'T BEEN GONE LONG - THERE WAS A KNIFE ON THE DECK, AND IT HADN'T EVEN RUSTED—

THAT'S STRANGE, NELSON - THERE'S BEEN NO REPORT OF ANY OTHER SALVAGE SHIP IN THESE WATERS FOR THREE YEARS - WE OURSELVES HAVE BEEN CRUISING HERE FOR A WEEK, AND WE'VE SEEN NO SIGN OF LIFE AT ALL

WELL, THERE'S ONLY ONE THING TO DO - I'LL HAVE TO SEND YOU DOWN AGAIN WITH CARLEY, TO SEE WHAT EVIDENCE YOU CAN PICK UP - THEY MAY HAVE LEFT SOMETHING BY WHICH WE CAN IDENTIFY THEM.

OKAY - SEND CARLEY AHEAD - I'LL BE WITH YOU IN A MINUTE....

ALL SET, CARLEY? I'LL DROP THE ACETYLENE TORCH AS SOON AS YOU HIT BOTTOM

AND SO CARLEY SETTLES BENEATH THE SURFACE, LITTLE KNOWING THE PHENOMENA HE AND NELSON ARE ABOUT TO WITNESS ~

SAY, ROD, DID YOU LEAVE THAT SIDE HATCH OPEN? OR WAS IT SPRUNG IN THE WRECK?

NO - IT WAS CLOSED WHEN I WAS DOWN BEFORE - THERE'S SOMETHING UNCANNY ABOUT THIS -

ON THE SEA BOTTOM THEY CONVERSE BY TELEPHONE ~

135

COME ON, ROD—LET'S GET INSIDE— TURN ON YOUR LIGHT—WE MAY NEED IT

GOOD LORD, CARLEY! WHAT'S THAT?

A SWIMMER, ROD! BUT~

IT CAN'T BE! NO HUMAN COULD LIVE IN THIS PRESSURE~YET NOW HE'S DISAPPEARED~AND HE WAS SWIMMING~HE CAN'T BE DEAD!

COME ON—LET'S FOLLOW HIM—HE CAN'T HAVE GONE FAR

BUT THE SWIMMER ELUDES THEM, AND WITH LONG STROKES OF HIS POWERFUL ARMS, RISES TO THE DECK OF THE SUNKEN SHIP—

HERE HE LOOKS CAUTIOUSLY ABOUT HIM, AND SEES THE CABLES RUNNING FROM THE DIVERS TO THE SURFACE OF THE WATER

THOSE ROBOTS—THEY CAN'T BE MEN! WHY, THEY'RE MECHANICAL—AND SO PONDEROUS— YET THEY'RE SHAPED LIKE MEN, AND CERTAINLY THEY'RE NOT FISH—I WONDER........ONE OF THEM HAD SOME KIND OF FIRE-WEAPON— I'D BETTER GET OUT OF HERE!

THESE MUST BE THE CONTROL WIRES—I'LL FIX IT SO THEY CAN'T FOLLOW ME!

WITH FIVE QUICK STROKES THE SWIMMER CUTS THE AIR-HOSES, TELEPHONE CABLES, AND ACETYLENE TORCH TUBE—!

136

HOLY SMOKE! OUR LINES ARE CUT! CALLING SURFACE - CALLING SURFACE! NO ANSWER!

THE DIVERS, REALIZING THEIR PREDICAMENT, QUICKLY SHUT THE AIR-VALVES IN THEIR HELMETS, THUS IMPRISONING THE AIR IN THEIR SUITS - TELEPHONE WIRES SEVERED THEY ARE CUT OFF FROM ALL COMMUNICATION

THE SUB-MARINER DARTS THROUGH THE DOOR, AND ATTACKS THE DIVERS!

STABBING ONE VIOLENTLY, HE DROPS HIS KNIFE, AND SEIZES THE OTHER'S HELMET, CRUSHING IT BETWEEN HIS POWERFUL HANDS.

ON DECK OF THE "RECOVERY," THE MATE SEES BUBBLES ON THE WATER'S SURFACE WHICH WARN HIM OF THE TRAGEDY BELOW

NELSON - CARLEY! NELSON! - THE WIRES ARE DEAD!

ANDERSON - GET INTO YOUR SUIT - YOU'LL HAVE TO GO BELOW - TAKE LIFE-LINES, A KNIFE, AND ANOTHER TORCH - AND HURRY!

AYE, SIR!

ALL RIGHT - SEND HIM DOWN FAST, BO'S'N!

AND IN A MOMENT, BELOW ~

ANDERSON FINDS THE CRUSHED BODIES OF CARLEY AND NELSON. - THE SUB-MARINER WATCHES FROM SECLUSION -

FRIGHTENED, AND RISKING "THE BENDS," ANDERSON HAULS HIMSELF RAPIDLY TO THE SURFACE -

BACK ON DECK. IN THE DECOMPRESSION CHAMBER, ANDERSON GASPS OUT HIS REPORT—THE MATE ORDERS ALL HANDS TO GET THE SHIP UNDER WEIGH ~

WE'LL HAVE TO REPORT THIS TO THE COAST-GUARD — PETERS, MAN THE ANCHOR WINCH!

FROM THE DEPTHS, THE SUB-MARINER SEES THE POWERFUL PROPELLORS BEGIN TO CHURN, AS THE ANCHOR IS HOISTED ~

WITH THE SPEED OF A BULLET, HE SPRINGS UPWARD, AND WITH SUPERHUMAN STRENGTH, SEIZES THE RUDDER!

JAMMING IT TO THE RIGHT, HE STOPS THE STARBOARD PROPELLOR WITH BARE HANDS!

IN THE ENGINE ROOM, THE FIRST ASSISTANT REPORTS EXCITEDLY TO THE BRIDGE ~

STARBOARD PROPELLOR FOULED, SIR!

WHAT'S THAT?!

GOOD LORD, SIR—THE RUDDER WINCH SEEMS OUT OF ORDER! THE SHIP WON'T RESPOND!

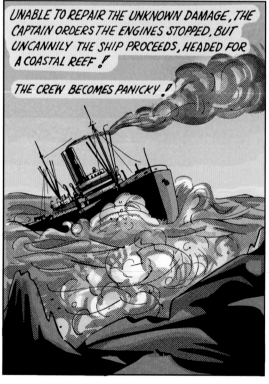

UNABLE TO REPAIR THE UNKNOWN DAMAGE, THE CAPTAIN ORDERS THE ENGINES STOPPED, BUT UNCANNILY THE SHIP PROCEEDS, HEADED FOR A COASTAL REEF!

THE CREW BECOMES PANICKY!

WITH EXTRAORDINARY STRENGTH, THE SUBMARINER GIVES THE UNFORTUNATE SHIP A TERRIFIC SHOVE — AND THE "RECOVERY" CRASHES HIGH ONTO THE ROCKS, SPLITTING COMPLETELY IN TWO!

ELATED AT THIS FEAT OF HIS OWN STRENGTH, THE SUB-MARINER DIVES BACK TO THE SUBMERGED WRECK ~

GATHERING THE DIVERS' BODIES IN HIS ARMS, HE SPEEDS OFF THROUGH THE WATER ~ HIS WINGED FEET PROPEL HIM, ROCKET-LIKE, INTO GREATER DEPTHS, AND PRESENTLY HE FACES A MAMMOTH DOOR IN A SECLUDED GROTTO ~ IT OPENS AT HIS COMMAND ~

DOMMA! OPEN!

HE ENTERS A HUGE, CHAPEL-LIKE CHAMBER ~

AND IS ADDRESSED BY A BEAUTIFULLY ROBED CREATURE ON THE THRONE AT THE FAR END OF THE HALL ~

WELL, NAMOR, PRIVILEGED ONE, WHAT MANNER OF PRIZE DOST THOU BRING US TODAY?

THAT I CANNOT TRUTHFULLY SAY, HOLY ONE – BUT THOU SHALT SEE FOR THYSELF – THESE I CAME UPON AND CONQUERED, SURPRISING THEM AS THEY RAIDED THE EARTH-MEN'S DERELICT~ THEY CAME FROM A FLOATING SHIP, WHICH I HAVE WRECKED WITH MY GREAT STRENGTH ~ I GIVE THEM TO YOU, AND PRAY YOU MAY BE PLEASED!

GREAT SHARKS, NAMOR! WHAT TYPE OF PRIZE DOST THOU CALL THESE? OPEN THEIR ENCASEMENTS - LET US SEE OF WHAT THEY ARE MADE!

WITH INFINITE CAUTION, THE HELMETS ARE UNSCREWED AND LIFTED OFF ~

HOLY MOTHER OF NEPTUNE! THEY ARE EARTH-MEN!!

CONGRATULATIONS, MY SON! YOU HAVE MADE A GOOD BEGINNING IN OUR WAR OF REVENGE!

WHY MOTHER!

KARAL, I COMMAND THEE TO OSSIFY THESE CREATURES ~ SET THEM IN THE ROYAL CHAMBER, WHERE THEY MAY BE SEEN AS EXAMPLES TO OUR WORTHY PEOPLE

DONE, YOUR HIGHNESS!

BUT MOTHER, I DON'T QUITE UNDERSTAND ~ WHY ARE THE EARTH-PEOPLE SO BAD? WASN'T MY FATHER AN EARTH-MAN?

YES, MY SON ~ AND A FINE MAN - BUT HIS PEOPLE WERE CRUEL ~ THEY INVADED OUR ANCIENT HOME DEEP IN THE WATERS AT THE SOUTH POLE, AND NEARLY EXTERMINATED OUR ENTIRE RACE ~ I MET YOUR FATHER IN THE YEAR 1920, WHEN.......

"A GREAT SHIP, THE 'ORACLE' CAME FROM AMERICA ON A SCIENTIFIC EXPEDITION ~ YOUR FATHER, COMMANDER LEONARD MᶜKENZIE, WAS THE CAPTAIN, AND THEY MADE THEIR BASE ON AN ICE-FLOE DIRECTLY ABOVE OUR CITY..."

"DURING THE WEEKS THAT FOLLOWED, WE WERE TORMENTED WITH BOMBARDMENTS OF HIGH EXPLOSIVES ~ OUR CASTLES WERE DEMOLISHED ~ OUR HUSBANDS, WIVES, MOTHERS, AND EVEN CHILDREN, WERE KILLED IN DROVES........."

"THE WHITE EARTH MEN WERE BLASTING US OUT OF EXISTENCE WITH THEIR INFERNAL 'SCIENTIFIK' INVESTIGATIONS' ~ SOON MANY MORE SHIPS ARRIVED, AND FINALLY, IN DESPERATION, OUR ELDERS COMMANDED AN ARMY TO BE FORMED, AND I, MOST NEARLY RESEMBLING THE FEMALE OF THE WHITE RACE, WAS INVESTED AS A SPY......"

THOU, FEN - BEAUTIFUL GODDESS OF THE SEALS - THOU SHALT FIND THY WAY INTO THE HANDS OF THESE WHITE MONSTERS, THERE TO WORK YOUR FEMININE WILES TO OUR RACIAL ADVANTAGE ~ GET THEE HENCE, WHILE THERE IS YET TIME!

"AND SO IT WAS, THAT, ON THE SAME NIGHT, I WAS FOUND HUNCHED UP AND SHIVERING, IN A SHIP'S HOLD, JUST AFT OF THE MAIN-MAST....."

GREAT HEAVENS! A STOWAWAY! CAPTAIN, COME QUICKLY!

"NOT REALIZING WHAT I WAS, OR WHY I WAS THERE, AND THINKING ME ONE OF THEIR OWN RACE, THEY HURRIED ME TO THE COMMANDER, WHO, GOOD MAN THAT HE WAS, DECIDED THAT I WAS INSUFFICIENTLY CLAD FOR THAT CLIMATE ~ AFTER GIVING ME HEAVY CLOTHES, IN WHICH I NEARLY SUFFOCATED, THEY FED ME SOME OF THEIR FOOD- WHAT IT WAS, I DIDN'T KNOW, BUT IT MADE ME VIOLENTLY ILL ~ THE COMMANDER TOOK PITY ON ME, AND, ALTHOUGH I COULD NOT UNDERSTAND HIS LANGUAGE, TRIED TO COMFORT ME WITH WORDS..."

"WITHIN A VERY SHORT TIME WE BECAME FAST FRIENDS, AND I BEGAN TO LEARN THEIR STRANGE TONGUE ~ THEY COULD NEVER UNDERSTAND, THOUGH, HOW I COULD SWIM SO MUCH IN THE EXTREMELY COLD WATER ~

OF COURSE I HAD TO, FREQUENTLY, FOR WE SUB-MARINERS CANNOT LIVE OUT OF WATER FOR LONGER THAN FIVE HOURS AT A STRETCH ~ AND MANY OF US CANNOT LIVE EVEN THAT LONG ~..."

"WELL, AS TIME WENT ON, THE COMMANDER AND I FELL IN LOVE, AND WERE MARRIED BY THEIR OWN RITUAL ~ AND ALL THE WHILE I WAS GIVING SECRET INFORMATION BACK TO OUR PEOPLE....."

WE CANNOT WIN, MASTER- THEY ARE TOO MIGHTY!

"AND THEY WERE TOO MIGHTY, FOR EVEN AS OUR ARMY ASSEMBLED FOR THE FIRST COUNTER-ATTACK, THERE CAME A TERRIBLE BOMBARDMENT FROM ABOVE - WHICH DESTROYED ALL BUT A MERE HANDFUL OF US!"

AND SO, MY SON, IT HAS TAKEN US TWENTY YEARS TO BUILD UP A RACE TO AVENGE THE BRUTAL HARM DONE US THEN ~ NOW, SINCE YOU ARE THE ONLY ONE OF US LEFT WHO CAN LIVE ON LAND AND IN WATER, AND WHO CAN ALSO FLY IN THE AIR, AND BECAUSE YOU HAVE THE STRENGTH OF A THOUSAND EARTH-MEN, IT IS YOUR DUTY TO LEAD US INTO BATTLE! YOU HAVE BEGUN WELL, BUT YOU MUST USE STRATEGY AND GREAT CARE ~ GO NOW TO THE LAND OF THE WHITE PEOPLE!

AND SO NAMOR, THE AVENGING SON, FACES THE SURFACE MEN OF THE WORLD, IN WHAT PROMISES TO BE MORTAL COMBAT!

141

IN THE ADJOINING CHAMBER, NAMOR MEETS HIS COUSIN, YOUNG DORMA - HE TELLS HER OF HIS COMMISSION, AND HIS PROPOSED TRIP -

OH NAMOR! HOW WONDERFUL! TAKE ME WITH YOU - PLEASE!

IT WILL BE TOO DANGEROUS, DORMA - BUT YOU MAY ACCOMPANY ME PART WAY - COME, NOW - WE MUST HURRY!

BUT WON'T WE HAVE TO TAKE SOME EQUIPMENT WITH US, NAMOR?

DECIDING THAT EQUIPMENT WILL ONLY HAMPER THEIR PROGRESS, THEY TRAVEL "LIGHT", AND LEAVE THE UNDERWATER CASTLE WITH THE HEARTFELT BEST WISHES OF THE ENTIRE TRIBE .....

AFTER TRAVELING FOR TWO DAYS AT LIGHTNING SPEED, THEY STOP FOR REST, AND COME TO THE SURFACE AT THE FIRST SIGN OF CIVILIZATION ....

THIS MUST BE CAPE ANNA LIGHTHOUSE, DORMA - IT GIVES ME AN IDEA - WE CAN START OUR CRUSADE RIGHT HERE - YOU SEE, IF WE DEMOLISH THIS LIGHT, IT WILL ENDANGER MANY SHIPS, AND PERHAPS DESTROY THEM! - IT WILL BE _OUR FIRST MOVE_!

THERE'S NO TELLING HOW MANY PEOPLE OCCUPY THE LIGHTHOUSE, SO WE MUST TAKE NO CHANCES - WHEN THE GUARD OPENS THE DOOR, I'LL JUMP HIM AND RUSH INSIDE TO WRECK THE CONTROLS - IF ANYONE COMES, YELL TO ME!

QUIETLY, NOW! I HEAR SOMEONE COMING!

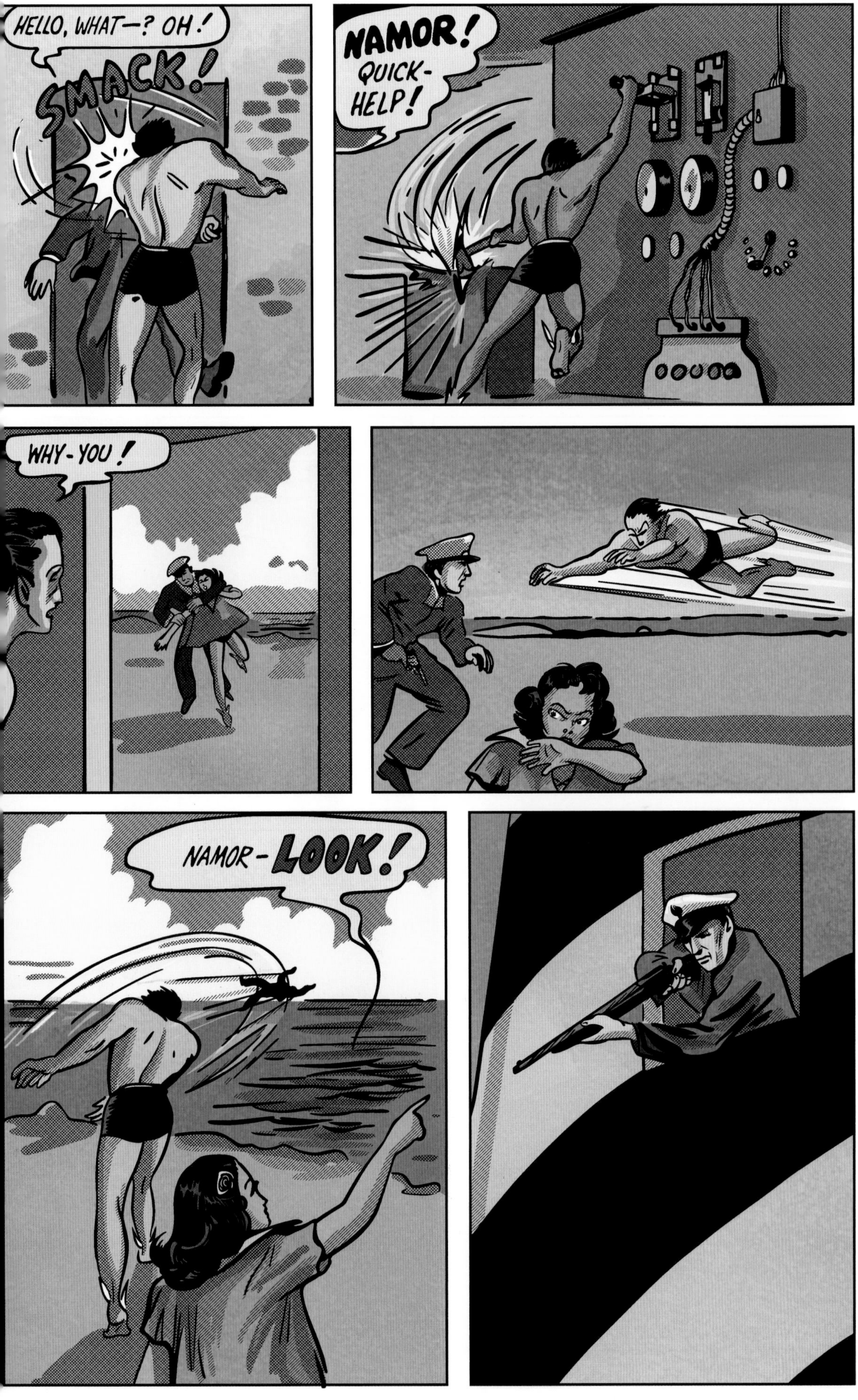
HELLO, WHAT—? OH!
SMACK!
NAMOR! QUICK- HELP!
WHY-YOU!
NAMOR-LOOK!

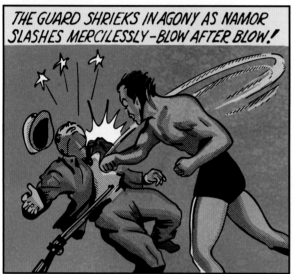

145

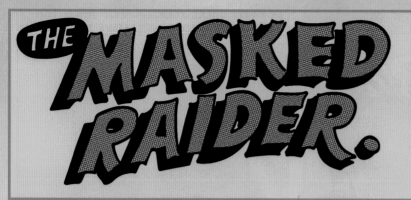

THE MASKED RAIDER.

CAL BRUNDER, POWERFUL RULER OF CACTUSVILLE, IS ATTEMPTING TO FORCE ALL OF THE SMALLER RANCHERS TO SELL OUT TO HIM, AT HIS OWN PRICE BRUNDER SEND HIS GUN-MEN TO CALL ON JIM — GARDLEY —

NOW YUH GIT BACK AN' TELL BRUNDER I'M NOT SELLING OUT!

UNSEEN BY GARDLEY ONE OF BRUNDER'S MEN SNEAKS UP BEHIND HIM.

UP WITH 'EM GARDLEY! BRUNDER AIN'T GONNA LIKE WOT YUH DID!

AW'RIGHT SLICK! LET'S TAKE HIM BACK T'TOWN!

AND DON'T TRY TUH MAKE NO GIT AWAY—IT AIN'T HEALTHY!

SOME DAY "SLICK", PEOPLE ARE GOING TO RUN YOUR CORRUPT GANG OUT OF THE COUNTRY. BRUNDER CAN'T KEEP BULL DOZIN' THE LITTLE RANCHERS MUCH LONGER!

WHY DON'T YOU GIT WISE TUH YORE SELF? WE COULD USE A MAN LIKE YOU IN OUR OUTFIT!

GARDLEY IS BROUGHT BEFORE BRUNDER, WHO IS THE REAL POWER IN CACTUSVILLE

HE LIKE TUH KILLED BENDS WIT' A BUSY ON THE JAW— HE SAID HE WOULDN'T SELL NOTHIN' EITHER

ALL RIGHT! SLICK!

SLICK YOU TALK TO THE OTHER RANCHERS..I'LL HANDLE FRIEND GARDLEY ALONE!

BRUNTER SOON REALIZES THAT GARDLEY IS UNAFRAID OF HIS THREATS.

NO USE WASTING ANY WORDS ON YOU — NOW I'LL GIVE SOME MEDICINE THAT WILL IN TIME CHANGE YOUR MIND!

BRUNDER SENDS FOR THE SHERIFF.
WHAT'S ON YORE MIND CAL? GARDLEY?? WHAT, ARE YUH TIED UP FER?

SHERIFF, MY BOY'S CAUGHT GARDLEY RED HANDED — RUSTLING MY STOCK!

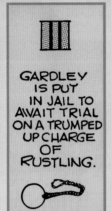

GARDLEY IS PUT IN JAIL TO AWAIT TRIAL ON A TRUMPED UP CHARGE OF RUSTLING.

GOSH A'MIGHTY KID — WHAT MADE YUH STEAL CATTLE —? YUH HAD A GOOD START, BUT NOW LOOK AT YUH!

BUT.. STEVE!

GARDLEY HAS PLENTY OF TIME TO THINK THINGS OVER.

POOR SHERIFF — I GUESS HE DOESN'T LIKE HIS JOB ANY TOO MUCH THESE DAYS — BOY, I'M IN A BAD SPOT!

IT'S TIME SOMEONE DID SOMETHING ABOUT THE BRUNDER GANG, AND I'M BEGINNING TO GET IDEAS.

YESSIR! IT MIGHT WORK?? I'M YOUNG AND STRONG— ...I'LL TRY IT — HEY— SHERIFF

HEARD YUH — WHA'D'YA WANT— HOME SICK A'READY?

HURRY STEVE! I'M — DYING.. ooooH.. I CAN'T STAND THIS.. OH MY STOMACH..... STEVE!

I'M COMIN' — YUH CAIN'T TAKE ON LIKE THIS — AN' YUH CAIN'T DIE! 'CAUSE YUH GOTTA GO ON TRIAL

SHERIFF.. LEAN CLOSER.... I'M DYING ! — I WANT TO... CONFESS!

AS THE SHERIFF BENDS A LITTLE CLOSER — A FIST, CRASHES INTO HIS CHIN —

SORRY STEVE, BUT I JUST COULDN'T STAY — I'LL ALSO NEED YOUR GUN !

LOCKING UP THE SHERIFF, GARDLEY STEPS OUTSIDE. THE STREET IS QUITE DESERTED .

THIS IS LUCK ....I'LL BORROW ONE OF THOSE HORSES, AND SHAKE LOOSE FROM THIS TOWN !

GARDLEY HEADS FOR THE HILLS

SAFE, FOR THE MOMENT, GARDLEY MAKES A CAMP IN THE HILLS

NOW OLD BOY, YOU, PRESENT SOMEWHAT OF A PROBLEM.

I HATE TO LET YOU GO OLD BOY — BUT YOU'D BE A DEAD GIVE A-WAY !

THEN, ONE NIGHT, GARDLEY, UNDER COVER OF DARKNESS, RAIDS HIS OWN RANCH FOR SUPPLIES. THE DAYS OF HIS DISAPPEARANCE BECOME WEEKS.

AT LAST MY DRAW IS FAST AND SMOOTH, AND OF LATE I HAVE MISSED ANY SHOTS !

NOW I MUST GET A TOP-NOTCH HORS SOMEWHERE !

ONE DAY GARDLEY DISCOVERS A MAGNIFICENT WILD HORSE.

BOY! HE SURE IS A BEAUTY — HE'LL FILL THE BILL, PERFECTLY!

IN SPITE OF GARDLEY'S EFFORTS THE HORSE REMAINS FREE

— THEN ONE DAY —

DOGGONE! HE'S CAUGHT HIMSELF!

THEN CAME DAYS OF THE UTMOST PATIENCE GRADUALLY JIM WON THE FRIENDSHIP OF THE HORSE, HE CALLED "LIGHTNING"

NOW FELLOW THE FUN IS GOING TO START!

LIGHTNING IS SADDLED AND GARDLEY CLIMBS ABOARD HIS MOUNT PREPARED FOR THE WORST.

LIGHTNING BREAKS INTO A RUN —

and GARDLEY IS MASTER.

PEOPLE ARE GOING TO HEAR A LOT ABOUT US, FROM NOW ON LIGHTNING!

④

JUBILANT OVER LIGHTNING'S ABILITIES, GARDLEY MAKES READY TO ADOPT A NEW ROLE THAT OF THE MASKED RAIDER.

I, JIM GARDLEY HEREBY MAKE A SOLEMN VOW TO FOREVER FIGHT THE LAWLESS... BRING JUSTICE TO THE OPPRESSED, AND HELP THE POOR — TO THIS END, I, THE MASKED RAIDER, DEDICATE MY LIFE TO THIS OATH!

SLICK, ROUND THE BOYS— BURN THE BLECK'S PLACE. WHEN THEY SEE THAT I MEAN BUSINESS...THEY WONT ACT SO VERY TOUGH!

I DON'T CARE IF ROWDY *HAS* FIVE ACES...THE GAMES OVER...WE'RE RIDIN'!

AWRIGHT

SLICK AND BRUNDER'S GUNSLINGERS, SET OUT FOR THE BLECK'S RANCH.

BUT BLECK A SMALL RANCHER SEES THEM FIRST—

DON'T YOU FELLOW'S COM NO CLOSER!

A BULLET REMOVES BLECK FROM THEIR PATH.

PING

THET'S DONE...LOOK'S LIKE MRS BLECK DIDN'T MAKE IT!

NEWS OF THE BURNING OF THE BLECK RANCH SPREAD LIKE WILD-FIRE.

BUT, KILLIN' AND BURNIN' THET'S GOIN' TO FAR

SHUT UP! WHAT RIGHT HAVE YOU TO THINK?

IF YUH ASK ME — I BET PEOPLE ARE GONNA GIT READY AND DO A BIT OF SELLIN' OUT!

THE DESPERATE RANCHERS AT LAST DECIDE TO TRY AND FIND A SOLUTION TO THEIR PROBLEM.

WE BETTER DO SOMETHING ABOUT BRUNDER! I'LL HEAD SOUTH — YUH GIT THE RANCHERS NORTH OF HERE!

..AND WE MEET IN LORDIN'S BARN AT EIGHT T'MORROW!

YUH BET WE'LL BE THERE! IT'S TIME WE HAD A MEETIN'!

LORDIN, A WISE AND RESPECTED MAN IS CHOSEN TO SPEAK TO THE WORRIED RANCHERS.

AS MUCH AS I HATE TUH ADMIT DEFEAT I SAY SELL — WE DON'T WANT NO MORE KILLIN'S.

HE'S RIGHT!

I'M STICKIN'!

YER FREE T' DECIDE FER YORE SELVES... BUT TUHMORRER I'M A'SELLIN' LORDIN'S RIGHT!

BACK IN TOWN BRUNDER HEARS OF THEIR DECISION.

HO! HO! I KNEW THEY'D SEE IT THAT WAY.

HEY SLICK! CALL BRUNDER.

IT'S ROWDY, BOSS

WHAT TH-?

THIS WAS PINNED TUH ROWDY'S BACK.. HE'S SHOT UP BAD!

BRUNDER— YOU AND YOUR GANG MUST PAY FOR ALL YOUR CRIMES.. I'M STARTING TO COLLECT. The Masked Raider

MEANWHILE OVER AT THE SHERIFF'S OFFICE AN UNEXPECTED CALLER ARRIVES

NOIV! HOW DO YOU STAND ON THE SUBJECT OF CLEANING UP THIS TOWN SHERIFF?

WH'WHO ARE YOU Y'Y'YORE MASKED!

IT WILL MEAN THAT YOU WILL HAVE TO OPENLY OPPOSE BRUNDER!

I'M WITH YUH STRANGER! I'M THROUGH CRAWLIN' T'HIM... I'LL TAKE MUH CHANCES AND PUT TH' TEETH BACK IN TH' LAW! YES-SIR!

OUTSIDE HUH! SO THET THE WAY THE WIND BLOWS—I KIN GIT'EM BOTH..TH'DOUBLE-CROSSIN SHERIFF!

JUST AS THE EAVES-DROPPER DECIDES TO SHOOT THE TWO UNSUSPECTING MEN, A CRONY ARRIVES.

JEST A MINUTE PAL...LET ME IN ON TH' FUN!

BUT THE MASKED RAIDER HEARING THEIR VOICES GOES OUT THE REAR DOOR.

WELL YOU FELLOWS ARE IN FOR A TREAT!

ALL RIGHT SHERIFF PUT THESE TWO AWAY—I'LL START THE ROUND-UP OF THE REST OF THE BRUNDER GANG!

SLICK, DO YOU WALK TO JAIL OR WILL I HAVE TO DRAG YOU?

YER MASKED!

152

THE LOUD VOICE OF SLICK BRINGS THE REMAINDER OF BRUNDER'S GANG TO HIS AID — BUT THE TOWNS-MEN RUSH TO THE AID OF THE "MASKED RAIDER".

GIT GOIN' HOSS! IT'S TOO HOT HERE!

AH! SO BRUNDER IS TRYING TO RUN OUT — NOT IF I CAN HELP IT!

COME ON LIGHTNING! LET'S GET HIM!!

THE MASKED RAIDER'S ROPE SNAGS BRUNDER AND — JERKS HIM FROM HIS HORSE.

WHAT TH'!

THERE YOU ARE MEN — THE BRUNDER GANG IS NO MORE!

BRUNDER'S FINISHED... BUT, WILL THE MASKED MAN TACKLE THE BIGGER GAME.?

The End

153

JUNGLE TERROR

A COMPLETE ADVENTURE STORY

by TOMM DIXON

AT THE FLORIDA PLANTATION HOME OF PROFESSOR ROBERTS, KEN MASTERS AND TIM ROBERTS, THE PROFESSOR'S NEPHEW ARE TALKING....

I TELL YOU, TIM — WE SHOULDN'T HAVE LET THE PROFESSOR GO INTO THAT JUNGLE! THREE MONTHS HAVE GONE BY AND WE HAVE NOT HEARD FROM HIM AS YET!

JUST BECAUSE SOMEONE TOLD HIM THAT A CERTAIN INDIAN TRIBE HAS A DIAMOND POSSESSING HYPNOTIC POWERS IS NO REASON FOR HIM TO GO ALONE INTO THE JUNGLE! WE'VE GOT TO FIND HIM, TIM — LET'S TAKE A LOOK AT THE MAP!

YES — HERE'S THE SPOT THE PROF. MARKED BEFORE HE LEFT, TIM!

GEE — IT SURE IS A DESOLATE SPOT, KEN!

I'LL SAY, SON! LOOK — DEEP IN THE AMAZON JUNGLE! WELL, THAT SETTLES IT, TIM — —

—WE'RE LEAVING THE FIRST THING IN THE MORNING, TIM! —AND WE'RE GOING BY AIR!

WHEE! I CAN'T WAIT TIL MORNING, KEN!!

BUT OUTSIDE THE WINDOW, A FIGURE LISTENS—

—AND A FEW MINUTES LATER!

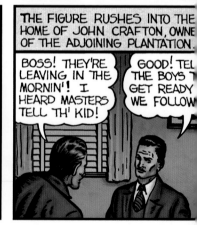

THE FIGURE RUSHES INTO THE HOME OF JOHN CRAFTON, OWNER OF THE ADJOINING PLANTATION.

BOSS! THEY'RE LEAVING IN THE MORNIN'! I HEARD MASTERS TELL TH' KID!

GOOD! TELL THE BOYS TO GET READY WE FOLLOW

THE NEXT MORNING KEN AND TIM ARE READY TO LEAVE.

OKAY, KEN LET'S GO!

TAKE A LAST LOOK AT FLORIDA, TIM, WE'RE HEADED TOWARD THE CARIBBEAN!

KEN!! THERE'S A PLANE FOLLOWING US -- SAY!! IT LOOKS LIKE -- IT IS --- THAT'S CRAFTON'S PLANE!! NOW I WONDER WHAT HE'S UP TO!!

HOURS LATER!

THEY'RE STILL FOLLOWING US, KEN!

LET 'EM COME! WE'RE OVER THE JUNGLE, TIM!

OH-OH! SOMETHING'S WRONG! MOTOR'S MISSING!! HOLD TIGHT, TIM—WE'RE GOIN' TO LAND IN THE TREES!

KEN CLIMBS FROM THE WRECKED PLANE CARRYING TIM WITH HIM!

OW—MY HEAD! ARE YOU OKAY, KEN?

YES, TIM—TAKE IT EASY! YOU'LL BE ALL RIGHT IN A FEW MINUTES!

BUT A FIGURE FOLLOWS KEN AND THE BOY AS THEY MAKE THEIR WAY THROUGH THE JUNGLE!

DON'T BE AFRAID, TIM— BUT I THINK WE'RE BEING FOLLOWED!

GOSH— SAVAGES!

A MOMENT LATER—

WHITE MAN STOP! WE TAKE TO CHIEF! COME!

MEANTIME, CRAFTON AND HIS MEN LAND IN THE JUNGLE AND SET OUT TO FIND KEN AND TIM.

STRAIGHT AHEAD, BOYS, AND STEP ON IT!

I'M KEEPIN' MY GUN HANDY, BOSS!

HERE'S WHAT WE DO—WE FOLLOW MASTERS AND TH' KID UNTIL THEY FIND PROFESSOR ROBERTS—THEN WE WAIT, AND WHEN THEY GET THE DIAMOND WE LET 'EM HAVE IT AND MAKE OUR WAY BACK TO THE PLANE!

HEY, BOSS TAKE IT EASY, MY FEET HURT!

B-BOSS! H-HELP! DO SOMETHING QUICK!

I GOT 'IM, BOSS!!

BANG! BANG!

NICE WORK, MIKE, BUT C'MON LET'S GET GOIN'! WE'VE GOT TO FIND WHAT'S HAPPENED TO MASTERS AN' THE KID!

I'LL SHOW THESE SAVAGES WHO'S BOSS 'ROUND HERE—

COMIN' BOSS!

—SUDDENLY A WHIZZING SOUND PIERCES THE AIR AND——

OW!

HE'S DEAD, SLUG! MUST'VE BEEN A POISONED ARROW—

DON'T MOV BOSS! THEY'RE AL AROUND US— I CAN SEE 'EM THROUGH THE BUSHES

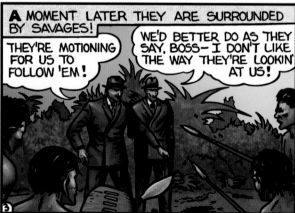

A MOMENT LATER THEY ARE SURROUNDED BY SAVAGES!

THEY'RE MOTIONING FOR US TO FOLLOW 'EM!

WE'D BETTER DO AS THEY SAY, BOSS—I DON'T LIKE THE WAY THEY'RE LOOKIN' AT US!

THE TWO MEN ARE LED TO THE NATIVE VILLAGE.

MEANWHILE KEN AND TIM ARE LED TO THE CHIEF'S HUT!

I'M OKAY NOW, KEN!

GOOD, TIM!

TAKE THEM TO THE PRISONER'S HUT—WE WILL KILL THEM LATER!

THIS IS GOOD! WE COME DOWN HERE TO GET YOUR UNCLE OUT OF A JAM AND WE GET IN ONE OURSELVES!

IN THERE— DO NOT TRY TO ESCAPE!

GOSH, KEN! NOW WE'LL NEVER FIND UNCLE JOHN!

AND AS THEY ENTER THE HUT!

KEN—LOOK! IT'S UNCLE JOHN!

TIM! KEN— WHAT ARE YOU TWO DOING DOWN HERE?

WE CAME AFTER YOU, PROF! BUT WHY ARE YOU A PRISONER? I THOUGHT YOU KNEW THIS TRIBE!

AT FIRST THEY WERE FRIENDLY, KEN—BUT WHEN THEY SAW I WAS AFTER THE HYPNOTIC DIAMOND THEY THREW ME IN HERE!

BUT LOOK! I'VE FOUND AN OPENING IN THIS CORNER—IT MUST LEAD SOMEWHERE—I'LL GO FIRST—WHEN THE COAST IS CLEAR, FOLLOW ME!

GO AHEAD, TIM! YOU'RE NEXT— BUT TAKE IT EASY—IT MIGHT BE A BIG DROP!

UNCLE JOHN IS HELPIN' ME FROM BELOW —C'MON, KEN!

SHALL I LET GO, UNCLE JOHN!

YES, TIM! GOSH—I HAD NO IDEA THIS PLACE WAS SO DEEP!

A FEW MINUTES LATER KEN JOINS THEM AND THE THREE SET OUT IN THE DARKNESS!

HANG CLOSE, TIM! SEE ANY- THING, KEN?

NO--WAIT— YES --A LIGHT!

GREAT SCOTT, KEN! THAT LIGHT—IT'S AS HOT AS A FURNACE—WHAT IS IT?

WOW! YOU'LL SEE, PROF! GET CLOSER!

DIAMONDS —MAN— DIAMONDS! NOT ONE, THOUSANDS!

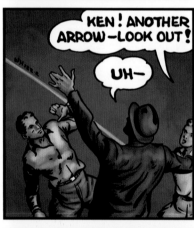

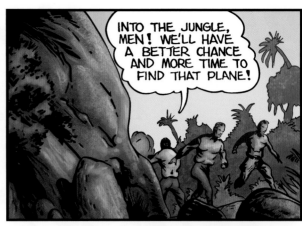

BURNING RUBBER

A Short Short Story About
The Auto Race Tracks

By Raymond Gill

THE crowd roared . . . with laughter! Bill Williams knew what they were laughing at, his coveted Blue Bird. Compared to the other cars in the race, the Blue Bird did look a bit shabby. But one thing was certain, there weren't any better mechanics or drivers than Bill and his able mechanic, Fred Turner.

"Everything's shipshape, Bill. You know, I feel kind of sorry for those other mugs. I'd hate to lose a race if I spent a lot of dough on a two tone chrom plated model."

"Fine. Well, I don't know, I'd give a lot to dress my Lady Bird here up with a lot of new feathers. I don't give a hoot what the crowd thinks myself, but I feel sorry for my 'Laddie's' sake.

"Cut it fella, I think you did pretty well digging up the entry fee. After all, you spent plenty for parts for your new super-charger."

"Yep, that's our only hope now. Don't kid yourself that we have any cinch. We have the best drivers in the business here today."

"What's the matter with you today Bill, I've never heard you talk like this before. You sound as though you've lost faith in our Blue Bird."

"No, not on your life. That's one thing I'll never do. I guess it got under my skin a little bit . . . those people laughing at her, I mean."

"That's better. By the way, doesn't Ann ever complain about your spending so much time with your 'Lady' here?"

"Yea, she was kidding me the other night[.]

"Well, there goes the signal, Bill. Mov[e] over."

"Oh, ah. . . . Listen old man, let me ta[ke] it alone this time. . . . I don't know why [I] want to. I . . . well, humor me this once, w[ill] you? I know I'll feel a lot better if I get o[ut] there alone. . . ."

"Ah, sure . . . sure, Bill. Anything you sa[y.] Only, be careful."

BILL shot ahead with a roar that surpris[ed] the smiling crowd that had gathered arou[nd] to poke fun at the Blue Bird.

He was hardly topped on the line when t[he] second starting signal was given. There we[re] eight cars in the race besides the Blue Bi[rd.] The combined noise of dozens of unmuffe[d] explosions thundered out into an increasi[ng] crescendo that thrilled some and annoy[ed] others.

To Bill it was sweet music . . . the power[ful] voice of his Lady Bird. Bill was in his glo[ry,] he could feel his whole body grow taught wi[th] a passionate desire to go faster, faster, fast[er.] The stiffer his body grew, the harder his f[oot] pressed the accelerator.

He was setting the pace, the other cars [di]rectly behind him, weaving back and for[th.] He was at his perfect ease now, he felt th[at] the Lady Bird was standing still and that t[he] track was some never ending ribbon that ke[pt]

olding in front of him. He was in a new
rld, a world all his own.

nn, the girl was literally sitting on the
;e of her seat as she watched the Blue Bird
dly rush on in meaningless velocity. Or so
seemed to her.

"Hello, Ann. Enjoying the race?"

"Fred! What are you doing up here? Why
:n't you in there with Bill?"

"Whoa, take it easy. He's just a bit moody,
;uess. He vants to be alone."

"Oh, Fred, I always feel better when you're
th him. If it's possible to feel good when
's throwing himself bodily into the face ot
e. You shouldn't have let him take it out
:re alone."

"Well, it's too late now to do anything about
t, besides, there's something you can do
help Bill. That's why I came up here."

"Yes, Fred. You know I'll do anything for
t grease monkey."

"That's the idea, calm down. I don't know
iat it is that's got everybody keyed up today.
e've all gone through these races before to-
ther."

"Yes, we have, Fred. But somehow I feel
at today it's all got to end. One way or the
ier."

"Ann, you know that we've spent a lot of
ne working on the Blue Bird these last few
onths. We always work hard on her before
race, but this time we've done something
ore than that. We've perfected a new gas
eder. I know Bill wouldn't want me to tell
u, but I feel that you have a right to know.
ll is in there right now, risking his life to test
This test is the final step. If it works, Bill
ill retire from the track. He told me so. If
fails . . . well . . ."

"Fred! Tell me. What if it doesn't work,
hat will happen? What can a gas feeder do
at will possibly crack him up?"

"Just this. That new feeder is mounted over
e engine, it feeds with a combined force of
avity and .pressure. If anything should go
rong, if it should spring the smallest leak
. . that hot motor will blow both him and
ie Blue Bird to kingdom come."

"Tell me, quickly Fred. What can I do that
ill help?"

"Well, you and Ruth Clerk, the daughter of
ie big motor magnet, C. G. Clark, are on
retty good terms, aren't you?"

"Why, yes. Ruth and I went to school to-
ether. Why?"

"Here's why. If you can get Ruth to get
ou in to see her father, now, before it's too
ite, we may be able to save the day . . . and
Bill's neck.".

"What am I supposed to do after I get in?"

"Here, show him these plans. It's the gas
feeder. If you can sell him on the idea of
manufacturing it, Bill could be flagged out of
the race before that temporary mounting
should blow."

"It's a deal. Give me those plans. You just
watch . . . he won't make more than one
more circle of the track . . . I'll see to that."

BILL, still madly kicking the gas pedal, was
now unconsciously wiping oil off his face
. . . suddenly he jerked himself back into stark
reality. The oil he's wiping off is thin. . . . Too
thin. . . . GASOLENE!

On the stands, Fred saw the thin shred of
smoke trailing the Blue Bird. Terror gripping
his heart, he called to Ann to hurry. . . . In
another moment. . . .

But Ann hadn't wasted any time. Fred's
nervous, scanning eyes finally located her,
down talking to the starter.

He also saw the Blue Bird, never slowing,
round the turn and come rocketing up the
straightway in front of the stands. Just as he
crossed the line the checkered flag waved
him out of the race. The other cars shot right
past him for the final lap. Bill leaped out of
the Blue Bird and took the situation in at a
glance. Of course, just like a woman. Ann
became nervous . . . couldn't stand a little
smoke . . . so she had him flagged out. She
didn't care if she was throwing all of his hard
work out of the window.

"Well, Ann, you did a beautiful job. I
couldn't have done better myself. And you
claim you care for me. Why, all you care about
is yourself. . . ."

"See here, see here. This young lady just
saved your life. A most ungrateful exhibition,
young man. A most ungrateful exhibition."

"Why, Mr. Clark. I . . . Oh, whats' the
use . . . she's probably queered that too. At
least if she let me finish the race I'd be in that
much. Oh, well."

"Young man, this young lady just explained
the fine points of your new gas feeder to me.
I'd like to have you drop in to my office this
afternoon, if you will, and we can come to
terms."

"What? Why didn't you tell me this before?
Wheeeeee? Oh, Ann, forgive me. . . . To the
devil with the race."

"Oh, ah, pardon me. But do remember me?
I'm Fred, your mechanic?"

"Fred. You old sonofagun. Isn't it wonderful?"

"It certinly is. The darn thing works! You
did manage to gain a whole lap on those birds!
They all had to go around an extra lap to
compete for second place!"

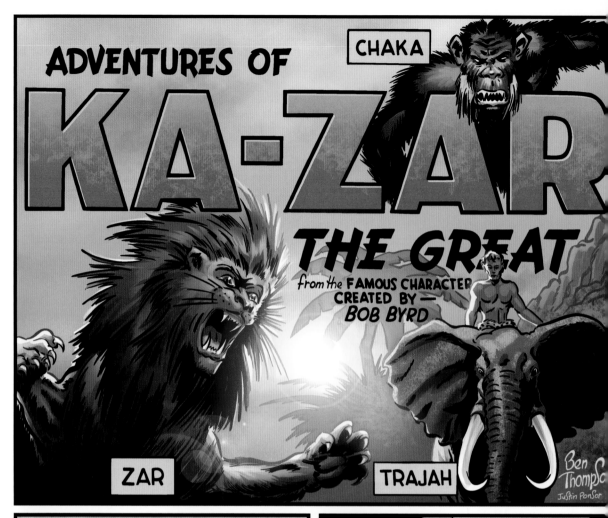

ADVENTURES OF KA-ZAR THE GREAT

CHAKA

from the FAMOUS CHARACTER CREATED BY— BOB BYRD

ZAR

TRAJAH

Ben Thompson
Justin Ponsor

JOHN RAND, YOUNG OWNER OF A RICH DIAMOND FIELD IN THE TRANSVAAL, IS FLYING FROM JOHANNESBURG TO CAIRO WITH HIS WIFE AND THEIR THREE-YEAR-OLD SON DAVID. OVER THE HEART OF THE **BELGIAN CONGO** THE PLANE DEVELOPS MOTOR TROUBLE AND RAND IS FORCED TO COME DOWN IN THE THICK, WILD **TROPICAL FOREST!!**

CONSTANCE!! HOLD DAVID..... I'M GOING TO LAND!!

THE PLANE DIVES INTO THE DENSE CONGO JUNGLE!

CONSTANCE! DAVID! ARE YOU HURT?

JOHN RAND STAGGERS OUT OF THE WRECK!!

TENDERLY, HE LIFTS HIS WIFE OUT OF THE BROKEN PLANE

MUMMY HURT?

MY LEG.... I THINK IT'S **BROKEN!!**

THERE'S A MEDICAL KIT IN THE PLANE.....I'LL FIX YOU UP IN A JIFFY!

WHILE HIS MOTHER WAS RECOVERING, YOUNG DAVID QUICKLY MADE FRIENDS WITH THE SMALL JUNGLE ANIMALS

DAILY, **ZAR,** LORD OF THE JUNGLE, WATCHES THE STRANGE TWO-LEGGED CUB**!!**

ANOTHER PAIR OF KEEN EYES WATCH THE BOY AS HE PLAYS NEAR THE EDGE OF THE SMALL CLEARING.

N'JAGA, THE LEOPARD, COULD WAIT NO LONGER!

LOOK, DADDY!

A WARNING CRY FROM DAVID'S MOTHER BRINGS JOHN RAND WITH A RIFLE....

ONE QUICK SHOT STOPS **N'JAGA** AND THE WOUNDED LEOPARD DASHES INTO THE JUNGLE WITHOUT HARMING DAVID!

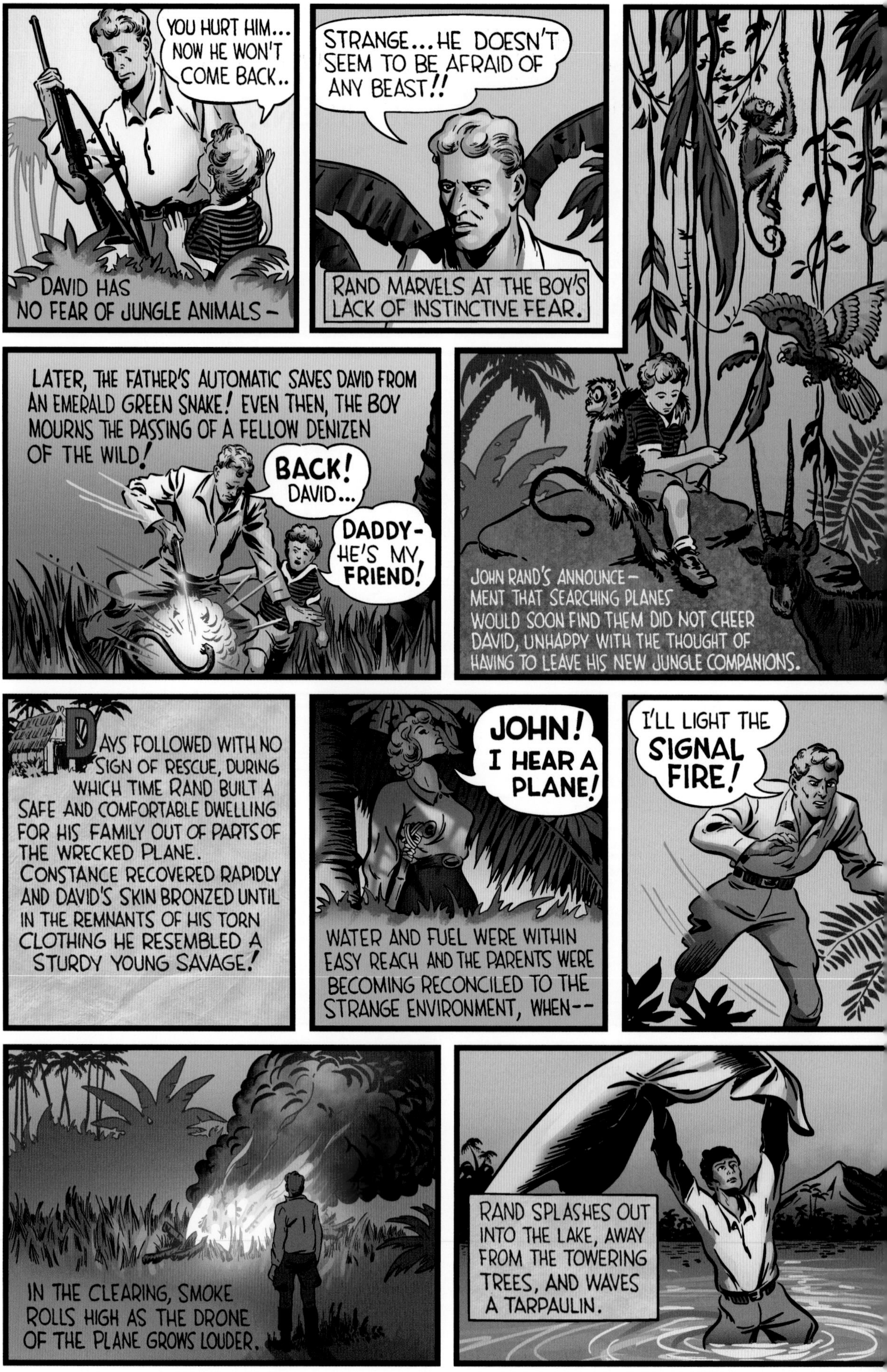
YOU HURT HIM... NOW HE WON'T COME BACK..
DAVID HAS NO FEAR OF JUNGLE ANIMALS –
STRANGE... HE DOESN'T SEEM TO BE AFRAID OF ANY BEAST!!
RAND MARVELS AT THE BOY'S LACK OF INSTINCTIVE FEAR.
LATER, THE FATHER'S AUTOMATIC SAVES DAVID FROM AN EMERALD GREEN SNAKE! EVEN THEN, THE BOY MOURNS THE PASSING OF A FELLOW DENIZEN OF THE WILD!
BACK! DAVID...
DADDY- HE'S MY FRIEND!
JOHN RAND'S ANNOUNCE– MENT THAT SEARCHING PLANES WOULD SOON FIND THEM DID NOT CHEER DAVID, UNHAPPY WITH THE THOUGHT OF HAVING TO LEAVE HIS NEW JUNGLE COMPANIONS.
DAYS FOLLOWED WITH NO SIGN OF RESCUE, DURING WHICH TIME RAND BUILT A SAFE AND COMFORTABLE DWELLING FOR HIS FAMILY OUT OF PARTS OF THE WRECKED PLANE. CONSTANCE RECOVERED RAPIDLY AND DAVID'S SKIN BRONZED UNTIL IN THE REMNANTS OF HIS TORN CLOTHING HE RESEMBLED A STURDY YOUNG SAVAGE!
JOHN! I HEAR A PLANE!
WATER AND FUEL WERE WITHIN EASY REACH AND THE PARENTS WERE BECOMING RECONCILED TO THE STRANGE ENVIRONMENT, WHEN--
I'LL LIGHT THE SIGNAL FIRE!
IN THE CLEARING, SMOKE ROLLS HIGH AS THE DRONE OF THE PLANE GROWS LOUDER.
RAND SPLASHES OUT INTO THE LAKE, AWAY FROM THE TOWERING TREES, AND WAVES A TARPAULIN.

NOT A SIGN OF RAND OR HIS PLANE..... NO CHANCE OF FINDING THEM IN THIS JUNGLE!

TURNING, THE PILOT CIRCLES TO THE NORTH WITHOUT SEEING THE SMOKE!

WITH A SINKING FEELING, RAND AND HIS WIFE WATCH THE PLANE DISAPPEAR!

POOH! THIS IS A BUSY HIGHWAY...THERE'LL BE ANOTHER ALONG SOON!

TRUE, THE PLANE CAME AGAIN THE NEXT DAY....AND ONE THE DAY AFTER, BUT EACH TIME IT WAS FARTHER FROM THEIR LONELY CAMP, UNTIL FINALLY, THEY CAME NO MORE.

THE DAY CAME WHEN CONSTANCE LAY IN THE HUT, CONSUMED BY A RAGING FEVER!!

SOON SHE DIED FROM THE RAVAGES OF THE TROPICAL FEVER. RAND WAS HEART-BROKEN...MORBIDLY HE TOYED WITH THE IDEA OF ENDING IT ALL .....LIFE HELD NO MEANING FOR HIM.

HIS WIFE'S LAST WISH HAD BEEN THAT THE BOY MUST LIVE. THAT THOUGHT, THAT CONVICTION, BROUGHT RAND BACK TO HIS SENSES. IMMEDIATELY HE BEGAN MAKING PLANS TO TREK BACK TO CIVILIZATION.

DAVID KNEW WHERE THE SWEETEST FLOWERS GREW FOR HIS MOTHER'S GRAVE.

THE HEAVY RAINS STOPPED AND RAND STUDIES THE MAP HE CARRIED IN THE AIRPLANE.

IT'S ABOUT **200** MILES TO THE NEAREST WHITE OUTPOST!

THAT EVENING, A TERRIBLE STORM LASHED THE JUNGLE.

AS GIANT BAOBAB TREES PLUNGED AND FELL, RAND SWEPT YOUNG DAVID INTO HIS ARMS AND RAN FOR THE SHELTER OF A CAVE.

A SIZZLING BOLT OF LIGHTNING SENDS A MAMMOTH TREE CRASHING DOWN ON **THEIR HEADS!**

RAND THRUSTS THE LAD ASIDE AS THE FALLING BAOBAB SENDS HIM SPINNING.

DO WE STILL HAVE TO START HOME SOON?

HOME?

QUICKLY, THE STORM PASSED AND RAND WAS NEXT CONSCIOUS OF BEING LED BACK TO THE HUT!

WHY THIS IS HOME, SON... HERE IN THIS CLEARING WHERE YOUR MOTHER IS!

I'M GLAD

JOHN RAND NEVER RECOVERED MENTALLY FROM THE BLOW THAT THE FALLING TREE STRUCK HIM. THOUGH RATIONAL IN EVERY OTHER RESPECT, HE LABORED UNDER THE DELUSION THAT THE JUNGLE WAS HIS HOME!

TOGETHER HE AND DAVID SURVIVED.... AND THRIVED. HIS BEARD BECAME A LUXURIANT GROWTH THAT **ZAR** MIGHT HAVE ENVIED.

SOME LATENT IMPULSE HAD MADE JOHN RAND TEACH HIS SON TO READ AND WRITE .... BUT DAVID PREFERRED PLAYING WITH HIS FRIENDS TO EVEN SUCH SIMPLE SCHOOLING.

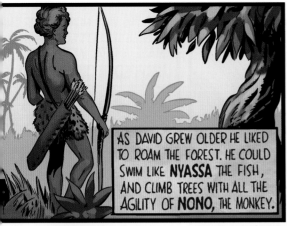

AS DAVID GREW OLDER HE LIKED TO ROAM THE FOREST. HE COULD SWIM LIKE **NYASSA** THE FISH, AND CLIMB TREES WITH ALL THE AGILITY OF **NONO**, THE MONKEY.

HE KNEW NOW WHY HIS FATHER HAD FIRED AT **N'JAGA** AND WHY HE KILLED THE GREEN SNAKE. HIS WAS THE CODE OF THE JUNGLE... KILL ONLY WHEN NECESSARY.

OON HE LEARNED TO TALK TO THE ANIMALS WITH STRANGE GUTTURAL SOUNDS AND FROM THAT DAY HE LIVED A HAPPIER LIFE.

THE JUNGLE LAD MET **QUOG**, THE WILD PIG, AND STAYED THAT BEAST'S STARTLED FLIGHT WITH A FRIENDLY CALL.

WHILE SWIMMING IN THE LAKE, HE WAS IN TURN STARTLED BY A GREAT BEAST THAT ROSE FROM THE S'HALLOWS ...**WAL-LAH**, THE HIPPOTAMUS.

HE HAD HIS FIRST VIEW OF **TRAJAH** AND LONGED TO RIDE ON THAT GREAT GRAY BACK!

A FLOATING SPECK IN THE SKY BROUGHT HIS EYES UPWARD. HE WATCHED **KRU**, THE BUZZARD, DROP TOWARDS THE EARTH.

THOUGH HE DID NOT KNOW IT, DAVID HAD ANOTHER COMPANION.... **ZAR** KEPT PACE WITH HIM AS HE RACED THROUGH THE JUNGLE!

167

QUICKLY, DAVID RAN TO WHERE **KRU** PERCHED IN A TREE-TOP.

THE STILLNESS WAS RENT BY A BLOOD-CURDLING ROAR...THAT OF **ZAR**...AND WITH A NOTE OF **FEAR!**

FOR, THE WISE MONARCH OF THE JUNGLE HAD ERRED! HE HAD MADE A FATAL MISSTEP AND LAY **TRAPPED IN QUICKSAND!!**

ZAR WAS UP TO HIS HAUNCHES NOW AND COULD NOT HOPE TO GAIN SOLID GROUND.

DAVID COULD SEE THE HOPELESS LIGHT IN THE LION'S AMBER EYES AND COULD NOT RESIST THE FORLORN APPEAL.

DESPERATELY HE SEIZED FALLEN BRANCHES AND THRUST THEM TOWARD **ZAR**...

INCH BY INCH **ZAR** DREW HIS TIRING BODY ACROSS THE TANGLE OF BOUGHS UNTIL....

FOR A FEW MINUTES **ZAR** LAY PANTING IN THE TALL GRASS WHILE **SHA**, HIS MATE, NUZZLED CLOSE. **ZAR** SURVEYED THE MAN CUB AND THERE A STRANGE PACT OF TRUCE WAS MADE.

....AT LAST HE STOOD FREE OF THE CLINGING SANDS!

I SMELL SMOKE!

NONSENSE! WE PUT OUR FIRE OUT BEFORE LEAVING

A WEEK AFTER THE RESCUE OF **ZAR**, DAVID AND HIS FATHER WERE EXPLORING THE FOREST, WHEN.....

THERE IT IS!!

SWIFTLY THEY TRAVELLED THROUGH THE TREES IN THE DIRECTION OF THE STRANGE SMOKE.

PEERING THROUGH THE BRANCHES, THEY SAW A BLACK MAN SQUATTING BEFORE A FIRE.

A SHORT DISTANCE AWAY, TWO OTHER BLACKS SCOOPED GRAVEL FROM A STREAM.... WATCHED BY A FAT WHITE MAN.

DROPPING TO THE GROUND, RAND STEPPED INTO THE CLEARING AND WALKED STRAIGHT TO THE GROUP.

FROM THEIR ACTIONS, DAVID KNEW THEY WERE ARGUING AND THAT HIS FATHER WAS COMMANDING THEM TO LEAVE!

HE ALSO SAW HIS FATHER TURN SLOWLY ON HIS HEEL AND START BACK TOWARDS THE BRUSH.

AT THAT MOMENT, **PAUL DE KRAFT**, WITH A HEART AS GREASY AS THE ROLLS OF FAT THAT COVERED HIS BODY, RAISED HIS GUN AND POINTED IT AT RAND'S BACK!

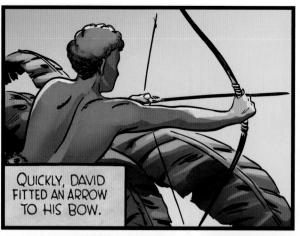

QUICKLY, DAVID FITTED AN ARROW TO HIS BOW.

JOHN RAND WAS AWARE OF A SUDDEN HUMMING BESIDE HIS EAR!

IN DE KRAFT'S ARM AN ARROW QUIVERED AND THE AUTOMATIC REVOLVER DROPPED TO THE GROUND!

DAVID AND HIS FATHER SILENTLY FADED INTO THE JUNGLE..... BUT, IF DAVID COULD HAVE SEEN THE DEVILS OF HATE LEERING OUT OF DE KRAFT'S EYES, HE WOULD HAVE PLACED ANOTHER ARROW IN THE MAN'S THROAT!

THIS JUNGLE IS SACRED TO YOUR MOTHER.... REMEMBER THAT, SON. NO ONE MUST BE ALLOWED TO PROFANE IT!

THAT NIGHT........

EMERALDS!! THAT'S WHAT I'VE STUMBLED ON IN THIS GOD-FORSAKEN STREAM!

AND SOME HALF-CRAZED HERMIT THINKS HE CAN ORDER ME FROM HERE! MUBANGI... GO FIND HIS CAMP AND SEE IF THERE ARE OTHERS!

IN A SHORT WHILE THE NATIVE RETURNS.....

I SAW, INKOSI, THE MAN AND BOY... NO OTHERS. THEY HAVE NO GUNS!

GOOD! THAT WILL MAKE IT EASIER!

AT DAWN DAVID WATCHED THE OTHER CAMP FROM A HIGH ROCK. IT APPEARED DESERTED. HAD THEY OBEYED HIS FATHER AND FLED IN THE NIGHT?

CAUTIOUSLY, DAVID APPROACHES THE TENT, PUZZLED THAT THEY COULD HAVE LEFT THEIR POSSESSIONS BEHIND.

HE FINGERED THE STRANGE ARTICLES AROUND THE CAMP.

FASCINATED, THE BOY STUDIES HIS REFLECTION IN A MIRROR!

HE DECIDES TO RETURN HOME ..... TO TELL HIS FATHER OF THE MANY WONDERFUL THINGS THE STRANGERS LEFT BEHIND.

A STACATTO CRACK PIERCES THE STILLNESS ...... DAVID REMEMBERS FAINTLY THE TIME HIS FATHER HAD FIRED AT **N'JAGA** AND SENSES .....**DANGER!!**

A **SECOND SHOT** ECHOES FROM THE DIRECTION OF HIS HOME AND DAVID WAITS NO LONGER!

THE HUT IS **AFIRE!!** DAVID LEAPS FORWARD WITH THE THOUGHT THAT HIS FATHER IS **INSIDE!**

171

AN OBJECT ON THE GROUND CAUGHT HIS EYE.

RAND, SHOT AND PAINFULLY WOUNDED, CRAWLED ALONG THE GROUND!

FATHER! WHAT HAPPENED?

WEAKLY, RAND MUMBLES A WARNING AS THE BOY, WITH THE STRENGTH OF A GROWN MAN, CARRIES HIS FATHER AWAY FROM THE FIRE.

DAVID FAILS TO SEE A NATIVE SNEAK AROUND THE BURNING SHELTER!

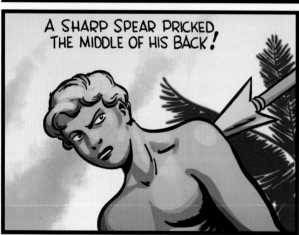

A SHARP SPEAR PRICKED THE MIDDLE OF HIS BACK!

BEFORE HE COULD ACT, DE KRAFT CAME ON THE RUN FROM THE JUNGLE.

FAT-FACE HAS WOUNDED MY FATHER.... AND FOR THAT **FAT-FACE SHALL DIE!**

DE KRAFT LAUGHED AT DAVID'S THREAT.

SPUNKY, EH? BUT, YOU'RE WRONG, KID. I DON'T WANT ANY WITNESSES TO THIS PARTY....AND **I'M GOING TO KILL YOU...... SEE?**

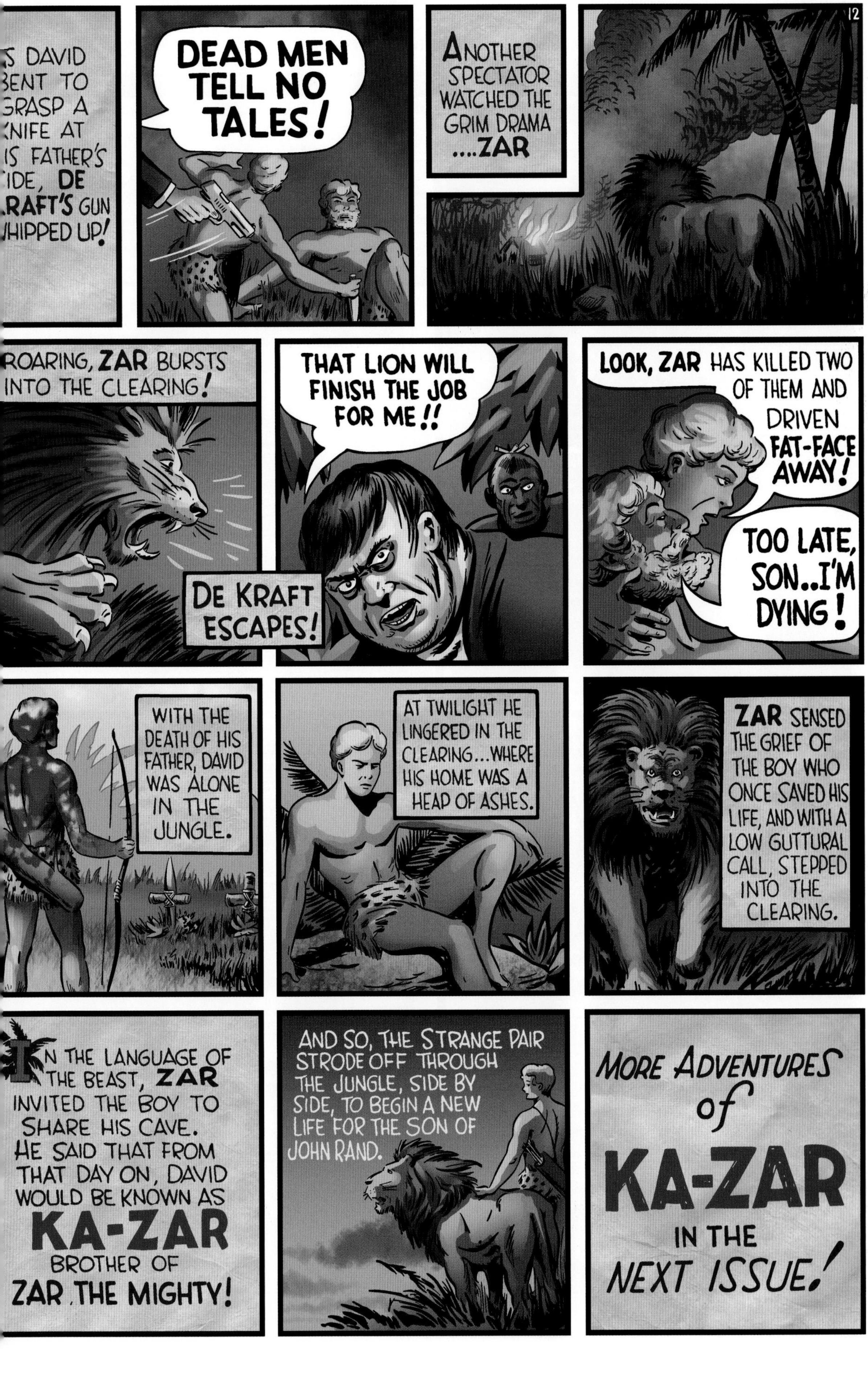

12
S DAVID BENT TO GRASP A KNIFE AT IS FATHER'S IDE, DE RAFT'S GUN WHIPPED UP!
DEAD MEN TELL NO TALES!
ANOTHER SPECTATOR WATCHED THE GRIM DRAMA ....ZAR
ROARING, ZAR BURSTS INTO THE CLEARING!
THAT LION WILL FINISH THE JOB FOR ME!!
DE KRAFT ESCAPES!
LOOK, ZAR HAS KILLED TWO OF THEM AND DRIVEN FAT-FACE AWAY!
TOO LATE, SON..I'M DYING!
WITH THE DEATH OF HIS FATHER, DAVID WAS ALONE IN THE JUNGLE.
AT TWILIGHT HE LINGERED IN THE CLEARING...WHERE HIS HOME WAS A HEAP OF ASHES.
ZAR SENSED THE GRIEF OF THE BOY WHO ONCE SAVED HIS LIFE, AND WITH A LOW GUTTURAL CALL, STEPPED INTO THE CLEARING.
IN THE LANGUAGE OF THE BEAST, ZAR INVITED THE BOY TO SHARE HIS CAVE. HE SAID THAT FROM THAT DAY ON, DAVID WOULD BE KNOWN AS KA-ZAR BROTHER OF ZAR, THE MIGHTY!
AND SO, THE STRANGE PAIR STRODE OFF THROUGH THE JUNGLE, SIDE BY SIDE, TO BEGIN A NEW LIFE FOR THE SON OF JOHN RAND.
MORE ADVENTURES of KA-ZAR IN THE NEXT ISSUE!

REFERENCE SCANS OF A PRINTED COPY OF *MARVEL COMICS* #1, USED DURING THE 2009 RESTORATION PROCESS TO ENSURE THAT THE REMASTERING WAS FAITHFUL TO THE ORIGINAL ISSUE'S ART AND COLORING.

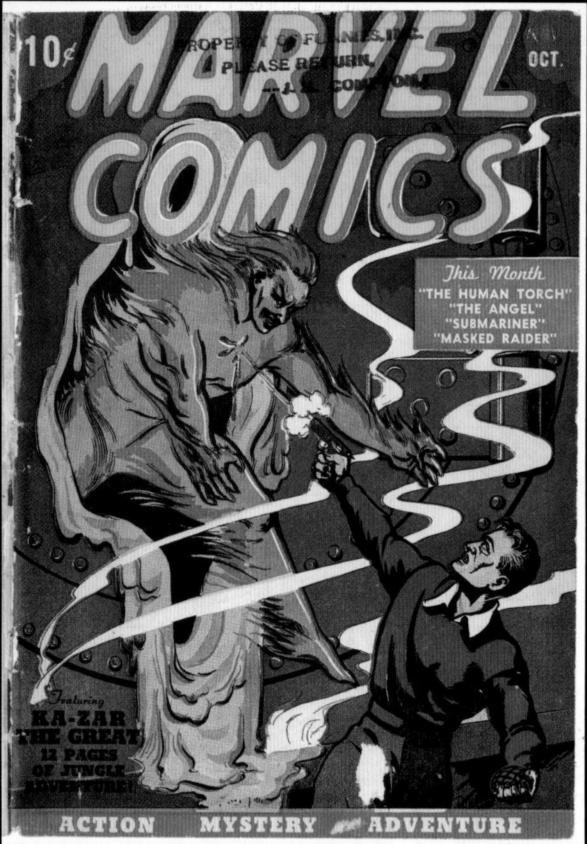

10¢
MARVEL COMICS
OCT.
PROPERTY OF FUNNIES, INC.
PLEASE RETURN.
This Month
"THE HUMAN TORCH"
"THE ANGEL"
"SUBMARINER"
"MASKED RAIDER"
Featuring
KA-ZAR THE GREAT
12 PAGES OF JUNGLE ADVENTURE!
ACTION MYSTERY AND ADVENTURE

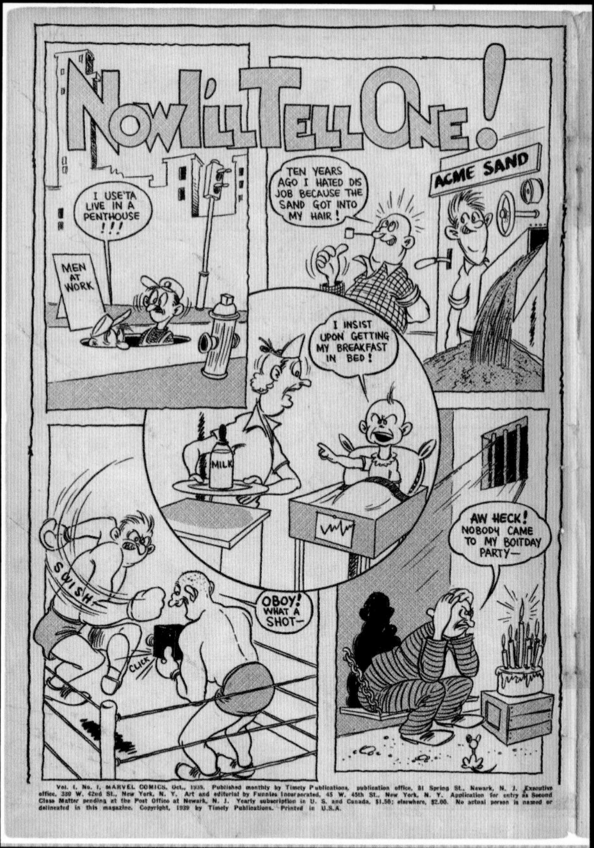

NOW I'LL TELL ONE!
I USE'TA LIVE IN A PENTHOUSE!!!
MEN AT WORK
TEN YEARS AGO I HATED DIS JOB BECAUSE THE SAND GOT INTO MY HAIR!
ACME SAND
I INSIST UPON GETTING MY BREAKFAST IN BED!
MILK
AW HECK! NOBODY CAME TO MY BOITDAY PARTY—
SWISH!
OBOY! WHAT A SHOT—
CLICK
Vol. 1, No. 1, MARVEL COMICS, Oct., 1939. Published monthly by Timely Publications, publication office, 81 Spring St., Newark, N. J. Executive office, 330 W. 42nd St., New York, N. Y. Art and editorial by Funnies Incorporated, 45 W. 45th St., New York, N. Y. Application for entry as Second Class Matter pending at the Post Office at Newark, N. J. Yearly subscription in U. S. and Canada, $1.50; elsewhere, $2.00. No actual person is named or delineated in this magazine. Copyright, 1939 by Timely Publications. Printed in U.S.A.

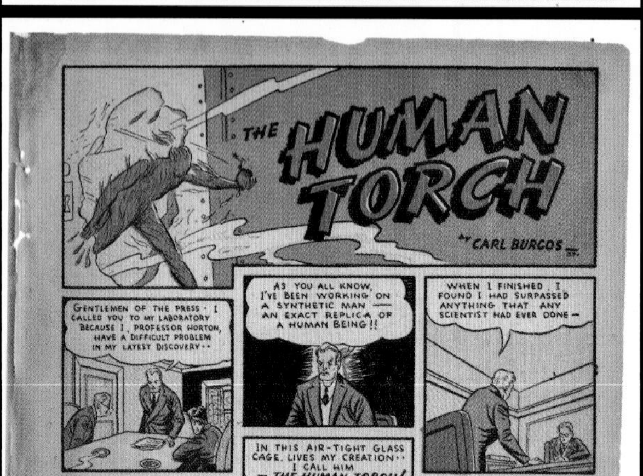

THE HUMAN TORCH
by CARL BURGOS
GENTLEMEN OF THE PRESS · I CALLED YOU TO MY LABORATORY BECAUSE I, PROFESSOR HORTON, HAVE A DIFFICULT PROBLEM IN MY LATEST DISCOVERY · ·
AS YOU ALL KNOW, I'VE BEEN WORKING ON A SYNTHETIC MAN — AN EXACT REPLICA OF A HUMAN BEING!!
WHEN I FINISHED, I FOUND I HAD SURPASSED ANYTHING THAT ANY SCIENTIST HAD EVER DONE —
IF YOU'LL FOLLOW ME, I'LL SHOW YOU WHY, EVEN I, FEAR THE MONSTROSITY WHICH I'VE CREATED!!
IN THIS AIR-TIGHT GLASS CAGE, LIVES MY CREATION · · I CALL HIM — THE HUMAN TORCH!
SOMETHING WENT WRONG WITH MY FIGURINGS SOMEWHERE · EVERY TIME THIS ROBOT THE HUMAN TORCH, CONTACTS OXYGEN IN THE AIR, HE BURSTS INTO FLAME! NOW WATCH!
AS HORTON ALLOWS SOME AIR INTO THE CAGE, THE OTHERS GASP IN TERROR! —
GOOD LORD! THAT FIGURE IS A WALL OF FIRE!!
HORTON, DESTROY THAT MAN, BEFORE SOME MAD-MAN CAN GRASP IT'S PRINCIPLES AND HURL IT AGAINST OUR CIVILIZATION!
NO!
SORRY, GENTLEMEN, BUT YOU SEE, DESTROYING HIM, DOES NOT ANSWER ANYTHING!!
THEN PERHAPS THE POWER OF THE PRESS WILL HELP CHANGE YOUR MIND!

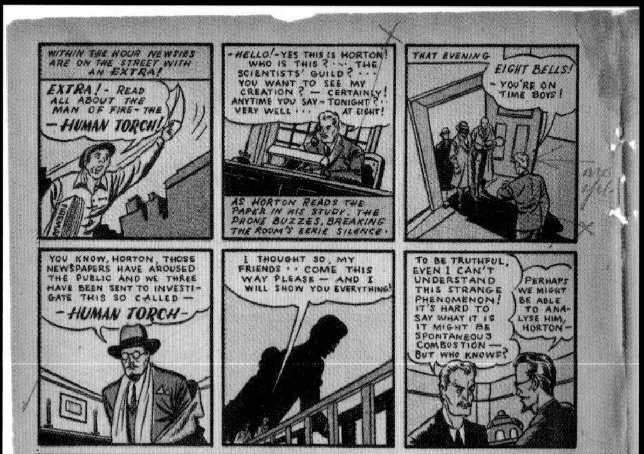

WITHIN THE HOUR NEWSIES ARE ON THE STREET WITH AN EXTRA!
EXTRA! — READ ALL ABOUT THE MAN OF FIRE — THE — HUMAN TORCH!
— HELLO! — YES THIS IS HORTON! WHO IS THIS? · · THE SCIENTISTS' GUILD? · · · YOU WANT TO SEE MY CREATION? — CERTAINLY! ANYTIME YOU SAY — TONIGHT? · · VERY WELL · · · AT EIGHT!
AS HORTON READS THE PAPER IN HIS STUDY, THE PHONE BUZZES, BREAKING THE ROOM'S EERIE SILENCE.
THAT EVENING
EIGHT BELLS! — YOU'RE ON TIME BOYS!
YOU KNOW, HORTON, THOSE NEWSPAPERS HAVE AROUSED THE PUBLIC AND WE THREE HAVE BEEN SENT TO INVESTIGATE THIS SO CALLED — HUMAN TORCH —
I THOUGHT SO, MY FRIENDS · · COME THIS WAY PLEASE — AND I WILL SHOW YOU EVERYTHING!
TO BE TRUTHFUL, EVEN I CAN'T UNDERSTAND THIS STRANGE PHENOMENON! IT'S HARD TO SAY WHAT IT IS IT MIGHT BE SPONTANEOUS COMBUSTION — BUT WHO KNOWS?
PERHAPS WE MIGHT BE ABLE TO ANALYSE HIM, HORTON —
— HE LOOKS HARMLESS ENOUGH · · DO YOU MIND FEEDING HIM SOME AIR, HORTON? — SO WE CAN MEASURE THE HEAT GIVEN WITH THIS PYROMETER? —
VERY WELL! —
AS AIR LEAKS IN THE WEIRD FLAME LIVENS LIKE A HELLISH FIRE!
GOOD LORD — THE HANDS OF THE METERS HAVE ALREADY GONE OFF THE DIALS! —
WHAT?
THE METER SNAPPED THE HEAT IS TOO GREAT! —
— AND YOU HAVE NO CONTROL OVER THE FLAME?
NONE WHAT SO EVER — THAT IS WHY I'M AFRAID!
2

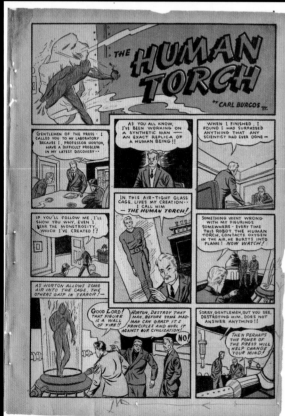

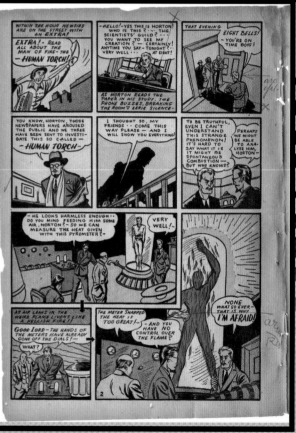

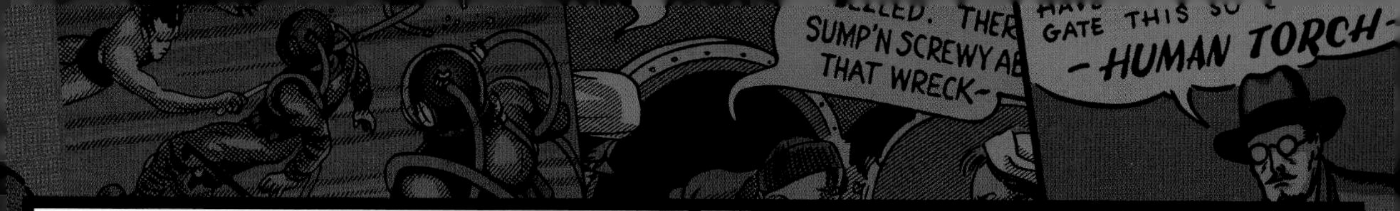
THAT WRECK-
-HUMAN TORCH-

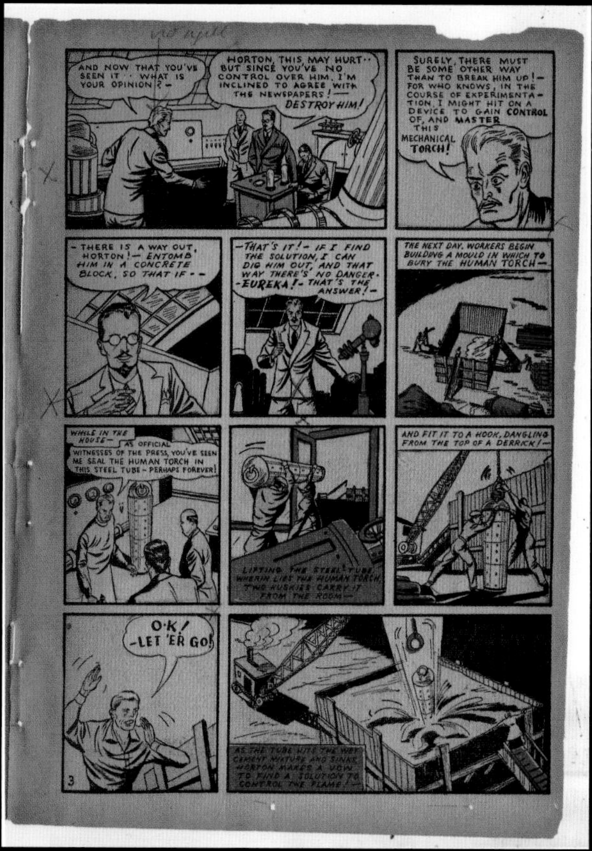
AND NOW THAT YOU'VE SEEN IT · · WHAT IS YOUR OPINION? –
HORTON, THIS MAY HURT · · BUT SINCE YOU'VE NO CONTROL OVER HIM, I'M INCLINED TO AGREE WITH THE NEWSPAPERS! — DESTROY HIM!
SURELY, THERE MUST BE SOME OTHER WAY THAN TO BREAK HIM UP! – FOR WHO KNOWS, IN THE COURSE OF EXPERIMENTATION, I MIGHT HIT ON A DEVICE TO GAIN CONTROL OF, AND MASTER THIS MECHANICAL TORCH!
– THERE IS A WAY OUT, HORTON! – ENTOMB HIM IN A CONCRETE BLOCK, SO THAT IF - -
–THAT'S IT! – IF I FIND THE SOLUTION, I CAN DIG HIM OUT, AND THAT WAY THERE'S NO DANGER. -EUREKA! – THAT'S THE ANSWER! –
THE NEXT DAY, WORKERS BEGIN BUILDING A MOULD IN WHICH TO BURY THE HUMAN TORCH –
WHILE IN THE HOUSE –
AS OFFICIAL WITNESSES OF THE PRESS, YOU'VE SEEN ME SEAL THE HUMAN TORCH IN THIS STEEL TUBE – PERHAPS FOREVER!
LIFTING THE STEEL TUBE, WHEREIN LIES THE HUMAN TORCH, TWO HUSKIES CARRY IT FROM THE ROOM –
AND FIT IT TO A HOOK, DANGLING FROM THE TOP OF A DERRICK! –
O·K! -LET 'ER GO!
AS THE TUBE HITS THE WET CEMENT MIXTURE AND SINKS, HORTON MAKES A VOW TO CONTROL THE FLAME! –
3

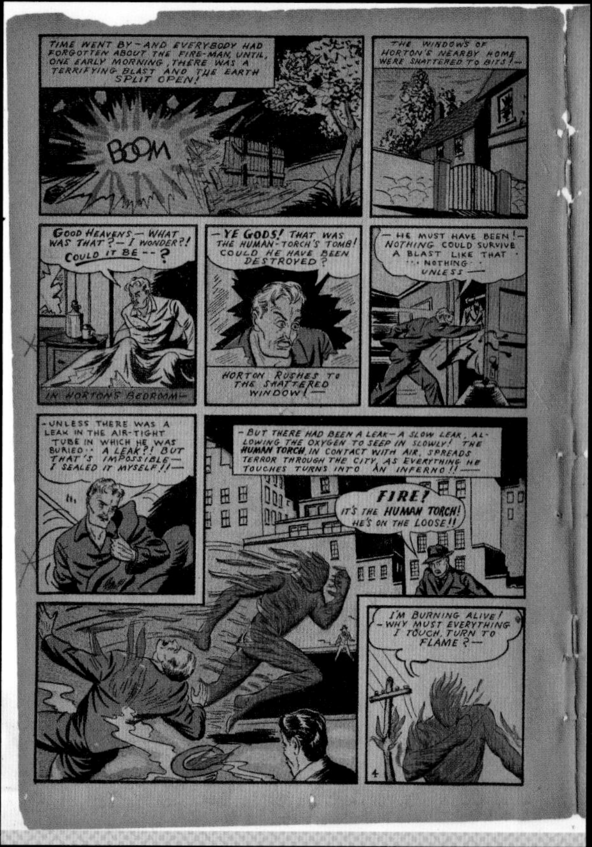
TIME WENT BY – AND EVERYBODY HAD FORGOTTEN ABOUT THE FIRE-MAN, UNTIL, ONE EARLY MORNING, THERE WAS A TERRIFYING BLAST AND THE EARTH SPLIT OPEN!
BOOM
THE WINDOWS OF HORTON'S NEARBY HOME WERE SHATTERED TO BITS! –
GOOD HEAVENS – WHAT WAS THAT? – I WONDER?! COULD IT BE - - ?
IN HORTON'S BEDROOM –
– YE GODS! THAT WAS THE HUMAN-TORCH'S TOMB! COULD HE HAVE BEEN DESTROYED?
HORTON RUSHES TO THE SHATTERED WINDOW! –
– HE MUST HAVE BEEN! – NOTHING COULD SURVIVE A BLAST LIKE THAT · · · · NOTHING · · UNLESS –
– UNLESS THERE WAS A LEAK IN THE AIR-TIGHT TUBE IN WHICH HE WAS BURIED · · A LEAK?! BUT THAT'S IMPOSSIBLE – I SEALED IT MYSELF!! –
– BUT THERE HAD BEEN A LEAK – A SLOW LEAK, ALLOWING THE OXYGEN TO SEEP IN SLOWLY! THE HUMAN TORCH, IN CONTACT WITH AIR, SPREADS TERROR THROUGH THE CITY, AS EVERYTHING HE TOUCHES TURNS INTO AN INFERNO!! –
FIRE! IT'S THE HUMAN TORCH! HE'S ON THE LOOSE!!
I'M BURNING ALIVE! – WHY MUST EVERYTHING I TOUCH, TURN TO FLAME? –
4

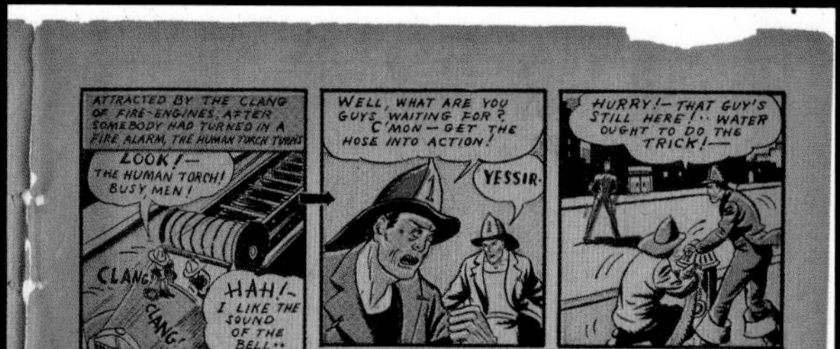
ATTRACTED BY THE CLANG OF FIRE-ENGINES, AFTER SOMEBODY HAD TURNED IN A FIRE ALARM, THE HUMAN TORCH TURNS
LOOK! – THE HUMAN TORCH! BUSY, MEN!
CLANG!
CLANG!
HAH! – I LIKE THE SOUND OF THE BELL · ·
WELL, WHAT ARE YOU GUYS WAITING FOR? C'MON – GET THE HOSE INTO ACTION!
YESSIR.
HURRY! – THAT GUY'S STILL HERE! · · WATER OUGHT TO DO THE TRICK! –
AS THE WATER SPURTS ONTO THE HUMAN-TORCH – A HISSING SOUND BELLOWS – A CLOUD OF SMOKE RISES · · BUT THE FIREMEN ARE DUMBFOUNDED, AS · · · –
GLORY BE! THE GUY'S LAUGHING! IT AIN'T HUMAN!!
HA! HA! HA! STOP – IT TICKLES!
KEEP POURING WATER ON HIM – THE FLAMES DYING DOWN! – I'M GOING TO GET HORTON!
AS THE HUMAN TORCH STEPS ON A HOSE, IT BURNS THROUGH, AND THE WATER SPURTS OUT
THE FLAMES ONCE AGAIN SHOOT UP, AND THE HUMAN TORCH IS ON THE LOOSE AGAIN! –
5

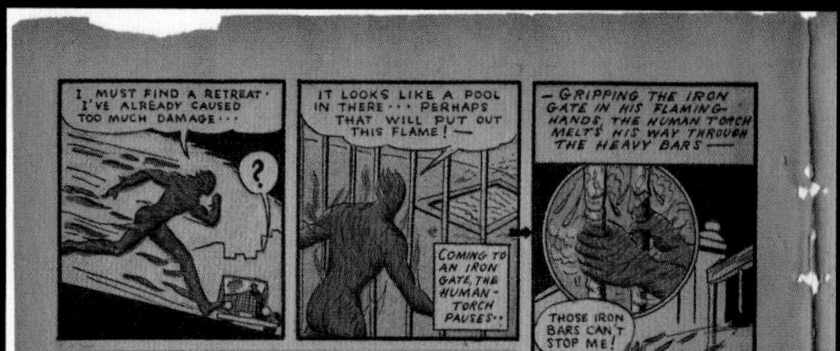
I MUST FIND A RETREAT · I'VE ALREADY CAUSED TOO MUCH DAMAGE · · ·
?
IT LOOKS LIKE A POOL IN THERE · · · PERHAPS THAT WILL PUT OUT THIS FLAME! –
COMING TO AN IRON GATE, THE HUMAN-TORCH PAUSES · ·
– GRIPPING THE IRON GATE IN HIS FLAMING-HANDS, THE HUMAN TORCH MELTS HIS WAY THROUGH THE HEAVY BARS –
THOSE IRON BARS CAN'T STOP ME!
LEAVING A TRAIL OF BLAZING GRASS, THE HUMAN-TORCH DIVES INTO THE POOL · · ·
MEANWHILE, IN THE HOUSE ON THE ESTATE WITH THE POOL
DAT'S FUNNY – DE GRASS 'ROUND DE POOL IS BOININ', SARDO!
YOU'RE NUTS, RED!
HUMAN-TO… ON LOOSE!
WAIT A MINUTE – DID YOU SAY BURNING?!! – THAT MEANS BUT ONE THING!
HUH?
NOW LISTEN – GET THE WINTER GLASS-COVER THAT FITS THE POOL – DRAW THE AIR OUT · · · THEN DRAIN THE WATER OUT! – HURRY! – DON'T ASK ANY QUESTIONS!
LATER!
HAH! – I THOUGHT SO! – IT'S THE HUMAN TORCH!!
SO WOT?
THAT'S WHAT I LIKE ABOUT YOU RED – YOU'RE SO STUPID!
I DON'T LIKE DAT KIND OF TALK – SARDO!
FORGET IT RED – WE GOT A MILLION-DOLLAR RACKET, AND DON'T NEED TO WORRY ABOUT COPS NOW!
6

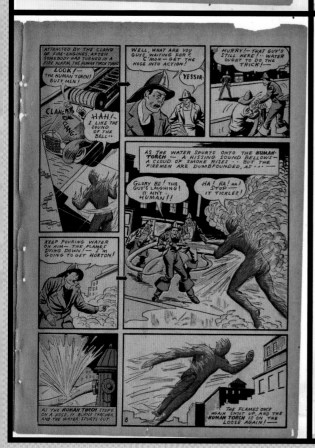

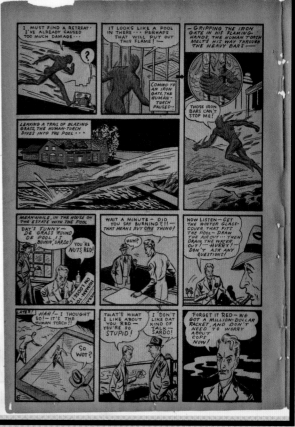

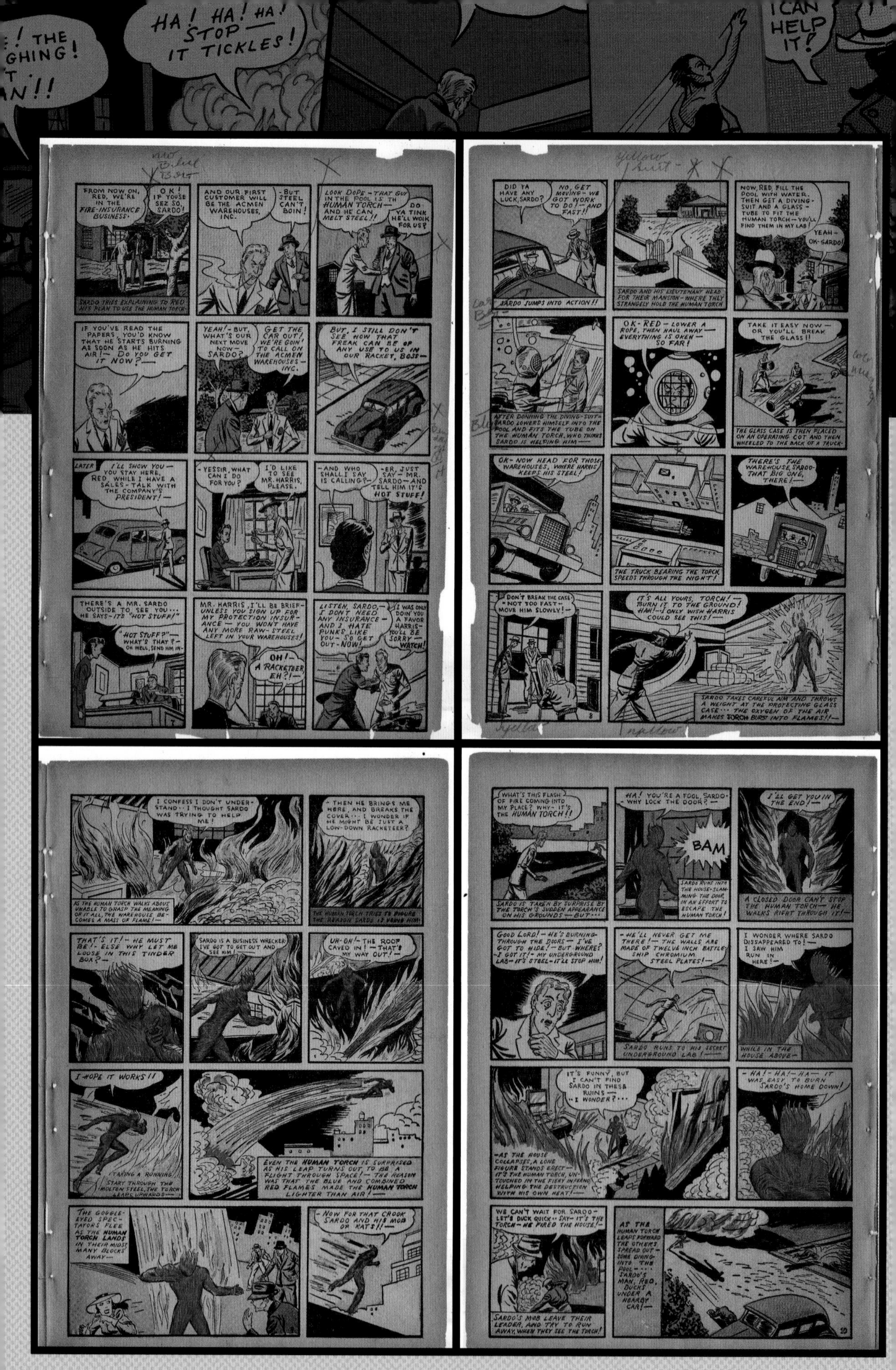

HA! HA! HA! STOP— IT TICKLES!
I CAN HELP IT!
FROM NOW ON, RED, WE'RE IN THE FIRE-INSURANCE BUSINESS.
OK! IF YOUSE SEZ SO, SARDO!
SARDO TRIES EXPLAINING TO RED HIS PLAN TO USE THE HUMAN TORCH
AND OUR FIRST CUSTOMER WILL BE THE ACMEN WAREHOUSES, INC.
-BUT STEEL CAN'T BOIN!
LOOK DOPE—THAT GUY IN THE POOL IS TH HUMAN TORCH—AND HE CAN MELT STEEL!!
DO YA TINK HE'LL WOIK FOR US?
IF YOU'VE READ THE PAPERS, YOU'D KNOW THAT HE STARTS BURNING AS SOON AS HE HITS AIR!—DO YOU GET IT NOW?—
YEAH!—BUT, WHAT'S OUR NEXT MOVE NOW—SARDO?
GET THE CAR OUT! WE'RE GOIN' TO CALL ON THE ACMEN WAREHOUSES—INC.
BUT, I STILL DON'T SEE HOW THAT FREAK CAN BE OF ANY USE TO US IN OUR RACKET, BOSS—
LATER
I'LL SHOW YOU—YOU STAY HERE, RED, WHILE I HAVE A SALES-TALK WITH THE COMPANY'S PRESIDENT!—
-YESSIR, WHAT CAN I DO FOR YOU?
I'D LIKE TO SEE MR. HARRIS, PLEASE.
-AND WHO SHALL I SAY IS CALLING?-
-ER, JUST SAY—MR. SARDO—AND TELL HIM IT'S HOT STUFF!
THERE'S A MR. SARDO OUTSIDE TO SEE YOU... HE SAYS—IT'S "HOT STUFF!"
"HOT STUFF?"—WHAT'S THAT?—OH WELL, SEND HIM IN—
MR. HARRIS, I'LL BE BRIEF—UNLESS YOU SIGN UP FOR MY PROTECTION INSURANCE—YOU WONT HAVE ANY MORE RAW-STEEL LEFT IN YOUR WAREHOUSES!
OH!—A RACKETEER, EH?!—
LISTEN, SARDO, I DON'T NEED ANY INSURANCE—AND I HATE PUNKS LIKE YOU—SO GET OUT—NOW!
I WAS ONLY DOIN' YOU A FAVOR HARRIS—YOU'LL BE SORRY—WATCH!
DID YA HAVE ANY LUCK, SARDO?
NO, GET MOVING—WE GOT WORK TO DO!—AND FAST!!
SARDO JUMPS INTO ACTION!!
SARDO AND HIS LIEUTENANT HEAD FOR THEIR MANSION—WHERE THEY STRANGELY HOLD THE HUMAN TORCH
NOW, RED, FILL THE POOL WITH WATER. THEN GET A DIVING-SUIT AND A GLASS-TUBE TO FIT THE HUMAN TORCH—YOU'LL FIND THEM IN MY LAB!
YEAH—OK—SARDO!
AFTER DONNING THE DIVING-SUIT SARDO LOWERS HIMSELF INTO THE POOL AND FITS THE TUBE ON THE HUMAN TORCH, WHO THINKS SARDO IS HELPING HIM—
OK—RED—LOWER A ROPE, THEN HAUL AWAY—EVERYTHING IS OKEH—SO FAR!
TAKE IT EASY NOW—OR YOU'LL BREAK THE GLASS!!
THE GLASS CASE IS THEN PLACED ON AN OPERATING COT AND THEN WHEELED TO THE BACK OF A TRUCK—
OK—NOW HEAD FOR THOSE WAREHOUSES, WHERE HARRIS KEEPS HIS STEEL!
THE TRUCK BEARING THE TORCH, SPEEDS THROUGH THE NIGHT!
THERE'S THE WAREHOUSE, SARDO—THAT BIG ONE, THERE!—
DON'T BREAK THE CASE—NOT TOO FAST—MOVE HIM SLOWLY!—
IT'S ALL YOURS, TORCH!—BURN IT TO THE GROUND! HAH!—I ONLY WISH HARRIS COULD SEE THIS!—
SARDO TAKES CAREFUL AIM AND THROWS A WEIGHT AT THE PROTECTING GLASS CASE... THE OXYGEN OF THE AIR MAKES TORCH BURST INTO FLAMES!!—
8
I CONFESS I DON'T UNDERSTAND.. I THOUGHT SARDO WAS TRYING TO HELP ME!
AS THE HUMAN TORCH WALKS ABOUT UNABLE TO GRASP THE MEANING OF IT ALL, THE WAREHOUSE BECOMES A MASS OF FLAME!—
-THEN HE BRINGS ME HERE, AND BREAKS THE COVER.. I WONDER IF HE MIGHT BE JUST A LOW-DOWN RACKETEER?
THE HUMAN TORCH TRIES TO FIGURE THE REASON SARDO IS USING HIM—
THAT'S IT!—HE MUST BE!—ELSE WHY LET ME LOOSE IN THIS TINDER BOX?—
SARDO IS A BUSINESS WRECKER! I'VE GOT TO GET OUT AND GET HIM!
UH-OH!—THE ROOF CAVED IN!—THAT'S MY WAY OUT!—
I HOPE IT WORKS!!
TAKING A RUNNING START THROUGH THE MOLTEN STEEL, THE TORCH LEAPS UPWARDS—
EVEN THE HUMAN TORCH IS SURPRISED AS HIS LEAP TURNS OUT TO BE A FLIGHT THROUGH SPACE!—THE REASON WAS THAT THE BLUE AND COMBINED RED FLAMES MADE THE HUMAN TORCH LIGHTER THAN AIR!—
THE GOGGLE-EYED SPECTATORS FLEE AS THE HUMAN TORCH LANDS IN THEIR MIDST MANY BLOCKS AWAY—
-NOW FOR THAT CROOK SARDO AND HIS MOB OF RATS!!—
WHAT'S THIS FLASH OF FIRE COMING INTO MY PLACE? WHY—IT'S THE HUMAN TORCH!!
SARDO IS TAKEN BY SURPRISE BY THE TORCH'S SUDDEN APPEARANCE ON HIS GROUNDS—BUT—
HA! YOU'RE A FOOL, SARDO—WHY LOCK THE DOOR?—
BAM
SARDO RUNS INTO THE HOUSE—SLAMMING THE DOOR, IN AN EFFORT TO ESCAPE THE HUMAN TORCH!
I'LL GET YOU IN THE END!—
A CLOSED DOOR CAN'T STOP THE HUMAN TORCH—HE WALKS RIGHT THROUGH IT!—
GOOD LORD!—HE'S BURNING THROUGH THE DOORS—I'VE GOT TO HIDE!—BUT WHERE?—I GOT IT!—MY UNDERGROUND LAB—IT'S STEEL—IT'LL STOP HIM!
-HE'LL NEVER GET ME THERE!—THE WALLS ARE MADE OF TWELVE INCH BATTLESHIP CHROMIUM STEEL PLATES!—
SARDO RUNS TO HIS SECRET UNDERGROUND LAB!—
I WONDER WHERE SARDO DISSAPPEARED TO!—I SAW HIM RUN IN HERE!—
WHILE IN THE HOUSE ABOVE—
IT'S FUNNY, BUT I CAN'T FIND SARDO IN THESE RUINS—I WONDER?...
-AS THE HOUSE COLLAPSES, A LONE FIGURE STANDS ERECT—IT'S THE HUMAN TORCH, UNTOUCHED IN THE FIERY INFERNO HELPING THE DESTRUCTION WITH HIS OWN HEAT!—
-HA!—HA!—HA—IT WAS EASY TO BURN SARDO'S HOME DOWN!
WE CAN'T WAIT FOR SARDO—LET'S DUCK QUICK—SAY—IT'S THE TORCH—HE FIRED THE HOUSE!—
SARDO'S MOB LEAVE THEIR LEADER, AND TRY TO RUN AWAY, WHEN THEY SEE THE TORCH!
AS THE HUMAN TORCH LEAPS FORWARD THE OTHERS SPREAD OUT—SOME DIVING INTO THE POOL... SARDO'S MAN, RED, DUCKS UNDER A NEARBY CAR!
10

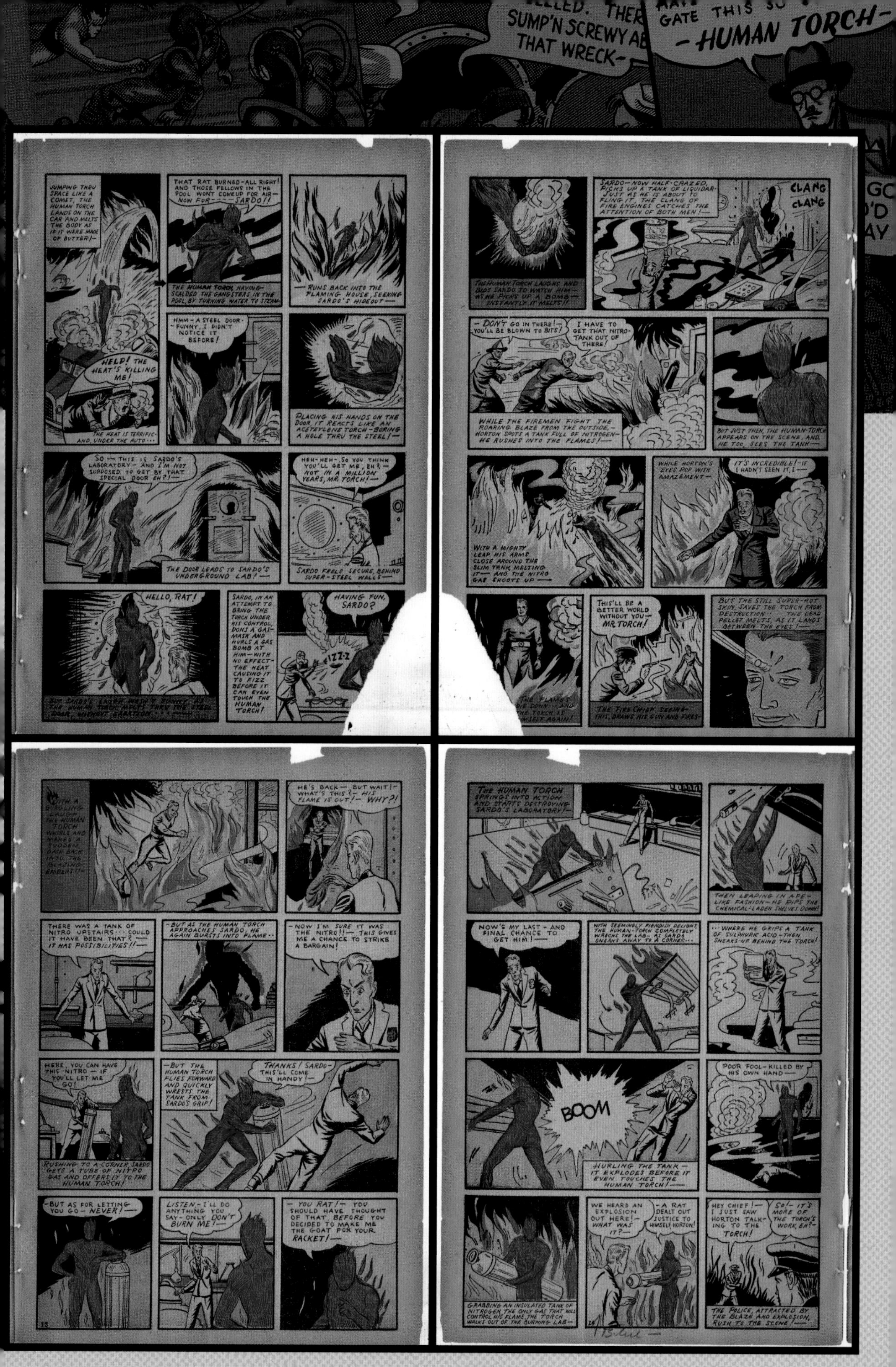
SUMP'N SCREWY AB
THAT WRECK-
GATE THIS SO
-HUMAN TORCH-
JUMPING THRU SPACE LIKE A COMET, THE HUMAN TORCH LANDS ON THE CAR AND MELTS THE BODY AS IF IT WERE MADE OF BUTTER!
HELP! THE HEAT'S KILLING ME!
THE HEAT IS TERRIFIC-AND, UNDER THE AUTO...
THAT RAT BURNED-ALL RIGHT! AND THOSE FELLOWS IN THE POOL WONT COME UP FOR AIR-NOW FOR---SARDO!!
THE HUMAN TORCH, HAVING SCALDED THE GANGSTERS IN THE POOL BY TURNING WATER TO STEAM-
-RUNS BACK INTO THE FLAMING HOUSE, SEEKING SARDO'S HIDEOUT-
HMM-A STEEL DOOR-FUNNY, I DIDN'T NOTICE IT BEFORE!
PLACING HIS HANDS ON THE DOOR, IT REACTS LIKE AN ACETYLENE TORCH-BORING A HOLE THRU THE STEEL!-
SO-THIS IS SARDO'S LABORATORY-AND I'M NOT SUPPOSED TO GET BY THAT SPECIAL DOOR EH?!-
THE DOOR LEADS TO SARDO'S UNDERGROUND LAB!-
HEH-HEH-SO YOU THINK YOU'LL GET ME, EH? NOT IN A MILLION YEARS, MR. TORCH!-
SARDO FEELS SECURE, BEHIND SUPER-STEEL WALLS-
HELLO, RAT!
SARDO, IN AN ATTEMPT TO BRING THE TORCH UNDER HIS CONTROL, DONS A GAS-MASK AND HURLS A GAS BOMB AT HIM-WITH NO EFFECT-THE HEAT CAUSING IT TO FIZZ BEFORE IT CAN EVEN TOUCH THE HUMAN TORCH!
HAVING FUN, SARDO?
FIZZ-Z
THE HUMAN TORCH LAUGHS AND BIDS SARDO TO WATCH HIM-AS HE PICKS UP A BOMB-INSTANTLY IT MELTS!!
SARDO-NOW HALF-CRAZED, PICKS UP A TANK OF LIQUIDAR-JUST AS HE IS ABOUT TO FLING IT, THE CLANG OF FIRE ENGINES CATCHES THE ATTENTION OF BOTH MEN!-
CLANG
CLANG
-DON'T GO IN THERE!-YOU'LL BE BLOWN TO BITS!
I HAVE TO GET THAT NITRO-TANK OUT OF THERE!
WHILE THE FIREMEN FIGHT THE ROARING BLAZE FROM THE OUTSIDE, HORTON SPOTS A TANK FULL OF NITROGEN-HE RUSHES INTO THE FLAMES!-
BUT JUST THEN, THE HUMAN-TORCH APPEARS ON THE SCENE, AND, HE TOO, SEES THE TANK-
WITH A MIGHTY LEAP HIS ARMS CLOSE AROUND THE SLIM TANK, MELTING IT-AND THE NITRO GAS SHOOTS UP-
WHILE HORTON'S EYES POP WITH AMAZEMENT-
IT'S INCREDIBLE!-IF I HADN'T SEEN IT, I-
THE FLAMES DIE DOWN---AND THE TORCH IS HIMSELF AGAIN!
THIS'LL BE A BETTER WORLD WITHOUT YOU-MR TORCH!
THE FIRE CHIEF SEEING-THIS, DRAWS HIS GUN AND FIRES-
BUT THE STILL SUPER-HOT SKIN, SAVES THE TORCH FROM DESTRUCTION.. THE LEAD PELLET MELTS, AS IT LANDS BETWEEN THE EYES!-
WITH A GURGLING LAUGH THE HUMAN TORCH WHIRLS AND MAKES A SUDDEN DASH BACK INTO THE BLAZING EMBERS!!-
HE'S BACK-BUT WAIT!-WHAT'S THIS?-HIS FLAME IS OUT!-WHY?!
THERE WAS A TANK OF NITRO UPSTAIRS...COULD IT HAVE BEEN THAT?-IT HAS POSSIBILITIES!!-
-BUT AS THE HUMAN TORCH APPROACHES SARDO, HE AGAIN BURSTS INTO FLAME..
-NOW I'M SURE IT WAS THE NITRO!!-THIS GIVES ME A CHANCE TO STRIKE A BARGAIN!
HERE, YOU CAN HAVE THIS NITRO-IF YOU'LL LET ME GO!
RUSHING TO A CORNER, SARDO GETS A TUBE OF NITRO GAS AND OFFERS IT TO THE HUMAN TORCH!
-BUT THE HUMAN TORCH FLIES FORWARD AND QUICKLY WRESTS THE TANK FROM SARDO'S GRIP!
THANKS! SARDO-THIS'LL COME IN HANDY!-
-BUT AS FOR LETTING YOU GO-NEVER!-
LISTEN,-I'LL DO ANYTHING YOU SAY-ONLY DON'T BURN ME!-
-YOU RAT!-YOU SHOULD HAVE THOUGHT OF THAT, BEFORE YOU DECIDED TO MAKE ME THE GOAT FOR YOUR RACKET!-
13
THE HUMAN TORCH SPRINGS INTO ACTION AND STARTS DESTROYING SARDO'S LABORATORY!-
THEN LEAPING IN APE-LIKE FASHION-HE RIPS THE CHEMICAL-LADEN SHELVES DOWN!
NOW'S MY LAST-AND FINAL CHANCE TO GET HIM!-
WITH SEEMINGLY FIENDISH DELIGHT, THE HUMAN-TORCH COMPLETELY WRECKS THE LAB-AS SARDO SNEAKS AWAY TO A CORNER...
...WHERE HE GRIPS A TANK OF SULPHURIC ACID-THEN SNEAKS UP BEHIND THE TORCH!
BOOM
HURLING THE TANK-IT EXPLODES BEFORE IT EVEN TOUCHES THE HUMAN TORCH!-
POOR FOOL-KILLED BY HIS OWN HAND-
GRABBING AN INSULATED TANK OF NITROGEN, THE ONLY GAS THAT WILL CONTROL HIS FLAME, THE TORCH WALKS OUT OF THE BURNING LAB-
WE HEARD AN EXPLOSION OUT HERE!-WHAT WAS IT?-
-A RAT DEALT OUT JUSTICE TO HIMSELF, HORTON!
14
HEY CHIEF!-I JUST SAW HORTON TALKING TO THE TORCH!
SO!-IT'S MORE OF THE TORCH'S WORK, EH?-
THE POLICE, ATTRACTED BY THE BLAZE AND EXPLOSION, RUSH TO THE SCENE!-

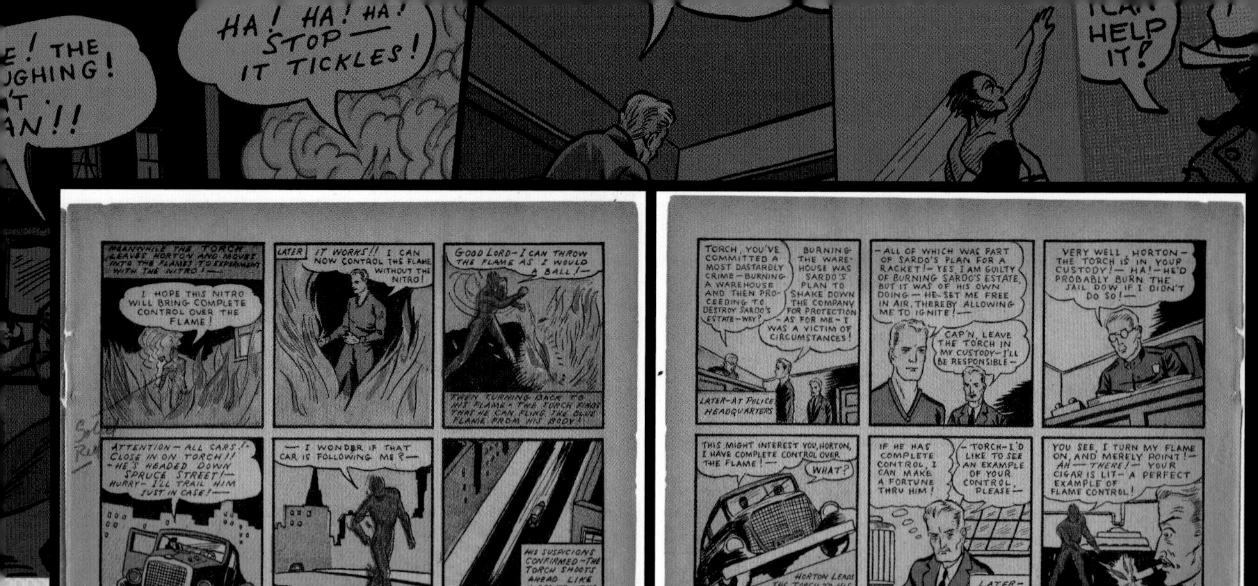

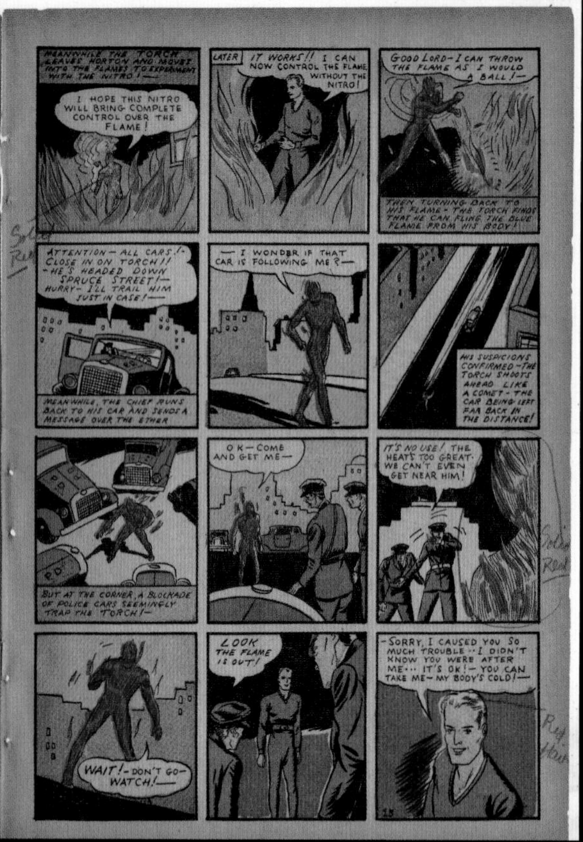
MEANWHILE THE TORCH LEAVES HORTON AND MOVES INTO THE FLAMES TO EXPERIMENT WITH THE NITRO!—
I HOPE THIS NITRO WILL BRING COMPLETE CONTROL OVER THE FLAME!
LATER
IT WORKS!! I CAN NOW CONTROL THE FLAME WITHOUT THE NITRO!
GOOD LORD—I CAN THROW THE FLAME AS I WOULD A BALL!—
THEN TURNING BACK TO HIS FLAME—THE TORCH FINDS THAT HE CAN FLING THE BLUE FLAME FROM HIS BODY!
ATTENTION—ALL CARS!—CLOSE IN ON TORCH!! —HE'S HEADED DOWN SPRUCE STREET!— HURRY—I'LL TRAIL HIM JUST IN CASE!—
MEANWHILE, THE CHIEF RUNS BACK TO HIS CAR AND SENDS A MESSAGE OVER THE ETHER
—I WONDER IF THAT CAR IS FOLLOWING ME?—
HIS SUSPICIONS CONFIRMED—THE TORCH SHOOTS AHEAD LIKE A COMET—THE CAR BEING LEFT FAR BACK IN THE DISTANCE!
BUT AT THE CORNER, A BLOCKADE OF POLICE CARS SEEMINGLY TRAP THE TORCH!—
O K—COME AND GET ME—
IT'S NO USE! THE HEAT'S TOO GREAT. WE CAN'T EVEN GET NEAR HIM!
WAIT!—DON'T GO—WATCH!—
LOOK THE FLAME IS OUT!
—SORRY, I CAUSED YOU SO MUCH TROUBLE··I DIDN'T KNOW YOU WERE AFTER ME··· IT'S OK!—YOU CAN TAKE ME—MY BODY'S COLD!—

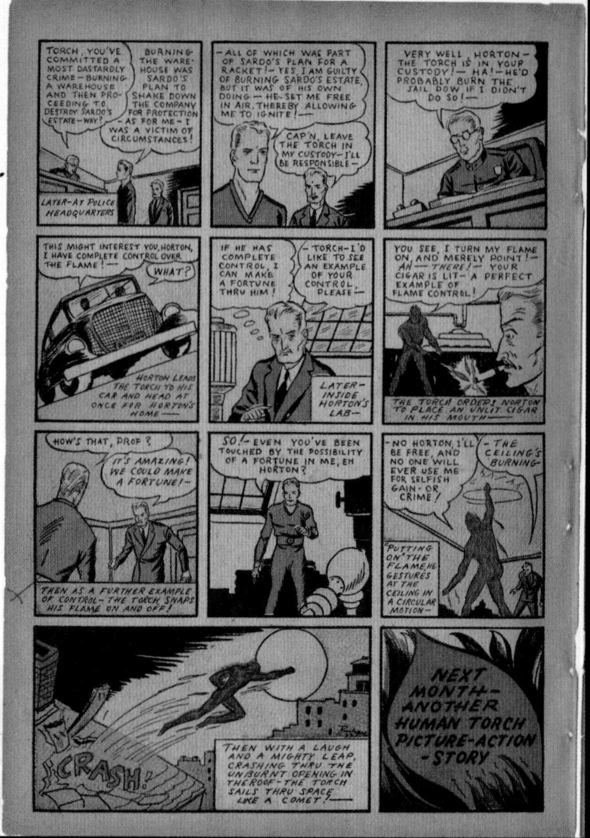
TORCH, YOU'VE COMMITTED A MOST DASTARDLY CRIME—BURNING A WAREHOUSE AND THEN PROCEEDING TO DESTROY SARDO'S ESTATE—WAY?
BURNING THE WAREHOUSE WAS SARDO'S PLAN TO SHAKE DOWN THE COMPANY FOR PROTECTION —AS FOR ME—I WAS A VICTIM OF CIRCUMSTANCES!
LATER—AT POLICE HEADQUARTERS
—ALL OF WHICH WAS PART OF SARDO'S PLAN FOR A RACKET!—YES, I AM GUILTY OF BURNING SARDO'S ESTATE, BUT IT WAS OF HIS OWN DOING—HE SET ME FREE IN AIR, THEREBY ALLOWING ME TO IGNITE!—
CAP'N, LEAVE THE TORCH IN MY CUSTODY—I'LL BE RESPONSIBLE—
VERY WELL, HORTON—THE TORCH IS IN YOUR CUSTODY!—HA!—HE'D PROBABLY BURN THE JAIL DOW IF I DIDN'T DO SO!—
THIS MIGHT INTEREST YOU, HORTON, I HAVE COMPLETE CONTROL OVER THE FLAME!—
WHAT?
HORTON LEADS THE TORCH TO HIS CAR AND HEAD AT ONCE FOR HORTON'S HOME—
IF HE HAS COMPLETE CONTROL, I CAN MAKE A FORTUNE THRU HIM!
—TORCH—I'D LIKE TO SEE AN EXAMPLE OF YOUR CONTROL, PLEASE!—
LATER—INSIDE HORTON'S LAB—
YOU SEE, I TURN MY FLAME ON, AND MERELY POINT!— AH—THERE!—YOUR CIGAR IS LIT—A PERFECT EXAMPLE OF FLAME CONTROL!
THE TORCH ORDERS NORTON TO PLACE AN UNLIT CIGAR IN HIS MOUTH—
HOW'S THAT, PROF?
IT'S AMAZING! WE COULD MAKE A FORTUNE!—
THEN AS A FURTHER EXAMPLE OF CONTROL—THE TORCH SNAPS HIS FLAME ON AND OFF!
SO!—EVEN YOU'VE BEEN TOUCHED BY THE POSSIBILITY OF A FORTUNE IN ME, EH HORTON?
—NO HORTON, I'LL BE FREE, AND NO ONE WILL EVER USE ME FOR SELFISH GAIN—OR CRIME!
—THE CEILING'S BURNING—
"PUTTING ON" THE FLAME, HE GESTURES AT THE CEILING IN A CIRCULAR MOTION—
CRASH!
THEN WITH A LAUGH AND A MIGHTY LEAP, CRASHING THRU THE UNBURNT OPENING IN THE ROOF—THE TORCH SAILS THRU SPACE LIKE A COMET!—
NEXT MONTH—ANOTHER HUMAN TORCH PICTURE-ACTION -STORY

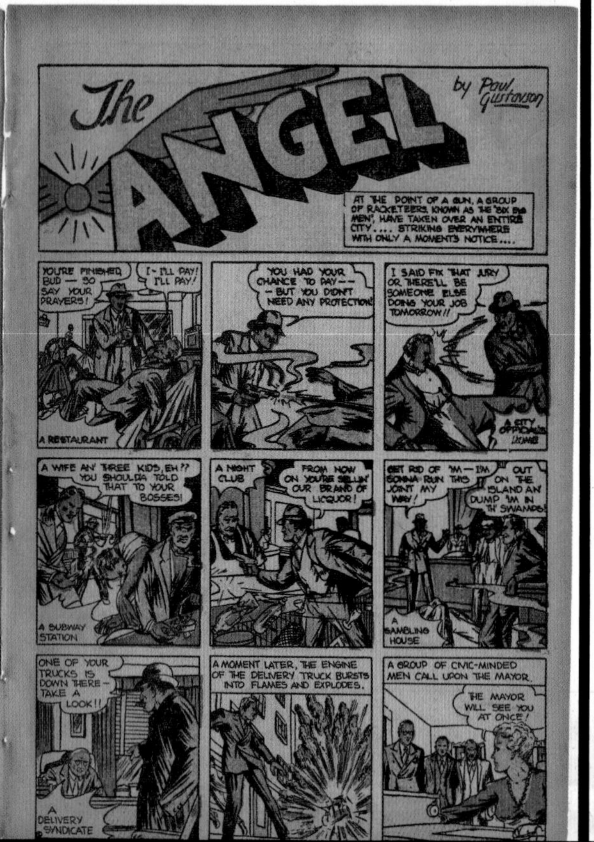
The ANGEL
by Paul Gustavson
AT THE POINT OF A GUN, A GROUP OF RACKETEERS, KNOWN AS THE "SIX BIG MEN", HAVE TAKEN OVER AN ENTIRE CITY.... STRIKING EVERYWHERE WITH ONLY A MOMENT'S NOTICE....
YOU'RE FINISHED, BUD — SO SAY YOUR PRAYERS!
I—I'LL PAY! I'LL PAY!
A RESTAURANT
YOU HAD YOUR CHANCE TO PAY—— —BUT YOU DIDN'T NEED ANY PROTECTION!
I SAID FIX THAT JURY OR THERE'LL BE SOMEONE ELSE DOING YOUR JOB TOMORROW!!
A CITY OFFICIAL'S HOME
A WIFE AN' THREE KIDS, EH?? YOU SHOULDA TOLD THAT TO YOUR BOSSES!
A SUBWAY STATION
A NIGHT CLUB
FROM NOW ON YOU'RE SELLIN' OUR BRAND OF LICQUOR!
GET RID OF 'IM—I'M GONNA RUN THIS JOINT MY WAY!
OUT ON THE ISLAND AN' DUMP 'IM IN TH' SWAMPS!
A GAMBLING HOUSE
ONE OF YOUR TRUCKS IS DOWN THERE—TAKE A LOOK!!
A DELIVERY SYNDICATE
A MOMENT LATER, THE ENGINE OF THE DELIVERY TRUCK BURSTS INTO FLAMES AND EXPLODES.
A GROUP OF CIVIC-MINDED MEN CALL UPON THE MAYOR.
THE MAYOR WILL SEE YOU AT ONCE!

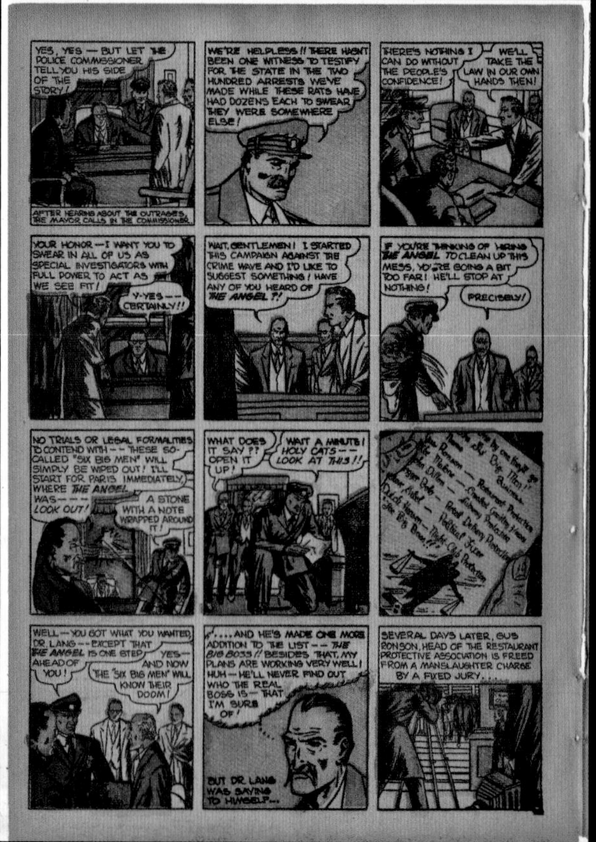
YES, YES — BUT LET THE POLICE COMMISSIONER TELL YOU HIS SIDE OF THE STORY!
AFTER HEARING ABOUT THE OUTRAGES, THE MAYOR CALLS IN THE COMMISSIONER.
WE'RE HELPLESS!! THERE HASN'T BEEN ONE WITNESS TO TESTIFY FOR THE STATE IN THE TWO HUNDRED ARRESTS WE'VE MADE WHILE THESE RATS HAVE HAD DOZENS EACH TO SWEAR THEY WERE SOMEWHERE ELSE!
THERE'S NOTHING I CAN DO WITHOUT THE PEOPLE'S CONFIDENCE!
WE'LL TAKE THE LAW IN OUR OWN HANDS THEN!
YOUR HONOR—I WANT YOU TO SWEAR IN ALL OF US AS SPECIAL INVESTIGATORS WITH FULL POWER TO ACT AS WE SEE FIT!
Y-YES——CERTAINLY!!
WAIT, GENTLEMEN! I STARTED THIS CAMPAIGN AGAINST THE CRIME WAVE AND I'D LIKE TO SUGGEST SOMETHING! HAVE ANY OF YOU HEARD OF THE ANGEL?!
IF YOU'RE THINKING OF HIRING THE ANGEL TO CLEAN UP THIS MESS, YOU'RE GOING A BIT TOO FAR! HE'LL STOP AT NOTHING!
PRECISELY!
NO TRIALS OR LEGAL FORMALITIES TO CONTEND WITH —— THESE SO-CALLED "SIX BIG MEN" WILL SIMPLY BE WIPED OUT! I'LL START FOR PARIS IMMEDIATELY, WHERE THE ANGEL WAS——— LOOK OUT!
A STONE WITH A NOTE WRAPPED AROUND IT!
WHAT DOES IT SAY?? OPEN IT UP!
WAIT A MINUTE! HOLY CATS—— LOOK AT THIS!!
WELL—YOU GOT WHAT YOU WANTED, DR. LANG——EXCEPT THAT THE ANGEL IS ONE STEP AHEAD OF YOU!
YES— AND NOW THE "SIX BIG MEN" WILL KNOW THEIR DOOM!
"....AND HE'S MADE ONE MORE ADDITION TO THE LIST —— THE BIG BOSS!! BESIDES THAT, MY PLANS ARE WORKING VERY WELL! HUH—HE'LL NEVER FIND OUT WHO THE REAL BOSS IS—THAT I'M SURE OF!
BUT DR LANG WAS SAYING TO HIMSELF...
SEVERAL DAYS LATER, GUS RONSON, HEAD OF THE RESTAURANT PROTECTIVE ASSOCIATION IS FREED FROM A MANSLAUGHTER CHARGE BY A FIXED JURY....

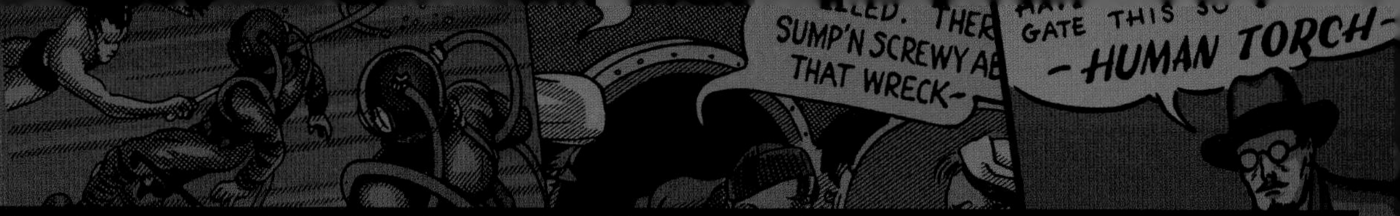
SUMP'N SCREWY AB
THAT WRECK-
GATE THIS
-HUMAN TORCH-

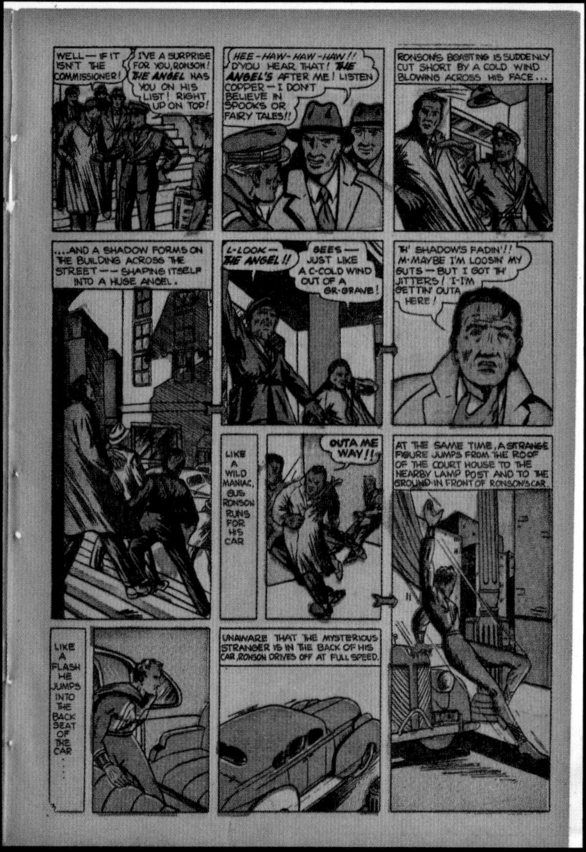
WELL — IF IT ISN'T THE COMMISSIONER!
I'VE A SURPRISE FOR YOU, RONSON! THE ANGEL HAS YOU ON HIS LIST! RIGHT UP ON TOP!
HEE-HAW-HAW-HAW!! D'YOU HEAR THAT! THE ANGEL'S AFTER ME! LISTEN COPPER — I DON'T BELIEVE IN SPOOKS OR FAIRY TALES!!
RONSON'S BOASTING IS SUDDENLY CUT SHORT BY A COLD WIND BLOWING ACROSS HIS FACE...
...AND A SHADOW FORMS ON THE BUILDING ACROSS THE STREET — SHAPING ITSELF INTO A HUGE ANGEL.
L-LOOK — THE ANGEL!!
GEES — JUST LIKE A C-COLD WIND OUT OF A GR-GRAVE!
TH' SHADOW'S FADIN'!! M-MAYBE I'M LOOSIN' MY GUTS — BUT I GOT TH' JITTERS! I-I'M GETTIN' OUTA HERE!
LIKE A WILD MANIAC, GUS RONSON RUNS FOR HIS CAR
OUTA ME WAY!!
AT THE SAME TIME, A STRANGE FIGURE JUMPS FROM THE ROOF OF THE COURT HOUSE TO THE NEARBY LAMP POST AND TO THE GROUND IN FRONT OF RONSON'S CAR.
LIKE A FLASH HE JUMPS INTO THE BACK SEAT OF THE CAR...
UNAWARE THAT THE MYSTERIOUS STRANGER IS IN THE BACK OF HIS CAR, RONSON DRIVES OFF AT FULL SPEED.

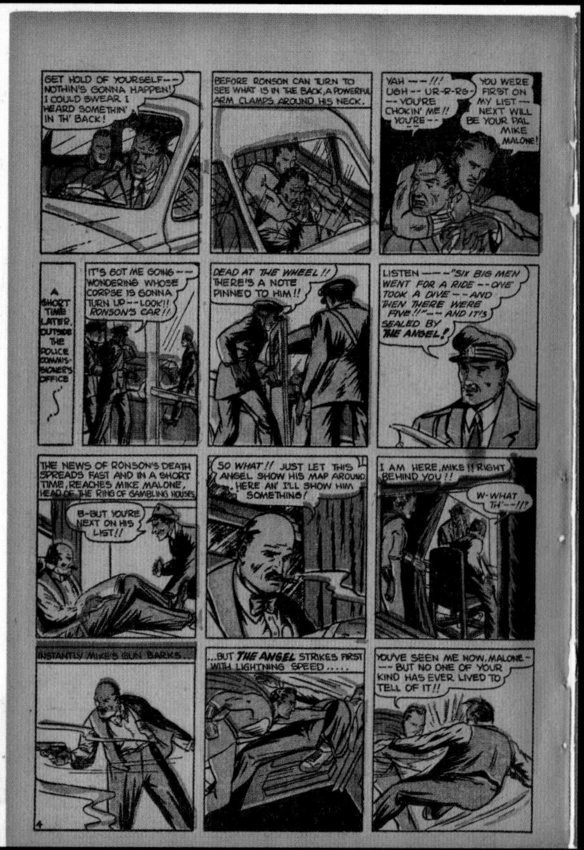
GET HOLD OF YOURSELF — NOTHIN'S GONNA HAPPEN! I COULD SWEAR I HEARD SOMETHIN' IN TH' BACK!
BEFORE RONSON CAN TURN TO SEE WHAT IS IN THE BACK, A POWERFUL ARM CLAMPS AROUND HIS NECK.
YAH ——!!! UGH — UR-R-RG — YOU'RE CHOKIN' ME!! YOU'RE —
YOU WERE FIRST ON MY LIST — NEXT WILL BE YOUR PAL MIKE MALONE!
A SHORT TIME LATER, OUTSIDE THE POLICE COMMISSIONER'S OFFICE
IT'S GOT ME GOING — WONDERING WHOSE CORPSE IS GONNA TURN UP — LOOK!! RONSON'S CAR!!
DEAD AT THE WHEEL!! THERE'S A NOTE PINNED TO HIM!!
LISTEN —— "SIX BIG MEN WENT FOR A RIDE — ONE TOOK A DIVE — AND THEN THERE WERE FIVE!!" — AND IT'S SEALED BY THE ANGEL!
THE NEWS OF RONSON'S DEATH SPREADS FAST AND IN A SHORT TIME, REACHES MIKE MALONE, HEAD OF THE RING OF GAMBLING HOUSES.
B-BUT YOU'RE NEXT ON HIS LIST!!
SO WHAT!! JUST LET THIS ANGEL SHOW HIS MAP AROUND HERE AN' I'LL SHOW HIM SOMETHING!
I AM HERE, MIKE!! RIGHT BEHIND YOU!!
W-WHAT TH' —!!?
INSTANTLY MIKE'S GUN BARKS...
...BUT THE ANGEL STRIKES FIRST WITH LIGHTNING SPEED.....
YOU'VE SEEN ME NOW, MALONE — BUT NO ONE OF YOUR KIND HAS EVER LIVED TO TELL OF IT!!
4

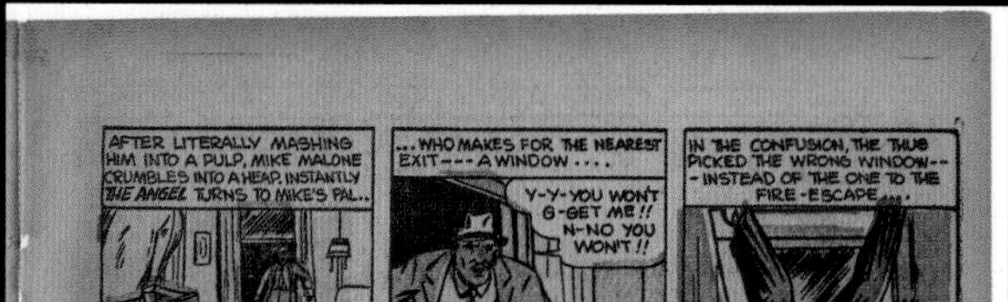
AFTER LITERALLY MASHING HIM INTO A PULP, MIKE MALONE CRUMBLES INTO A HEAP. INSTANTLY THE ANGEL TURNS TO MIKE'S PAL...
...WHO MAKES FOR THE NEAREST EXIT — A WINDOW....
Y-Y-YOU WON'T G-GET ME!! N-NO YOU WON'T!!
IN THE CONFUSION, THE THUG PICKED THE WRONG WINDOW — INSTEAD OF THE ONE TO THE FIRE-ESCAPE....
MEANWHILE, A WOMAN QUIETLY OPENS THE DOOR AND PLACES A NOTE ON THE TABLE FOR THE ANGEL...
"YOU CAN CROSS NUMBER THREE OFF YOUR LIST — HE WAS THE ONE THAT WENT THROUGH THE WINDOW! NUMBER FOUR IS WAITING FOR YOU — BE CAREFUL!!"
QUICKLY, THE ANGEL RUSHES INTO THE HALL TO SEE WHO HAD LEFT THE NOTE FOR HIM, ONLY TO GET A GLIMPSE OF A WOMAN ENTERING THE ELEVATOR....
H-M-M-M!! IT LOOKS AS IF THERE ARE OTHER THAN CIVIC REASONS WHY THESE MEN ARE TO BE DONE AWAY WITH! VERY INTERESTING — SO NUMBER FOUR IS WAITING FOR ME!!
WHILE IN ONE OF THE UNDERWORLD'S DENS, TRIGGER BOLO, HEAD OF THE RETAIL-DELIVERY PROTECTIVE ASSOCIATION, WAITS FOR THE ANGEL.
ALL SET TRIGGER
SO THE ANGEL'S GONNA DO AWAY WITH ME EH?! MY TRIGGER FINGER'S ITCHIN', SO SEE THAT YOU BRING HIM IN HERE!!
WE GOTCHA, BOSS!
NICE HOLE TRIGGER HAS — FIT FOR ONLY RATS TO LIVE IN!!
THAT'S RIGHT — BE NICE AND QUIET!!
5

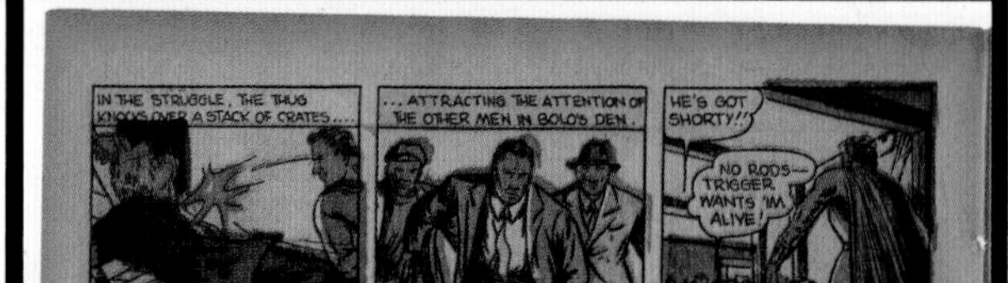
IN THE STRUGGLE, THE THUG KNOCKS OVER A STACK OF CRATES....
...ATTRACTING THE ATTENTION OF THE OTHER MEN IN BOLO'S DEN.
HE'S GOT SHORTY!!
NO RODS — TRIGGER WANTS 'IM ALIVE!
SEEING THE GUNMEN RUSHING TOWARD HIM, THE ANGEL COUNTER-ATTACKS WITH THE FURY OF A CHARGING LION!
BUT CANNOT WITHSTAND THE TREMENDOUS ODDS AGAINST HIM.
GOT HIS HANDS TIED?
YEAH!
GOOD WORK, BOYS! SO YOU WERE GONNA GET RID OF ME, EH!! UP AGAINST THE WALL WITH 'IM!!
AT THAT MOMENT, THE MYSTERIOUS WOMAN THAT LEFT THE WARNING NOTE FOR THE ANGEL STEPS INTO THE ROOM.
NOT HERE, TRIGGER! THAT'S AN ORDER!
SEE THIS TOMMY-GUN! IT'S GONNA CUT YOU TO PIECES — VERY SLOWLY!
OK — STAND BACK, BOYS!

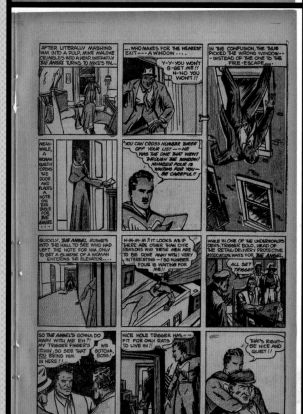

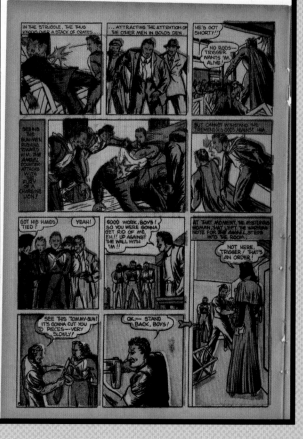

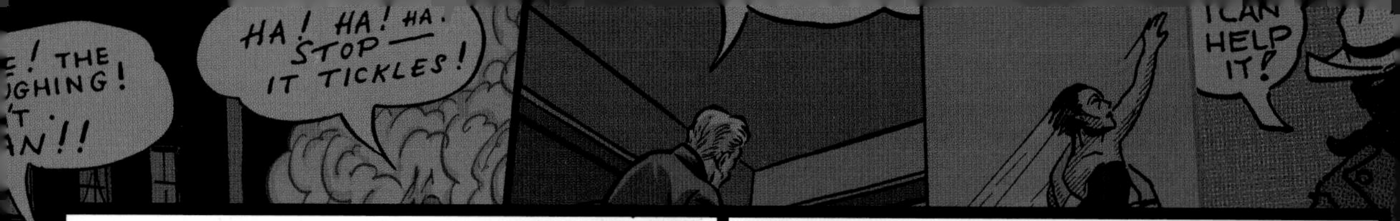

HA! HA! HA.
STOP—
IT TICKLES!
HELP IT!

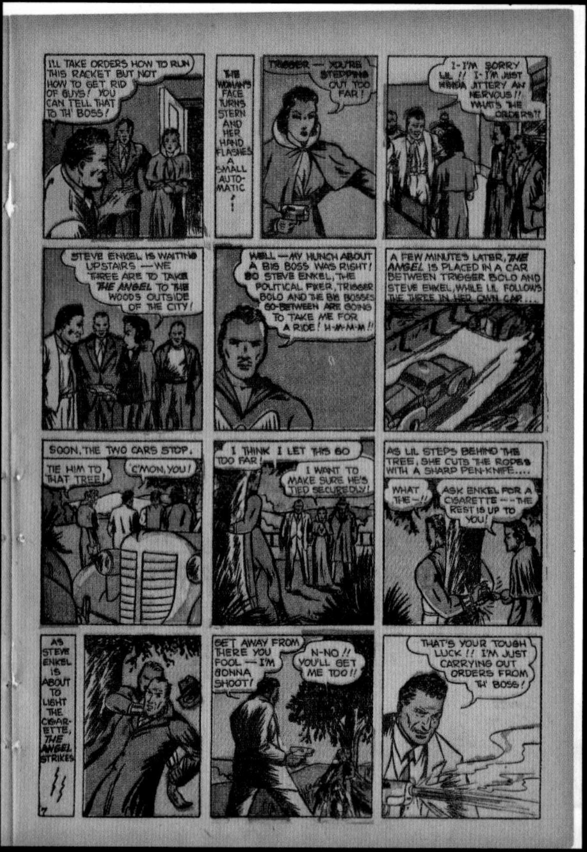

I'LL TAKE ORDERS HOW TO RUN THIS RACKET BUT NOT HOW TO GET RID OF GUYS! YOU CAN TELL THAT TO TH' BOSS!
THE WOMAN'S FACE TURNS STERN AND HER HAND FLASHES A SMALL AUTOMATIC!
TRIGGER — YOU'RE STEPPING OUT TOO FAR!
I-I'M SORRY LIL!! I-I'M JUST KINDA JITTERY AN' NERVOUS!! WHAT'S THE ORDERS?!
STEVE ENKEL IS WAITING UPSTAIRS —WE THREE ARE TO TAKE THE ANGEL TO THE WOODS OUTSIDE OF THE CITY!
WELL —MY HUNCH ABOUT A BIG BOSS WAS RIGHT! SO STEVE ENKEL, THE POLITICAL FIXER, TRIGGER BOLO AND THE BIG BOSS'S GO-BETWEEN ARE GOING TO TAKE ME FOR A RIDE! H-M-M-M!!
A FEW MINUTES LATER, THE ANGEL IS PLACED IN A CAR BETWEEN TRIGGER BOLO AND STEVE ENKEL, WHILE LIL FOLLOWS THE THREE IN HER OWN CAR....
SOON, THE TWO CARS STOP.
TIE HIM TO THAT TREE!
C'MON, YOU!
I THINK I LET THIS GO TOO FAR!
I WANT TO MAKE SURE HE'S TIED SECURELY!
AS LIL STEPS BEHIND THE TREE, SHE CUTS THE ROPES WITH A SHARP PEN-KNIFE....
WHAT THE--!!
ASK ENKEL FOR A CIGARETTE -- THE REST IS UP TO YOU!
AS STEVE ENKEL IS ABOUT TO LIGHT THE CIGARETTE, THE ANGEL STRIKES!
GET AWAY FROM THERE YOU FOOL —I'M GONNA SHOOT!
N-NO!! YOU'LL GET ME TOO!!
THAT'S YOUR TOUGH LUCK!! I'M JUST CARRYING OUT ORDERS FROM TH' BOSS!

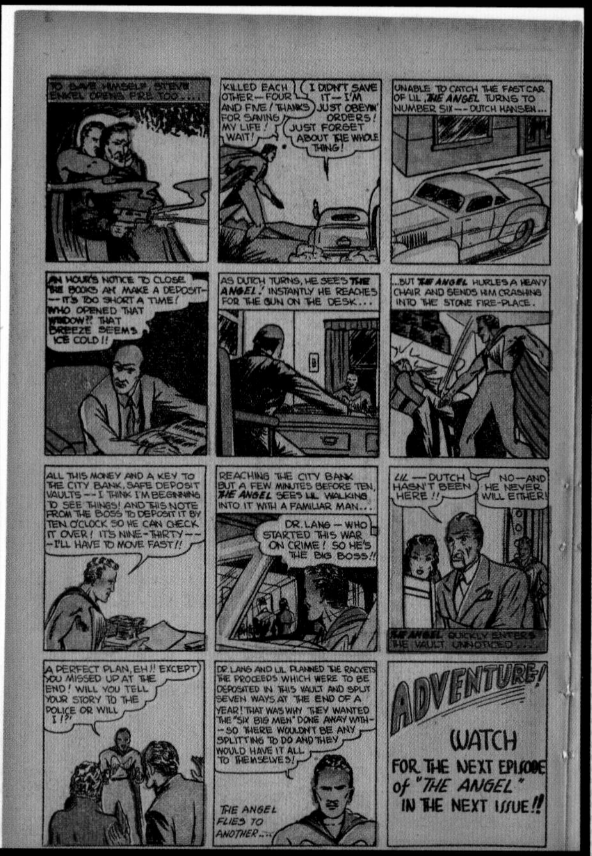

TO SAVE HIMSELF, STEVE ENKEL OPENS FIRE TOO.....
KILLED EACH OTHER—FOUR AND FIVE! THANKS FOR SAVING MY LIFE! WAIT!
I DIDN'T SAVE IT—I'M JUST OBEYIN' ORDERS! JUST FORGET ABOUT THE WHOLE THING!
UNABLE TO CATCH THE FAST CAR OF LIL, THE ANGEL TURNS TO NUMBER SIX--DUTCH HANSEN...
AN HOUR'S NOTICE TO CLOSE THE BOOKS AN' MAKE A DEPOSIT--IT'S TOO SHORT A TIME! WHO OPENED THAT WINDOW?! THAT BREEZE SEEMS ICE COLD!!
AS DUTCH TURNS, HE SEES THE ANGEL! INSTANTLY HE REACHES FOR THE GUN ON THE DESK...
...BUT THE ANGEL HURLS A HEAVY CHAIR AND SENDS HIM CRASHING INTO THE STONE FIRE-PLACE.
ALL THIS MONEY AND A KEY TO THE CITY BANK SAFE DEPOSIT VAULTS--I THINK I'M BEGINNING TO SEE THINGS! AND THIS NOTE FROM THE BOSS TO DEPOSIT IT BY TEN O'CLOCK SO HE CAN CHECK IT OVER! IT'S NINE-THIRTY---I'LL HAVE TO MOVE FAST!!
REACHING THE CITY BANK BUT A FEW MINUTES BEFORE TEN, THE ANGEL SEES LIL WALKING INTO IT WITH A FAMILIAR MAN...
DR. LANG — WHO STARTED THIS WAR ON CRIME! SO HE'S THE BIG BOSS!!
LIL — DUTCH HASN'T BEEN HERE!!
NO—AND HE NEVER WILL EITHER!
THE ANGEL QUICKLY ENTERS THE VAULT UNNOTICED....
A PERFECT PLAN, EH!! EXCEPT YOU MISSED UP AT THE END! WILL YOU TELL YOUR STORY TO THE POLICE OR WILL I!?
DR. LANG AND LIL PLANNED THE RACKETS THE PROCEEDS WHICH WERE TO BE DEPOSITED IN THIS VAULT AND SPLIT SEVEN WAYS AT THE END OF A YEAR! THAT WAS WHY THEY WANTED THE "SIX BIG MEN" DONE AWAY WITH--SO THERE WOULDN'T BE ANY SPLITTING TO DO AND THEY WOULD HAVE IT ALL TO THEMSELVES!
THE ANGEL FLIES TO ANOTHER....
ADVENTURE!
WATCH FOR THE NEXT EPISODE of "THE ANGEL" IN THE NEXT ISSUE!!

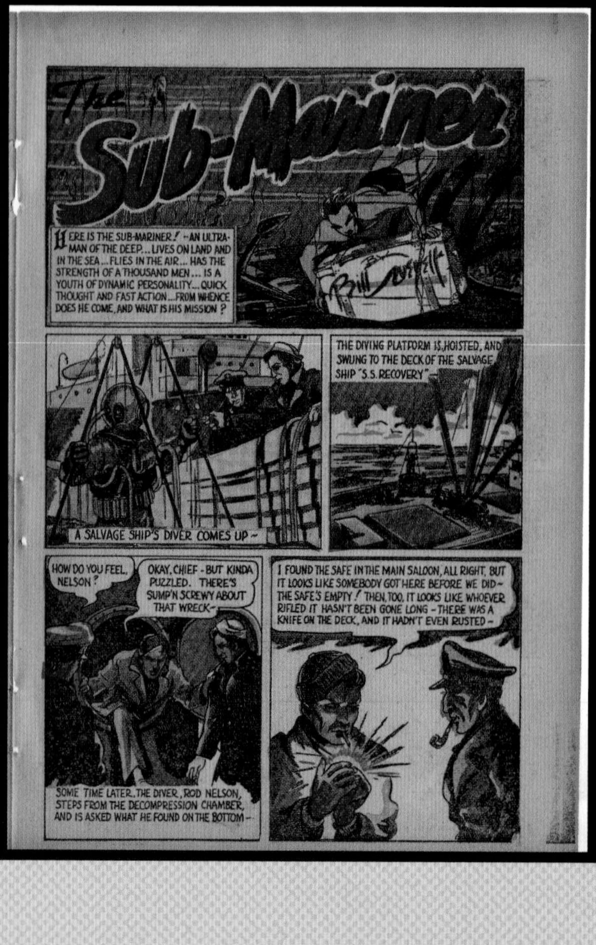

The Sub-Mariner
HERE IS THE SUB-MARINER! —AN ULTRA-MAN OF THE DEEP... LIVES ON LAND AND IN THE SEA... FLIES IN THE AIR... HAS THE STRENGTH OF A THOUSAND MEN... IS A YOUTH OF DYNAMIC PERSONALITY... QUICK THOUGHT AND FAST ACTION... FROM WHENCE DOES HE COME, AND WHAT IS HIS MISSION?
A SALVAGE SHIP'S DIVER COMES UP~
THE DIVING PLATFORM IS HOISTED, AND SWUNG TO THE DECK OF THE SALVAGE SHIP "S.S. RECOVERY"~
HOW DO YOU FEEL, NELSON?
OKAY, CHIEF - BUT KINDA PUZZLED. THERE'S SUMP'N SCREWY ABOUT THAT WRECK~
SOME TIME LATER, THE DIVER, ROD NELSON, STEPS FROM THE DECOMPRESSION CHAMBER, AND IS ASKED WHAT HE FOUND ON THE BOTTOM~
I FOUND THE SAFE IN THE MAIN SALOON, ALL RIGHT, BUT IT LOOKS LIKE SOMEBODY GOT HERE BEFORE WE DID - THE SAFE'S EMPTY! THEN, TOO, IT LOOKS LIKE WHOEVER RIFLED IT HASN'T BEEN GONE LONG - THERE WAS A KNIFE ON THE DECK, AND IT HADN'T EVEN RUSTED -

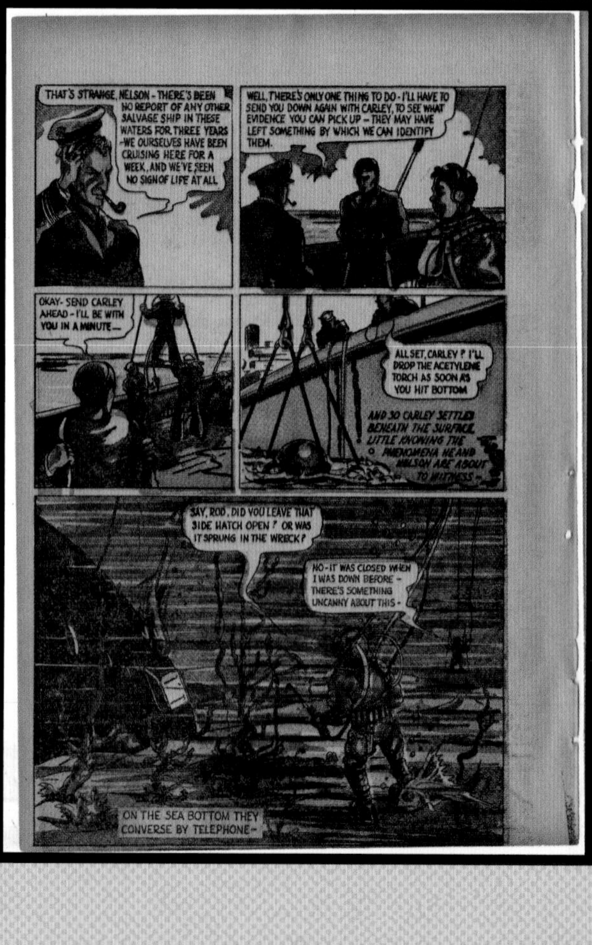

THAT'S STRANGE, NELSON - THERE'S BEEN NO REPORT OF ANY OTHER SALVAGE SHIP IN THESE WATERS FOR THREE YEARS - WE OURSELVES HAVE BEEN CRUISING HERE FOR A WEEK, AND WE'VE SEEN NO SIGN OF LIFE AT ALL
WELL, THERE'S ONLY ONE THING TO DO - I'LL HAVE TO SEND YOU DOWN AGAIN WITH CARLEY, TO SEE WHAT EVIDENCE YOU CAN PICK UP - THEY MAY HAVE LEFT SOMETHING BY WHICH WE CAN IDENTIFY THEM.
OKAY - SEND CARLEY AHEAD - I'LL BE WITH YOU IN A MINUTE—
ALL SET, CARLEY? I'LL DROP THE ACETYLENE TORCH AS SOON AS YOU HIT BOTTOM
AND SO CARLEY SETTLED BENEATH THE SURFACE, LITTLE KNOWING THE PHENOMENA HE AND NELSON ARE ABOUT TO WITNESS~
SAY, ROD, DID YOU LEAVE THAT SIDE HATCH OPEN? OR WAS IT SPRUNG IN THE WRECK?
NO - IT WAS CLOSED WHEN I WAS DOWN BEFORE - THERE'S SOMETHING UNCANNY ABOUT THIS -
ON THE SEA BOTTOM THEY CONVERSE BY TELEPHONE~

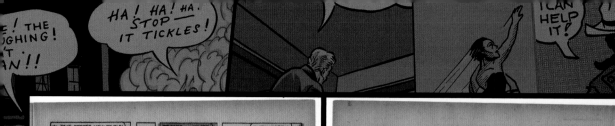

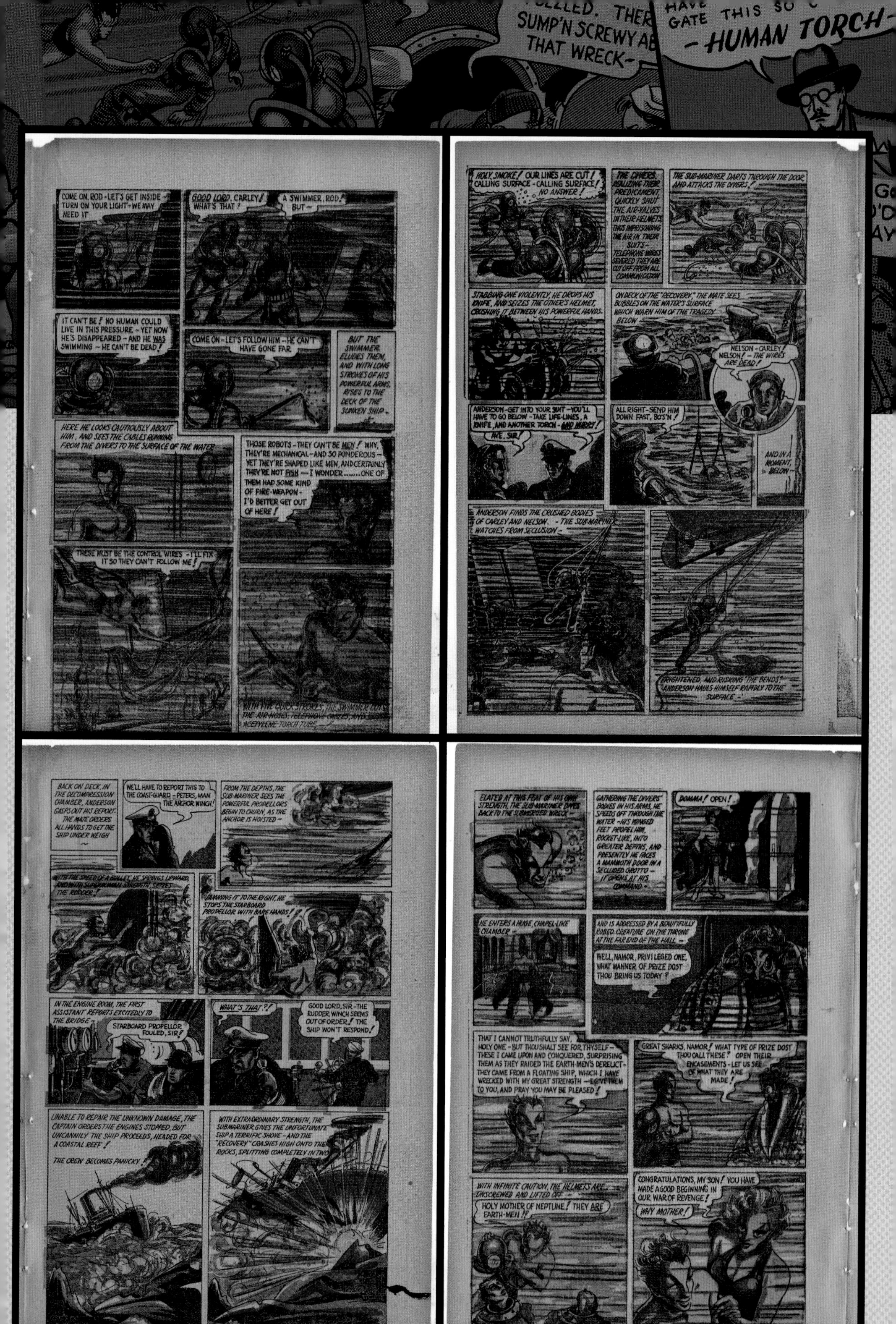
COME ON, ROD - LET'S GET INSIDE - TURN ON YOUR LIGHT - WE MAY NEED IT
GOOD LORD, CARLEY! WHAT'S THAT?
A SWIMMER, ROD! BUT -
IT CAN'T BE! NO HUMAN COULD LIVE IN THIS PRESSURE - YET NOW HE'S DISAPPEARED - AND HE WAS SWIMMING - HE CAN'T BE DEAD!
COME ON - LET'S FOLLOW HIM - HE CAN'T HAVE GONE FAR
BUT THE SWIMMER ELUDES THEM, AND WITH LONG STROKES OF HIS POWERFUL ARMS, RISES TO THE DECK OF THE SUNKEN SHIP -
HERE HE LOOKS CAUTIOUSLY ABOUT HIM, AND SEES THE CABLES RUNNING FROM THE DIVERS TO THE SURFACE OF THE WATER -
THOSE ROBOTS - THEY CAN'T BE MEN! WHY, THEY'RE MECHANICAL - AND SO PONDEROUS - YET THEY'RE SHAPED LIKE MEN, AND CERTAINLY THEY'RE NOT FISH — I WONDER....... ONE OF THEM HAD SOME KIND OF FIRE-WEAPON - I'D BETTER GET OUT OF HERE!
THESE MUST BE THE CONTROL WIRES - I'LL FIX IT SO THEY CAN'T FOLLOW ME!
WITH FIVE QUICK STROKES, THE SWIMMER CUTS THE AIR-HOSES, TELEPHONE CABLES, AND ACETYLENE TORCH TUBE -
HOLY SMOKE! OUR LINES ARE CUT! CALLING SURFACE - CALLING SURFACE! NO ANSWER!
THE DIVERS, REALIZING THEIR PREDICAMENT, QUICKLY SHUT THE AIR-VALVES IN THEIR HELMETS, THUS IMPRISONING THE AIR IN THEIR SUITS - TELEPHONE WIRES SEVERED THEY ARE CUT OFF FROM ALL COMMUNICATION
THE SUB-MARINER DARTS THROUGH THE DOOR AND ATTACKS THE DIVERS!
STABBING ONE VIOLENTLY, HE DROPS HIS KNIFE, AND SEIZES THE OTHER'S HELMET, CRUSHING IT BETWEEN HIS POWERFUL HANDS.
ON DECK OF THE "RECOVERY," THE MATE SEES BUBBLES ON THE WATER'S SURFACE WHICH WARN HIM OF THE TRAGEDY BELOW -
NELSON - CARLEY! NELSON! - THE WIRES ARE DEAD!
ANDERSON - GET INTO YOUR SUIT - YOU'LL HAVE TO GO BELOW - TAKE LIFE-LINES, A KNIFE, AND ANOTHER TORCH - AND HURRY!
AYE, SIR!
ALL RIGHT - SEND HIM DOWN FAST, BO'S'N!
AND IN A MOMENT, BELOW -
ANDERSON FINDS THE CRUSHED BODIES OF CARLEY AND NELSON. - THE SUB-MARINER WATCHES FROM SECLUSION -
FRIGHTENED, AND RISKING "THE BENDS," ANDERSON HAULS HIMSELF RAPIDLY TO THE SURFACE -
BACK ON DECK, IN THE DECOMPRESSION CHAMBER, ANDERSON GASPS OUT HIS REPORT - THE MATE ORDERS ALL HANDS TO GET THE SHIP UNDER WEIGH ~
WE'LL HAVE TO REPORT THIS TO THE COAST-GUARD - PETERS, MAN THE ANCHOR WINCH!
FROM THE DEPTHS, THE SUB-MARINER SEES THE POWERFUL PROPELLORS BEGIN TO CHURN, AS THE ANCHOR IS HOISTED -
WITH THE SPEED OF A BULLET, HE SPRINGS UPWARD, AND WITH SUPERHUMAN STRENGTH, SEIZES THE RUDDER!
JAMMING IT TO THE RIGHT, HE STOPS THE STARBOARD PROPELLOR WITH BARE HANDS!
IN THE ENGINE ROOM, THE FIRST ASSISTANT REPORTS EXCITEDLY TO THE BRIDGE -
STARBOARD PROPELLOR FOULED, SIR!
WHAT'S THAT?!
GOOD LORD, SIR - THE RUDDER WINCH SEEMS OUT OF ORDER! THE SHIP WON'T RESPOND!
UNABLE TO REPAIR THE UNKNOWN DAMAGE, THE CAPTAIN ORDERS THE ENGINES STOPPED, BUT UNCANNILY THE SHIP PROCEEDS, HEADED FOR A COASTAL REEF!
THE CREW BECOMES PANICKY!
WITH EXTRAORDINARY STRENGTH, THE SUBMARINER GIVES THE UNFORTUNATE SHIP A TERRIFIC SHOVE - AND THE "RECOVERY" CRASHES HIGH ONTO THE ROCKS, SPLITTING COMPLETELY IN TWO
ELATED AT THIS FEAT OF HIS OWN STRENGTH, THE SUB-MARINER DIVES BACK TO THE SUBMERGED WRECK -
GATHERING THE DIVERS' BODIES IN HIS ARMS, HE SPEEDS OFF THROUGH THE WATER - HIS WINGED FEET PROPEL HIM, ROCKET-LIKE, INTO GREATER DEPTHS, AND PRESENTLY HE FACES A MAMMOTH DOOR IN A SECLUDED GROTTO - IT OPENS AT HIS COMMAND -
DOMMA! OPEN!
HE ENTERS A HUGE, CHAPEL-LIKE CHAMBER -
AND IS ADDRESSED BY A BEAUTIFULLY ROBED CREATURE ON THE THRONE AT THE FAR END OF THE HALL -
WELL, NAMOR, PRIVILEGED ONE, WHAT MANNER OF PRIZE DOST THOU BRING US TODAY?
THAT I CANNOT TRUTHFULLY SAY, HOLY ONE - BUT THOU SHALT SEE FOR THYSELF - THESE I CAME UPON AND CONQUERED, SURPRISING THEM AS THEY RAIDED THE EARTH-MEN'S DERELICT - THEY CAME FROM A FLOATING SHIP, WHICH I HAVE WRECKED WITH MY GREAT STRENGTH - I GIVE THEM TO YOU, AND PRAY YOU MAY BE PLEASED!
GREAT SHARKS, NAMOR! WHAT TYPE OF PRIZE DOST THOU CALL THESE? OPEN THEIR ENCASEMENTS - LET US SEE OF WHAT THEY ARE MADE!
WITH INFINITE CAUTION, THE HELMETS ARE UNSCREWED AND LIFTED OFF -
HOLY MOTHER OF NEPTUNE! THEY ARE EARTH-MEN!!
CONGRATULATIONS, MY SON! YOU HAVE MADE A GOOD BEGINNING IN OUR WAR OF REVENGE!
WHY MOTHER!

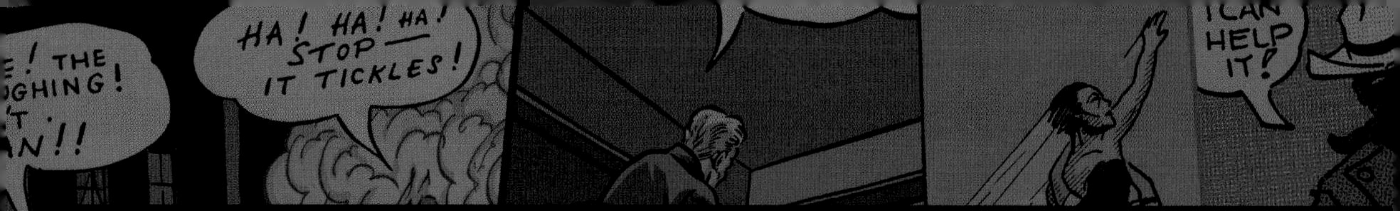
HA! HA! HA! STOP— IT TICKLES!

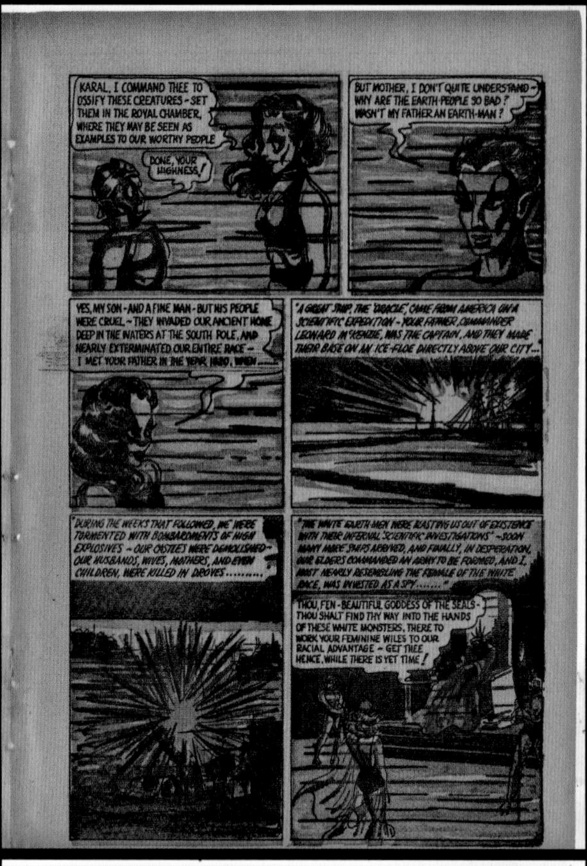
KARAL, I COMMAND THEE TO OSSIFY THESE CREATURES - SET THEM IN THE ROYAL CHAMBER, WHERE THEY MAY BE SEEN AS EXAMPLES TO OUR WORTHY PEOPLE
DONE, YOUR HIGHNESS!
BUT MOTHER, I DON'T QUITE UNDERSTAND - WHY ARE THE EARTH-PEOPLE SO BAD? WASN'T MY FATHER AN EARTH-MAN?
YES, MY SON - AND A FINE MAN - BUT HIS PEOPLE WERE CRUEL ~ THEY INVADED OUR ANCIENT HOME DEEP IN THE WATERS AT THE SOUTH POLE, AND NEARLY EXTERMINATED OUR ENTIRE RACE - I MET YOUR FATHER IN THE YEAR 1920, WHEN .....
"A GREAT SHIP, THE 'ORACLE', CAME FROM AMERICA ON A SCIENTIFIC EXPEDITION - YOUR FATHER, COMMANDER LEONARD M'KENZIE, WAS THE CAPTAIN, AND THEY MADE THEIR BASE ON AN ICE-FLOE DIRECTLY ABOVE OUR CITY..."
"DURING THE WEEKS THAT FOLLOWED, WE WERE TORMENTED WITH BOMBARDMENTS OF HIGH EXPLOSIVES ~ OUR CASTLES WERE DEMOLISHED - OUR HUSBANDS, WIVES, MOTHERS, AND EVEN CHILDREN, WERE KILLED IN DROVES ...."
"THE WHITE EARTH-MEN WERE BLASTING US OUT OF EXISTENCE WITH THEIR INFERNAL 'SCIENTIFIC INVESTIGATIONS' ~ SOON MANY MORE SHIPS ARRIVED, AND FINALLY, IN DESPERATION, OUR ELDERS COMMANDED AN ARMY TO BE FORMED, AND I, MOST NEARLY RESEMBLING THE FEMALE OF THE WHITE RACE, WAS INVESTED AS A SPY ......"
THOU, FEN - BEAUTIFUL GODDESS OF THE SEALS - THOU SHALT FIND THY WAY INTO THE HANDS OF THESE WHITE MONSTERS, THERE TO WORK YOUR FEMININE WILES TO OUR RACIAL ADVANTAGE ~ GET THEE HENCE, WHILE THERE IS YET TIME!

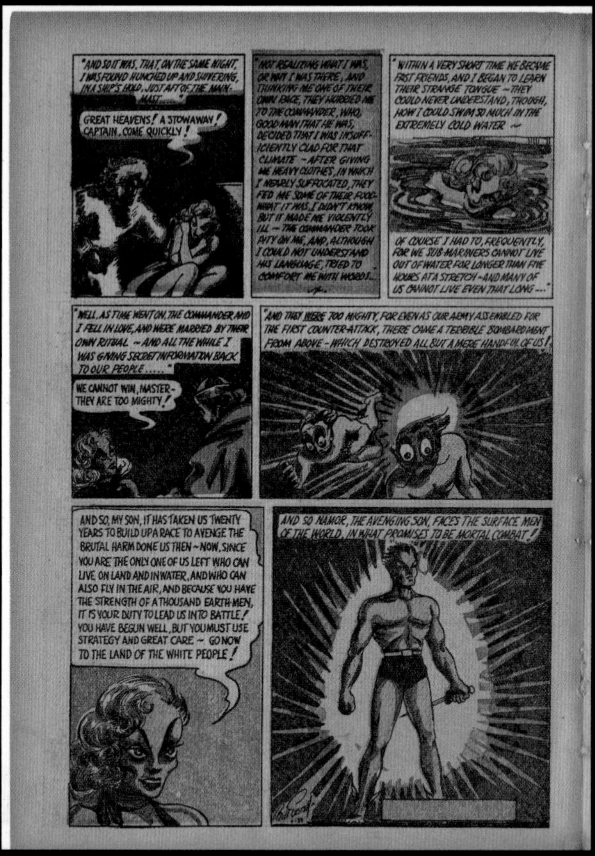
"AND SO IT WAS, THAT, ON THE SAME NIGHT, I WAS FOUND HUNCHED UP AND SHIVERING, IN A SHIP'S HOLD, JUST AFT OF THE MAIN-MAST ....."
GREAT HEAVENS! A STOWAWAY! CAPTAIN, COME QUICKLY!
"NOT REALIZING WHAT I WAS, OR WHY I WAS THERE, AND THINKING ME ONE OF THEIR OWN RACE, THEY HURRIED ME TO THE COMMANDER, WHO, GOOD MAN THAT HE WAS, DECIDED THAT I WAS INSUFFICIENTLY CLAD FOR THAT CLIMATE ~ AFTER GIVING ME HEAVY CLOTHES, IN WHICH I NEARLY SUFFOCATED, THEY FED ME SOME OF THEIR FOOD - WHAT IT WAS, I DIDN'T KNOW, BUT IT MADE ME VIOLENTLY ILL ~ THE COMMANDER TOOK PITY ON ME, AND, ALTHOUGH I COULD NOT UNDERSTAND HIS LANGUAGE, TRIED TO COMFORT ME WITH WORDS..."
"WITHIN A VERY SHORT TIME WE BECAME FAST FRIENDS, AND I BEGAN TO LEARN THEIR STRANGE TONGUE ~ THEY COULD NEVER UNDERSTAND, THOUGH, HOW I COULD SWIM SO MUCH IN THE EXTREMELY COLD WATER ~
OF COURSE I HAD TO, FREQUENTLY, FOR WE SUB-MARINERS CANNOT LIVE OUT OF WATER FOR LONGER THAN FIVE HOURS AT A STRETCH ~ AND MANY OF US CANNOT LIVE EVEN THAT LONG ---"
"WELL, AS TIME WENT ON, THE COMMANDER AND I FELL IN LOVE, AND WERE MARRIED BY THEIR OWN RITUAL ~ AND ALL THE WHILE I WAS GIVING SECRET INFORMATION BACK TO OUR PEOPLE ....."
WE CANNOT WIN, MASTER - THEY ARE TOO MIGHTY!
"AND THEY WERE TOO MIGHTY, FOR EVEN AS OUR ARMY ASSEMBLED FOR THE FIRST COUNTER-ATTACK, THERE CAME A TERRIBLE BOMBARDMENT FROM ABOVE - WHICH DESTROYED ALL BUT A MERE HANDFUL OF US!"
AND SO, MY SON, IT HAS TAKEN US TWENTY YEARS TO BUILD UP A RACE TO AVENGE THE BRUTAL HARM DONE US THEN ~ NOW, SINCE YOU ARE THE ONLY ONE OF US LEFT WHO CAN LIVE ON LAND AND IN WATER, AND WHO CAN ALSO FLY IN THE AIR, AND BECAUSE YOU HAVE THE STRENGTH OF A THOUSAND EARTH-MEN, IT IS YOUR DUTY TO LEAD US INTO BATTLE! YOU HAVE BEGUN WELL, BUT YOU MUST USE STRATEGY AND GREAT CARE ~ GO NOW TO THE LAND OF THE WHITE PEOPLE!
AND SO NAMOR, THE AVENGING SON, FACES THE SURFACE MEN OF THE WORLD, IN WHAT PROMISES TO BE MORTAL COMBAT!

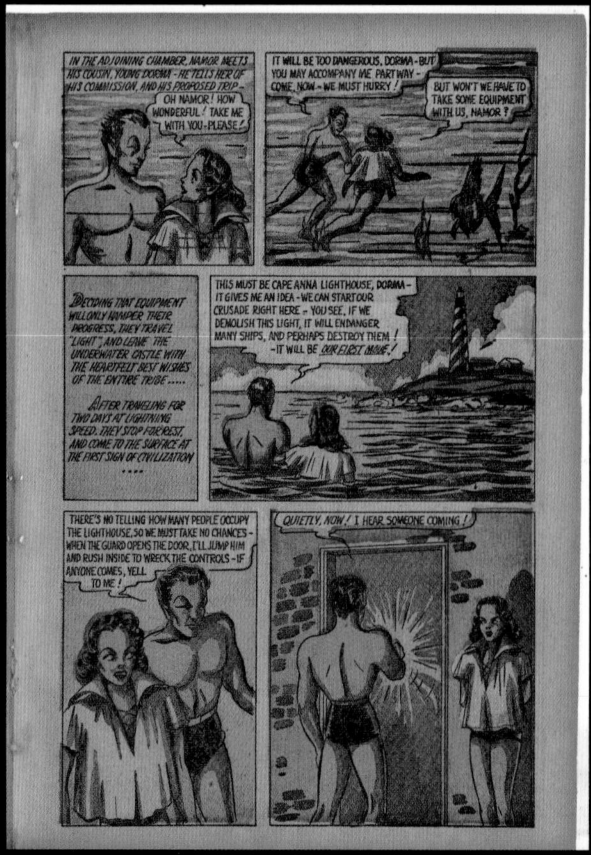
IN THE ADJOINING CHAMBER, NAMOR MEETS HIS COUSIN, YOUNG DORMA - HE TELLS HER OF HIS COMMISSION, AND HIS PROPOSED TRIP -
OH NAMOR! HOW WONDERFUL! TAKE ME WITH YOU - PLEASE!
IT WILL BE TOO DANGEROUS, DORMA - BUT YOU MAY ACCOMPANY ME PARTWAY - COME, NOW - WE MUST HURRY!
BUT WON'T WE HAVE TO TAKE SOME EQUIPMENT WITH US, NAMOR?
DECIDING THAT EQUIPMENT WILL ONLY HAMPER THEIR PROGRESS, THEY TRAVEL "LIGHT", AND LEAVE THE UNDERWATER CASTLE WITH THE HEARTFELT BEST WISHES OF THE ENTIRE TRIBE .....
AFTER TRAVELING FOR TWO DAYS AT LIGHTNING SPEED, THEY STOP FOR REST, AND COME TO THE SURFACE AT THE FIRST SIGN OF CIVILIZATION ....
THIS MUST BE CAPE ANNA LIGHTHOUSE, DORMA - IT GIVES ME AN IDEA - WE CAN START OUR CRUSADE RIGHT HERE - YOU SEE, IF WE DEMOLISH THIS LIGHT, IT WILL ENDANGER MANY SHIPS, AND PERHAPS DESTROY THEM! - IT WILL BE OUR FIRST MOVE!
THERE'S NO TELLING HOW MANY PEOPLE OCCUPY THE LIGHTHOUSE, SO WE MUST TAKE NO CHANCES - WHEN THE GUARD OPENS THE DOOR, I'LL JUMP HIM AND RUSH INSIDE TO WRECK THE CONTROLS - IF ANYONE COMES, YELL TO ME!
QUIETLY, NOW! I HEAR SOMEONE COMING!

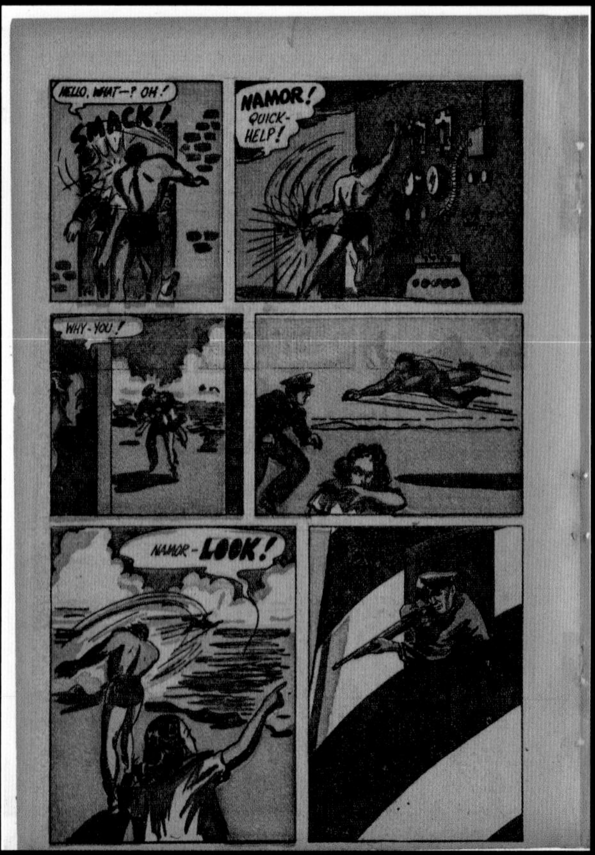
HELLO, WHAT—? OH!
SMACK!
NAMOR! QUICK - HELP!
WHY - YOU!
NAMOR - LOOK!

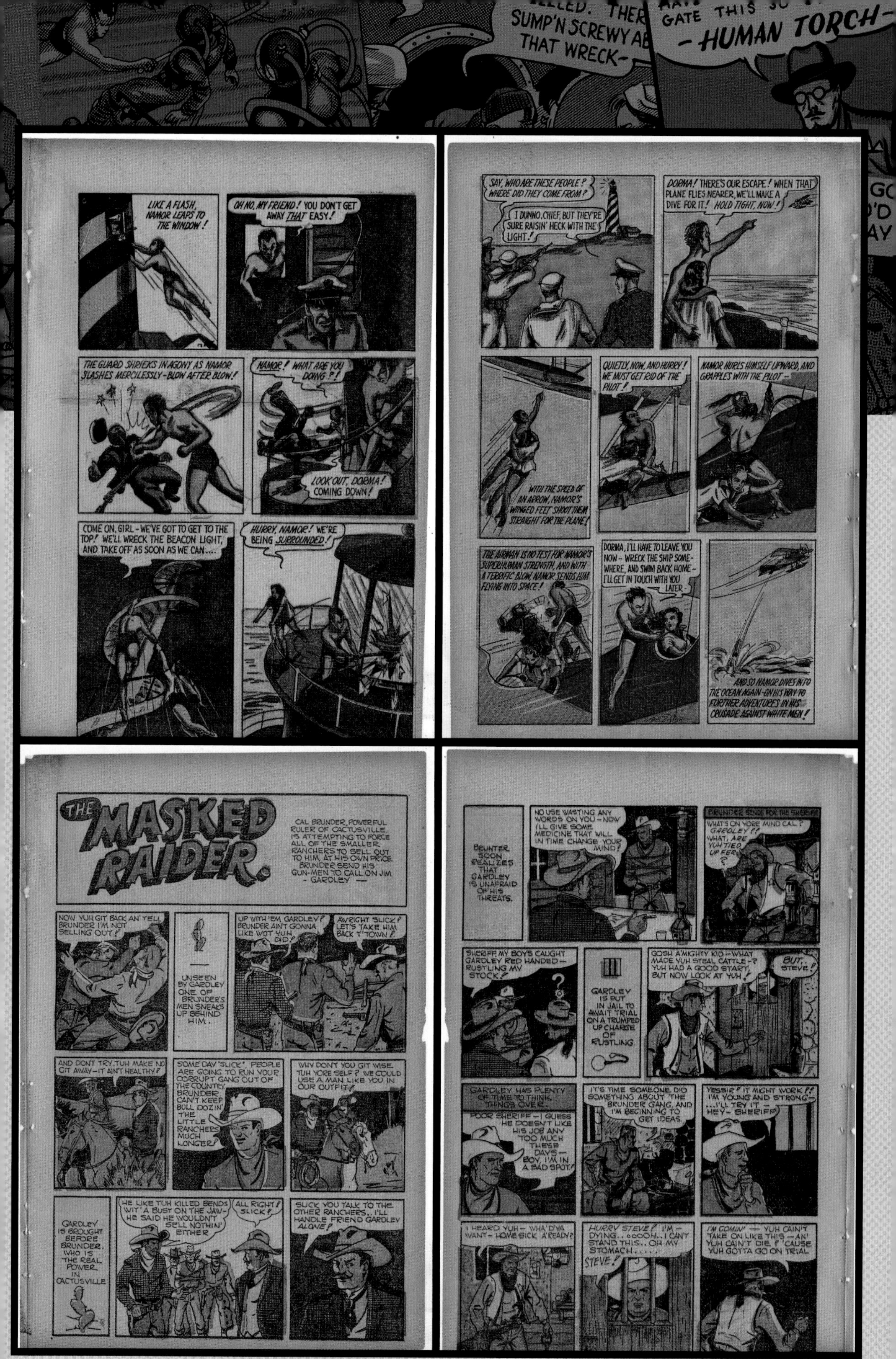
THAT WRECK-
-HUMAN TORCH-
LIKE A FLASH, NAMOR LEAPS TO THE WINDOW!
OH NO, MY FRIEND! YOU DON'T GET AWAY THAT EASY!
THE GUARD SHRIEKS IN AGONY AS NAMOR SLASHES MERCILESSLY-BLOW AFTER BLOW!
NAMOR! WHAT ARE YOU DOING?!
LOOK OUT, DORMA! COMING DOWN!
COME ON, GIRL-WE'VE GOT TO GET TO THE TOP! WE'LL WRECK THE BEACON LIGHT, AND TAKE OFF AS SOON AS WE CAN....
HURRY, NAMOR! WE'RE BEING SURROUNDED!
SAY, WHO ARE THESE PEOPLE? WHERE DID THEY COME FROM?
I DUNNO, CHIEF, BUT THEY'RE SURE RAISIN' HECK WITH THE LIGHT!
DORMA! THERE'S OUR ESCAPE! WHEN THAT PLANE FLIES NEARER, WE'LL MAKE A DIVE FOR IT! HOLD TIGHT, NOW!
WITH THE SPEED OF AN ARROW, NAMOR'S WINGED FEET SHOOT THEM STRAIGHT FOR THE PLANE!
QUIETLY, NOW, AND HURRY! WE MUST GET RID OF THE PILOT!
NAMOR HURLS HIMSELF UPWARD, AND GRAPPLES WITH THE PILOT-
THE AIRMAN IS NO TEST FOR NAMOR'S SUPERHUMAN STRENGTH, AND WITH A TERRIFIC BLOW, NAMOR SENDS HIM FLYING INTO SPACE!
DORMA, I'LL HAVE TO LEAVE YOU NOW - WRECK THE SHIP SOMEWHERE, AND SWIM BACK HOME - I'LL GET IN TOUCH WITH YOU LATER-
AND SO NAMOR DIVES INTO THE OCEAN AGAIN-ON HIS WAY TO FURTHER ADVENTURES IN HIS CRUSADE AGAINST WHITE MEN!
THE MASKED RAIDER
CAL BRUNDER, POWERFUL RULER OF CACTUSVILLE, IS ATTEMPTING TO FORCE ALL OF THE SMALLER RANCHERS TO SELL OUT TO HIM, AT HIS OWN PRICE. BRUNDER SEND HIS GUN-MEN TO CALL ON JIM - GARDLEY —
NOW YUH GIT BACK AN' TELL BRUNDER I'M NOT SELLING OUT!
UNSEEN BY GARDLEY ONE OF BRUNDER'S MEN SNEAKS UP BEHIND HIM.
UP WITH 'EM GARDLEY! BRUNDER AIN'T GONNA LIKE WOT YUH DID!
AWRIGHT SLICK! LET'S TAKE HIM BACK T'TOWN!
AND DON'T TRY TUH MAKE NO GIT AWAY-IT AIN'T HEALTHY!
SOME DAY "SLICK", PEOPLE ARE GOING TO RUN YOUR CORRUPT GANG OUT OF THE COUNTRY. BRUNDER CAN'T KEEP BULL DOZIN' THE LITTLE RANCHERS MUCH LONGER!
WHY DON'T YOU GIT WISE TUH YORE SELF? WE COULD USE A MAN LIKE YOU IN OUR OUTFIT!
GARDLEY IS BROUGHT BEFORE BRUNDER, WHO IS THE REAL POWER IN CACTUSVILLE
HE LIKE TUH KILLED BENDS WIT' A BUST ON THE JAW-HE SAID HE WOULDN'T SELL NOTHIN' EITHER
ALL RIGHT! SLICK!
SLICK YOU TALK TO THE OTHER RANCHERS.. I'LL HANDLE FRIEND GARDLEY ALONE!
BRUNTER SOON REALIZES THAT GARDLEY IS UNAFRAID OF HIS THREATS.
NO USE WASTING ANY WORDS ON YOU-NOW I'LL GIVE SOME MEDICINE THAT WILL IN TIME CHANGE YOUR MIND!
BRUNDER SENDS FOR THE SHERIFF
WHAT'S ON YORE MIND CAL? GARDLEY?! WHAT, ARE YUH TIED UP FER?
SHERIFF, MY BOYS CAUGHT GARDLEY RED HANDED-RUSTLING MY STOCK!
GARDLEY IS PUT IN JAIL TO AWAIT TRIAL ON A TRUMPED UP CHARGE OF RUSTLING.
GOSH A'MIGHTY KID-WHAT MADE YUH STEAL CATTLE-? YUH HAD A GOOD START, BUT NOW LOOK AT YUH!
BUT.. STEVE!
GARDLEY HAS PLENTY OF TIME TO THINK THINGS OVER.
POOR SHERIFF-I GUESS HE DOESN'T LIKE HIS JOB ANY TOO MUCH THESE DAYS-BOY, I'M IN A BAD SPOT!
IT'S TIME SOMEONE DID SOMETHING ABOUT THE BRUNDER GANG, AND I'M BEGINNING TO GET IDEAS
YESSIR! IT MIGHT WORK!! I'M YOUNG AND STRONG-...I'LL TRY IT-HEY-SHERIFF!
I HEARD YUH-WHA'D'YA WANT-HOME SICK A'READY?
HURRY STEVE! I'M-DYING..oooOH..I CAN'T STAND THIS..OH MY STOMACH.....
STEVE!
I'M COMIN'-YUH CAIN'T TAKE ON LIKE THIS-AN' YUH CAIN'T DIE! 'CAUSE YUH GOTTA GO ON TRIAL

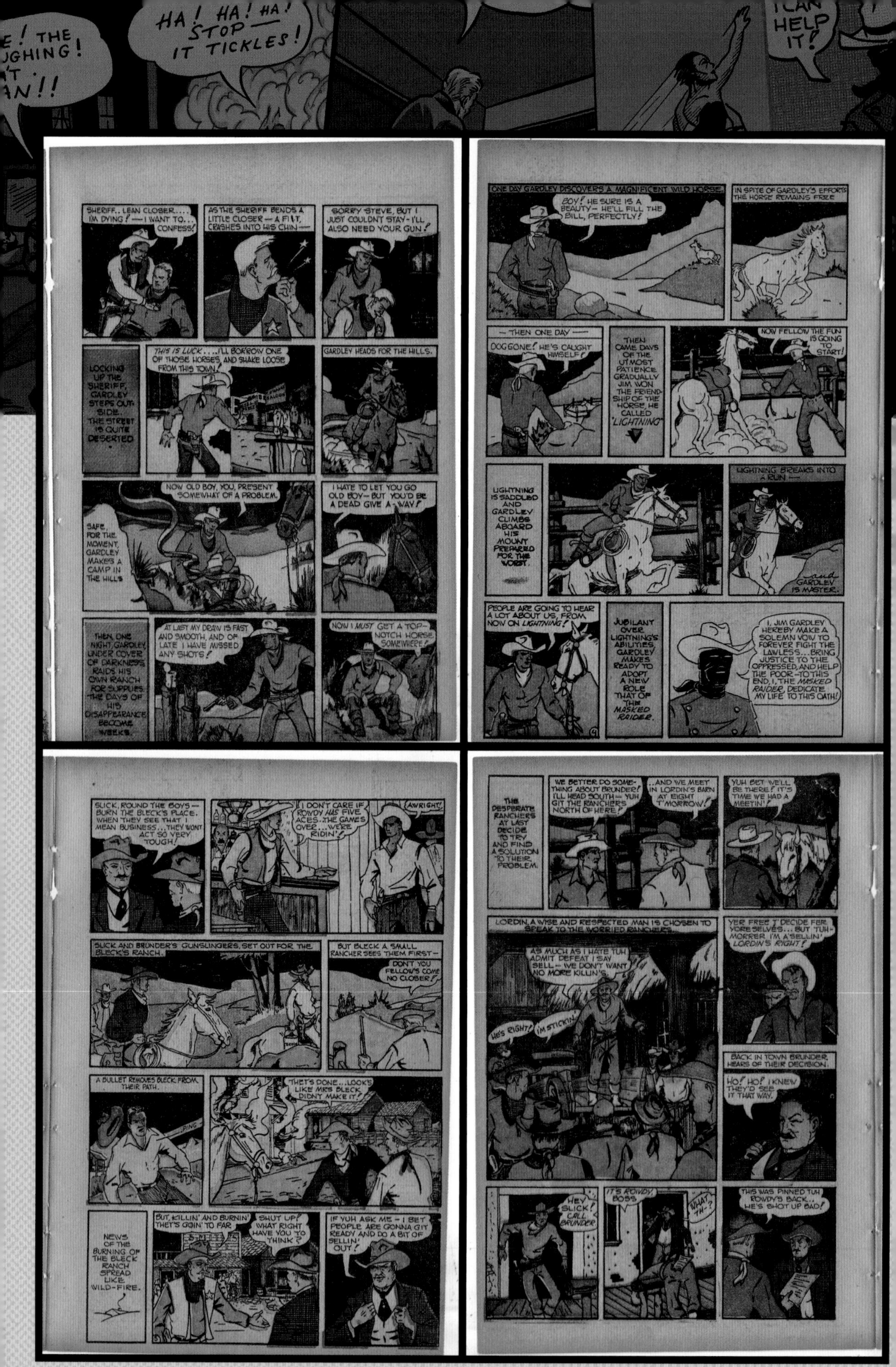

HA! HA! HA! STOP — IT TICKLES!
SHERIFF.. LEAN CLOSER.... I'M DYING! — I WANT TO... CONFESS!
AS THE SHERIFF BENDS A LITTLE CLOSER — A FIST CRASHES INTO HIS CHIN —
SORRY STEVE, BUT I JUST COULDN'T STAY - I'LL ALSO NEED YOUR GUN!
LOCKING UP THE SHERIFF, GARDLEY STEPS OUTSIDE. THE STREET IS QUITE DESERTED.
THIS IS LUCK....I'LL BORROW ONE OF THOSE HORSES, AND SHAKE LOOSE FROM THIS TOWN!
SALOON
GARDLEY HEADS FOR THE HILLS.
SAFE, FOR THE MOMENT, GARDLEY MAKES A CAMP IN THE HILLS
NOW OLD BOY, YOU PRESENT SOMEWHAT OF A PROBLEM.
I HATE TO LET YOU GO OLD BOY— BUT YOU'D BE A DEAD GIVE A-WAY!
THEN, ONE NIGHT, GARDLEY, UNDER COVER OF DARKNESS, RAIDS HIS OWN RANCH FOR SUPPLIES. THE DAYS OF HIS DISAPPEARANCE BECOME WEEKS.
AT LAST MY DRAW IS FAST AND SMOOTH, AND OF LATE I HAVE MISSED ANY SHOTS!
NOW I MUST GET A TOP-NOTCH HORSE SOMEWHERE!
ONE DAY GARDLEY DISCOVERS A MAGNIFICENT WILD HORSE.
BOY! HE SURE IS A BEAUTY— HE'LL FILL THE BILL, PERFECTLY!
IN SPITE OF GARDLEY'S EFFORTS THE HORSE REMAINS FREE
— THEN ONE DAY —
DOGGONE! HE'S CAUGHT HIMSELF!
THEN CAME DAYS OF THE UTMOST PATIENCE. GRADUALLY JIM WON THE FRIENDSHIP OF THE HORSE. HE CALLED "LIGHTNING"
NOW FELLOW THE FUN IS GOING TO START!
LIGHTNING IS SADDLED AND GARDLEY CLIMBS ABOARD HIS MOUNT PREPARED FOR THE WORST.
LIGHTNING BREAKS INTO A RUN —
and GARDLEY IS MASTER.
PEOPLE ARE GOING TO HEAR A LOT ABOUT US, FROM NOW ON LIGHTNING!
JUBILANT OVER LIGHTNING'S ABILITIES, GARDLEY MAKES READY TO ADOPT A NEW ROLE THAT OF THE MASKED RAIDER.
I, JIM GARDLEY HEREBY MAKE A SOLEMN VOW TO FOREVER FIGHT THE LAWLESS... BRING JUSTICE TO THE OPPRESSED, AND HELP THE POOR—TO THIS END, I, THE MASKED RAIDER, DEDICATE MY LIFE TO THIS OATH!
9
SLICK, ROUND THE BOYS— BURN THE BLECK'S PLACE. WHEN THEY SEE THAT I MEAN BUSINESS... THEY WONT ACT SO VERY TOUGH!
I DON'T CARE IF ROWDY HAS FIVE ACES...THE GAMES OVER... WE'RE RIDIN'!
AWRIGHT!
SLICK AND BRUNDER'S GUNSLINGERS SET OUT FOR THE BLECK'S RANCH.
BUT BLECK A SMALL RANCHER SEES THEM FIRST—
DON'T YOU FELLOWS COME NO CLOSER!
A BULLET REMOVES BLECK FROM THEIR PATH.
PING
THET'S DONE... LOOKS LIKE MRS. BLECK DIDN'T MAKE IT!
NEWS OF THE BURNING OF THE BLECK RANCH SPREAD LIKE WILD-FIRE.
BUT, KILLIN' AND BURNIN' THET'S GOIN' TO FAR
SHUT UP! WHAT RIGHT HAVE YOU TO THINK?
IF YUH ASK ME— I BET PEOPLE ARE GONNA GIT READY AND DO A BIT OF SELLIN' OUT!
THE DESPERATE RANCHERS AT LAST DECIDE TO TRY AND FIND A SOLUTION TO THEIR PROBLEM.
WE BETTER DO SOMETHING ABOUT BRUNDER! I'LL HEAD SOUTH— YUH GIT THE RANCHERS NORTH OF HERE!
...AND WE MEET IN LORDIN'S BARN AT EIGHT T'MORROW!
YUH BET WE'LL BE THERE! IT'S TIME WE HAD A MEETIN'!
LORDIN, A WISE AND RESPECTED MAN IS CHOSEN TO SPEAK TO THE WORRIED RANCHERS.
AS MUCH AS I HATE TUH ADMIT DEFEAT I SAY SELL— WE DON'T WANT NO MORE KILLIN'S.
HE'S RIGHT!
I'M STICKIN'!
YER FREE T' DECIDE FER YORE SELVES... BUT TUH-MORRER, I'M A-SELLIN'! LORDIN'S RIGHT!
BACK IN TOWN BRUNDER HEARS OF THEIR DECISION.
HO! HO! I KNEW THEY'D SEE IT THAT WAY.
HEY SLICK! CALL BRUNDER
IT'S ROWDY, BOSS
WHAT TH-?
THIS WAS PINNED TUH ROWDY'S BACK... HE'S SHOT UP BAD!

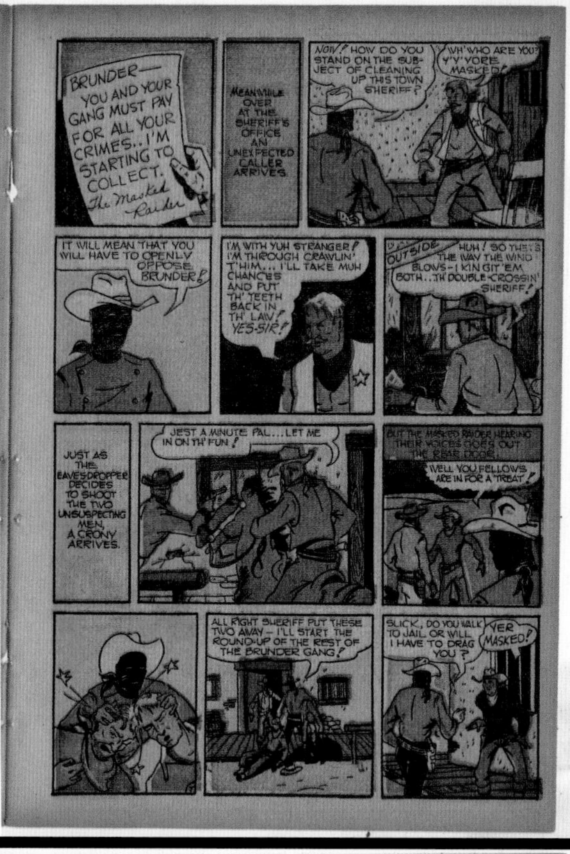
BRUNDER— YOU AND YOUR GANG MUST PAY FOR ALL YOUR CRIMES.. I'M STARTING TO COLLECT. The Masked Raider
MEANWHILE OVER AT THE SHERIFF'S OFFICE AN UNEXPECTED CALLER ARRIVES.
NOW! HOW DO YOU STAND ON THE SUBJECT OF CLEANING UP THIS TOWN SHERIFF?
WH' WHO ARE YOU? Y'Y'YORE MASKED!
IT WILL MEAN THAT YOU WILL HAVE TO OPENLY OPPOSE BRUNDER!
I'M WITH YUH STRANGER! I'M THROUGH CRAWLIN' T'HIM... I'LL TAKE MUH CHANCES AND PUT TH' TEETH BACK IN TH' LAW! YES-SIR!
OUTSIDE
HUH! SO THET'S THE WAY THE WIND BLOWS—I KIN GIT 'EM BOTH..TH' DOUBLE-CROSSIN' SHERIFF!
JUST AS THE EAVESDROPPER DECIDES TO SHOOT THE TWO UNSUSPECTING MEN, A CRONY ARRIVES.
JEST A MINUTE PAL... LET ME IN ON TH' FUN!
BUT THE MASKED RAIDER HEARING THEIR VOICES GOES OUT THE REAR DOOR.
WELL YOU FELLOWS ARE IN FOR A "TREAT"!
ALL RIGHT SHERIFF PUT THESE TWO AWAY—I'LL START THE ROUND-UP OF THE REST OF THE BRUNDER GANG!
SLICK, DO YOU WALK TO JAIL OR WILL I HAVE TO DRAG YOU?
YER MASKED!

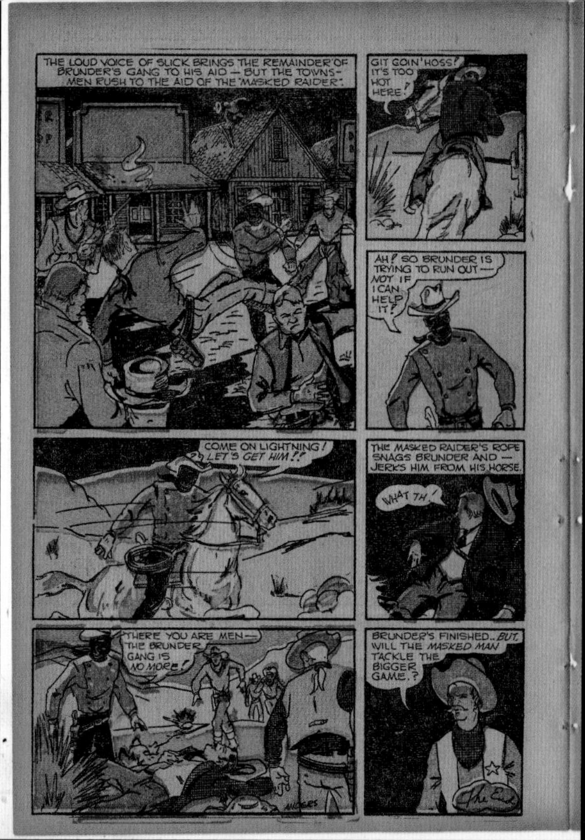
THE LOUD VOICE OF SLICK BRINGS THE REMAINDER OF BRUNDER'S GANG TO HIS AID—BUT THE TOWNSMEN RUSH TO THE AID OF THE "MASKED RAIDER".
GIT GOIN' HOSS! IT'S TOO HOT HERE!
AH! SO BRUNDER IS TRYING TO RUN OUT— NOT IF I CAN HELP IT!
COME ON LIGHTNING! LET'S GET HIM!!
THE MASKED RAIDER'S ROPE SNAGS BRUNDER AND—JERKS HIM FROM HIS HORSE.
WHAT TH'!
THERE YOU ARE MEN— THE BRUNDER GANG IS NO MORE!
BRUNDER'S FINISHED.. BUT, WILL THE MASKED MAN TACKLE THE BIGGER GAME.?
The End

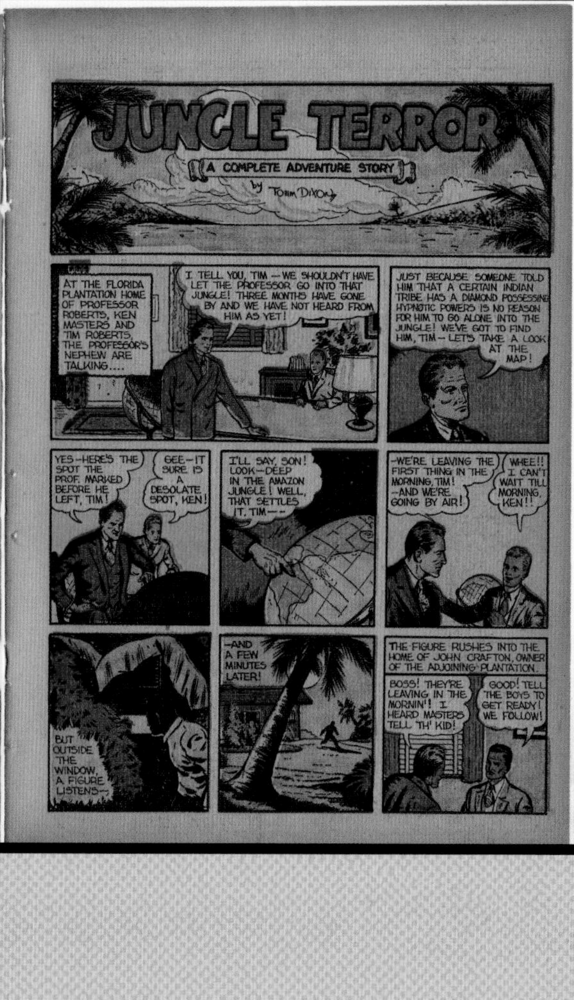
JUNGLE TERROR
A COMPLETE ADVENTURE STORY
by TOMM DIXON
AT THE FLORIDA PLANTATION HOME OF PROFESSOR ROBERTS, KEN MASTERS AND TIM ROBERTS, THE PROFESSOR'S NEPHEW ARE TALKING....
I TELL YOU, TIM—WE SHOULDN'T HAVE LET THE PROFESSOR GO INTO THAT JUNGLE! THREE MONTHS HAVE GONE BY AND WE HAVE NOT HEARD FROM HIM AS YET!
JUST BECAUSE SOMEONE TOLD HIM THAT A CERTAIN INDIAN TRIBE HAS A DIAMOND POSSESSING HYPNOTIC POWERS IS NO REASON FOR HIM TO GO ALONE INTO THE JUNGLE! WE'VE GOT TO FIND HIM, TIM—LET'S TAKE A LOOK AT THE MAP!
YES—HERE'S THE SPOT THE PROF. MARKED BEFORE HE LEFT, TIM!
GEE—IT SURE IS A DESOLATE SPOT, KEN!
I'LL SAY, SON! LOOK—DEEP IN THE AMAZON JUNGLE! WELL, THAT SETTLES IT, TIM——
—WE'RE LEAVING THE FIRST THING IN THE MORNING, TIM! —AND WE'RE GOING BY AIR!
WHEE!! I CAN'T WAIT TILL MORNING, KEN!!
BUT OUTSIDE THE WINDOW, A FIGURE LISTENS—
—AND A FEW MINUTES LATER!
THE FIGURE RUSHES INTO THE HOME OF JOHN CRAFTON, OWNER OF THE ADJOINING PLANTATION.
BOSS! THEY'RE LEAVING IN THE MORNIN'! I HEARD MASTERS TELL TH' KID!
GOOD! TELL THE BOYS TO GET READY! WE FOLLOW!

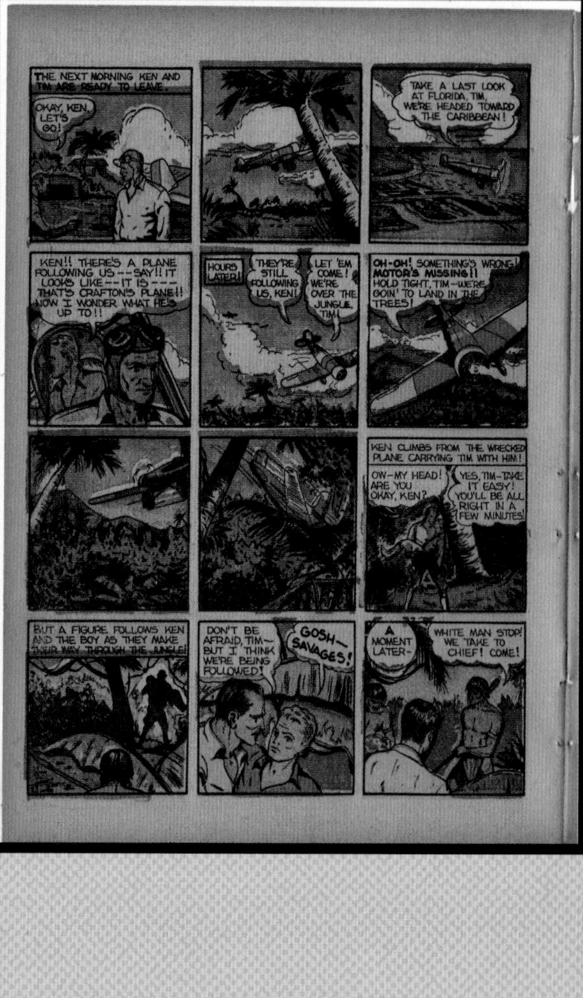
THE NEXT MORNING KEN AND TIM ARE READY TO LEAVE.
OKAY, KEN, LET'S GO!
TAKE A LAST LOOK AT FLORIDA, TIM, WE'RE HEADED TOWARD THE CARIBBEAN!
KEN!! THERE'S A PLANE FOLLOWING US——SAY!! IT LOOKS LIKE——IT IS——— THAT'S CRAFTON'S PLANE!! NOW I WONDER WHAT HE'S UP TO!!
HOURS LATER!
THEY'RE STILL FOLLOWING US, KEN!
LET 'EM COME! WE'RE OVER THE JUNGLE, TIM!
OH-OH! SOMETHING'S WRONG! MOTOR'S MISSING!! HOLD TIGHT, TIM—WE'RE GOIN' TO LAND IN THE TREES!
KEN CLIMBS FROM THE WRECKED PLANE CARRYING TIM WITH HIM!
OW—MY HEAD! ARE YOU OKAY, KEN?
YES, TIM—TAKE IT EASY! YOU'LL BE ALL RIGHT IN A FEW MINUTES!
BUT A FIGURE FOLLOWS KEN AND THE BOY AS THEY MAKE THEIR WAY THROUGH THE JUNGLE!
DON'T BE AFRAID, TIM— BUT I THINK WE'RE BEING FOLLOWED!
GOSH— SAVAGES!
A MOMENT LATER—
WHITE MAN STOP! WE TAKE TO CHIEF! COME!

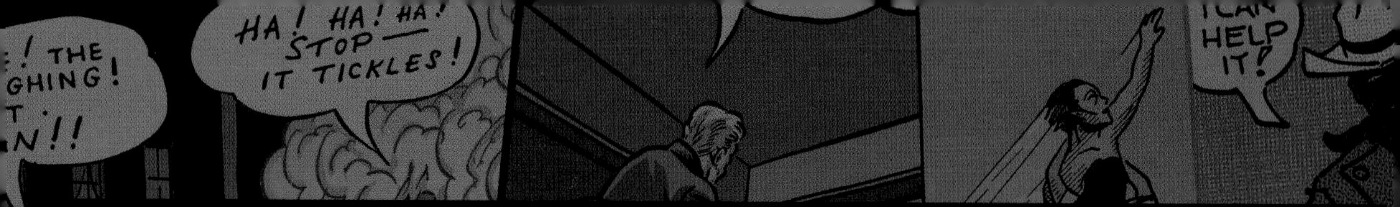

E! THE
GHING!
T
N!!
HA! HA! HA! STOP— IT TICKLES!
I CAN HELP IT!

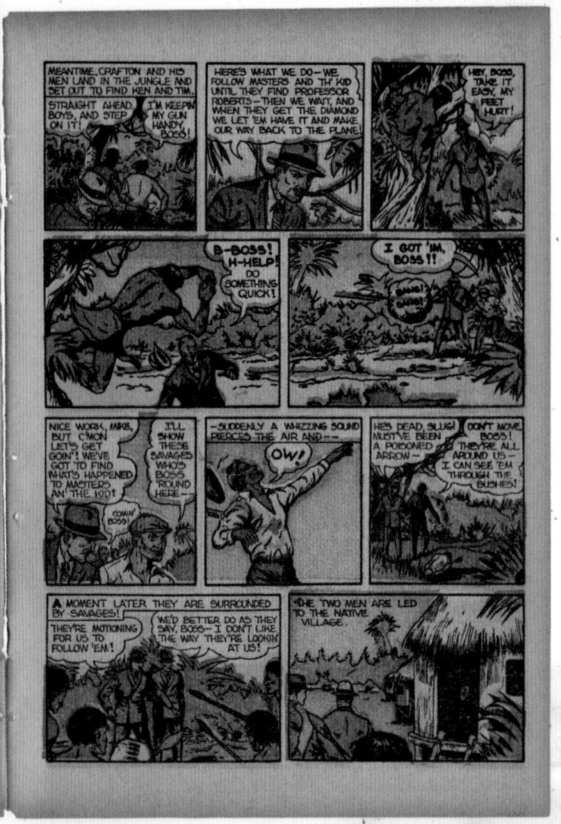

MEANTIME, CRAFTON AND HIS MEN LAND IN THE JUNGLE AND SET OUT TO FIND KEN AND TIM.
STRAIGHT AHEAD, BOYS, AND STEP ON IT!
I'M KEEPIN' MY GUN HANDY, BOSS!
HERE'S WHAT WE DO—WE FOLLOW MASTERS AND TH' KID UNTIL THEY FIND PROFESSOR ROBERTS—THEN WE WAIT, AND WHEN THEY GET THE DIAMOND WE LET 'EM HAVE IT AND MAKE OUR WAY BACK TO THE PLANE!
HEY, BOSS, TAKE IT EASY, MY FEET HURT!
B-BOSS! H-HELP! DO SOMETHING QUICK!
I GOT 'IM, BOSS!!
BANG! BANG!
NICE WORK, MIKE, BUT C'MON LET'S GET GOIN'! WE'VE GOT TO FIND WHAT'S HAPPENED TO MASTERS AN' THE KID!
I'LL SHOW THESE SAVAGES WHO'S BOSS 'ROUND HERE--
COMIN' BOSS!
—SUDDENLY A WHIZZING SOUND PIERCES THE AIR AND--
OW!
HE'S DEAD, SLUG! MUST'VE BEEN A POISONED ARROW—
DON'T MOVE, BOSS! THEY'RE ALL AROUND US— I CAN SEE 'EM THROUGH THE BUSHES!
A MOMENT LATER THEY ARE SURROUNDED BY SAVAGES!
THEY'RE MOTIONING FOR US TO FOLLOW 'EM!
WE'D BETTER DO AS THEY SAY, BOSS—I DON'T LIKE THE WAY THEY'RE LOOKIN' AT US!
THE TWO MEN ARE LED TO THE NATIVE VILLAGE.

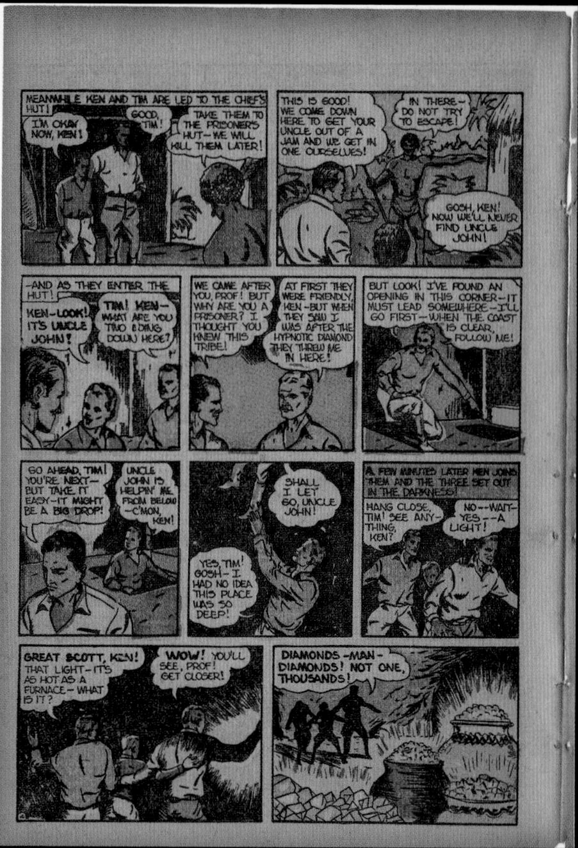

MEANWHILE KEN AND TIM ARE LED TO THE CHIEF'S HUT!
I'M OKAY NOW, KEN!
GOOD, TIM!
TAKE THEM TO THE PRISONER'S HUT—WE WILL KILL THEM LATER!
THIS IS GOOD! WE COME DOWN HERE TO GET YOUR UNCLE OUT OF A JAM AND WE GET IN ONE OURSELVES!
IN THERE— DO NOT TRY TO ESCAPE!
GOSH, KEN! NOW WE'LL NEVER FIND UNCLE JOHN!
—AND AS THEY ENTER THE HUT!
KEN—LOOK! IT'S UNCLE JOHN!
TIM! KEN— WHAT ARE YOU TWO S-DING DOWN HERE?
WE CAME AFTER YOU, PROF! BUT WHY ARE YOU A PRISONER? I THOUGHT YOU KNEW THIS TRIBE!
AT FIRST THEY WERE FRIENDLY, KEN—BUT WHEN THEY SAW I WAS AFTER THE HYPNOTIC DIAMOND THEY THREW ME IN HERE!
BUT LOOK! I'VE FOUND AN OPENING IN THIS CORNER—IT MUST LEAD SOMEWHERE—I'LL GO FIRST—WHEN THE COAST IS CLEAR, FOLLOW ME!
GO AHEAD, TIM! YOU'RE NEXT— BUT TAKE IT EASY—IT MIGHT BE A BIG DROP!
UNCLE JOHN IS HELPIN' ME FROM BELOW —C'MON, KEN!
SHALL I LET GO, UNCLE JOHN!
YES, TIM! GOSH—I HAD NO IDEA THIS PLACE WAS SO DEEP!
A FEW MINUTES LATER KEN JOINS THEM AND THE THREE SET OUT IN THE DARKNESS!
HANG CLOSE, TIM! SEE ANYTHING, KEN?
NO—WAIT— YES—A LIGHT!
GREAT SCOTT, KEN! THAT LIGHT—IT'S AS HOT AS A FURNACE—WHAT IS IT?
WOW! YOU'LL SEE, PROF! GET CLOSER!
DIAMONDS—MAN—DIAMONDS! NOT ONE, THOUSANDS!

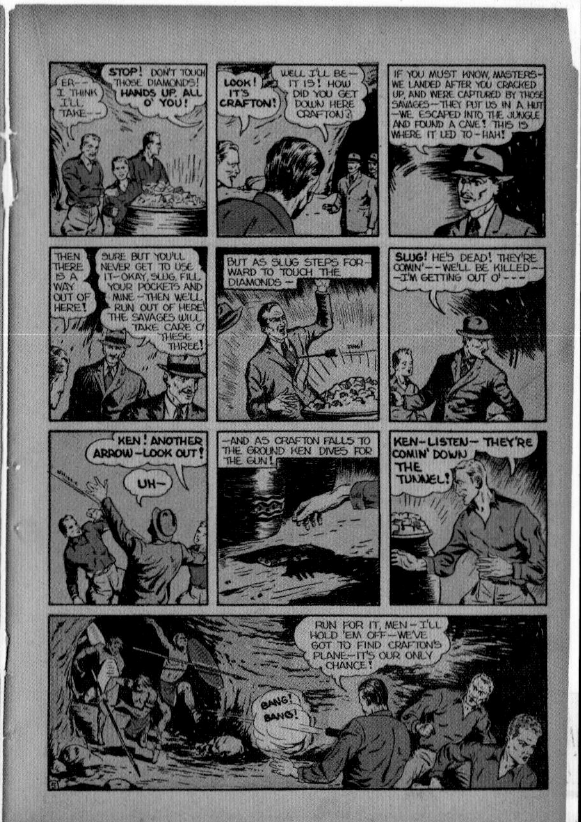

ER— I THINK I'LL TAKE—
STOP! DON'T TOUCH THOSE DIAMONDS! HANDS UP, ALL O' YOU!
LOOK! IT'S CRAFTON!
WELL I'LL BE— IT IS! HOW DID YOU GET DOWN HERE CRAFTON?
IF YOU MUST KNOW, MASTERS— WE LANDED AFTER YOU CRACKED UP, AND WERE CAPTURED BY THOSE SAVAGES—THEY PUT US IN A HUT —WE ESCAPED INTO THE JUNGLE AND FOUND A CAVE! THIS IS WHERE IT LED TO—HAH!
THEN THERE IS A WAY OUT OF HERE!
SURE BUT YOU'LL NEVER GET TO USE IT—OKAY, SLUG, FILL YOUR POCKETS AND MINE—THEN WE'LL RUN OUT OF HERE! THE SAVAGES WILL TAKE CARE O' THESE THREE!
BUT AS SLUG STEPS FORWARD TO TOUCH THE DIAMONDS—
SLUG! HE'S DEAD! THEY'RE COMIN'—WE'LL BE KILLED— I'M GETTING OUT O'—
KEN! ANOTHER ARROW—LOOK OUT!
UH—
—AND AS CRAFTON FALLS TO THE GROUND KEN DIVES FOR THE GUN!
KEN—LISTEN— THEY'RE COMIN' DOWN THE TUNNEL!
RUN FOR IT, MEN—I'LL HOLD 'EM OFF—WE'VE GOT TO FIND CRAFTON'S PLANE—IT'S OUR ONLY CHANCE!
BANG! BANG!

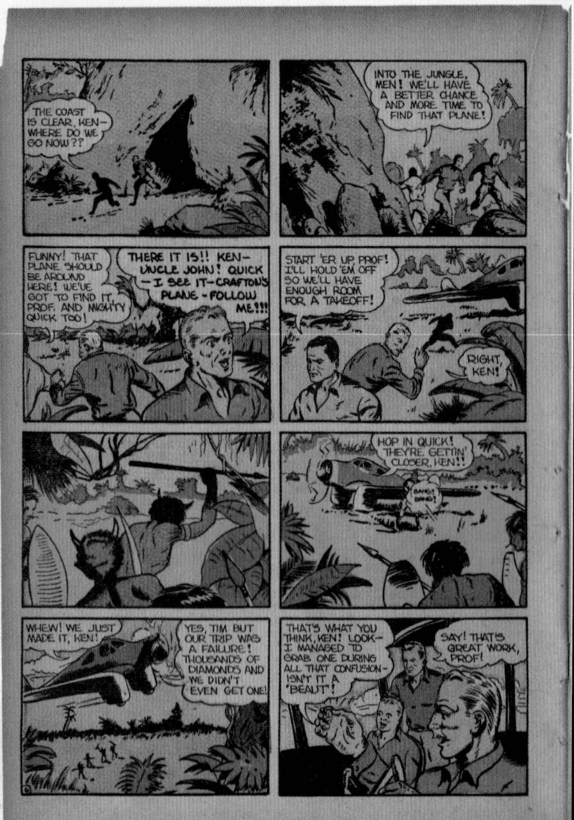

THE COAST IS CLEAR, KEN— WHERE DO WE GO NOW??
INTO THE JUNGLE, MEN! WE'LL HAVE A BETTER CHANCE AND MORE TIME TO FIND THAT PLANE!
FUNNY! THAT PLANE SHOULD BE AROUND HERE! WE'VE GOT TO FIND IT, PROF, AND MIGHTY QUICK TOO!
THERE IT IS!! KEN— UNCLE JOHN! QUICK —I SEE IT—CRAFTON'S PLANE—FOLLOW ME!!!
START 'ER UP PROF! I'LL HOLD 'EM OFF SO WE'LL HAVE ENOUGH ROOM FOR A TAKEOFF!
RIGHT, KEN!
HOP IN QUICK! THEY'RE GETTIN' CLOSER, KEN!!
BANG! BANG!
WHEW! WE JUST MADE IT, KEN!
YES, TIM BUT OUR TRIP WAS A FAILURE! THOUSANDS OF DIAMONDS AND WE DIDN'T EVEN GET ONE!
THAT'S WHAT YOU THINK, KEN! LOOK— I MANAGED TO GRAB ONE DURING ALL THAT CONFUSION— ISN'T IT A 'BEAUT'!
SAY! THAT'S GREAT WORK, PROF!

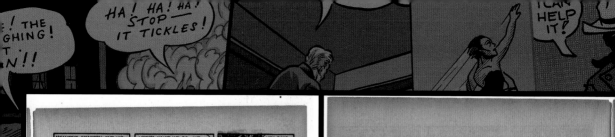

BURNING RUBBER

A Short Short Story About
The Auto Race Tracks

By Raymond Gill

THE crowd roared . . . with laughter! Bill Williams knew what they were laughing at, his coveted Blue Bird. Compared to the other cars in the race, the Blue Bird did look a bit shabby. But one thing was certain, there weren't any better mechanics or drivers than Bill and his able mechanic, Fred Turner.

"Everything's shipshape, Bill. You know, I feel kind of sorry for those other mugs. I'd hate to lose a race if I spent a lot of dough on a two tone chrom plated model."

"Fine. Well, I don't know, I'd give a lot to dress my Lady Bird here up with a lot of new feathers. I don't give a hoot what the crowd thinks myself, but I feel sorry for my 'Laddie's' sake.

"Cut it fella, I think you did pretty well digging up the entry fee. After all, you spent plenty for parts for your new super-charger."

"Yep, that's our only hope now. Don't kid yourself that we have any cinch. We have the best drivers in the business here today."

"What's the matter with you today Bill, I've never heard you talk like this before. You sound as though you've lost faith in our Blue Bird."

"No, not on your life. That's one thing I'll never do. I guess it got under my skin a little bit . . . those people laughing at her, I mean."

"That's better. By the way, doesn't Ann ever complain about your spending so much time with your 'Lady' here?"

"Yea, she was kidding me the other night."

"Well, there goes the signal, Bill. Move over."

"Oh, ah. . . Listen old man, let me take it alone this time. . . . I don't know why I want to. I . . . well, humor me this once, will you? I know I'll feel a lot better if I get out there alone. . . ."

"Ah, sure . . . sure, Bill, Anything you say, Only, be careful."

BILL shot ahead with a roar that surprised the smiling crowd that had gathered around to poke fun at the Blue Bird.

He was hardly topped on the line when the second starting signal was given. There were eight cars in the race besides the Blue Bird. The combined noise of dozens of unmuffeled explosions thundered out into an increasing crescendo that thrilled some and annoyed others.

To Bill it was sweet music . . . the powerful voice of his Lady Bird. Bill was in his glory, he could feel his whole body grow taught with a passionate desire to go faster, faster, faster. The stiffer his body grew, the harder his foot pressed the accelerator.

He was setting the pace, the other cars directly behind him, weaving back and forth. He was at his perfect ease now, he felt that the Lady Bird was standing still and that the track was some never ending ribbon that kept unfolding in front of him. He was in a new world, a world all his own.

Ann, the girl was literally sitting on the edge of her seat as she watched the Blue Bird madly rush on in meaningless velocity, Or so it seemed to her.

"Hello, Ann. Enjoying the race?"

"Fred! What are you doing up here? Why aren't you in there with Bill?"

"Whoa, take it easy. He's just a bit moody, I guess. He vants to be alone."

"Oh, Fred, I always feel better when you're with him. If it's possible to feel good when he's throwing himself bodily into the face of fate. You shouldn't have let him take it out there alone. . . ."

"Well, it's too late now to do anything about that, besides, there's something you can do to help Bill. That's why I came up here."

"Yes, Fred. You know I'll do anything for that grease monkey."

"That's the idea, calm down. I don't know what it is that's got everybody keyed up today. We've all gone through these races before together."

"Yes, we have, Fred. But somehow I feel that today it's all got to end. One way or the other."

"Ann, you know that we've spent a lot of time working on the Blue Bird these last few months. We always work hard on her before a race, but this time we've done something more than that. We've perfected a new gas feeder. I know Bill wouldn't want me to tell you, but I feel that you have a right to know. Bill is in there right now, risking his life to test it. This test is the final step. If it works, Bill will retire from the track. He told me so. If it fails . . . well . . . ?"

"Fred! Tell me. What if it doesn't work, what will happen? What can a gas feeder do that will possibly crack him up?"

"Just this. That new feeder is mounted over the engine, it feeds with a combined force of gravity and pressure. If anything should go wrong, if it should spring the smallest leak . . . that hot motor will blow both him and the Blue Bird to kingdom come."

"Tell me, quickly Fred. What do I do that will help?"

"Well, you and Ruth Clerk, the daughter of the big motor magnet, C. G. Clark, are on pretty good terms, aren't you?"

"Why, yes. Ruth and I went to school together. Why?"

"Here's why. If you can get Ruth to get you in to see her father, now, before it's too late, we may be able to save the day . . . and Bill's neck."

"What am I supposed to do after I get in?"

"Here, show him these plans. It's the gas feeder. If you can sell him on the idea of manufacturing it, Bill could be flagged out of the race before that temporary mounting should blow."

"It's a deal. Give me those plans. You just watch . . . he won't make more than one more circle of the track . . . I'll see to that."

BILL, still madly kicking the gas pedal, was now unconsciously wiping oil off his face . . . suddenly he jerked himself back into stark reality. The oil he's wiping off is thin. . . . Too thin. . . . GASOLENE!

On the stands, Fred saw the thin shred of smoke trailing the Blue Bird. Terror gripping his heart, he called to Ann to hurry. . . . In another moment. . . .

But Ann hadn't wasted any time. Fred's nervous, scanning eyes finally located her, down talking to the starter.

He also saw the Blue Bird, never slowing, round the turn and come rocketing up the straightway in front of the stands. Just as he crossed the line the checkered flag waved him out of the race. The other cars shot right past him for the final lap. Bill leaped out of the Blue Bird and took the situation in at a glance. Of course, just like a woman. Ann became nervous . . . couldn't stand a little smoke . . . so she had him flagged out. She didn't care if she was throwing all of his hard work out of the window.

"Well, Ann, you did a beautiful job. I couldn't have done better myself. And you claim you care for me. Why, all you care about is yourself. . . ."

"See here, see here. This young lady just saved your life. A most ungrateful exhibition, young man. A most ungrateful exhibition."

"Why, Mr. Clark. I . . . Oh, whats' the use . . . she's probably queered that too. At least if she let me finish the race I'd be in that much. Oh, well."

"Young man, this young lady just explained the fine points of your new gas feeder to me. I'd like to have you drop in to my office this afternoon, if you will, and we can come to terms."

"What? Why didn't you tell me this before? Wheeeeee? Oh, Ann, forgive me. . . . To the devil with the race."

"Oh, ah, pardon me. But do remember me? I'm Fred, your mechanic?"

"Fred. You old sonofagun. Isn't it wonderful?"

"It certinly is. The darn thing works! You did manage to gain a whole lap on those birds! They all had to go around an extra lap to compete for second place!"

ADVENTURES OF

CHAKA
KA-ZAR
THE GREAT

from the FAMOUS CHARACTER
CREATED BY BOB BYRD

ZAR   TRAJAH

JOHN RAND, YOUNG OWNER OF A RICH DIAMOND FIELD IN THE TRANSVAAL, IS FLYING FROM JOHANNESBURG TO CAIRO WITH HIS WIFE AND THEIR THREE-YEAR-OLD SON DAVID, OVER THE HEART OF THE BELGIAN CONGO THE PLANE DEVELOPS MOTOR TROUBLE AND RAND IS FORCED TO COME DOWN IN THE THICK, WILD TROPICAL FOREST!!

CONSTANCE!! HOLD DAVID.....I'M GOING TO LAND!!

THE PLANE DIVES INTO THE DENSE CONGO JUNGLE!

CONSTANCE! DAVID! ARE YOU HURT?

JOHN RAND STAGGERS OUT OF THE WRECK!!

TENDERLY, HE LIFTS HIS WIFE OUT OF THE BROKEN PLANE

MUMMY HURT?

MY LEG.... I THINK IT'S BROKEN!!

THERE'S A MEDICAL KIT IN THE PLANE....I'LL FIX YOU UP IN A JIFFY!

WHILE HIS MOTHER WAS RECOVERING, YOUNG DAVID QUICKLY MADE FRIENDS WITH THE SMALL JUNGLE ANIMALS

DAILY, ZAR, LORD OF THE JUNGLE, WATCHES THE STRANGE TWO-LEGGED CUB!!

ANOTHER PAIR OF KEEN EYES WATCH THE BOY AS HE PLAYS NEAR THE EDGE OF THE SMALL CLEARING.

N'JAGA, THE LEOPARD, COULD WAIT NO LONGER!

LOOK, DADDY!

A WARNING CRY FROM DAVID'S MOTHER BRINGS JOHN RAND WITH A RIFLE....

ONE QUICK SHOT STOPS N'JAGA AND THE WOUNDED LEOPARD DASHES INTO THE JUNGLE WITHOUT HARMING DAVID!

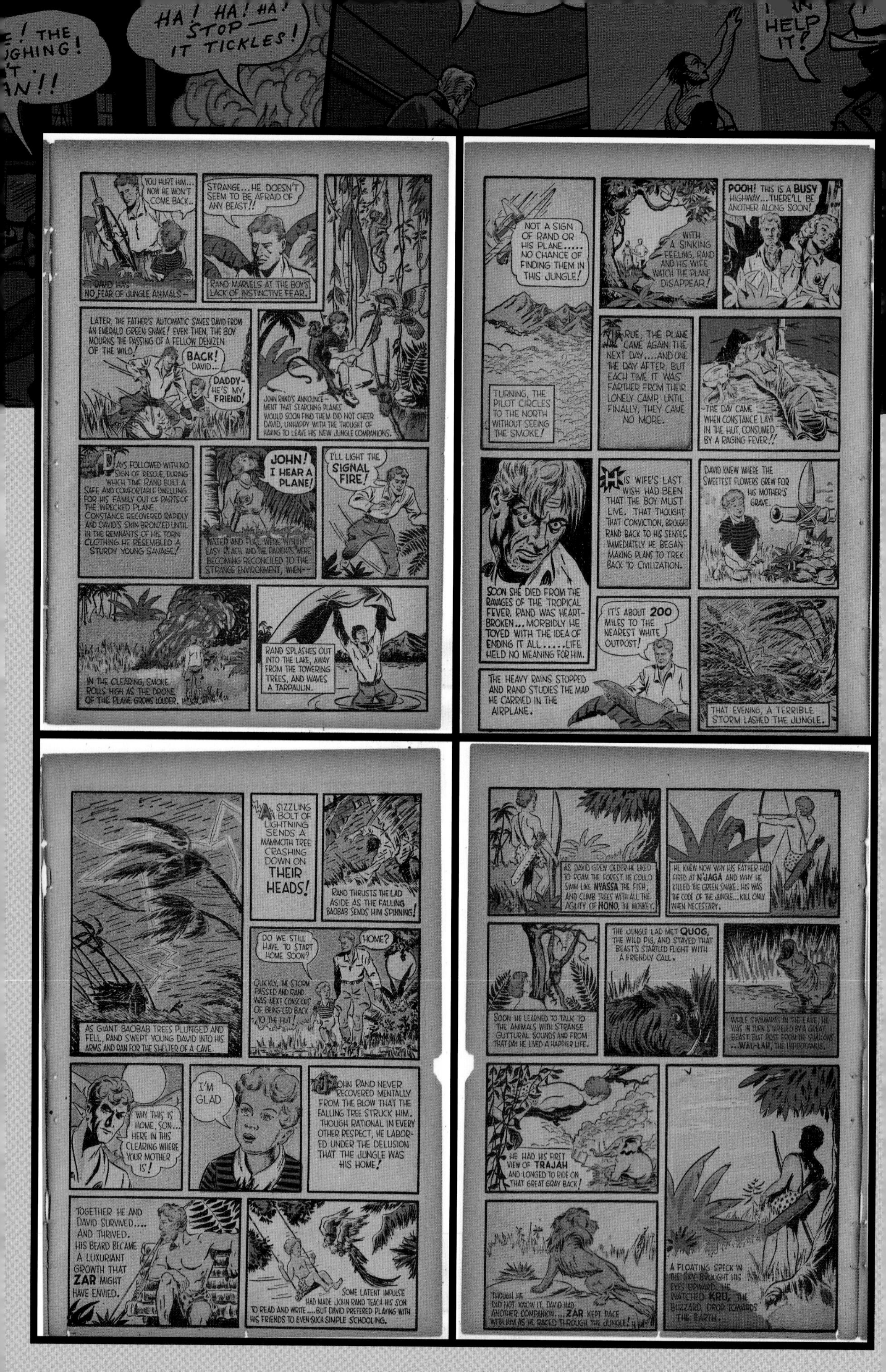
HA! HA! HA! STOP— IT TICKLES!
HELP IT!
YOU HURT HIM... NOW HE WON'T COME BACK..
DAVID HAS NO FEAR OF JUNGLE ANIMALS—
STRANGE...HE DOESN'T SEEM TO BE AFRAID OF ANY BEAST!!
RAND MARVELS AT THE BOY'S LACK OF INSTINCTIVE FEAR.
LATER, THE FATHER'S AUTOMATIC SAVES DAVID FROM AN EMERALD GREEN SNAKE! EVEN THEN, THE BOY MOURNS THE PASSING OF A FELLOW DENIZEN OF THE WILD!
BACK! DAVID...
DADDY— HE'S MY FRIEND!
JOHN RAND'S ANNOUNCEMENT THAT SEARCHING PLANES WOULD SOON FIND THEM DID NOT CHEER DAVID, UNHAPPY WITH THE THOUGHT OF HAVING TO LEAVE HIS NEW JUNGLE COMPANIONS.
DAYS FOLLOWED WITH NO SIGN OF RESCUE, DURING WHICH TIME RAND BUILT A SAFE AND COMFORTABLE DWELLING FOR HIS FAMILY OUT OF PARTS OF THE WRECKED PLANE. CONSTANCE RECOVERED RAPIDLY AND DAVID'S SKIN BRONZED UNTIL IN THE REMNANTS OF HIS TORN CLOTHING HE RESEMBLED A STURDY YOUNG SAVAGE!
JOHN! I HEAR A PLANE!
WATER AND FUEL WERE WITHIN EASY REACH AND THE PARENTS WERE BECOMING RECONCILED TO THE STRANGE ENVIRONMENT, WHEN—
I'LL LIGHT THE SIGNAL FIRE!
IN THE CLEARING, SMOKE ROLLS HIGH AS THE DRONE OF THE PLANE GROWS LOUDER.
RAND SPLASHES OUT INTO THE LAKE, AWAY FROM THE TOWERING TREES, AND WAVES A TARPAULIN.
NOT A SIGN OF RAND OR HIS PLANE..... NO CHANCE OF FINDING THEM IN THIS JUNGLE!
TURNING, THE PILOT CIRCLES TO THE NORTH WITHOUT SEEING THE SMOKE!
WITH A SINKING FEELING, RAND AND HIS WIFE WATCH THE PLANE DISAPPEAR!
POOH! THIS IS A BUSY HIGHWAY...THERE'LL BE ANOTHER ALONG SOON!
TRUE, THE PLANE CAME AGAIN THE NEXT DAY....AND ONE THE DAY AFTER, BUT EACH TIME IT WAS FARTHER FROM THEIR LONELY CAMP, UNTIL FINALLY, THEY CAME NO MORE.
THE DAY CAME WHEN CONSTANCE LAY IN THE HUT, CONSUMED BY A RAGING FEVER!!
SOON SHE DIED FROM THE RAVAGES OF THE TROPICAL FEVER. RAND WAS HEART-BROKEN... MORBIDLY HE TOYED WITH THE IDEA OF ENDING IT ALL.....LIFE HELD NO MEANING FOR HIM.
HIS WIFE'S LAST WISH HAD BEEN THAT THE BOY MUST LIVE. THAT THOUGHT, THAT CONVICTION, BROUGHT RAND BACK TO HIS SENSES. IMMEDIATELY HE BEGAN MAKING PLANS TO TREK BACK TO CIVILIZATION.
DAVID KNEW WHERE THE SWEETEST FLOWERS GREW FOR HIS MOTHER'S GRAVE.
IT'S ABOUT 200 MILES TO THE NEAREST WHITE OUTPOST!
THE HEAVY RAINS STOPPED AND RAND STUDIES THE MAP HE CARRIED IN THE AIRPLANE.
THAT EVENING, A TERRIBLE STORM LASHED THE JUNGLE.
AS GIANT BAOBAB TREES PLUNGED AND FELL, RAND SWEPT YOUNG DAVID INTO HIS ARMS AND RAN FOR THE SHELTER OF A CAVE.
A SIZZLING BOLT OF LIGHTNING SENDS A MAMMOTH TREE CRASHING DOWN ON THEIR HEADS!
RAND THRUSTS THE LAD ASIDE AS THE FALLING BAOBAB SENDS HIM SPINNING!
DO WE STILL HAVE TO START HOME SOON?
HOME?
QUICKLY, THE STORM PASSED AND RAND WAS NEXT CONSCIOUS OF BEING LED BACK TO THE HUT!
WHY THIS IS HOME, SON... HERE IN THIS CLEARING WHERE YOUR MOTHER IS!
I'M GLAD
JOHN RAND NEVER RECOVERED MENTALLY FROM THE BLOW THAT THE FALLING TREE STRUCK HIM. THOUGH RATIONAL IN EVERY OTHER RESPECT, HE LABORED UNDER THE DELUSION THAT THE JUNGLE WAS HIS HOME!
TOGETHER HE AND DAVID SURVIVED.... AND THRIVED. HIS BEARD BECAME A LUXURIANT GROWTH THAT ZAR MIGHT HAVE ENVIED.
SOME LATENT IMPULSE HAD MADE JOHN RAND TEACH HIS SON TO READ AND WRITE... BUT DAVID PREFERED PLAYING WITH HIS FRIENDS TO EVEN SUCH SIMPLE SCHOOLING.
AS DAVID GREW OLDER HE LIKED TO ROAM THE FOREST. HE COULD SWIM LIKE NYASSA THE FISH, AND CLIMB TREES WITH ALL THE AGILITY OF NONO, THE MONKEY.
HE KNEW NOW WHY HIS FATHER HAD FIRED AT N'JAGA AND WHY HE KILLED THE GREEN SNAKE. HIS WAS THE CODE OF THE JUNGLE... KILL ONLY WHEN NECESSARY.
SOON HE LEARNED TO TALK TO THE ANIMALS WITH STRANGE GUTTURAL SOUNDS AND FROM THAT DAY HE LIVED A HAPPIER LIFE.
THE JUNGLE LAD MET QUOG, THE WILD PIG, AND STAYED THAT BEAST'S STARTLED FLIGHT WITH A FRIENDLY CALL.
WHILE SWIMMING IN THE LAKE, HE WAS IN TURN STARTLED BY A GREAT BEAST THAT ROSE FROM THE SHALLOWS ...WAL-LAH, THE HIPPOTAMUS.
HE HAD HIS FIRST VIEW OF TRAJAH AND LONGED TO RIDE ON THAT GREAT GRAY BACK!
THOUGH HE DID NOT KNOW IT, DAVID HAD ANOTHER COMPANION.... ZAR KEPT PACE WITH HIM AS HE RACED THROUGH THE JUNGLE!
A FLOATING SPECK IN THE SKY BROUGHT HIS EYES UPWARD. HE WATCHED KRU, THE BUZZARD, DROP TOWARDS THE EARTH.

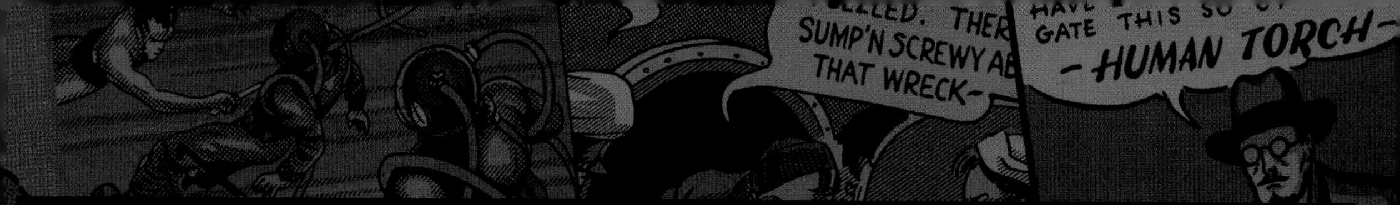
THAT WRECK-
-HUMAN TORCH-

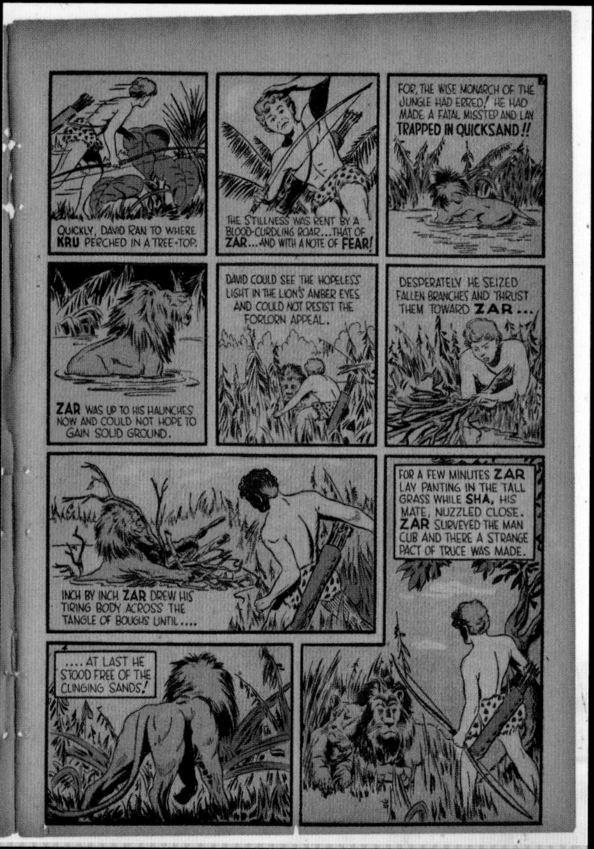
QUICKLY, DAVID RAN TO WHERE KRU PERCHED IN A TREE-TOP.
THE STILLNESS WAS RENT BY A BLOOD-CURDLING ROAR... THAT OF ZAR... AND WITH A NOTE OF FEAR!
FOR, THE WISE MONARCH OF THE JUNGLE HAD ERRED! HE HAD MADE A FATAL MISSTEP AND LAY TRAPPED IN QUICKSAND!!
ZAR WAS UP TO HIS HAUNCHES NOW AND COULD NOT HOPE TO GAIN SOLID GROUND.
DAVID COULD SEE THE HOPELESS LIGHT IN THE LION'S AMBER EYES AND COULD NOT RESIST THE FORLORN APPEAL.
DESPERATELY HE SEIZED FALLEN BRANCHES AND THRUST THEM TOWARD ZAR...
INCH BY INCH ZAR DREW HIS TIRING BODY ACROSS THE TANGLE OF BOUGHS UNTIL....
.... AT LAST HE STOOD FREE OF THE CLINGING SANDS!
FOR A FEW MINUTES ZAR LAY PANTING IN THE TALL GRASS WHILE SHA, HIS MATE, NUZZLED CLOSE. ZAR SURVEYED THE MAN CUB AND THERE A STRANGE PACT OF TRUCE WAS MADE.

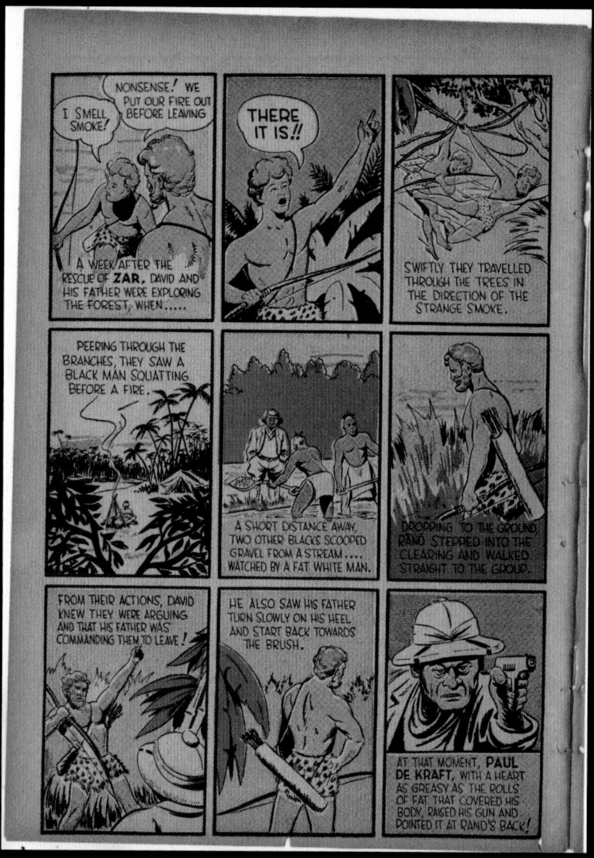
A WEEK AFTER THE RESCUE OF ZAR, DAVID AND HIS FATHER WERE EXPLORING THE FOREST, WHEN.....
I SMELL SMOKE!
NONSENSE! WE PUT OUR FIRE OUT BEFORE LEAVING
THERE IT IS!!
SWIFTLY THEY TRAVELLED THROUGH THE TREES IN THE DIRECTION OF THE STRANGE SMOKE.
PEERING THROUGH THE BRANCHES, THEY SAW A BLACK MAN SQUATTING BEFORE A FIRE.
A SHORT DISTANCE AWAY, TWO OTHER BLACKS SCOOPED GRAVEL FROM A STREAM.... WATCHED BY A FAT WHITE MAN.
DROPPING TO THE GROUND, RAND STEPPED INTO THE CLEARING AND WALKED STRAIGHT TO THE GROUP.
FROM THEIR ACTIONS, DAVID KNEW THEY WERE ARGUING AND THAT HIS FATHER WAS COMMANDING THEM TO LEAVE!
HE ALSO SAW HIS FATHER TURN SLOWLY ON HIS HEEL AND START BACK TOWARDS THE BRUSH.
AT THAT MOMENT, PAUL DE KRAFT, WITH A HEART AS GREASY AS THE ROLLS OF FAT THAT COVERED HIS BODY, RAISED HIS GUN AND POINTED IT AT RAND'S BACK!

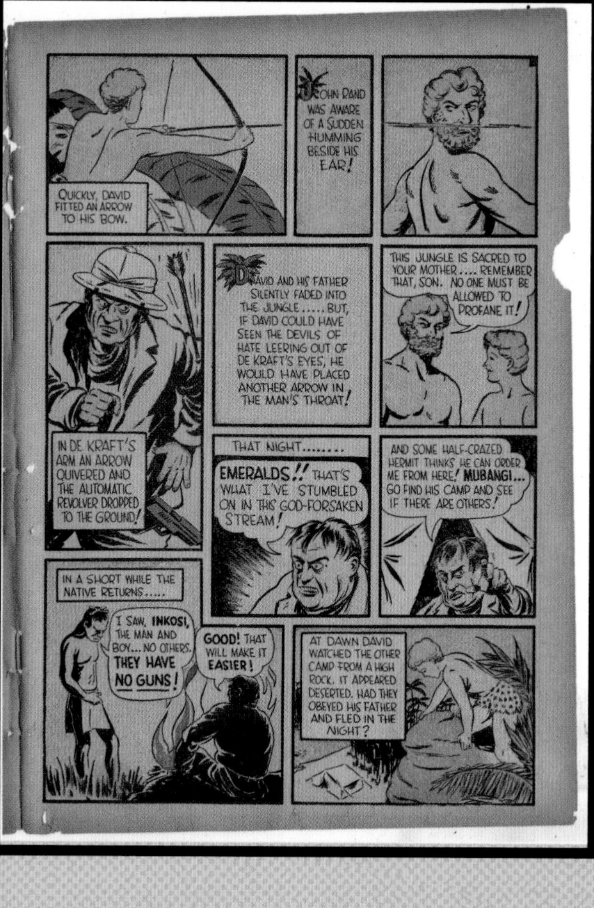
QUICKLY, DAVID FITTED AN ARROW TO HIS BOW.
JOHN RAND WAS AWARE OF A SUDDEN HUMMING BESIDE HIS EAR!
IN DE KRAFT'S ARM AN ARROW QUIVERED AND THE AUTOMATIC REVOLVER DROPPED TO THE GROUND!
DAVID AND HIS FATHER SILENTLY FADED INTO THE JUNGLE..... BUT, IF DAVID COULD HAVE SEEN THE DEVILS OF HATE LEERING OUT OF DE KRAFT'S EYES, HE WOULD HAVE PLACED ANOTHER ARROW IN THE MAN'S THROAT!
THIS JUNGLE IS SACRED TO YOUR MOTHER.... REMEMBER THAT, SON. NO ONE MUST BE ALLOWED TO PROFANE IT!
THAT NIGHT........
EMERALDS!! THAT'S WHAT I'VE STUMBLED ON IN THIS GOD-FORSAKEN STREAM!
AND SOME HALF-CRAZED HERMIT THINKS HE CAN ORDER ME FROM HERE! MUBANGI... GO FIND HIS CAMP AND SEE IF THERE ARE OTHERS!
IN A SHORT WHILE THE NATIVE RETURNS.....
I SAW, INKOSI, THE MAN AND BOY... NO OTHERS. THEY HAVE NO GUNS!
GOOD! THAT WILL MAKE IT EASIER!
AT DAWN DAVID WATCHED THE OTHER CAMP FROM A HIGH ROCK. IT APPEARED DESERTED. HAD THEY OBEYED HIS FATHER AND FLED IN THE NIGHT?

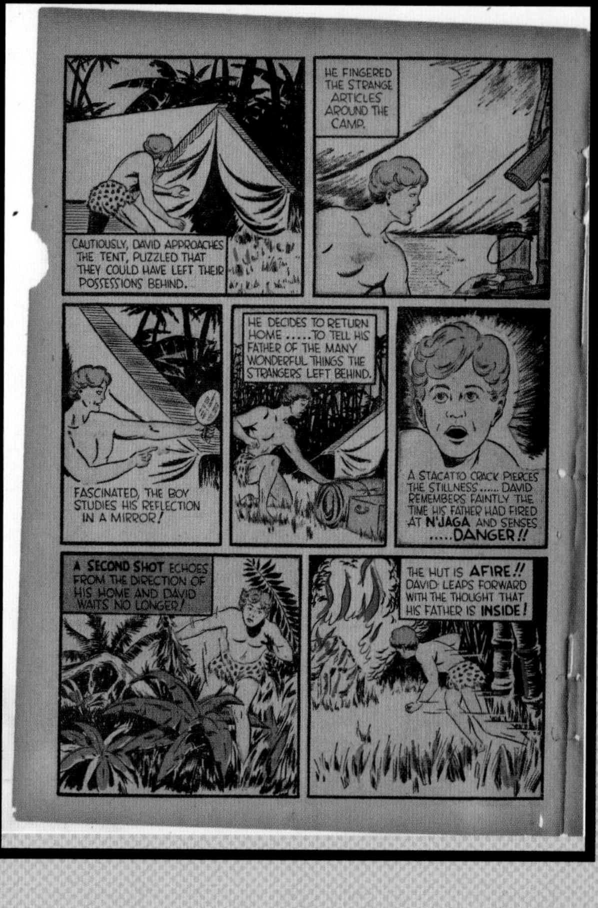
CAUTIOUSLY, DAVID APPROACHES THE TENT, PUZZLED THAT THEY COULD HAVE LEFT THEIR POSSESSIONS BEHIND.
HE FINGERED THE STRANGE ARTICLES AROUND THE CAMP.
FASCINATED, THE BOY STUDIES HIS REFLECTION IN A MIRROR!
HE DECIDES TO RETURN HOME.....TO TELL HIS FATHER OF THE MANY WONDERFUL THINGS THE STRANGERS LEFT BEHIND.
A STACATTO CRACK PIERCES THE STILLNESS...... DAVID REMEMBERS FAINTLY THE TIME HIS FATHER HAD FIRED AT N'JAGA AND SENSES .....DANGER!!
A SECOND SHOT ECHOES FROM THE DIRECTION OF HIS HOME AND DAVID WAITS NO LONGER!
THE HUT IS AFIRE!! DAVID LEAPS FORWARD WITH THE THOUGHT THAT HIS FATHER IS INSIDE!

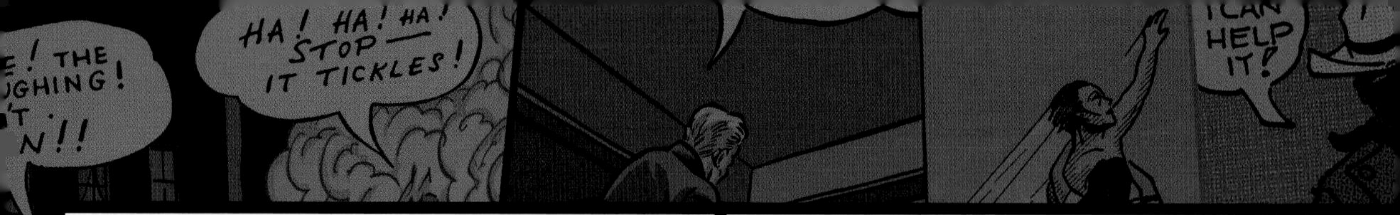

HA! HA! HA! STOP — IT TICKLES!
HELP IT!

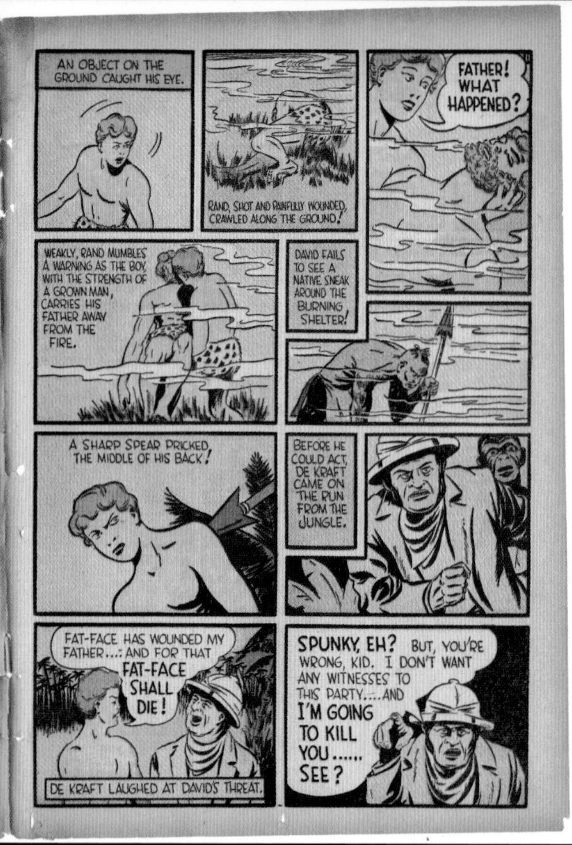

AN OBJECT ON THE GROUND CAUGHT HIS EYE.
RAND, SHOT AND PAINFULLY WOUNDED, CRAWLED ALONG THE GROUND!
FATHER! WHAT HAPPENED?
WEAKLY, RAND MUMBLES A WARNING AS THE BOY, WITH THE STRENGTH OF A GROWN MAN, CARRIES HIS FATHER AWAY FROM THE FIRE.
DAVID FAILS TO SEE A NATIVE SNEAK AROUND THE BURNING SHELTER!
A SHARP SPEAR PRICKED THE MIDDLE OF HIS BACK!
BEFORE HE COULD ACT, DE KRAFT CAME ON THE RUN FROM THE JUNGLE.
FAT-FACE HAS WOUNDED MY FATHER...: AND FOR THAT FAT-FACE SHALL DIE!
DE KRAFT LAUGHED AT DAVID'S THREAT.
SPUNKY, EH? BUT, YOU'RE WRONG, KID. I DON'T WANT ANY WITNESSES TO THIS PARTY.....AND I'M GOING TO KILL YOU...... SEE?

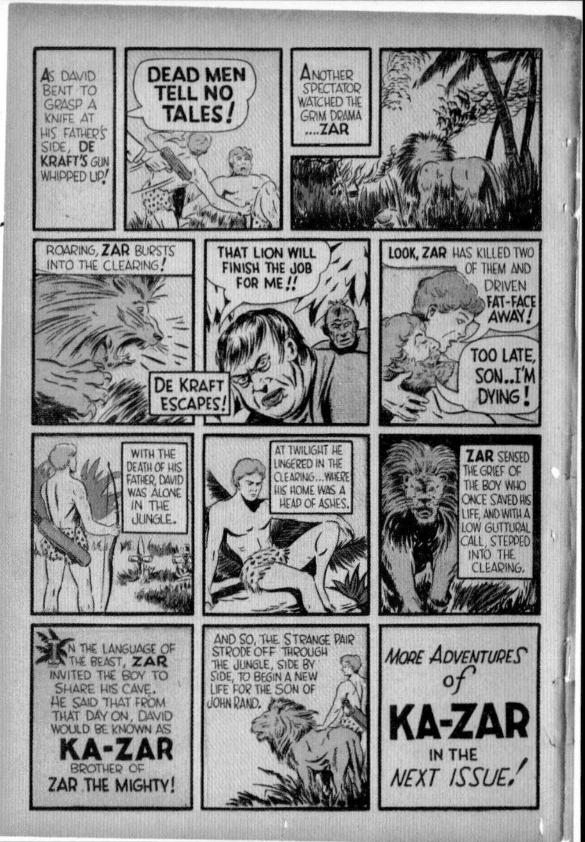

AS DAVID BENT TO GRASP A KNIFE AT HIS FATHER'S SIDE, DE KRAFT'S GUN WHIPPED UP!
DEAD MEN TELL NO TALES!
ANOTHER SPECTATOR WATCHED THE GRIM DRAMA ....ZAR
ROARING, ZAR BURSTS INTO THE CLEARING!
THAT LION WILL FINISH THE JOB FOR ME!!
DE KRAFT ESCAPES!
LOOK, ZAR HAS KILLED TWO OF THEM AND DRIVEN FAT-FACE AWAY!
TOO LATE, SON..I'M DYING!
WITH THE DEATH OF HIS FATHER, DAVID WAS ALONE IN THE JUNGLE.
AT TWILIGHT HE LINGERED IN THE CLEARING...WHERE HIS HOME WAS A HEAP OF ASHES.
ZAR SENSED THE GRIEF OF THE BOY WHO ONCE SAVED HIS LIFE, AND WITH A LOW GUTTURAL CALL, STEPPED INTO THE CLEARING.
IN THE LANGUAGE OF THE BEAST, ZAR INVITED THE BOY TO SHARE HIS CAVE. HE SAID THAT FROM THAT DAY ON, DAVID WOULD BE KNOWN AS KA-ZAR BROTHER OF ZAR THE MIGHTY!
AND SO, THE STRANGE PAIR STRODE OFF THROUGH THE JUNGLE, SIDE BY SIDE, TO BEGIN A NEW LIFE FOR THE SON OF JOHN RAND.
MORE ADVENTURES of KA-ZAR IN THE NEXT ISSUE!

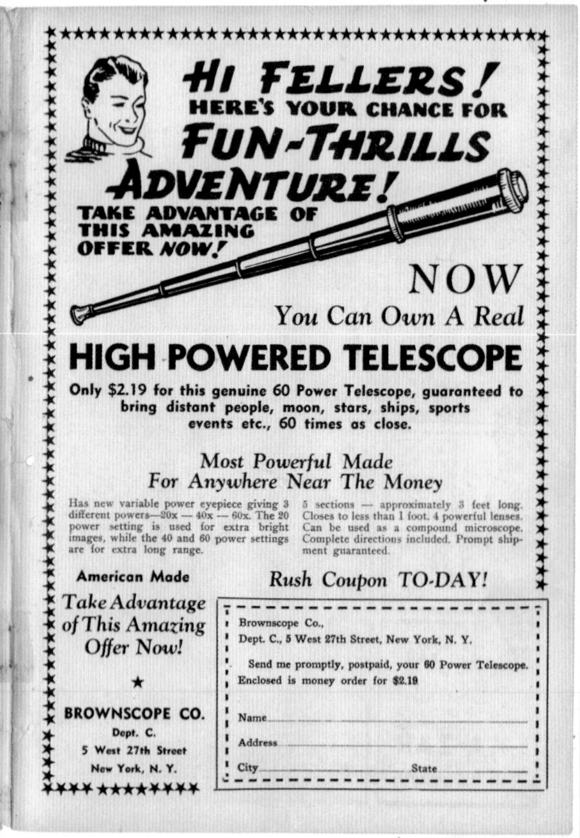

HI FELLERS! HERE'S YOUR CHANCE FOR FUN-THRILLS ADVENTURE!
TAKE ADVANTAGE OF THIS AMAZING OFFER NOW!
NOW
You Can Own A Real
HIGH POWERED TELESCOPE
Only $2.19 for this genuine 60 Power Telescope, guaranteed to bring distant people, moon, stars, ships, sports events etc., 60 times as close.
Most Powerful Made For Anywhere Near The Money
Has new variable power eyepiece giving 3 different powers—20x — 40x — 60x. The 20 power setting is used for extra bright images, while the 40 and 60 power settings are for extra long range.
5 sections — approximately 3 feet long. Closes to less than 1 foot. 4 powerful lenses. Can be used as a compound microscope. Complete directions included. Prompt shipment guaranteed.
American Made
Rush Coupon TO-DAY!
Take Advantage of This Amazing Offer Now!
BROWNSCOPE CO. Dept. C. 5 West 27th Street New York, N. Y.
Brownscope Co., Dept. C., 5 West 27th Street, New York, N. Y.
Send me promptly, postpaid, your 60 Power Telescope. Enclosed is money order for $2.19
Name
Address
City
State

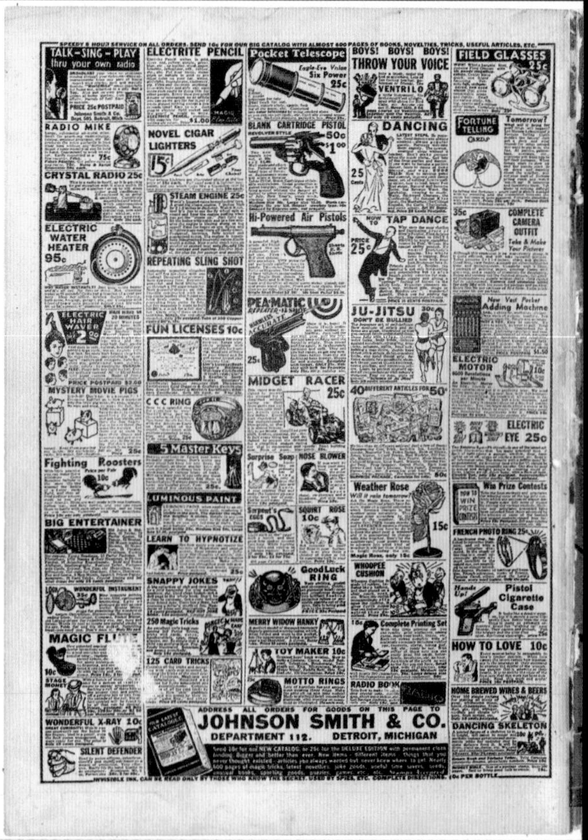

TALK-SING-PLAY thru your own radio
ELECTRITE PENCIL
Pocket Telescope 25c
BOYS! BOYS! BOYS! THROW YOUR VOICE
FIELD GLASSES 25c
RADIO MIKE
NOVEL CIGAR LIGHTERS 15c
BLANK CARTRIDGE PISTOL
DANCING
FORTUNE TELLING
CRYSTAL RADIO 25c
STEAM ENGINE 25c
Hi-Powered Air Pistols
TAP DANCE
COMPLETE CAMERA OUTFIT
ELECTRIC WATER HEATER 95c
REPEATING SLING SHOT
PEA-MATIC
JU-JITSU
FUN LICENSES 10c
MIDGET RACER 25c
MYSTERY MOVIE PIGS
CCC RING
ELECTRIC MOTOR
ELECTRIC EYE 25c
5 Master Keys
Fighting Roosters
Weather Rose
LUMINOUS PAINT
BIG ENTERTAINER
LEARN TO HYPNOTIZE
SNAPPY JOKES
Good Luck RING
Pistol Cigarette Case
250 Magic Tricks
MERRY WIDOW HANKY
Complete Printing Set
HOW TO LOVE 10c
125 CARD TRICKS
TOY MAKER 10c
MOTTO RINGS
HOME BREWED WINES & BEERS
WONDERFUL X-RAY 10c
DANCING SKELETON
SILENT DEFENDER
ADDRESS ALL ORDERS FOR GOODS ON THIS PAGE TO
JOHNSON SMITH & CO.
DEPARTMENT 112. DETROIT, MICHIGAN

A HOT SELLER, *MARVEL COMICS #1* FLEW OFF THE NEWSSTANDS ON AUGUST 31, 1939, AND SOLD OUT ITS ORIGINAL PRINTING WITHIN A WEEK. A SECOND PRINTING OF 800,000 COPIES WAS HASTILY SHOT OFF THE PRESSES WITH A REVISED INDICIA AND NOVEMBER OVERPRINT STAMP ADDED TO FRANK R. PAUL'S COVER.

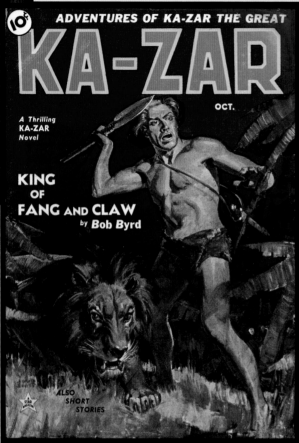

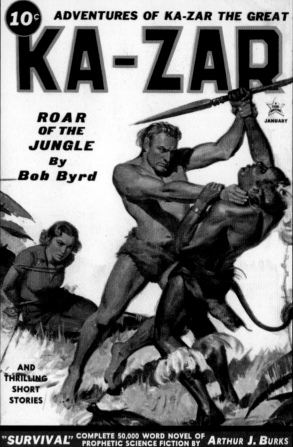

TIMELY EDITOR MARTIN GOODMAN'S FIRST TITLE BEARING THE NAME "MARVEL," THE PULP MAGAZINE *MARVEL SCIENCE STORIES* DEBUTED WITH AN AUGUST 1938 COVER DATE. COVER ART BY **NORMAN SAUNDERS**.

UNCANNY
TALES

REVELRY
IN

APR.-MAY
15¢

EXCITING STORIES OF HORROR AND TERROR

MYSTERY
TALES

SEPT.

15¢

SOULS FOR
SATAN'S
CREATURES
eerie novelet by
RUSSELL GRAY

BRIDES

BILL EVERETT WAS AN INCOMPARABLE TALENT AND AN EARLY COMIC BOOK AUTEUR. THIS PHOTOGRAPH OF
EVERETT WAS TAKEN SHORTLY BEFORE HE CREATED HIS SIGNATURE CHARACTER, THE TEMPESTUOUS SUB-MARINER.

TODAY A COPY OF *MARVEL COMICS #1* WILL COST YOU A BIT MORE THAN THE THIN DIME REQUESTED IN THESE HOUSE ADS FROM *COMPLETE DETECTIVE* (OCTOBER 1939) AND *WESTERN NOVELETS #139* (DECEMBER 1939).

MARVEL COMICS #1, PAGE 36 ORIGINAL ART BY BILL EVERETT

The Story of the Human Torch!

Carl Burgos' HOT IDEA

"He called to my attention the fact that I was letting down my public. As he spoke the room seemed to fill with boys and girls, all shouting hotly that they wanted a new character. Screaming with this artificial fever, I told them all to go to the Devil! At this they rushed in and grabbed me, and I fainted.

"When I awoke, I was lying on a bed of red hot coals. I figured that it must be the large furnace of the building. I was terrified for an instant, until I realized that I could stand the heat. I was burning.

"Outside the door of the furnace I could hear the laughter of my publisher and the children, but it was rapidly fading for the roar of the fire was filling my ears. A hot draft fanned the flames and I could feel myself being drawn up into the chimney. I seemed to float, my body was lighter than the air, and for a horrible minute I found myself hurtling up through the sooty brick chimney.

CARL BURGOS was sitting half way between his drawing board and his typewriter when we barged into his compact little studio. "How's about an interview, Carl?" we asked.

"Fire away!"

We learned that he was born in New York City, in uptown Manhattan, about two dozen years ago. He told us that he had gone to school there and had held every job he ever had in that city.

We queried him on the HUMAN TORCH.

"You'd be surprised how I happened upon the HUMAN TORCH," he said.

"IT was on the Fourth of July last year, a beastly hot day. The heat moved across my drawing board in heavy waves so thick I could feel it. To make matters worse, I had just had a hot discussion with my publisher. He wanted a new character, something brand new, an angle that had never been done before.

"I was all hot and bothered. I racked my brain until my head began to swim. At my wit's end, I decided to lie down for a while and try to cool off.

"I lay there for about fifteen minutes, like a man sick with jungle fever, my pulse pounding. The room seemed to take on a red glow.

"Suddenly into the room stormed my publisher, demanding to know where the new character was. In a daze I told him to go to the Devil, that gentleman being rather on my mind. I hoped that he would go away, but he didn't. His turning only added to the rapidly mounting heat of the room.

"LIKE any other skyrocket, I shot to a great height in a blazing arc. I was relieved to find that I was gradually drifting back to earth.

"I finally alighted on the roof of an office building, and I quickly ran to cover as my blaring feet were leaving smoking prints on the tar roof. In the building I heaved a sigh of relief for I recognized it as the place where my publisher had his office. I believed that if he could do this to me he should know how to make me normal again. I went to his office, being careful to walk only on the tile flooring.

"I pushed open the frosted glass door and stood face to face with him. The red glow from my body lighted up his face. His astonishment turned to delight and he called the members of his staff. As they all crowded around him he cried pointing to me, 'There's our new character, a HUMAN TORCH!'

"Burned up, I rushed at him, but stumbled. Then the scene faded.

"When I regained consciousness, I was lying on the floor of my studio feeling much better than before it all happened."

"But Carl," we smiled, "you tell it as if it had really happened."

He looked us squarely in the eyes. "You may not believe me, but my publisher was not a bit surprised when I showed him my new feature—the HUMAN TORCH. He acted as if he had known it all the time!"

We left shortly after that, closing the door quietly behind us. **END**

ZZLED. THER
SUMP'N SCREWY AB
THAT WRECK—
HAVE
GATE THIS SO C
— HUMAN TORCH—

Bill Everett's HURRICANE

The Story of THE SUB-MARINER!

• • •

"**T**HAT'S another story. You see, when we returned to the east coast, I found just as much adventure as I did in the west. What I mean is, I got myself a job on a seagoing tramp that went from Maine to Florida.

"On one run, when we were still a day out at Florida, one of those native Floridian hurricanes hit us broadsides. It shook that old tub like it was a toy. I happened to be at the wheel, and the full force of the storm spun it like a top. One of the bigger men took over for the minute, for there was another job to be done. The wireless antenna had been blown down, and it meant a climb up the slippery rope stays to the top of the mast. I was elected.

"I climbed into my oilskins and started up. The wind cut my face and hands, and I had all I could do to hold on. The rigging was wet and slippery. My job was to carry that loose wire up and tie it back to the mast. Well, I finally reached the top, and stood upright on the crosstrees. The wind lashed my oils and they cracked like thunder. Suddenly, after I had done my job, I felt myself being swept off my perch into thin air!

"I grabbed, and luckily caught the end of a rope. I swung there, half dazed for a moment, only to realize that my hand was slowly slipping off the wet hemp. Below I could see the washed deck glaring up at me. The cold wind had numbed my spirit, and a strange feeling came over me, I felt I was not alone.

"Something seemed to take hold of me and lift me, bodily, back onto the crosstrees. I lay there for a moment, and when I finally got a grip on myself, I looked up to see who, or what, had helped me.

"**THERE WAS NO ONE THERE!**"

IT was raining pretty hard when we reached Bill Everett's apartment-studio, a dramatic background for the story we hoped to get.

"Hello, Bill," we smiled, "mind if we annoy you for a while?"

"Come on in," Bill said beaming. "I was hoping someone would drop in on me tonight."

True to style, he made us feel right at home. "We've come to ask you to tell us something about yourself, and how you started to write about the SUB-MARINER. Do you mind?"

"Well," Bill said, "I was born in Newton, Massachusetts, and I'm still young enough to be in that first draft—if and when. When I was very young my folks went out to Arizona. We stayed there until after I finished high school.

"But, my folks decided to go back to Massachusetts, and I decided to go back to school. I went to the Vesper George Art School where I made up my mind that I would make art a career.

"While I was studying, I worked in a large advertising agency, but I wasn't satisfied. I wanted to do newspaper work, so I landed a job on the NEW YORK HERALD TRIBUNE, after doing a turn on the art staff of the BOSTON TRAVELER. Later I was the art director of a national magazine, but there my flare for cartooning was somewhat stifled, so I free-lanced around until I broke into this field, as the Art Editor of Funnies, Inc., the outfit that creates the features that appear in MARVEL COMICS."

"But, Bill," we asked, "where did you pick up the idea for the SUB-MARINER?"

WE couldn't help but notice the sincere look in Bill's eyes as he spoke. "Whew, that was a corker, Bill. But, where does the SUB-MARINER come in?"

He smiled that slow smile of his and said. "Who knows? To me it was HE who helped me that night.

"For the duration of that trip I was constantly reminded of Coleridge's ANCIENT MARINER, the poem that tells about the supernatural powers of the sea. I suppose that had some bearing on my title, SUB-MARINER.

"To me, I owe my life to that something—whether wind, a strong subconscious motion, or a supernatural being. But I shall always think of it as my friend . . . THE SUB-MARINER."

END

FANTASY MASTERPIECES #9 (JUNE 1967) REPRINTED THE HUMAN TORCH STORY FROM MARVEL COMICS #1, AS WELL AS SEVERAL OTHER GOLDEN AND SILVER AGE TALES. COVER ART BY **GIL KANE**.

INTRODUCTION

arvel Comics #1 is a milestone in the history of comic books. It not only intro-duced two of the greatest super heroes of the era now known as "The Golden Age", it also gave a start, and ultimately a name, to the most successful pub-lisher of comic books in the United States today.

That publishing company would become known, decades later, as Marvel Comics, and it still continues to publish the adventures of The Human Torch and The Sub-Mariner. In 1939, however, the firm was known as Timely Publica-tions, one of several companies owned and operated by an enterprising young man named Martin Goodman.

In 1932, with the country in the depths of a devastating depression, Goodman had launched his first pulp magazine, a collection of cowboy tales called **Complete Western Book**. Among the many that followed it were **Detective Short Stories, Uncanny Tales**, and **Marvel Science Stories**. Crime, horror, and sci-ence fiction were staple elements of the pulp magazines, which presented fast-moving fiction printed on cheap paper and wrapped in luridly colored covers. In their contents, the pulps were ancestors of the comic books, and pulp publishers like Goodman used their expertise in newsstand distribution to become key figures in the growth of the new medium.

Comic books had been around in one form or another for years, but had really come into their own in 1938 with the introduction of a character called Superman, who demonstrated that colorfully costumed heroes gifted with strange powers could be more appealing to young readers than reprints of old newspaper strips. Within a few months, super heroes were popping up everywhere.

When **Marvel Comics** appeared, however, it offered readers something a little different. The typical super hero was something of a Boy Scout, a two-dimensional figure who never wavered from his oath to do good and right wrongs. Marvel characters didn't necessarily find things that easy to figure out. The Human Torch, an artificial being created in a laboratory, was terrified when he discovered that he could burst into flame. Everybody else seemed to consider him a menace, and only criminals even pretended to befriend him. His creator was willing to betray him for a quick buck, and nobody stopped to think of him as a potential hero. The Sub-Mariner seemed even more like a villain. The prince of an undersea race, he had a human father and thus wasn't really at home even among his own people, but he had an abiding hatred for surface dwellers, and more than a touch of malice in his makeup. He was redeemed only by a hint that there might be justice in his cause, that perhaps mankind was despoiling the planet.

In short, these unusual characters with their muddled motives were forerunners of the mixed-up super heroes that later brought Marvel Comics to the forefront of the industry. The Sub-Mariner was a young rebel, The Human Torch suffered from an identity crisis, and comic books were never quite the same again.

How did Martin Goodman happen to acquire such an awesome twosome for his first effort in the field? It was sheer luck, really. Goodman and his staff had no experience in creating comics, so he commissioned the contents of **Marvel Comics #1** from a company called Funnies Incorporated.

6

PUBLISHED IN 1990, THE *MARVEL COMICS #1 50TH ANNIVERSARY HC* FEATURED NEW TEXT PIECES BY **LES DANIELS** AND **ROY THOMAS**.

Funnies Inc. was, in the parlance of the time, a "shop," a company with the talent to produce comic books but without the capital to publish them. Lloyd Jacquet ran the business, and his chief salesman was Frank Torpey, who set up a meeting with pulp publisher Goodman and convinced him that comic books were the wave of the future. Goodman's gamble paid off handsomely, and eventually he offered Torpey a job as a member of his own sales staff.

The art director at Funnies Inc., Bill Everett, didn't have to look far to find at least one feature for **Marvel Comics**—he had already created Prince Namor, The Sub-Mariner, for a comic book that never got published. **Motion Picture Funnies Weekly** had been intended as a premium to be given out at movie theaters, but there had been so little interest from economy-minded exhibitors that the project was scuttled, and only a handful of office copies have survived. Ecologically-minded like his hero was, Everett recycled The Sub-Mariner, and with that decision became the creator of Marvel's first super hero.

Carl Burgos, the father of The Human Torch, was Everett's friend as well as his colleague. They were contemporaries, both born in 1917, and had worked together for another publisher before joining Funnies Inc. and taking on the **Marvel Comics** commission. According to Everett, he and Burgos sometimes met in a bar after work to kick around ideas, and The Torch came out of one such session. The fire vs. water concept was a natural, and it was all but inevitable that The Torch and Namor would eventually clash. The classic crossover ran through issues eight, nine, and ten of what by then was called **Marvel Mystery Comics**. Publisher Martin Goodman had added the "Mystery" to the title beginning with the second issue, but nobody seems to remember why.

Goodman also had some input into **Marvel Comics #1**. He decided that The Human Torch was the character who would make the greatest impact on the cover, and then gave the assignment to one of his regular pulp magazine artists, Frank R. Paul. The Torch went on to appear on almost every cover of the title's ten year run. Goodman also had some evident influence in the choice of one of the back-up characters, Ka-Zar. This jungle hero, a fairly obvious imitation of Tarzan, was the title character of a Goodman pulp magazine that appeared for three issues back in 1936. Funnies Inc. staffer Ben Thompson created the comic book version, based on the prose pieces by Bob Byrd. Ka-Zar didn't last long, but he has returned often enough over the years to be assured of his place in the Marvel Universe. That's more than can be said for The Masked Raider, an ersatz Lone Ranger depicted by Al Anders. The story "Jungle Terror," by Tom Dixon, was a one-shot, and the prose piece "Burning Rubber" was only included because it qualified the comic book for magazine mailing rates. The Angel is another matter. This ruthless vigilante, whose methods of dealing with criminals leave the authorities unnerved, strikes a modern note since such characters have recently come into vogue, but in fact he was the type of avenging

BY LES DANIELS

angel found frequently in the pulps. Perhaps for this reason, he was reportedly the favorite of publisher Goodman, who featured him on a few covers before he realized who the stars really were. Created by Paul Gustavson, The Angel enjoyed a healthy run in his day, but seems unlikely to make a major comeback since his name was later bestowed on one of the original X-Men.

By today's standards, the writing and drawing in **Marvel Comics #1** seem crude. Most of its contributors were relative newcomers to the field, working rapidly for a few dollars a page, and usually providing scripts, pencils, inks and even lettering without any assistance. Some went on to do much more polished work—notably Bill Everett, who was contributing elegant Sub-Mariner pages just before his death in 1973. But there was enough energy and innovation in Marvel's first offering to capture the public's imagination, and this title was soon joined by others like **Daring Mystery** and **Mystic**.

Late in 1939, writer-artist Joe Simon was hired away from Funnies Inc. to serve as Marvel-Timely's first editor. Simon and his partner Jack Kirby created **Captain America Comics**, the company's biggest seller. The Human Torch and The Sub-Mariner got their own titles, and a youngster named Stan Lee was added to the staff. The quality of the comics improved and sales jumped as World War II broke out. More titles were added: **U.S.A, All Winners, Young Allies, All Select**. Stan Lee had been editor for years when the super heroes ran out of steam in 1949, but the company carried on, publishing humor, horror, westerns, war, whatever sold.

In 1961, Martin Goodman suggested to Stan Lee that the time might be ripe for a super hero revival; Lee and Jack Kirby responded by creating **The Fantastic Four**. One member of the quartet was a new version of The Human Torch, and the villain in the fourth issue, still strangely sympathetic, was The Sub-Mariner. The company finally adopted Marvel Comics as its official name, and a renaissance of the super hero began with the introduction of characters like The Incredible Hulk, Spider-Man, Thor, Iron Man, The Avengers, The X-Men, and a host of others.

Marvel has gone from strength to strength, until today it dominates the field, but it all started here, with **Marvel Comics #1**. The Torch and The Sub-Mariner have sometimes been dismissed as "gimmick" characters, dependent on the elements of fire and water for their appeal, but in fact it is the personalities of these first Marvel heroes that set them apart. Far from being defined by their powers, these heroes are troubled by them, and must strive to define themselves in a world that seems to have no place for them. In these simple stories is the germ of the modern Marvel style.

What you are holding is a reproduction of this extraordinarily rare publication, which even in mediocre condition is worth thousands of dollars. A copy in mint condition was recently sold for $82,000, which is apparently the highest price ever paid for a single comic book. You may not feel it is the best you have ever read, but it is certainly one of the most important.

You have history in your hands.

—Les Daniels

! THE
GHING!
T
N
HA! HA. HA!
STOP—
IT TICKLES!
I CAN
HELP
IT?

THE TORCH THAT LIT THE WAY

O ne of the two pillars of talent upon which rested the success of Timely Comics' earliest days was the Sub-Mariner's creator, Bill Everett.

The other was Carl Burgos, creator of the first Human Torch.

Born in New York in 1917, Burgos attended the famous National Academy of Design, and in his late teens drifted into working for Harry "A" Chesler, head of one of the first of the so-called "comic shops."

The comics shops, in case it isn't explained elsewhere in this landmark reprinting of **Marvel Comics #1**, were groups of writers and artists who, laboring away in some loft or office somewhere, produced entire issues of comic books from start to finish, then delivered them *en toto* to the publisher, who simply had them printed up—and copyrighted—in his (ye publisher's) name.

This, you see, allowed publishers to leap headlong from putting out other types of magazines into the burgeoning new field of comic books, without the fuss and bother of setting up their own organizations. All they had to do was sign the checks.

This was the brave new world young Carl Burgos entered circa 1938.

Sometimes he'd work for a comics shop, at other times directly for a comics publisher. Burgos's first solo strip was something which has been reported variously as "Stoney Dawson" or "Rocky Dawson." Either way, it was clearly a stepping-stone (you should excuse the expression) to better things.

Those "better things" evidently began when he went to work for Centaur Publications, home of such deathless new heroes as Speed Centaur and Detective Eye (respectively, a crime-smashing centaur and a crime-smashing giant flying eye). Burgos's main contribution to the line was a crime-smashing android called the Iron Skull.

From first to last, it seems, androids were to be a Burgos mainstay.

By 1939—there've been at least two or three different versions printed of how it came about—Carl was working with a go-getter named Lloyd Jacquet and a good friend, writer/artist Bill Everett, as part of a new comics shop which Jacquet christened "Funnies, Incorporated."

According to an interview I did with Everett in 1972, Funnies, Inc.'s sales manager was a friend of pulp-mag publisher Martin Goodman, who wanted to get into comics in the wake of the recent success of **Action Comics** and Superman.

For this venture, Everett created the Sub-Mariner—and Carl Burgos created the Human Torch.

The resultant comic: **Marvel Comics #1**, which for reasons best known only to God and Martin Goodman (if them!) became **Marvel Mystery Comics** with its second issue.

The Torch was evidently considered the hotter property of the two, for Goodman commissioned a different artist to do a cover of that hero. No swimming-suit could compete with the sight of a man on fire!

The Torch, of course, wasn't really human at all. He was actually merely the second (but not the last) of Burgos's awesome androids.

Still, it was the Torch, who after all even worked for the New York Police Department, was generally on the side of the human race in those epic early battles with the Sub-Mariner, while Prince Namor was usually out for revenge and/or conquest.

All too soon, everybody, including Burgos, tended to *forget* the Torch's android state, and to treat him as if

BY ROY THOMAS

he were human from head to toe. From 1939-49, the Torch appeared in all 92 issues of **Marvel Mystery**, in all 35 issues of **The Human Touch**, and in dozens of other Timely mags—and to the best of my knowledge, after the first year or so at most, there was never another hint of the Torch's being an android until his origin was retold in the final issue of **Marvel Mystery**! As a kid who started reading Torch stories circa 1945-46, I remember how shocked I was when I found out.

Burgos never made great claims for his artwork. Still, though doubtless with help from assistants, he drew (and perhaps wrote) the Torch until he, like Everett, went into the armed services soon after Pearl Harbor. As reported by Burgos in the invaluable *Steranko History of Comics*, he "started in the Air Corps, took infantry ranger training, went overseas as a rifleman, was transferred to the Signal Corps, and came back in the engineers."

While Burgos was out of town—*way* out of town—others stepped into the breach to draw the Torch's increasingly warlike adventures: Syd Shores, Carl Pfeufer, Mike Sekowsky, Don Rico, Al Gabriele, Jimmy Thompson, *et al*.

Burgos drew some more comics after he was mustered out of the service. In 1954 the Torch was revived briefly. His android origin was again told, then again ignored. Art was by the likes of Russ Heath and Dick Ayers—and, unless I miss my guess, one Carl Burgos, who was on the Timely staff at the time.

But, though during this period Burgos made the jump from comics into the advertising field, which was to be his profession of choice for the rest of his life, he wasn't quite done with comic books yet.

In the early/middle 1960s, when the new Marvel Comics Group was just getting up a full head of steam, Burgos returned to draw a story or two starring Giant-Man—not to mention a brash youngster named Johnny Storm, who had become the only Human Torch which the Woodstock Generation was to know.

Soon afterward, he became editor of Eerie Publications, which put out black-and-white horror comics and the like. And, circa 1966, he both drew and probably at least co-created a hero named—Captain Marvel.

No, not the kid who shouted "Shazam!" and changed into the World's Mightiest Mortal—or Captain Mar-Vell, that gallant Kree officer who later died of cancer—or the current light-bending lady who used to chair the Avengers.

Burgos's Captain Marvel was—you guessed it—an *android*.

In the aftermath of the mid-60s Batman TV craze, everybody and his brother was coming out with super heroes. And since the Captain Marvel name had been lying around for more than a decade, Burgos and Eerie decided to use that well-known monicker for a hero who—well, let's just say that when he shouted the word "Split!" his arms and legs (maybe his head, too—I forget) went flying in every direction to slug or kick or butt criminals. Then he'd yell "Zam!"—and all the errant members would swiftly rejoin themselves to his robotic torso.

This Captain Marvel was not Burgos's finest hour—but hey, nobody's perfect.

Myself, I never met Carl Burgos personally.

I always wanted to, of course, being the Golden Age groupie I was and am.

For years I wanted to lock him and Bill Everett up in a room together somewhere, and not let either of them out until they had straightened up a lot of weighty matters such as:

Did the two of them *really* create the Torch and Sub-Mariner as opposites, over drinks in the Webster Bar—or did Namor exist a bit earlier, since he was also published in that freebie black-and-white called *Motion*

Picture Funnies Weekly?

Which of those frantic Torch-vs.-Namor free-for-alls was it that, according to legend, was produced over one frantic weekend with everybody squirreled up in a hotel suite, wildly scribbling away, with Burgos drawing the Torch figures and Everett the Namor figures while others wrote, inked, did backgrounds, lettered, etc.?

Did Lloyd Jacquet really offer Bill Everett and three other guys (*not* counting Burgos) the chance to go in 50-50 with him in 1939 on Funnies, Inc., as Everett told Jim Steranko—or did Funnies, Inc., originally consist of the trio of Jacquet, Everett, and Burgos, as *Burgos* told Steranko elsewhere on the very same page of his history?

I don't suppose we'll ever know.

I only spoke once to Burgos before his death. In 1977 I finally talked with him by phone between New York and my new home in Los Angeles. I was putting together an annual for Marvel's World War Two opus, **The Invaders**, and I wanted desperately to have the solo chapters of Torch, Subby, and Captain America illustrated by Golden Age greats.

Carl said he'd be happy to do the Torch chapter, but later withdrew at the last minute for obscure reasons. I was fortunate to get Alex Schomburg, who'd done so many great Timely covers during the war years, to fill in for him: still, I've always regretted not getting the chance to work, even once, with the creator of the Human Torch. Carl Burgos died in 1984.

But the Torch himself, and his published adventures, remain—already spanning more than five decades in one incarnation or another, and destined perhaps to still be crying "Flame on!" as the twentieth century turns into the twenty-first.

And what better way to light our way into a new millennium—than with the glow of a Human Torch?

BILL E. & ME

t is an ancient Mariner,

And he stoppeth one of three...

So begins Samuel Taylor Coleridge's epic poem **The Rime of the Ancient Mariner,** which many of us muddled through in school and a few of us probably enjoyed, even if we never totally understood it. One of those who did enjoy the poem, as he enjoyed most things related to the sea, was **Bill Everett,** the creator of Prince Namor, the Sub-Mariner—who was partly named after Coleridge's poem.

Bill Everett was a friend of mine.

As a fan of the Sub-Mariner since the late 1940s, I was thrilled when, not long after I became Stan Lee's assistant editor at Marvel in 1965, the great Bill Everett suddenly showed up in the Marvel Bullpen and announced that he was ready to go back to work.

Actually, Bill, who'd lately been working for a paper firm in Massachusetts, had made an abortive return to comics the year before, when he'd illustrated **DAREDEVIL #1** for Stan as editor and writer. However, the strains of moonlighting had led to severe deadline problems, and Bill had never been overly scrupulous about deadlines when he was holding down just *one* job—so after that single issue, Stan and Bill had called off their collaboration by mutual consent.

But now Bill was back, and Stan was glad to see him, for Marvel was growing by leaps and bounds (*I'd* landed a job there, hadn't I?), and there was always room for one more talented cartoonist. Bill's plan was to stay in New York City during the week, and return to New England—and his family—on weekends.

But he needed a place to stay when he was in town.

And since my fellow Missourian and comics writer Gary Friedrich and I had just moved into an apartment of our own, we volunteered to put Bill up those four or five nights a week.

Volunteered? We were ecstatic—especially me. It gave me a chance to talk at length with one of the talents I most admired from the so-called Golden Age of Comics, of which he'd been such an integral part.

Bill's work on Sub-Mariner in the late 40s had been fairly standard fare storywise, though enlivened by his highly individualistic art style, and in 1965 I had only seen a few of his earliest stories. But his all-too-brief revival of Namor in 1954–55 I considered then (as I still do) to be one of the super-hero highlights of the 1950s, or any other decade.

Anyway, Bill moved, part-time, into our second-floor pad at 177A Bleecker Street, between MacDougal and Sullivan Streets—in the heart of Manhattan's Greenwich Village.

Like I said, this was 1965—the blossoming of the counterculture movement. Every night beneath our streetside window, across from the studio of a prominent sculptor, a virtual Sargasso Sea of motorcycles revved and roared in front of the trendy hand-painting establishment that occupied the first floor directly under us. Occasionally, we could even hear ourselves think.

Our digs were a "railroad apartment"—one in which the rooms are strung out in a straight row. Theoretically, you could stand in the narrow living room (which was maybe a whole ten feet wide) and fire a bullet through the narrow kitchen and the narrow bedroom into the wall of the narrow bathroom.

A REMINISCENCE BY **ROY THOMAS**

How we squeezed Bill, as well, into this tiny space still puzzles me, but somehow we did it. He'd sleep on the couch or the bed (assuming anyone could tell the difference), without complaint. He and Gary drove me crazy with the cigarette butts they left everywhere. Everywhere.

Though he was twice our age, Bill somehow fit right in with the Bohemian atmosphere. Probably better than I did. The three of us hung out in espresso joints and bars, being jostled by peaceniks and protesters.

Of course, it was hardly an idyllic time for Bill, as he was separated for days at a time from his wife and his daughter Wendy. And, truth to tell, he wasn't exactly the most productive member of the Bullpen this time around.

His first assignment was to pick up where Steve Ditko had abruptly left off on **DR. STRANGE**. Bill did a creditable job, co-creating Umar the Unrelenting with Stan. He even gave our apartment's address to the good Doctor's mansion, which it has retained to this day, against all logic and logistics.

But in that very first story, which called for a flashback of Doc and Clea in an earlier adventure, Bill cleverly sidestepped several hours' worth of drawing by pasting up panels from the Ditko story being recapped instead of redrawing the scenes in his own style. Stan was understandably not too happy about Bill's ingenuity, even though it had probably taken him longer to paste up the pages than it would have to draw the scene himself.

Still, Stan, like Marvel's publisher Martin Goodman, always had a weak spot in his heart for Bill, who'd been a part of that very first issue of **Marvel Comics** already a quarter of a century in the past.

Bill himself was never one to look back; at least, he'd rarely initiate the reminiscences. But once I'd get him started, the memories would pour out, first there in that Greenwich Village hole—then later, after a quite convincing death threat from a landlord who took issue with the theory and practice of rent control had caused us to depart Bleecker Street, in my apartment on the more fashionable Upper East Side.

Bill's memories were colored with time, of course, and some of them were doubtless more accurate than others, but they were a joy to listen to.

Among many other things, he told me how—

As a young man, he'd come within an ace of going on an expedition to the Polar Regions with the famous Admiral Byrd;

He and cartoonist Carl Burgos had met circa 1938–39 at the Centaur Comic Group, where he created "Skyrocket Steele," then "Dirk the Demon," and finally an early and intriguing super-hero called "Amazing-Man."

He and Burgos had left Centaur to join an organization called Funnies, Inc., which put together ("packaged") entire comic books for publishers, on a freelance basis;

The Sub-Mariner and Burgos' creation, the Human Torch, became the two main features in **Marvel Comics #1**

COPYRIGHT © 1978 ROY THOMAS
ART BY MARIE SEVERIN

...UZZLED. THER
SUMP'N SCREWY AB
THAT WRECK—
HAVE
GATE THIS SO C
— HUMAN TORCH—

which Funnies, Inc. packaged for pulp-mag publisher Martin Goodman, who was starting Timely Comics, forerunner of Marvel Comics;

Bill gave Namor his own distinctive flying method—wings on his feet—by borrowing them from a statue of the Roman god Mercury;

He gave his hero his name by writing lots of words backward on a piece of paper—and "Namor" was the one that looked best;

He, Burgos and a ragtag team of writers and artists worked long, sleepless weekends to complete a Torch/Namor battle story, with Everett and Burgos each penciling the figures of his own hero;

He came up with a weird illustrative technique for the first two Sub-Mariner stories, to give a greater illusion of underwater action (thereby inadvertently making those stories almost impossibly difficult to reprint in 1990!);

He had a young fan named Jack Lemmon, who wanted very much to grow up and be a cartoonist himself ("Wonder what ever happend to that kid!" he'd laugh);

Bill developed two more underwater heroes—"Hydroman" and "The Fin"—because he *liked* doing underwater heroes;

When the Sub-Mariner's comic folded in 1949, he switched over to doing horror comics without missing a beat, and got to enjoy doing them every bit as much;

He and artists Joe Maneely and John Severin caroused and "lost Fridays" (*i.e.*, paydays) as Marvel/Timely staffers in the mid-1950s...

Namor's comic outlasted both the Torch and Captain America in that short-lived 1950s revival because a producer was showing an interest in doing a "Sub-Mariner" TV series starring movie star Richard Egan, and nobody was likely to build a show around a hero who'd been canceled, right?;

Bill himself got an early tip that the economic axe was about to fall on Timely Comics staffers in 1957, and dug out early to avoid the rush;

He finally called up Stan about getting back into comic books after seeing a piece on them in *Playboy* and figuring that maybe there was still a career for him in comics, after all.

Yeah, Bill told me all that—once, twice, many times, once I'd get him started.

He'd have a drink (he had 'way too many drinks, but eventually became a proud, proselytizing, and far-from-anonymous mainstay of Alcoholics Anonymous for several years before his death in 1973), and he'd tell me lots of things.

Most of which, alas, I've forgotten over the years that have flowed under the bridge since then.

One thing, though, he never did get around to telling me:

How to stop wishing, every time I stop and think about it, that Bill Everett were still around to tell me his stories all over again.

MARVEL MASTERWORKS:
GOLDEN AGE MARVEL COMICS VOL. 1 HC (2004)
INTRODUCTION EXCERPT BY ROY THOMAS

What you hold in your hands is both a marvel—
and a mystery!

Until the 1990s, it was virtually unheard of, and all
but undreamed of, that any comics company would
ever publish faithful full-color reprints of the early
comic book stories, whether as facsimile editions
or as actual books.

But things began to change in 1990, both at Marvel
and elsewhere. In that year Marvel, for its part,
published a hardcover quasi-reprint of *Marvel
Comics #1*, the title that had started it all for merry
Martin Goodman, accountant turned pulp-mag
publisher turned comic book entrepreneur with
his Timely Comics Group. This was followed in
the late '90s by reprints of three quality-paper,
comics-format reprints of sought-after stories in
two trade-paperback volumes of *The Golden Age
of Marvel*, and by two primo hardcovers reprinting
all the Captain America stories from the first ten,
Simon-and-Kirby-produced issues of that title.

The latter whetted our appetites for a series
reprinting, issue by issue, of the great early editions
of *Marvel Mystery Comics*, which had introduced
Timely's first two great heroes, the Human Torch
and the Sub-Mariner, to a world that had been
breathlessly waiting for them without knowing it.

And now we have it: *Marvel Comics #1* and *Marvel
Mystery Comics #2-4*, together again for the first
time. And what a package it is!

Oh, it's easy enough to find fault with the writing and
art—to call them "primitive" (as if primitivism were
de facto a bad thing) or "childish" (as if they weren't
scripted and drawn precisely with kids in mind, or
as if kid-oriented material wasn't worth doing)—
and, I might add, as if folks a few decades down
the road aren't going to make equally disparaging
remarks about today's favorites, wondering why
they aren't up to the obviously superior and eternal
standards of 2070.

To appreciate the all-important comics reproduced
in this volume, it helps to have a sense of historical
perspective—of being able to put oneself in shoes
made in the first half of the 20th century, and go
for a nice long unhurried walk, stopping to smell
the roses (and the pulp paper) along the way.

For something was being born in America at
the end of the 1930s—something relatively new
under the sun, insofar as anything ever *can* be
new—something no other generation had ever
experienced in quite the same way.

Two new things, actually.

Comic books—and super heroes.

I won't waste time here debating whether the comic
art form is descended lineally from *The Yellow Kid*
in 1896, or the work of Rudolph Töpffer in Germany
in the mid-19th century, or Egyptian hieroglyphics,
or even the pictures carved in caves in Spain and
France during the Stone Age. Such speculation is
all very interesting, but in the end it doesn't matter.
Comic books—*real* comic books as we know them
today—were born in the mid-1930s, and they were
a definite mutation from what had come before.

So were super heroes.

You can find precursors for any individual super
hero, of course. The Human Torch and Sub-Mariner?
Well, shucks, Superman was there "first," right? Only
thing is, Zorro and The Phantom and the super-
powered hero of Philip Wylie's novel *Gladiator* and
even Popeye were there before *him*—and Tarzan
and John Carter of Mars before *them*—and Hercules
and Perseus and Theseus long before any of that
bunch! Point being: once someone conceived the
notion of a man (or woman) with super-powers,
walking (and sometimes leaping or even flying)
amid humankind in our modern technological
society, the dam had burst.

Marvel Comics #1 was such a cascading torrent of
a comic book.

Martin Goodman probably had only a vague idea
of what he wanted when he decided in 1939 to
switch some of his publishing activities from
pulp magazines with names like *Marvel Science
Stories* and *Ka-Zar* to the burgeoning new field
of comic books. Supposedly, a business associate
named Frank Torpey convinced Goodman to get
into comics, and Goodman was reportedly forever
grateful, with Torpey receiving a $25 a week stipend
for years afterward.

Goodman himself was smart enough to realize that
super heroes, a new phenomenon in said new field,
were what was making those four-color mags leap
off the nation's newsstands into the hands of kids
(and the occasional adult) with a dime to spare at
the tail end of the Great Depression. So he probably
told Lloyd Jacquet, the head of a comics-producing
"shop" known as Funnies, Inc., to produce for
him the wall-to-wall contents of a comic book
with a super hero or two in it. But not *only* super
heroes, because in 1939 everybody was still hedging
their bets. Yeah, there might be a guy in a mask

and tights up front and on the cover, but inside he had backup: jungle heroes not named Tarzan and magicians not named Mandrake and masked cowboys not called the Lone Ranger and private detectives not named Sam Spade. Thus, Goodman wound up with Ka-Zar, and the Masked Raider, and with Ferret the Mystery Detective (at least by issue #4)—even if there never was a magician hero in *Marvel Mystery*. Plus there were gag cartoons. You hadda have gag cartoons—one-pagers, one *panel*, even—just to break things up, even on the inside covers, maybe, where you didn't have to pay for color, while you waited for the advertising revenue to start pouring in.

Lloyd Jacquet wasn't a particularly creative guy himself, but he didn't have to be. He had Bill Everett and Carl Burgos and Paul Gustavson and some other guys working for him who *were* creative. In the case of Everett and Burgos, very creative. And in the case of Everett—very, *very* creative.

Nobody knows precisely how the Human Torch and the Sub-Mariner (let alone the Angel) came to be in the package that Jacquet's studio produced, which became *Marvel Comics #1*. When he and I roomed together in the late 1960s, Bill Everett told me he had no idea which had come first—his Namor or Burgos' Torch. Did water lead to fire—or fire to water—or was it all just some amazing coincidence spawned by two guys working near each other at drawing desks? Sure, also in 1939 there was this short-lived black-and-white comic called *Motion Picture Funnies Weekly* which printed the first eight pages of what became the 12-page initial "Sub-Mariner" story in *Marvel #1*, but nobody to date has nailed down precisely how the one led to the other—or even been able to prove with 100% certainty which one came first.

It's even been claimed now and again that Bill Everett got the idea for the Sub-Mariner from an unproduced movie serial (maybe one that had some connection with *Motion Picture Funnies Weekly?*) that dealt with Atlantis as a sunken civilization— and besides, Republic Pictures' second serial, in 1936, had been titled *The Undersea Kingdom*, although its inhabitants were air-breathers. But there was no authentic source, no paper trail, for the former theory—not even a plausible quote from a 1930s movie executive or scriptwriter. The whole hypothesis reads to this writer, frankly, like somebody's pipe dream. Bill E. himself told me in an interview circa 1970 that he'd "always been interested in anything nautical"—that he'd also been fascinated by anything to do with Atlantis, including the psychic readings of the famed Edgar Cayce—that he could have gone on one of Admiral Byrd's legendary expeditions to one of the Poles "if I'd wanted to." But what Bill had really needed to do was make a living, so he concocted a story about a half-man, half-fish from the Antarctic, wrote down the word "Roman" backward for his name, and that was it. He never used the word "Atlantis,"

because "Atlantis to me was another world and a world that existed and I still believe it does, somewhere… But the idea of a submerged continent came from Atlantis."

When I spoke with Torch creator Carl Burgos once or twice over the phone—I never met the man, alas—I never got around to asking him about the conception of his own hero, but it was probably much the same as Bill's. He had to make a buck— and in 1939 making up a super hero had been the way to do it, if you wanted to be a comic book artist and/or writer. Maybe neither man was thinking consciously of the fact that Superman's publishers had already sued an early imitator called Wonder Man out of existence because he had the same powers as Jerry Siegel and Joe Shuster's creation— but the fact remains that, whether instinctively or cold-bloodedly, Carl and Bill conceived characters who *weren't* just imitations of another hero. Each had his own super-power, his own gimmick, his own *raison d'être*. One was an android who burst into flame when exposed to the air—the other a merman. They would blaze (and swim) new trails all their own.

In terms of personality, too, they were originally something less than standardly heroic. At first, the Torch wasn't much more than a force of unleashed nature, charging around in a world he never made and wondering why everything he touched turned to flame. Why indeed? And the Sub-Mariner was the next thing to an out-and-out villain, at least if you looked at it from the viewpoint of the NYPD, the Army, or just John Q. Citizen trying to get home on the elevated train and finding that some guy with a triangular head and wings on his feet had ripped it right out from under you! Namor, in particular, had a well-developed personality that was years ahead of its time, and would find its ultimate echo and reincarnation in *Fantastic Four* and the other comics launched by Stan Lee, Jack Kirby, and Steve Ditko in the early 1960s and after.

But, you can read all that wonderment for yourself, and draw your own conclusions about what it all means. No need for me to connect all the dots for you. You'll see the wheels turning, the synapses synapting, as Bill and Carl and the others spin their titanic tales for you. The kid inside you will undoubtedly wonder what's going to happen *next* issue. No wonder you won't quite know—they didn't know themselves! They were, quite literally, making it up as they went along.

But, while you're marveling—don't forget to *enjoy*! These are classic stories you're about to read (some of them, anyway)—milestones in comics history.

And a lot of them are genuine, unadulterated *fun*!

—Roy Thomas
2004

INTRODUCTION
BY WILL MURRAY

The late summer of 1939 signaled the approaching ten year anniversary of the Stock Market Crash of 1929. For a grim and gloomy decade, the United States had been mired in the Great Depression. No end lay in sight. No one imagined that the solution to America's economic recovery lay in Europe, where German leader Adolf Hitler had been annexing and absorbing neighboring nations like a ravenous tiger.

In early September, Hitler's gray legions unexpectedly devoured Poland in a full-out invasion. World War II had ignited. Europe quickly plunged into an abyss of death and destruction never before witnessed by history.

As Americans read the headlines in the security of an ocean's distance from the warring European nations, they began to sense that they too would be drawn into the spreading Nazi holocaust.

Yet there was hope in the air. The 1939 New York World's Fair had opened in April, showcasing the exciting World of Tomorrow. In the world of popular entertainment, big things were brewing. Hollywood was having its best year ever. This was the golden year of *Gone with the Wind, The Wizard of Oz, Mr. Smith Goes to Washington,* and similar cinematic classics. Radio was going nationwide, and attracting big name stars like Fred Allen and Jack Benny. *The Shadow* and *The Lone Ranger* were top-rated programs. The new medium of television, its development stalled by the Depression, was said to be just around the corner. And another new medium, an offshoot of the pulp fiction magazine crossed with immensely popular newspaper comic strips, was booming.

Comic books had been around for most of the 1930s. But not until the advent of Superman in 1938 did sales skyrocket into the stratosphere. Kids and adults were snapping up copies of *Action Comics,* as well as *Detective Comics* featuring Batman. Hearing of million-copy print runs, other publishers began jumping in. A revolutionary new kind of American hero was emerging from this novel new art form—the super hero! The Golden Age of Comic books had dawned.

The newspaper scare heads that summer failed to record another beginning. In Manhattan, a beleaguered publisher named Martin Goodman received the inaugural issue of *Marvel Comics* in his office in the McGraw-Hill Building. It was his first foray into the fresh field of comic books. He also hoped it would become the salvation of his shaky pulp publishing enterprise.

As Goodman extracted from a messenger envelope the advance copy, still warm from the heat of the presses, he absorbed the vivid Frank R. Paul cover, showing the Human Torch burning through a bank vault, a frightened robber's bullets melting against his superheated chest, and frowned critically at the slightly off-register printing. Covers were the most important element of any magazine. The searing scarlet of the Torch, the red-and-yellow of the Marvel Comics title logo, jumped out. But would they grab the kids?

Martin Goodman, circa 1942

Opening the magazine, Goodman's editorial heart must have stopped. The interior printing was a disaster! Colors were inconsistent and wildly off-register. His lead hero, the Human Torch, changed color without rhyme or reason. The Sub-Mariner strip with its elegant penwork on craft-tint paper printed as muddy as its sea-bottom setting. Worse, the lettering was smudged and difficult to read.

Seeking a standout cover, Goodman had gone to the extra expense of using process color separation instead of the flat primary palette employed by other comic houses—all for nothing!

Suddenly it no longer mattered whether or not the enhanced cover enticed prospective readers to purchase *Marvel Comics* #1. Once they began reading, kids would throw down the shoddy package in utter disgust, never to bother with another—as no doubt Martin Goodman felt like doing at that very moment, 70 years ago.

He picked the phone to cancel *Marvel Comics.* After just one issue, Goodman was through with comic books forever.

In that very same moment, the future Marvel Universe trembled on the brink of eternity. Captain America. Spider-Man. The Hulk. Thor. The Fantastic Four. And countless others, were about to become still-born. The careers of creative giants such as Stan Lee, Jack Kirby, Carl Burgos, Bill Everett, Steve Ditko, and many more, hung in the balance. An exciting world of entertainment, modern myth and soaring super-heroic escape tottered on the brink of being de-created.

And Martin Goodman was about to make what could be the most disastrous decision of his professional life.

Martin Goodman had entered the world of magazine publishing at the worst possible time in 20th century. He could never imagine that he was laying the foundations for a mighty multimedia empire.

The year was 1933. By most accounts, the darkest of the Great Depression. Magazines and their publishers were in desperate trouble. Distributors were going out of business. The great pulp chains that had boomed with the prosperity of the Roaring Twenties were crashing. Fiction House. Clayton. Dell. Fawcett. And many lesser houses. By the beginning of 1933, most were bankrupt or had suspended operations indefinitely. Some would never rise again.

Among these foundering publishers was pioneer Hugo Gernsback, the founder of *Amazing Stories*, the first science-fiction magazine. He too was in dire financial straights. Ironically, this cash-strapped futurist's own future looked bleak.

Working in Gernsback's circulation department were Louis Horace Silberkleit and Martin Goodman. Goodman soon became a publisher's representative for Eastern Distribution Company, traveling the country, pushing magazines like *Amazing Stories* and Harry Steeger's new Popular Publications line to distributors. The 25-year-old Brooklynite had come up the hard way, hitchhiking across country, riding the rails and living in hobo camps while he figured out what to do with his life. It wouldn't be easy. Goodman had only a 4th grade education. Magazines fascinated him as a youngster. Family legend has it that he would cut and paste prototypes of his own out of existing periodicals.

By contrast, Silberkleit was seven years older, a college graduate and registered pharmacist, with a degree from New York Law School. He too joined Eastern. They seemed improbable prospective partners.

Louis Silberkleit

Then Eastern News collapsed, temporarily taking down several pulp houses with it. Goodman had made a lot of contacts and more than a few friends. Seeing their ships going down, he and Silberkleit decided to team up and found their own company.

For in this chaos, Silberkleit and Goodman saw opportunity. The nation was just as much in need of a good ten-cent pulp magazine as before. Probably more, with the millions of newly unemployed swelling in numbers by the week.

The key to this lay in the print shops of America. Printing houses were suffering just as much as magazine publishers. More so, since a publisher could suspend operations until market conditions improved, as Fiction House did for a year. Or they could simply fold their tent and go out of business.

Not so a printer. Those huge Hoe offset presses cost millions of dollars. You couldn't just idle them. There were unbreakable union printer contracts to contend with too. But the presses had to be fed to stay solvent. That was the real bottom line.

One of Goodman's future rivals, Harry Donenfeld, owned the Donny Press. He specialized in printing risqué girlie magazines like Frank Armer's *Pep* and *Spicy Stories*. When the publishers of these magazines started sinking, they owed him a ton of money. In good times, Donenfeld might have written off that debt, but not in hard times. He needed those magazines to fuel his print shop. So like other printers of that Depression era, he made his debtors an offer they could not refuse: he would continue printing their titles in return for a fat share in future profits. Some, Donenfeld simply took over for debt. He also partnered up with Eastern's Paul Sampliner to launch a new distribution outfit, Independent News Distribution.

By this rough process was founded the paper empire that is today DC Comics.

Silberkleit and Goodman did not possess that ability. They knew a different side of the pulp business. The distribution and circulation side. Recognizing that desperate printers were willing to extend credit to startup publishers in the hope of some modest return, they found one willing to work with them. All they needed was something to print.

Here again hard times were their chief ally. Pulp magazine writers were also suffering. Back in 1932-33, more than one orphaned fictioneer was found dead from self-inflicted wounds, his pockets stuffed with rejection slips. Many had moved up to the slick magazines or hardcover publishers, and were suddenly without open markets. But they had equity in old stories from years past.

As Silberkleit's editor, Martin Goodman offered to buy second-serial rights to older books and short stories and reprint them. He paid only a fraction of a cent, but for hungry writers, it was found money in tough times.

Thus was born *Western Supernovel Magazine.* No one, not even Goodman, suspected that his policy of reprinting old stories planted the seeds for the future *Marvel Comics.*

Why Westerns? No doubt Silberkleit and Goodman knew that the Western genre was one of the most reliable in the field. It had been so clear back to the days of the dime novel. A publisher could hardly fail to make a profit on a solidly edited Western pulp.

In 1933, Western magazines were just coming out of a slump. Fewer Western titles were being published, and there was a glut of manuscripts floating around. The bankrupt Clayton chain had dumped the unpublished inventory of its cancelled *Cowboy Stories* onto the market at fire-sale prices. Goodman may have snapped up a few himself.

For the new venture, Silberkleit and Goodman took the name Newsstand Publications. They set up shop in a hole-in-the wall office in the same Manhattan building where Gernsback and Frank Armer, a former employee of Eastern's successor, Independent News, were headquartered. Depending on whim, the address of the building was either 52 Park Place or the back-door entrance, 60 Murray Street.

That first issue cover-featured "Jess Roundtree, Texas Ranger" by Dane Coolidge. It was billed as a $2.00 novel, no doubt to entice readers to overlook its hefty cover price—15 cents. Other stories were by Steve Payne, Clee Woods and Edgar L. Cooper, half-forgotten now but big names back in the day.

The new magazine was dated May 1933. Joseph Cragin's cover was classic stuff: a redheaded cowpoke was pulling at his shooting iron while a bullet whisked his Stetson clean off his head. By the second issue, it became *Complete Western Book Magazine*, apparently because Frank Armer of Super Magazines complained. He had just announced *Super-Western Stories.*

Western Supernovel Magazine (May 1933), art by Jospeh Cragin

Goodman hired some of the top names in cowboy fiction. Soon the covers boasted "All Stories Brand New." It wasn't long before Newsstand became a reliable "down-river" pulp house—which meant a dump market. If the better-paying editors rejected your story, you could always peddle it to Goodman for a fraction of a cent a word. He would in turn protect your reputation by slapping a house name like James Hall on it.

Newsstand expanded carefully. *Black Book Detective* and *Romantic Love Secrets* arrived in the summer of 1933. The latter title was issued as by Graham Publications. It folded the following summer, and was replaced by *The Black Rider Western.* It was the first Newsstand pulp built around a single character. Goodman purchased the rights to a novel by top author Oscar Schisgall, then hired a revolving group of obscure pulpsters to pen sequels. The character's resemblance to the radio's popular *Lone Ranger* serial was a major consideration.

Western Novels and Short Stories premiered with an April 1934 cover date. Then came disaster. Mutual Magazine Distributing went belly-up that summer, owing Silberkleit over $23,000 for sold magazines. He could not pay his Chicago printer, W. F. Hall. So Goodman and another Silberkleit associate, A. Lincoln Hoffman, cut a common Depression deal: They would continue publishing if Hall extended credit and became their publishing "angel."

Silberkleit sold out his interest, quickly launching *Double-Action Western* under the Winford imprint. He was soon running a parallel operation. Whatever Goodman published, Silberkleit mirrored it. Goodman and Hoffman divided the surviving titles among them, with Hoffman operating as Ranger Publications, Spencer Publications and others, sometimes contributing stories to his own magazines under pen names to save money. Manuscripts were purchased through Hoffman's Publishers and Producers Exchange. Gradually, carefully, they worked their way back to profitability.

Ka-Zar #1 (Oct. 1937), art by John W. Scott

Early in 1935, Goodman added three new titles, *Western Fiction Magazine, All Star Detective* and *All Star Fiction.* Each carried a new house imprint: A Star Magazine. Later that year Goodman launched the Western Fiction Publishing Company arm of his growing operation. He continued to pour out Western pulps, *Wild Western Novels, Best Western,* and *Quick-Trigger Western Novel Magazine.*

In the fall of 1936, Goodman moved into the RKO Building on 6th Avenue. He rebranded part of his chain, dubbing it the Red Circle line. Old pulp hands noticed that his trademark resembled the famous bullseye slug used by Fiction House. But the ploy evidently worked, as did the vivid covers by J. W. Scott, A. Leslie Ross and Norman Saunders.

Ka-Zar came along in 1936, under a new imprint, Manvis. The jungle hero was the first star in the future Marvel firmament, and his adventures were avidly read by a teenager named Stanley Martin Lieber—later to call himself Stan Lee. No one knows who the nominal author of Ka-Zar really was. The only other Red Circle story bylined Bob Byrd was the work of Thomson Burtis. Launched with an October cover date to coincide with the release of MGM's *Tarzan Escapes,* the title lasted only three issues. But Ka-Zar would live again.

Late in 1936, after a change in distributors, Hoffman suspended operations. The two associates went their separate ways. Months later, Hoffman sold out to Thrilling Publications. Goodman stood alone. Pushing into fresh genre territory, he added *Star Sports*, *Best Love* and *True Crime* to his line.

Interviewed by *Literary Digest* on the state of the industry in 1937, Goodman was spotlighted as "a young pulpeteer" who oversaw a string of 14 titles with a combined circulation of 400,000 a month. His top sellers were *Complete Western*, *Best Western*, *Star Sports Stories*, *Western Short Stories* and *Western Fiction*. Asked his formula for success, Goodman famously remarked, "If you get a title that catches on, then add a few more, you're in for a nice profit." He also observed, "Fans are not interested in quality." Goodman would soon learn differently.

Already a shrewd businessman, Goodman collected all returns from the metropolitan New York area, and shipped them to England, netting him a penny a copy profit on 200,000 copies every month. In modern money, he was raking in an extra $30,000 a month this way.

Red Circle expanded again in the fall of 1937, adding *Gunsmoke Western*, *Two-Gun Western Novels*, *Six-Gun Western*, *Western Short Stories*, *Detective Short Stories*, *Complete Adventure Magazine*, *Complete Sport* and *Sports Action*. Most were edited by "Ward Marshall" and "James Randall." Goodman and younger brother Sidney Charles toiled behind those fictitious bylines.

One issue of *Star Detective*, dated March 1937, seemed to look far into the future with its lead novel by the mysterious R.V. Romero, entitled "The X-Man." The hero was an undercover sleuth. Another nascent star in the unborn universe.

True Crime Magazine (July 1936), art by John W. Scott

New titles kept coming. *Top-Notch Detective* and *Top-Notch Western*. *Best Sports* and *Real Sports*. *Detective Mysteries*. *Sky Devils*. *Real Confessions*. If one failed to sell, Goodman simply folded it and started a similar title. The pulp genres were fixed. It was simply a matter of finding a catchy title that grabbed readers, he believed.

A new challenge reared up after the stock market crashed again in October 1937. Coming after a year of what looked like economic recovery, this was a huge blow to the national mood. It threw the pulp houses into disarray. Titles were cancelled all that autumn.

Martin Goodman responded by slashing his word rates and increasing the use of reprints. The old-line pulp houses were furious. Some paid top author's rates and only charged ten cents a copy. Goodman was offering old retreads and asking fifteen cents per issue. To add insult to injury, some of those recycled stories were retitlings of tales first published by the rival houses.

No one recalls who filed the first complaint. But the Federal Trade Commission began investigating Red Circle Magazines. The charge? It seems laughable today: Selling unlabelled reprints to an unsuspecting public. Goodman typically changed the story title, byline and often the characters' names. The FTC saw this as an unfair trade practice.

To be fair to Martin Goodman, he was not the only pulp publisher to operate on that basis. Louis Silberkleit's Atlas Fiction Group was also targeted. But many of the old-time pulp chains were themselves guilty of similar practices. The difference was, they reprinted stories from their own back files.

After only five years in the business, Goodman's Red Circle bullet had become a bullseye—and he was the target. He continued publishing, of course, hiring Robert O. Erisman away from Silberkleit to be his pulp editor. Immediately, the line underwent dramatic changes as new writers were discovered and groomed. Goodman continued to take advantage of the fact that perfectly good pulp stories were often rejected for idiosyncratic reasons. The line became known for its off-center heroes, off-trail plots, and steadfast avoidance of what Goodman derided as "sappy" stories.

Marvel Science Stories #1 (Aug. 1938), art by Norman Saunders

Marvel Science Stories debuted in the Summer of 1938. It was controversial from the start, mixing as it did science-fiction pulp tales with off-the-wall sex and sadism. It also marked the first use of the magic name *Marvel*.

Red Circle comprised some 25 titles by 1938, including nine Westerns, four detective titles, five sports pulps and various others. With a ruthless efficiency, Goodman dropped the faltering *Star Detective* and another weak title, replacing them with *Mystery Tales* and *Uncanny Tales*—whose masthead typography was later recycled for *Marvel Comics* #1. Both appealed to the "weird menace" reader. By volume, Goodman was one of the most prolific pulp publishers. Increasingly however, it was clear that the handwriting was on the wall. It was only a matter of time before the FTC acted…

Enter Frank Torpey.

A friend of Goodman's, Torpey was the salesman for Funnies Inc., a new outfit that had failed to penetrate the burgeoning comic book business with a one-shot theater giveaway called *Motion Picture Funnies Weekly* and was now seeking to package original strips for other publishers. He introduced Goodman to Funnies, Inc. owner Lloyd Jacquet, and they poured over the best-selling comics titles, *Superman* chief among them. Goodman must have been astounded when he heard circulation figures. Publishers had not seen such sell-through numbers since the boom days of the Roaring Twenties.

There was another attraction: Comic strip artists worked cheap. Cheaper than hungry pulp writers selling second serial rights. Even if the new venture bombed, it was unlikely to lose much money.

Goodman set up his new outfit, which he called Timely Publications, installing his brother Abe as publisher to keep it separate from his troubled Red Circle line. Using the buzzword that he'd used for *Marvel Science Stories,* he dubbed the first title, *Marvel Comics.* The coincidence of the first syllable with his own first name may not have been entirely coincidental. Officially, Goodman's title was managing editor.

Motion Picture Funnies Weekly #1 (1939), art by Fred Schwab

The features were conceptualized by the staff of Funnies, Inc., with Goodman having approval over the final selection. Artists Bill Everett and Carl Burgos (*né* Max Finkelstein) brainstormed Prince Namor, The Sub-Mariner and The Human Torch jointly.

"We were asked to develop all new characters," Everett explained in *The Steranko History of Comics.* "Carl and I were quite close friends, and we usually held our story conferences very informally over a drink. We were discussing the new book in the Webster bar and between us, whether it was his idea or mine or a combination of both, we decided on using the two elements, fire and water. We did that because everything else was being used at the time. It happened to be a lucky guess. We talked about what we could do with them and if I'm not mistaken, the idea of a character turning himself into flame came first. Carl called him the Human Torch.

"Then we discussed the natural opposite of fire…water. What could we do with a character and water? That was my part of it…I called him the Sub-Mariner after the poem and for the name Namor, I simply spelled 'Roman' backwards. …In those days, we didn't have writers unless we wanted to hire them ourselves. Almost everybody created their own features and both wrote and drew them, I was no different. I began thinking about the Sub-Mariner and his ice kingdom under Antarctica. The wings on his feet were inspired by the statue of Mercury. The concept of the Sub-Mariner came naturally to me, just like it was something that had to be told."

"We just called them characters," Burgos added. "The word super hero didn't exist until much later. When we created them, we never knew which characters would catch on. We just did the best we could."

The choice of a star character was a no-brainer to the cover-conscious Goodman. Red sold covers. The fiery Human Torch would be the lead feature. This was an early decision, as evidenced by the origin story's unusually long length—16 pages. Although the story text mentions the Torch's red and blue flames, he was colored a solid red with touches of yellow—although in one panel the anonymous colorist reversed them.

For a cover, Goodman went outside Funnies, Inc. Frank R. Paul had been the premier cover artist for Hugo Gernsback, and supplied both covers and interior illustrations for *Marvel Science* and its new companion title, *Dynamic Science Stories.* Paul executed a cover depicting a much more demonic Human Torch than Carl Burgos ever imagined.

The Angel came next. With his blue outfit and penchant for dropping down from high places, he might have been mistaken

Marvel Comics #1 (Sept. 1939), art by Frank R. Paul

for a debonair, mustached Superman. Leslie Charteris' popular detective hero, The Saint, was the main inspiration—although The Angel also threw a frightening symbolic shadow *à la* The Shadow. The Angel's debut story resembles *The Saint in New York,* which was adapted by RKO in 1938. Calling himself Paul Gustavson, Finnish immigrant Karl Paul Gustafson wrote and drew the feature, never bothering with an origin story.

Al Anders' "The Masked Raider" was a Western strip in the Lone Ranger tradition. The Lone Ranger was among the hottest media properties of 1939. The radio show had been building a steady audience since 1933, but the release of the Republic serial *The Lone Ranger Rides Again* earlier in the year broke Saturday matinee box-office records. No doubt Goodman was thinking of the Masked Rider pulp when a name was chosen for him.

One feature had previously appeared in *Motion Picture Funnies Weekly,* Jacquet's abortive attempt to launch his own title earlier in '39. Bill Everett's "Sub-Mariner" had to be expanded with four new pages, but the addition of color over the careful craft-tint shading produced poor results. The only stand-alone story, "Jungle Terror," was by Art Pinajian, working under the pen name of Tomm Dixon.

Rounding out the book was a character out of Goodman's pulp past. It was no accident Ka-Zar the Great was revived in comics form. The first Tarzan movie since 1936's *Tarzan Escapes* had been released in June. The storyline for MGM's *Tarzan Finds a Son*—a young boy survives a jungle plane crash—paralleled Ka-Zar's origin in striking ways. Goodman was not about to let a perfect publicity opportunity go sailing past uncaptured. Ben Thompson illustrated the serialized adaptation of the pulp novels.

Younger brother Arthur Goodman once recalled that at the last minute, a feature prepared for *Marvel* #1 was unceremoniously jettisoned from that historic roster. Legal or creative reasons were cited. Since DC Comics had recently crushed Victor Fox's Wonder Man over similarities to Superman, it's easy to speculate that the concept killed might have been deemed legally risky.

Funnies, Inc. payment records show that The Masked Raider was the final feature paid for, thus making it the most likely candidate to have replaced the dropped idea, although Ka-Zar the Great or the standalone "Jungle Terror" can't be discounted.

Bill Everett's "The Sub-Mariner" from the black-and-white *Motion Picture Funnies Weekly* #1 (1939)

Goodman packed that first issue with lead heroes—few fillers. The reader got a lot of value for his dime. The topliners were the strangest super heroes ever seen up to that time. An android and an amphibian. Outlaws both—although the Torch would soon join the police force in his assumed civilian identity. While individual stories were largely self-contained, character continuity carried the strips from issue to issue, giving the impression of a Saturday matinee movie serial. No doubt this was a key part of the marketing strategy.

When the package was assembled, Goodman sent it to a printer in Newark, New Jersey, selected no doubt with an eye to economy. A careful businessman, Goodman initially only dipped his toe in to the four-color forest. Approximately 80,000 copies were printed for a limited East Coast release. Perhaps, like some pulp publishers, he planned to ship unspoiled returns to Western states as a way of reducing waste.

As a publisher, Martin Goodman had a reputation for being fast on the trigger. Through his network of industry contacts, he was plugged into the national distribution net. Final returns typically took three months to come in. Goodman worked the phones the first week, and if he didn't like what he heard, he'd cut his losses by canceling an underperforming title.

But before any of that could happen, bigger things were in the wind. The world outside his 42nd Street office seemed to be going crazy.

On August 26, Germany ordered all her luxury liners to drop their passengers at the nearest port and steam for home without delay. Stranded tourists were thrown into a blind panic. A mad scramble to find alternate accommodations ensued. The Atlantic became jammed with commercial liners fleeing Continental Europe. War was coming. And everyone knew it.

Amid that chaos, understanding that people curtailed their spending in uncertain conditions, Martin Goodman canceled *Marvel Comics* #1, thinking that with its disastrous printing, it was doubly doomed.

But he worked the phones anyway. Goodman needed to know how badly he was going to be burned by the poorly printed failure of a comic book.

To his utter astonishment, *Marvel* #1 was flying off the stands. Within a week of its official on-sale date of Thursday August 31, it had sold out completely!

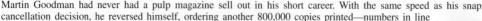

Martin Goodman had never had a pulp magazine sell out in his short career. With the same speed as his snap cancellation decision, he reversed himself, ordering another 800,000 copies printed—numbers in line with Superman's reported sales. Since *Marvel Comics* was a monthly, he had a November cover-date overprinted over the old October slug and the indicia modified. The second printing would have a full six weeks to sell. And sell it did.

Perhaps Goodman thought that this was further confirmation of his adage, "Fans aren't interested in quality," but he realized the new field of comics was a publishing goldmine. He reactivated plans for issue #2, scheduling a revised release date of October 13.

The lineup continued as before, but with another former *Motion Pictures Funnies* strip, American Ace, replacing "Jungle Terror." Goodman also tinkered with the two key sales features—the title and cover.

A Bill Everett Sub-Mariner cover rough was set aside in favor of the costumed Angel, in full flight, attacking

Bill Everett's unused *Marvel Comics* #2 cover rough (1939)

warplanes emblazoned with pseudo-swastikas. The cover by Charles J. Mazoujian—Art Pinajian's cousin—was not based on Paul Gustavson's Angel story in that issue, but a second Angel text story, also illustrated by Mazoujian. "Death-Bird Squadron" by pulp writer David C. Cooke depicted a version of The Angel, possessing flight and super-strength never seen in his own strip, beating off Nazi bombers over besieged Poland. Goodman was using the headlines to sell his revived magazine. It wouldn't be long before real swastikas were decorating his comics covers.

A photostat of Mazoujian's cover survives to this day. It shows clearly that The Angel's face was cleaned up to remove his pencil mustache and make him look younger—and sufficiently like Superman to fool wide-eyed kids in 1939. For the Man of Steel, little more than a year old, was already appearing in two comic books and a syndicated newspaper strip.

The logo was also redesigned to read *Marvel Mystery Comics*, with the word Mystery superimposed over Comics. Why? No one today can say. Theories range from the improbable inspiration of Marvel Mystery Oil to the likely one that Goodman thought that first issue of *Marvel Comics* needed a bold new look after the shoddy Newark printing job. This time Goodman employed the Greater Buffalo Press—which printed most of the nation's Sunday newspaper sections—to produce the magazine.

Simultaneously, he retitled *Marvel Science Stories*. It became *Marvel Tales*. The December 1939 issue cover-featured "The Angel from Hell." Goodman was on an angel kick that month.

With the third issue, Goodman settled on a final logo, using the version of the word Marvel that had formerly graced *Marvel Science Stories*. A new cover artist debuted. Another Red Circle pulpster, Alex Schomburg would soon become the "face" of the Timely line. Here again, a shaven-faced Angel took the cover spot. Was Goodman trolling for Superman readers? How else to explain the absence of the Torch or Sub-Mariner?

Prince Namor finally won a cover with issue #4. Schomburg's portrayal was a peek into the near future. Sub-Mariner was depicted battling Nazi sailors on a swastika-emblazoned German submarine. Pearl Harbor lay over a year in the future, but the Battle of the Atlantic was well underway. Nazi raiders were sinking commercial vessels at will. By year's end, 165 Allied ships had been sent to the bottom. Goodman knew that war sold magazines. And it would really sell them once the U.S. entered World War II.

The World War II storyline was Bill Everett's. Although Funnies, Inc. had staff scripters like John H. Compton and Ray Gillman, Burgos, Gustavson and Everett toiled alone. "In the beginning," Everett noted, "I did it any way I wanted because I had no supervision. I made up the dialogue as I went along—usually when I lettered it."

With this issue, the lineup was shaken up. The Ferret, by Irwin Hasen with pulp writer R. B. S. "Bob" Davis writing as Stockbridge Winslow, would not last long. But Steve Dahlman's robotic Electro was a striking strip that might have been consulted by Stan Lee 30 years in the future when Iron Man was being conceived. Its contemporary 1940 origins are easy to trace: One of the sensations of the New York World's Fair was a giant golden robot called…Elektro!

Only four issues in, Goodman was moving fast to consolidate his new enterprise. He lured artist Joe Simon away from Funnies, Inc. and asked the 26-year-old newspaper artist from Rochester, New York to produce new features to supplement the material Jacquet was providing. Simon's Torch knockoff, The Fiery Mask, had so impressed Goodman he scheduled it for the lead feature in *Daring Mystery Comics* #1, then asked for more of the same.

"Martin Goodman confided to me why he wanted a second and third fiery crime-fighter," Simon once wrote. "It was a tactic to discourage other publishers from imitating the popular 'Human Torch.' Goodman would use this same strategy throughout his career as a comic book publisher, well into the Marvel years, sometimes suffering temporary losses himself in an effort to choke out the competition."

Goodman was learning fast. The slant of *Marvel Mystery Comics* quickly became super heroes vs. weird horror. Goodman was rumored be a reader of *Weird Tales*. But Simon also had a flare for the bizarre. They worked well together.

"Martin Goodman carried that company on his back, despite the fact that he had a very tender ass," recalls Simon. "Martin was very canny in business plus he also had a strong nose for story content. Martin didn't give me a significant amount of editorial guidance. He let me go unleashed. Possibly because he was surrounded by a bunch of relatives who were way out of their element when it came to story and art. Martin was very pleased with the way I took over his other magazines. I was very lucky to have the experience from the newspaper days."

The early Timely team consisted of Martin's surviving brothers, Abe, Arthur and Dave, as well as brother-in-law Robert Solomon. Simon also remembered that among confidants, Goodman was known familiarly as Moe.

It was a highly competitive time. Everyone was jumping into the exploding comics field. Louis Silberkleit had been vying with Goodman for the same pulp niche. Predictably, he published *Blue Ribbon Comics* #1 a month after Timely started up. A few issues later, it was retitled *Blue Ribbon Mystery Comics*. Unbeknownst to Goodman, Timely's bookkeeper, Maurice Coyne, was the *M* in MLJ Magazines (working with Louis Silberkleit and John Goldwater.) He was another Gernsback alum.

Mere months after the debut of *Marvel Comics*, Fawcett launched Captain Marvel. Goodman countered with Marvel Boy and The Black Marvel. Marvel Boy was quickly rechristened The Young Avenger, perhaps under legal pressure. The Black Marvel soon vanished, probably for similar reasons. Simultaneously in the summer of 1940, Timely, Silberkleit and Quality Comics released new strips entitled Hercules. The lawyers were as busy as the artists.

"We were always trying for new characters," Simon recounted. "We had a lot of failures, we had a lot of marginal characters, but we kept trying new ones."

The first Timely character to be revamped was the Torch. Burgos redrew him with an expressive face for *Marvel Mystery* #4. When it didn't take, his blue costume was recolored red. To this day, when a Marvel character falters, he's not abandoned, he's reinvented. It would happen to The Torch, Sub-Mariner and Ka-Zar. Even the lackluster Masked Raider later reincarnated in the 1950s as the Black Rider.

Gimmicks sold comic books. With a magazine full of colorful characters, perhaps it was inevitable that some would meet. But this had never before been done in comics. Ka-Zar and Sub-Mariner were serials, with lots of continuity. Namor and the Torch soon crossed over as arch-antagonists.

"That was an idea that Carl and I dreamed up," Everett claimed. "We considered the fact that the two characters and their opposing elements had separate stories and wondered what could happen if we got them together as rivals to fight each other."

Goodman loved the idea. With typical enthusiasm for a hot idea, he wanted the entire thing produced over a weekend. "All we knew was that The Torch and Namor had to have a fight," recounted Everett. They enlisted pulp writers John H. Compton and Jack D'Arcy to script the elaborate storyline. "Carl and I worked on the team-ups together. I'd draw my character, he'd draw his and, like them, we'd argue constantly because we wanted to."

The Masked Raider reborn, *Black Rider* #8 (March 1950) with Stan Lee posing in the hero's costume.

It was another sellout. And another creative innovation that would reverberate decades ahead into the Marvel years. The beginnings of the Marvel action formula of super heroes in conflict were taking shape.

Goodman later explained his thinking this way: "I think the comic-book field suffers from the same thing TV does. After a few years, an erosion sets in. You still maintain loyal readers, but you lose a lot more readers than you're picking up. That's why we have so many super-hero characters, and run super heroes together. Even if you take two characters that are weak sellers and run them together in the same book, somehow, psychologically, the reader feels he's getting more. You get the Avenger[s] follower and the Sub-Mariner follower. Often you see a new title do great on the first issue and then it begins to slide off…."

Expansion came rapidly. *Daring Mystery Comics* was a clone of the flagship title, but with a constantly changing roster of features. *Mystic Comics* followed. Neither caught on, but *Mystic* produced one hit hero—Stan Lee's The Destroyer. A cover was mocked up for a *Zephyr Comics.* No doubt Goodman spotted the title as a loser, and killed it. Simon & Kirby's *Red Raven* was cancelled after one issue. Another famous snap decision. This one stuck.

"He would make these decisions at the drop of a hat," Stan Lee revealed to Roy Thomas. "He would say, 'Let's put out a new book. Let's change this title to something else. Let's drop this, let's substitute this for that.' It was always happening. He lived with the sales figures. He had those pages of sales figures in front of him all the time, and that's what he based all his decisions on."

Lee had come aboard in 1940. Although still in his teens and related to his "Uncle Martin" by marriage, he learned fast and displayed a creative flair that would reverberate clear into the 21st century.

"He was quite a gentle guy," Lee says of Goodman. "If you looked at him you would say, this wasn't a guy who led a rough and tumble life. He was slender and quiet, kind of classy-looking. I liked him very much. He didn't bluster around and pull his weight. He was fun to be with. I enjoyed talking to him. He was an interesting conversationalist. He had a wry sense of humor. He loved golf. In later years, he loved to play Scrabble."

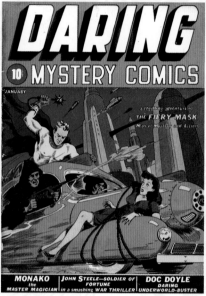

Daring Mystery Comics #1 (Jan. 1940), art by Alex Schomburg

Just out of high school, Lee missed out on the beginnings of Timely Comics. "All I remember was that I thought he was very happy with the way the first book did," he notes. "That's what made him decide to stay in the comic book business. He had a fella named Frank Torpey, who worked for him. Frank was a sort of jack all trades. He ran errands—just a loyal guy who was always around. I had heard it was Frank who had talked him into doing a comic book, and because of that he was grateful and always kept him around."

Mystic Comics #1 (March 1940), art by Alex Schomburg

The Human Torch and Sub-Mariner soon spun off into their own titles. Goodman never seemed to shake the idea that his pet hero, The Angel, was a sleeping giant. After he gave up on him as a cover character with *Marvel Mystery* #12, the Angel was added to the *Sub-Mariner* title as a co-feature. In 1941, Goodman announced a new pulp, *The Angel Detective*, saturating his pulps with multiple ads. A variation on the Timely Angel, the new project was cancelled after only one issue.

Timely's home run came when Simon and artist Jack Kirby's electrifying *Captain America Comics* debuted at the end of 1940. "I did that with Martin Goodman," recalls Simon. "We were passing sketches back and forth before Kirby was even in on it. We just gave Kirby scripts, and layouts. Before Kirby got it, we had the costume and everything. Martin was trying to talk me into doing a great effort on the art, to try to get the first issue out before Hitler got killed. Kirby was begging us to let him do the whole book."

Wisely, Simon acquiesced. "It was a good testing ground for me," Kirby later recalled. "The first issue was meant to look more like a movie than a traditional comic book. Movies were what I knew best, and I wanted to tell stories the way they did. I guess I'm just a frustrated director."

"Now the first issue of *Captain America* had Hitler as the villain," Simon continues. "And the whole reason we put that out was because America was in a patriotic frenzy. Also, everybody was looking for interesting villains. Bob Kane and Bill Finger and the others we coming up with some very interesting ones, and they were selling. So I thought of what kind of a villain to come up with? And there was only one that the whole world hated—and that was Adolf Hitler. So he was our villain. We had the villain first and then we came up with Captain America."

It was a huge gamble. Only once before had a publisher committed an entire magazine to a new and unproven character—and that was the disastrous *Red Raven.* But Martin Goodman believed in Captain America. In later years, Timely promotional material credited Goodman with launching a crusade to wake America up to the Nazi threat through his publications, while modern commentators have suggested the publisher's Jewish background provided the insight and motivation to do so.

"The whole country was anti-Hitler," Lee countered. "Hitler seemed to be the closet equivalent to Satan that anyone could ever find…The things we were reading that Hitler was doing—conquering Czechoslovakia, Poland, all those countries—it looked like he wanted to gobble up the world. I think it went way past that the comic book publishers were Jewish. We were just making Hitler the villain."

"World War II lent itself to good dramas," Kirby noted. "The whole thing could have been written by some hack out of Warner Bros. It was a black and white issue with a villain who was so completely evil that it was just made to order. Anything you did in World War II was an act of nobility. If you hung Hitler or killed hundreds of Germans, you were on the side of the angels."

Captain America was the first Timely title to sell nearly a million copies a month. The Simon & Kirby look took the industry by storm. And the action formula they devised became the new Timely house style. Goodman hired Joe Simon to become his in-house editor and began phasing out Funnies, Inc. "Just do comic books," Goodman told Simon. "Come up with new ideas. This business is getting competitive and we can't keep putting out this crap for very long."

Over at MLJ comics, Louis Silberkleit and new partner John Goldwater saw the new hero with his triangular shield as a knockoff of their own patriotic super hero, The Shield, who wore a similar chest protector.

"So Martin brought me in there and we had a conference with John Goldwater," Simon says. "I suggested to Goldwater that we'll change the shield to round to be more unique. Anyway, he had to agree to it. He couldn't argue against it. The thing that ticked off Martin the most was that before we left, John Goldwater brought out a contract he wanted me and Jack Kirby to sign—he wanted to steal us away from Martin. So Martin got very mad about it."

Goodman would have been furious to know that it was Coyne who had suggested that Simon ask for a royalty on *Captain America Comics*. Goodman agreed. Later Coyne whispered into Simon's ear that most of Timely's overhead had been put on that one title, resulting in drastically reduced royalties. Simon and Kirby moved on—not to MLJ, but to DC Comics.

Joe Simon's original Captain America design

The void was filled by Stan Lee and artist Syd Shores, who had been hired by Simon as an inker. "My first job on staff was to ink the cover for *Captain America* #1," recalled Shores. "I don't think I inked the *whole* first issue. I think that Jack did that one himself. I'm not sure, but shortly afterwards I was inking Cap regularly and a host of others. Stan joined the staff just about then, and there grew an enormous amount of staffers within a short while. Some of the guys who'd been freelancing now came on staff, people like Bill Everett and Carl Burgos, while Stan had worked into doing some writing. When Simon and Kirby left in 1942 Stan did all the writing and was given the position of editorial director, while I was the art director, although I got called 'associate editor' in the books that were put out around then."

Ultimately, Lee worked with Goodman longer than anyone else. "In some ways he was a genius," recalled Lee to *Overstreet's Comic Book Quarterly*. "He had one of the best senses of what the public wanted to read than anybody I've ever known. He instinctively would know…'Stan, I think we ought to do more war stories,' or 'I think we ought to have more villains on the covers.' He was wonderful on covers. Martin taught me everything I knew about covers and I became pretty good at them, because they were the most important part of our business.

"Mainly," adds Lee, "the thing he was interested in is: are we putting out a magazine in a field that seems hot. If he found that Western comics were selling well, he made sure we were putting out Western comics. If he felt that animated-type comics, like *Terry-Toons*, were selling well, he wanted to be sure that we had enough animated comics. Beyond that his primary concern was the covers. He was very insistent that the covers be done a certain way, and he was right. He felt that the covers were very important. They had to catch the perspective reader's eye. He had different theories. Have bright colors. Contrasting colors. Not too much dialogue. A big picture. Basically something that would catch your eye."

In those days, that meant the prolific and panoramic Alex Schomburg, who was given the creative freedom to do whatever he wanted. "I seldom submitted pencil roughs," he once said. "They bought sight unseen—just as long as the Japs showed their ugly teeth and glasses and the Nazis looked like bums."
"I remember…hearing Martin tell me time and again how great a cover illustrator Alex was, and how he wished we had

more like him," Stan Lee professed. "We used to wonder how he managed to get so much detail in every cover. No matter how difficult the scene, no matter how many people, Alex drew them clearly, accurately and excitingly. If he had to draw a bridge, you'd see every rivet, every girder in the structure. If he drew a crowd scene, you'd see everyone in the crowd doing something specific and interesting."

Explained Simon, "Martin Goodman's covers had every inch of space taken up with action, in the background and stuff going on, so that kids would look at it like a puzzle."

Oddly enough, Goodman took a casual attitude toward the ever-growing roster of Timely super heroes. "We never talked much about super heroes," says Lee, "because super heroes were nothing special then. We had all kind of books. Whatever he thought was trend at the moment. In those days, he was putting everything he could get into the comics. There was no continuity. They'd be a guy in a cape or a cloak. They'd be a guy who was just a detective. They'd be Ka-Zar. Remember, in the very early days, he didn't do his own strips. He bought them from a company called Funnies."

Goodman instead kept a weather eye toward new trends. During the war, pulps and comics were devoured by soldiers in the field and stateside readers alike. Returns were almost non-existent. But paper was scarce. To keep expanding, he killed most of his five surviving pulps, saving only *Complete Western Book Magazine,* transfering Robert Erisman to the comics division.

All-Winners Comics #13 (Fall 1944), an archetypal packed puzzle-style Schomburg cover

"Goodman had a good paper allocation and diverted much of it from his pulps to the comics," remembered artist Vince Fago. "That's how we were able to out-produce much of the competition."

For, having carved out a solid niche in the comic book industry, Goodman reverted to a publishing strategy from his pulp days. He sought to flood the market while it was still hot, seizing newsstand space the way troops occupied enemy territory: to keep the competition from gaining a foothold.

"Martin and Stan knew they needed to put a new accent on the books," Fago explained to Jim Amash. "Goodman was interested in me because of my humor background; they wanted more humor comics for the soldiers. They also wanted to tone down the hero comics and thought I had the background to do it. They knew that, if I could put that into the work of the people who worked for me, it would be good for the company. And Martin would be my watchdog. Anything I put into the books and he didn't like, he'd let me know."

Fago temporarily took over Lee's duties while the latter served in the Army. "I started editing when Timely moved from the McGraw-Hill Building to the Empire State Building," he told *Alter Ego.* "I think that was in August of 1942…Stan never really worked as an editor in the Empire State Building until after the war. I was the editor when we moved."

Thanks to Walt Disney, Hollywood animated movies were enjoying a boom. *Daring Mystery Comics* was converted into a humor title, *Comedy Comics. Joker Comics, Krazy Comics* and *Terry-Toons Comics* (featuring a licensed Mighty Mouse) followed. It was the first of many course corrections Goodman instituted at Timely.

In January 1942, the United States was fully embroiled in World War II, and the Federal Trade Commission finally rendered its judgment. It found that Martin Goodman and his old crony Louis Silberkleit "falsely represented that their books and other publications contained original, complete and unabridged novels." Both publishers had to sign stipulations admitting wrongdoing and promising to cease and desist. But neither probably cared. The pulp field was in its death throes. Timely forged on with their Nazi-busting super heroes, while MLJ discovered its own gold mine through its phenomenally successful teenage character, Archie Andrews. The loss of star artists Everett, Burgos, Gustavson and Shores to the armed forces slowed the Timely juggernaut not at all.

This was the pinnacle of the Golden Age of Comics. Prematurely silver-haired, and wearing a perpetual bow tie, Goodman presided over a bustling empire of comics and other magazines. Once Stan Lee had firm control over the editorial and art direction side of the business, Goodman dispensed with the services of Funnies, Inc. Artists worked on salary in the busy bullpen. Writers like science-fiction pioneer Ray Cummings and daughter Betty, as well as future best-seller Mickey Spillane, scripted features. Bonuses were handed out every three months. Goodman often sat in on lunchtime poker games. Times were good at Timely Comics.

By all accounts, it was run as an old-fashioned paternalistic enterprise. Recalled artist Allen Bellman, "Martin

Goodman was indeed a great guy. He spoke softly and it is my feeling that he treated the staff well. Though air conditioning was in use at the time, but because of the war only electric fans were available to us. Every Wednesday, and in the summertime he allowed the staff to take off in the afternoon, that's when Syd Shores and I went to Ebbets Field to watch the Brooklyn Dodgers play. He produced one or two Broadway plays which never made it to the top. One was *Love on Leave,* and much of the audience were staff members. We were all given free tickets. There are some who may not agree with me that Martin Goodman was indeed a gentleman, but he was a good businessman, tough but fair."

"Martin Goodman used to lie back in a big chaise lounge," Vince Fago related, "and he'd look at the sales charts every day. He was counting his money. He had been a hustler who'd had a rough life and he was trying to live it up. Goodman did things the hard way, but he succeeded. …The print runs were 250,000 to 500,000 copies. Sometimes we'd put out five books a week or more. You'd see the numbers come back and could tell that Goodman was a millionaire. The comics were what gave him that chaise lounge."

Super-hero sales began faltering when the overseas military market began drying up at war's end. Goodman abandoned the genre without stalling or sentiment. "I remember that during the war I was drawing The Patriot feature," Allen Bellman explained to Timely scholar Dr. Michael J. Vassallo. "As soon as the war was over, so was The Patriot! So I knew that super-hero features were stalling. Martin Goodman was no fool…I'm sure the public was sick of heroes fighting Nazi and Axis villains. While the war was on, it was good propaganda. When the true horror of the Nazi regime was exposed to the world it likely made super heroes seem silly in comparison."

Goodman moved into popular new genres—crime comics, titles like *Miss America, Pasty Walker* and *Millie the Model* aimed at young girls, and teenage comics like *Georgie,* a blatant attempt to grab Archie readers. *Georgie* led to problems, both in-house and out, according to artist and editor Al Jaffee.

"Martin Goodman was not a creative man; all he thought about was business," Jaffee related to *Alter Ego's* Jim Amash. "Here's an example of a Martin Goodman edict: we were all told to put cross-hatching on the back of Georgie's head because *Archie* had it, and those comics were big sellers. That was so ridiculous! Is that what made *Archie* so popular, or was it good stories?"

Dave Berg wrote and drew *Georgie.* He recalled being summoned to meet MLJ's John Goldwater, who wanted Berg to testify in a plagiarism suit against Timely. Berg flatly refused. "The next time I saw Goodman," he informed *Alter Ego,* "I told him about it. He said, 'But I have a golf game with him tomorrow.' I asked, 'Are you going to keep it?' 'Of course,' Goodman said. 'Business is business and golf is golf.'"

Goodman also returned to the familiar territory of the Western, reviving defunct Red Star Western pulp titles as comic books. In their new guise, they outsold their pulp ancestors. Two-Gun Kid and Kid Colt, Outlaw, became Timely's new stars.

Years of producing Westerns had not prepared him to foresee all related trends. "I went to Martin Goodman one time," said Timely editor Don Rico, "and I said, 'Look, we're doing a whole lot of Westerns; how about instead of imagining things, let's use the real West.' He was excited as hell. He said, 'What do you have in mind? What kind of a hero?' I said, 'How about a guy like Wyatt Earp?' He said, 'Who? Who'd ever go for a guy with a name like Wyatt Earp?'"

Five years later, when *The Life and Legend of Wyatt Earp* became the top-rated TV Western, Rico recalled that Goodman apologized to him, then instructed Stan Lee to produce a *Wyatt Earp* comic book.

Horror began booming in the late 1940s, and Goodman flooded the stands with mystery and horror comic books, some revivals of his old pulp titles, *Mystery Tales* and *Uncanny Tales.* In 1949, *Marvel Mystery Comics* jettisoned its last super heroes and was retitled *Marvel Tales* after the old generic pulp. It became simply another Goodman fantasy comic, indistinguishable from all the others.

For the postwar era was a boom-and-bust period for the Timely tribe. "Martin Goodman had about six or seven companies," Vince Fago recalled. "If he was ever sued or went bankrupt, he'd still have these other companies! Goodman knew the hard times, and though things were going great, he banked on things changing later. And he was right."

Marvel Tales #93 (Aug. 1949), art attributed to Martin Nodell

During the 1946 magazine glut that caused expanding publishers to drastically pull back in the face of ruinous returns, Martin Goodman was unusually aggressive. "For years," Gil Kane recounted in *Alter Ego,* "Timely would have three 'units,' and they would turn out 25 Western comics, 25 love comics, and they'd run them each for about six or seven months, until they'd absolutely drown the market, and it seemed to me that then they'd just fire everybody and pull out."

The advent of network television in the late 1940s altered the four-color landscape forever. "TV was kicking the hell

! THE
GHING!
T
N!

HA! HA! HA!
STOP—
IT TICKLES!

I CAN
HELP
IT?

out of a great number of comics," Goodman once observed. "A book like *Donald Duck* went from two and a quarter million monthly sales to about 200,000. You couldn't give the animated stuff away, the Disney stuff, because of TV. TV murdered it. Because if a kid spends Saturday morning looking at the stuff, what parent is going to give the kid another couple of dimes to buy the same thing again?"

Simultaneously parental attacks on comic books as a bad influence on children in magazines, newspapers, books and Senate hearings took their toll. "Goodman was a rather shy person who blushed very easily," recounted artist Dave Gantz in *Alter Ego.* "You could tell what he was thinking by the color of his face. The comic book business had gone through many ups and downs, and there was a time when Goodman had trouble relaxing. So we made up a bunch of posters that said 'Relax!' in comic book lettering with lots of exclamation points and put them up in his office. You could do anything but relax with these posters!"

Adventures Into Terror #43 (Nov. 1950), art by Russ Heath

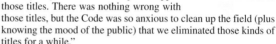

The Golden Age was over. The newly established Comics Code Authority decreed what could be published and what material was no longer permissible. "In the beginning," revealed Stan Lee in *Overstreet's Comic Book Quarterly,* "I think they said 'We don't want any horror stories.' We had been publishing books like *Adventures Into Terror* and *Journey Into Mystery*, and I think we just dropped those titles. There was nothing wrong with those titles, but the Code was so anxious to clean up the field (plus knowing the mood of the public) that we eliminated those kinds of titles for a while."

"Timely publisher Martin Goodman used to close shop at the drop of hat," lamented artist John Romita. "If expenses got too high, he'd say 'the hell with it,' and close shop. Nobody had any protection because there were no pension plans, no severance pay or insurance plans, or savings plans. Everyone who worked in comics were flying by the seat of their pants."

It had happened in 1949, when Goodman discovered a closet full of unusable inventory art worth thousands of dollars. "They kept buying stuff in order to stay ahead of the game," editor Al Jaffee told *Alter Ego.* "When you're putting out thirty or forty books a month, you're in big trouble if you fall behind. You won't be able to fill those magazines. That's why you stockpile work. …In comics, especially in those days, things went out of fashion very quickly. For example, you have a stockpile of humor work and teenage books became hot. Or horror comics become big and you've still got all this extra teenage stuff."

Artist Joe Sinnott recalled what happened next: "Stan called me and said, 'Joe, Martin Goodman told me to suspend operations because I have all this artwork in-house and have to use it up before I can hire you again.' It turned out to be six months, in my case."

It was the end of the Timely bullpen. The loss of so many salaried artists freed up substantial money, and Goodman next turned his attention to starting his own distribution company, Atlas News Company. He continued to produce product at an astonishing rate, cementing his position as publisher of the largest comic book chain in America. New talent came on board—future stars like John Romita, Dick Ayers, Gene Colan, Don Heck, John Buscema, Steve Ditko, John Severin, Stan Goldberg, and the amazingly versatile Joe Maneely. But Goodman remained an industry follower, not a leader.

"Martin believed he had his finger on the pulse beat of the country," observed Don Rico. "From where I sat, he was just a guy who knew how to shovel product onto the shelves and make a buck. He usually arrived on the tail end of a trend."

Goodman was forever trying to knock down his competition. One strategy was to cover-date his titles a month or two ahead of other publishers, hoping to trick news dealers into prematurely taking rival titles off-sale, choking circulation. In a dog-eat-dog business, Goodman saw this as simple self-preservation. "This field is full of pirates," he complained.

Yet in a bizarre business move, late in 1956, Goodman dissolved Atlas to go with American News. He was stunned when American went out of business April of '57, orphaning his many titles. It was Martin Goodman's darkest hour. It was almost Marvel's end, too. Artist and colorist Stan Goldberg remembered, "DC wanted to buy all of Timely's titles. They offered around $15,000 because they wanted to own Captain America, Sub-Mariner, and the Human Torch.

$15,000 was a lot of money then, but Martin Goodman still had his magazines and was a millionaire. Goodman said, 'Aw, what's $15,000 going to mean to me? I'll hold onto these titles. Why should I give it to them?' This was probably the smartest thing he ever did."

Ironically DC's distribution arm, Independent News, took over—but with severe product restrictions. After that, Magazine Management, as Goodman was calling the company, became a marginal operation of 16 bimonthly titles trembling on the brink of cancellation.

"The comic book business hit rock bottom," Lee recalled in *FOOM*. "My publisher said to me, 'Stan, we have to let the whole staff go. I'm just going to keep you, but I want you to fire everybody.' I said, "I can't do it!' He said, 'You'd better,' and he went off to Florida, while I was given the job of firing more people than I could count."

One of the casualties was *Marvel Tales*. After 159 issues, it was no more. Goodman's last pulps were quietly folded, including the one that started it all—*Complete Western Book Magazine*. He focused on his lucrative line of men's magazines, becoming such a remote figure that long-time freelancers like artist Dick Ayers today say, "I never met the guy!"

Recalled Lee, "When we would finish a cover of something, I would bring it in and show it to Martin. He stayed mostly within the confinement of his executive office."

Stan's brother, Larry Lieber, came on board as Lee's sole freelance scripter. "When I started writing," he told *Comics Scene*, "I said to Martin Goodman, 'Tell me, how would you describe the comic industry?' He said, 'I'd call it a dying industry.' And it was just hanging on. They'd put out these few books. Stan was there alone and he was making most of the corrections himself."

Ayers vividly remembers Lee saying at this time, "'Dick, it's time to get out of the business.' The way he put it, his uncle walked by the office and wouldn't even wave to him. It was like the ship was sinking and we all had to get off."

When Westerns and fantasy titles peaked in the early 1960s, Goodman looked once again at his circulation figures—as well as those of competitors he had access to. He saw that DC was reviving its dormant super heroes. A team book called *Justice League of America* was breaking prevailing sales records. Goodman ordered Lee to do something similar.

Lee recalled Goodman suggesting, "You could use our old Human Torch and Sub-Mariner and maybe Captain America. That'll save you from having to dream up any new characters."

Knowing he had to satisfy Goodman, Lee flirted with bringing back the old pre-war Timely super heroes, who had briefly teamed up as the All-Winners Squad in 1946, but who had all flopped during a brief 1953 revival.

All-Winners Comics #21 (Winter 1946)
art by Syd Shores

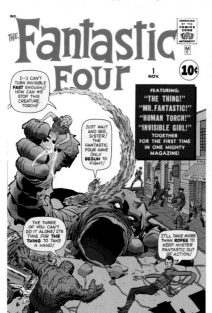

"I really wanted to do something different," Lee asserted. "That's why I didn't want to do the Torch and the Sub-Mariner. I wanted to create a new group."

By that time, Jack Kirby was back in the fold. He too was eager to return to super heroes. Together they produced *The Fantastic Four*—and here the Marvel Universe truly ignited. Alan Shepard Jr. had just become the first American in space. The Space Race was on, and Lee and Kirby gave the world a new breed of astronaut super heroes. Reimagined versions of the Human Torch and the Sub-Mariner were key to the rebirth. Naturally, The Torch and Prince Namor tangled at the earliest opportunity. Before long, Captain America would be revived by Lee and Kirby. Even Ka-Zar was resurrected.

Soon, the company officially rebranded itself as Marvel Comics, a name it had flirted with years before, but which had never stuck.

"When we saw how well the books were starting to sell," Lee recalled, "I figured we ought to change our name and give ourselves a whole new image. So we thought about it a while and came up with the name Marvel, because that was the name of the first book we ever published, *Marvel Mystery Comics*."

The Fantastic Four #1 (Nov. 1961), art by Jack Kirby & uncredited

Now it was Marvel forever. Timely-style character crossovers

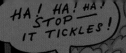

May 1963 house ad celebrating the success of the newly minted Marvel Comics Group and its rapidly expanding line of heroes

became a hallmark of the line. Fans dubbed it the Marvel Universe. Sales soared. DC and Archie Comics—the former MLJ—copied Marvel shamelessly.

"Our competitors couldn't understand why our stuff was selling," Lee revealed to the New York *Times*' Saul Braun. "They would have a super hero see a monster in the street and he'd say, 'Oh, a creature, I must destroy him before he crushes the world.' And they'd have another super hero in another book see a monster and say, 'Oh, a creature, I must destroy him before he crushes the world.' It was so formularized. I said to my writers, 'Is that what you'd say in real life?' If you saw a monster coming down the street, you'd say, 'Gee, there must be a masquerade party going on.'"

Goodman capitalized on what he saw working. Once *The Fantastic Four* and *The Amazing Spider-Man* were established, he ordered Lee to duplicate them. *The X-Men* and *Daredevil* resulted. When *Daredevil* #1 fell behind schedule, Lee and Kirby hastily cobbled together *The Avengers* out of second-tier super heroes and Goodman was finally presented with a Justice League to call his own. Bill Everett and Carl Burgos returned to the fold—although the latter soon left, unhappy with the new Human Torch and complaining "If I knew how much trouble and heartbreak that character would cause me, I would never have bothered!"

With a long memory for competitor's sales figures and a patient eye on lapsing trademarks, Goodman initiated new incarnations of abandoned properties like Captain Marvel and the Ghost Rider. When Lee showed him a new super-hero team dubbed "The Mutants," Goodman balked at the uncommercial title, and so it became *The X-Men*. (Earlier, he had vetoed "The Fabulous Four" in favor of *The Fantastic Four*.)

Thirty years of publishing had honed his editorial instincts. Larry Lieber saw him this way: "He had a very good feel of what the average reader would like or wouldn't like. He had read a lot. He was self-educated. He came from a poor family and worked his way up. He also knew good writing. But he knew it from the point of view of the average reader. He knew what would go and what wouldn't, and he had good taste. I don't know that he could create things himself, but if he saw something good I think he knew it."

Yet Martin Goodman never lost his fast-draw ways when it came to killing fledgling magazines. Famous Goodman premature cancellations include Lee and Kirby's *Two-Gun Kid* and *The Hulk,* as well as Neal Adams' *X-Men,* John Buscema's *Silver Surfer* and Roy Thomas and Barry Smith's *Conan the Barbarian*—which went on to great success after yet another last-minute stay of execution. Once, he killed a new Marvel science-fiction strip, Starhawk, the minute he saw the character, growling that "rockets, rayguns and robots" never sold comic books.

The most famous of all was of course Spider-Man, whom Goodman dismissed with a curt, "You can't make a hero out of a spider. People hate spiders!" preferring to push Ant-Man instead. Stan Lee convinced him to print the origin by reminding him that one of the most popular pulp heroes of the 1930s was The Spider. Stubbornly, Goodman cancelled *Amazing Fantasy* after that initial offering, shelving a second Spider-Man adventure and the rest of *Amazing Fantasy* #16. When final sales figures were calculated, Goodman once more reversed himself. *The Amazing Spider-Man* went on to become the most successful hero of the Marvel Universe.

When Martin Goodman sold Marvel Comics in 1968, his age had caught up to the silvery color of his hair. He stayed on as publisher until 1972. Marvel circulation was peaking, thanks to a brilliant strategic move that allowed the company to finally surpass sales of arch-rival DC Comics. Goodman mandated that all Marvel titles increase size and jump to 25 cents. DC followed suit. After only a month, Goodman cut back to 20 cents. DC held to the higher price for a brutal year. Goodman predicted DC would take a bath, and they did. He retired, vindicated and victorious.

When Marvel supplanted DC as industry leader, Goodman returned to take the staff out to dinner at a restaurant where DC staffers usually celebrated their hard-won sales superiority.

Today, the mighty Marvel multimedia entertainment empire spans the entire globe. Never in his wildest dreams could Martin Goodman have imagined what would grow out of that single misprinted 64-page comic magazine 70 marvelous years ago….

Will Murray has been called the Indiana Jones of pulp fiction and popular culture research for his innumerable articles on subjects as diverse as H.P. Lovecraft and Big Nose Serrano. The author of over 50 books and novels in series ranging from Doc Savage to The Destroyer, he had written prose stories starring Spider-Man, Ant-Man, and The Hulk for various Marvel anthologies, as well as other classic characters, including Superman, Batman, Wonder Woman, The Phantom, The Spider, The Avenger, and The Green Hornet. His novel Nick Fury, Agent of S.H.I.E.L.D.: Empyre, *published in 2000, eerily anticipated the operational details of the September 11, 2001 terrorist attacks on New York and Washington D.C. A Marvel comics reader since 1962, Murray co-created, with artist Steve Ditko, the most powerful mutant in the current Marvel Universe, the unbeatable Squirrel Girl. He is also the literary agent for the estate of Lester Dent, creator of Doc Savage.*

BIBLIOGRAPHY

Allen, Michael. "Stan 'The Man' Lee." *Overstreet's Comic Book Quarterly* Vol. 1 #4, April-June 1994.

Amash, Jim. "I Let People Do Their Jobs!" *Alter Ego* Vol. 3 #11 November 2001.

Amash, Jim. "A Long Glance at Dave Gantz." *Alter Ego* Vol. 3 #13 March 2002

Amash, Jim. "The Goldberg Variations." *Alter Ego* Vol.3 #18 October 2002.

Amash, Jim. "You Do the Best You Can…" *Alter Ego* Vol. 3 #26, July 2003.

Amash, Jim. "It Was a Fun Time!" *Alter Ego* Vol. 3 #35 April 2004.

Amash, Jim. "Captain America was a Dirty Name!" *Alter Ego* Vol. 3 #35 April 2004.

Amash, Jim. "He Left This Planet Too Soon To Go To Artists' Heaven!" *Alter Ego* Vol. 3 # 51 August 2005.

Amash, Jim. "They Depended on [The Super-Heroes] To Keep Us Afloat." *Alter Ego* Vol. 3 #57 March 2006.

Amash, Jim. "Who is *Bob Deschamps* and Why Is He Saying all Those Crazy Things About Timely?"
      Alter Ego Vol. 3 #20 January 2003.

Benton, Mike. *Superhero Comics of the Silver Age.* Taylor Publishing Company, 1991.

Benton, Mike. *Superhero Comics of the Golden Age.* Taylor Publishing Company, 1992.

Bradfield, Harriet. "New York Market Letter" *Writer's Digest,* 1933-45.

Braun, Saul. "Shazam! Here Comes Captain Relevant." *New York Times* May 2, 1971.

Daniels, Les. *Marvel.* Harry N. Abrams, 1991.

Daniels, Les. *DC Comics.* Bullfinch, 1995.

Duin, Steve and Richardson, Mike. *Comics Between the Panels.* Dark Horse Comics, 1998.

Eisner, Will. *Will Eisner's Shop Talk.* Dark Horse Comics, 2001.

Evanier, Mark. *Kirby: King of Comics.* Harry N. Abrams, 2008.

Everett, Bill. "Letter to Jerry DeFuccio." *Robin Snyder's History of Comics* Vol. 2 #7, July 1991.

Goulart, Ron. *Great History of Comics.* Contemporary Books, 1986.

Gustafson, Jon. *Chroma: The Art of Alex Schomburg.* Father Tree Press, 1986.

Hewetson, Alan. "Syd Shores." *Now and Then Times.* Vol. 1 #2 November 1973.

Jones, Gerard. *Men of Tomorrow.* Basic Books, 2004.

Kraft, David Anthony. "The FOOM Interview: Stan Lee." *FOOM* #17 March 1977.

Lammers, Tom. *Tales of the Implosion, a History of the 1957 Atlas Implosion.* Privately published 2005.

Lee, Stan. "Introduction." *Marvel Masterworks The Fantastic Four: Vol. 1.* Marvel, 1987.

Lee, Stan, and George Mair. *Excelsior!: The Amazing Life of Stan Lee.* Boxtree, 2002.

Mathieu, Aron. "Any Rights Today." *Writer's Digest,* October 1943.

Milo, George. *The Comics Journal Library Volume One: Jack Kirby.* Fantagraphics Books 2002.

Moore, Scotty. "Schomburg's War." *Overstreet's Comic Book Quarterly* Vol. 1 #6, October-December 1994.

Morrow, John. "Joe Simon on Captain America." *The Jack Kirby Collector* Vol. 2 #3 January, 1995.

Murray, Will. "Project Captain America Declassified." *Comics Scene Vol. 2* #14 August 1990.

Murray, Will. "The American Hero." *Comics Scene Yearbook* Vol.1 #1 1992.

Murray, Will. "The Inker Who Saved Marvel Comics." *Comics Scene* Vol. 2 #49 January 1995.

Murray, Will. "Monster Master." *Comics Scene* Vol. 2 #52, September 1995.

Murray, Will. "DC's Tangled Roots!" *Comic Book Marketplace* Vol. 2 #53 November 1997.

Murray, Will. "Joe Simon: Look Back with Humor!" *Comic Book Marketplace* Vol. 2 #62 August 1998.

Murray, Will. "Stan Lee Looks Back." *Comics Scene 2000* Vol. 3 #1 Spring 2000.

Murray, Will. "Joe Simon: On Creating Icons." *Comics Buyers Guide* #1418 January 19, 2001.

Nicholls, Stan. "Comics Man." *Comics Scene Yearbook* Vol. 1 #1 1992.

Simon, Joe, with Jim Simon. *The Comic Book Makers.* Vanguard Productions 2003.

Simon, Joe. "The Creator of Captain America Meets the Creator of The Human Torch." *Alter Ego* Vol. 3 #36 May 2004.

Steranko, Jim. *The Steranko History of Comics.* Supergraphics, 1970.

Thomas, Roy "Everett on Everett." *Alter Ego* Vol. 1 #11, 1978.

Thomas, Roy. " 'Stan Was the Prince…' Gil Kane on Timely Comics." *Alter Ego* Vol. 3 #3 Winter 1999-2000.

Thomas, Roy. "So You Want a Job, Eh?" *Alter Ego* Vol. 3 #6 Autumn 2000.

Thomas, Roy. "Fifty Years on the 'A' List." *Alter Ego* Vol. 3 #9, July 2201.

Thomas, Roy. "Comics Were Great!" *Alter Ego* Vol. 3 #2 November 2001.

Thomas, Roy. "I Wish Wal-Mart Sold Memory!" *Alter Ego* Vol. 2 #35 April 2004.

Vassallo, Dr. Michael J. "Two Timely Talks with Allen Bellman." *Alter Ego* Vol. 3 #32. January 2004.

Vassallo, Dr. Michael J. "Vince Fago and The Timely Funny Animal Dept." Comicartville Library.
      Comicartville.com 2003.

Woolfolk, William. "Perseverance Chapter 6." *Robin Snyder's The Comics.* Vol. 6 #8 August, 1995.

Wyman, Jr., Ray. *The Art of Jack Kirby.* The Blue Rose Press, 1992.

—. "Federal Trade Commission Orders and Complaints, 1942-45." *Trade Regulation*
      Reporter, Ninth Edition, 1945.

—. "Big Business in Pulp Thrillers" *Literary Digest* January 23, 1937.

—. "Jack Kirby & Don Rico." *Mysticogyfil* Vol #1 #2 May 1975.

—. "Meet the Editor. "Robert O. Erisman" *The Writer's Journal,* November 1940.

—. "Literary Market Tips." *The Author and Journalist,* 1933-1945.

In addition, the following persons gave generously of their time and knowledge: Stan Lee, Joe Simon, Larry Lieber, Dick Ayers, Roy Thomas, Allen Bellman, David McDonnell, Ron Goulart, Mark Evanier, Joe Lovece, Michael Feldman, Frank Motler, Dr. Michael J. Vassallo, Matt Moring, John Locke, Robert. K. Wiener, Mark Trost and Stephen Fishler.

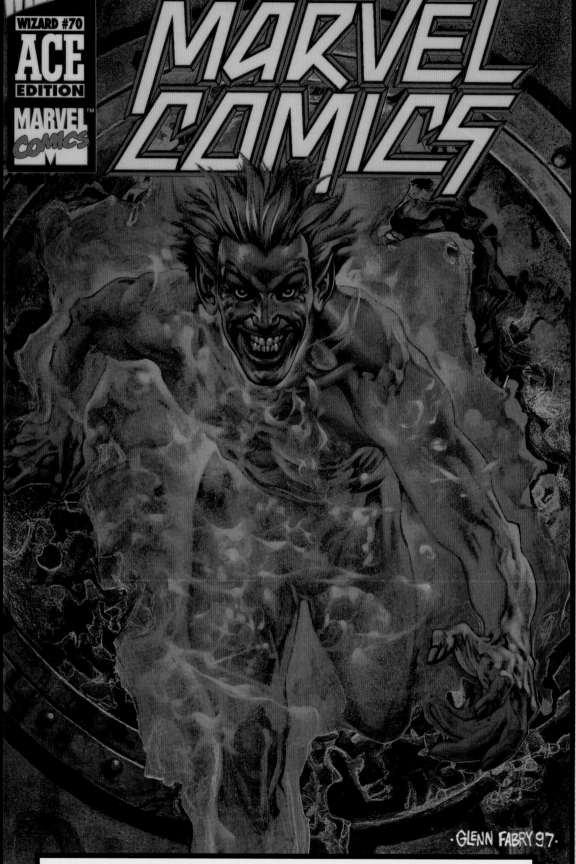

IN 1997, *MARVEL COMICS #1*'S HUMAN TORCH, SUB-MARINER AND KA-ZAR STORIES WERE REPRINTED AS *WIZARD ACE EDITION #16*. OUTER AND INNER COVER ART BY **GLENN FABRY**.

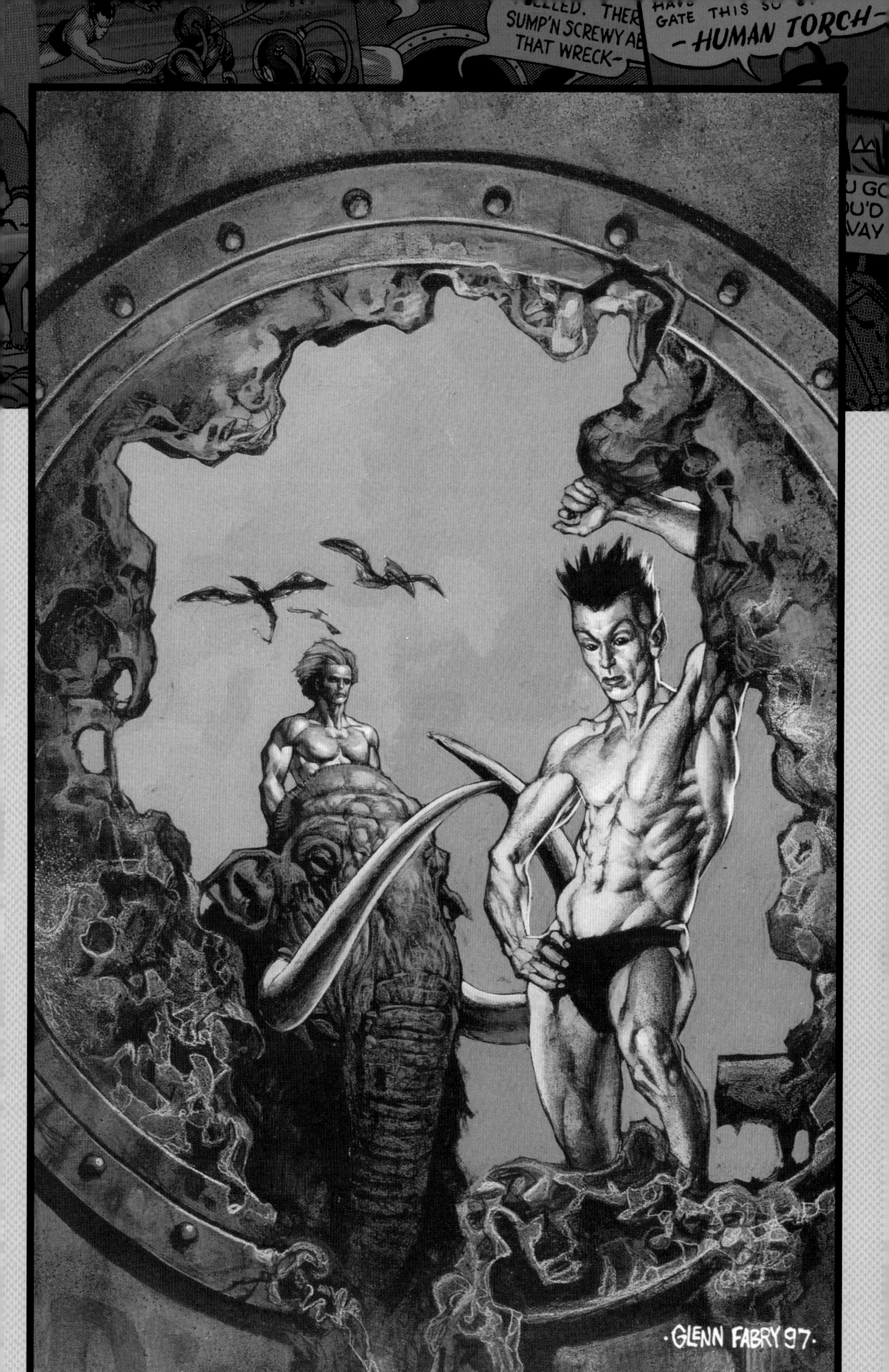
SUMP'N SCREWY AB
THAT WRECK-
GATE THIS
-HUMAN TORCH-
·GLENN FABRY 97·

JELENA KEVIC DJURDJEVIC'S COVER FOR THE *MARVEL COMICS #1 70TH ANNIVERSARY EDITION* WAS
ALSO USED AS THE COVER OF THE *GOLDEN AGE MARVEL COMICS OMNIBUS VOL. 1 HC.*

FRANK R. PAUL & DEAN WHITE'S VARIANT COVER FOR THE *MARVEL COMICS #1 70TH ANNIVERSARY EDITION*
WAS ALSO USED AS THE COVER OF *MARVEL MASTERWORKS: GOLDEN AGE MARVEL COMICS VOL. 1 TPB* (2011).

MARVEL COMICS #1'S ICONIC COVER HAS BEEN THE SUBJECT OF SEVERAL HOMAGES OVER THE YEARS.

MARVEL ZOMBIES 2 #2 (JANUARY 2008) COVER ART BY **ARTHUR SUYDAM**

*THE TORCH #2 (DECEMBER 2009) COVER ART BY **ALEX ROSS***

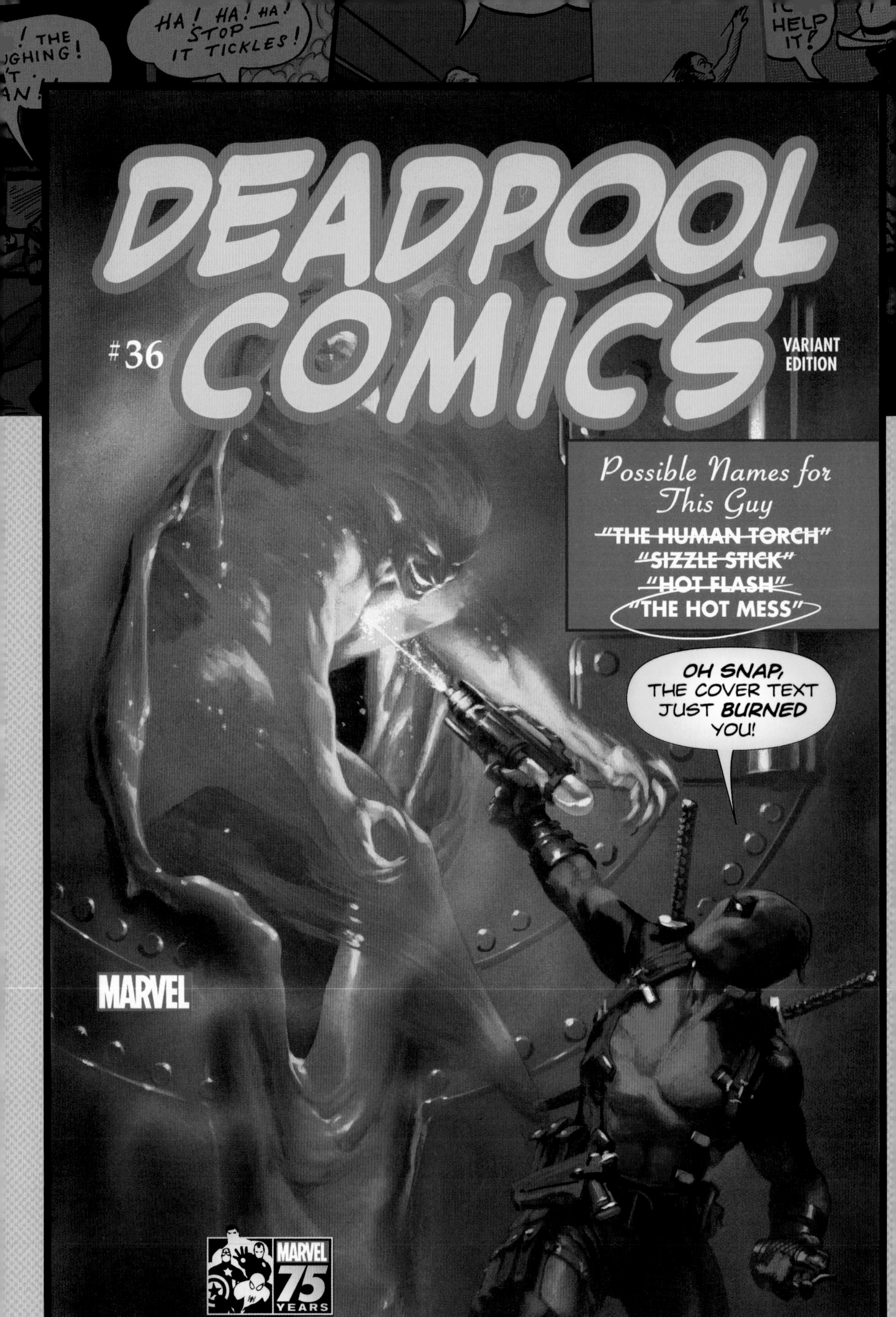
HA! HA! HA! STOP— IT TICKLES!
DEADPOOL COMICS
#36
VARIANT EDITION
Possible Names for This Guy
"THE HUMAN TORCH"
"SIZZLE STICK"
"HOT FLASH"
"THE HOT MESS"
OH SNAP, THE COVER TEXT JUST BURNED YOU!
MARVEL
MARVEL 75 YEARS
TACOS
BURRITOS
CHIMIS

DEADPOOL #36 (DECEMBER 2014) 75TH ANNIVERSARY VARIANT COVER ART BY **GABRIELE DELL'OTTO**